Derivation and Explanation in the Minimalist Program

Generative Syntax

General Editor: David Lightfoot

Recent work in generative syntax has viewed the language faculty as a system of principles and parameters, which permit children to acquire productive grammars triggered by normal childhood experiences. The books in this series serve as an introduction to particular aspects or modules of this theory. They presuppose some minimal background in generative syntax, but meet the tutorial needs of intermediate and advanced students. Written by leading figures in the field, the books also contain sufficient fresh material to appeal to the highest level.

Derivation and Explanation in the Minimalist Program

Edited by
Samuel David Epstein and
T. Daniel Seely

Blackwell Publishing

© 2002 by Blackwell Publishers Ltd
a Blackwell Publishing company

350 Main Street, Malden, MA 02148–5018, USA
108 Cowley Road, Oxford OX4 1JF, UK
550 Swanston Street, Carlton, Victoria 3053, Australia
Kurfürstendamm 57, 10707 Berlin, Germany

The right of Samuel David Epstein and T. Daniel Seely to be identified as the Authors of the Editorial Material in this Work has been asserted in accordance with the UK Copyright, Designs, and Patents Act 1988.

First published 2002 by Blackwell Publishers Ltd

Library of Congress Cataloging-in-Publication Data

Derivation and explanation in the Minimalist Program / edited by Samuel David Epstein and T. Daniel Seely.
     p. cm. — (Generative syntax; 6)
     Includes bibliographical references and index.
     ISBN 0–631–22732–6 (alk. paper) — ISBN 0–631–22733–4 (pbk.: alk. paper)
     1. Minimalist theory (Linguistics) 2. Generative grammar. 3. Explanation (Linguistics) I. Epstein, Samuel David. II. Seely, T. Daniel. III. Series.
P158.28 .D47 2003
415—dc21

2002004859

A catalogue record for this title is available from the British Library.

Set in 10/12pt Palatino
by Graphicraft Ltd, Hong Kong
Printed and bound in the United Kingdom
by MPG Books Ltd, Bodmin, Cornwall

For further information on
Blackwell Publishing, visit our website:
http://www.blackwellpublishing.com

Contents

Acknowledgments

We thank David Lightfoot, Series Editor, and Steve Smith, Editorial Director, for their interest in and support of this project. In addition, we are indebted to Tami Kaplan, Associate Acquisitions Editor in Linguistics at Blackwell for her extraordinarily professional and personable assistance throughout all stages of the preparation of the manuscript. Thanks also to Sarah Coleman, assistant editor, for her help. We are, of course, very grateful to our contributors for their willingness to participate in this project, for their hard work, and for their patience. We also thank each of us for tolerating the other (some more than others, and conversely). Finally, we thank Noam Chomsky for the generative revolution and for his support of this project.

This book is dedicated, in reverse chronological order to: Charlie, Piper, Sylvie, Molly, Hannah and Elaine. Also to Josh. And to our parents Peggy and Thomas Seely; and Lucy Epstein (1920–99) and Joseph Epstein (1917–93).

Samuel David Epstein
T. Daniel Seely

List of Contributors

Michael Brody, Department of Phonetics and Linguistics, University College London, UK.

Chris Collins, Department of Modern Languages and Linguistics, Cornell University, USA.

Samuel David Epstein, Department of Linguistics, University of Michigan, USA.

John Frampton, Department of Mathematics, Northeastern University, USA.

Sam Gutmann, Department of Mathematics, Northeastern University, USA.

Norbert Hornstein, Department of Linguistics, University of Maryland, USA.

Richard S. Kayne, Department of Linguistics, New York University, USA.

Hisatsugu Kitahara, Institute of Cultural and Linguistic Studies, Keio University, Japan.

James McCloskey, Department of Linguistics, University of California at Santa Cruz, USA.

Norvin Richards, Department of Linguistics and Philosophy, MIT, USA.

Esther Torrego, Linguistics Program, Department of Hispanic Studies, University of Massachusetts at Boston, USA.

Juan Uriagereka, Department of Linguistics, University of Maryland, USA.

T. Daniel Seely, Program in Linguistics, Eastern Michigan University, USA.

Jan-Wouter Zwart, Department of Linguistics, University of Groningen, The Netherlands.

Introduction: On the Quest for Explanation

Samuel David Epstein and
T. Daniel Seely

1 Explanation through minimization

Anyone seeking to understand how humans acquire the knowledge they have, and interested in explicitly characterizing what the knowledge is, must engage in the development of a theory. Whenever asking "What exactly is X?" and "How does it develop?" and seeking an explanatory answer, the only way to proceed is to construct a theory, however preliminary or undetailed. In linguistics, once one postulates, e.g., "noun," one has engaged in theory construction. Since the goal of any theory is to explain things, the further question we all must address is "To what extent is this goal achieved?" If engaged in serious rational inquiry, the question can't be avoided. Addressing it requires that we be analytical and reflective about our proposals. In this regard, Chomsky, acknowledging the possibility that the Minimalist Program might well be "wrong," writes of its merits as follows:

> the Minimalist Program, right or wrong, has a certain therapeutic value. It is all too easy to succumb to the temptation to offer a purported explanation for some phenomenon on the basis of assumptions that are of roughly the order of complexity of what is to be explained. . . . Minimalist demands at least have the merit of . . . sharpening the question of whether we have a genuine explanation or a restatement of a problem in other terms.   (Chomsky 1995: 233–4)

Expressing this same commitment to critical reflection, Whitehead wrote:

> the progress of biology and psychology has probably been checked by the uncritical assumption of half truths. If science is not to degenerate into a medley of *ad hoc* hypotheses, it must become philosophical and must enter upon a thorough criticism of its own foundations.[1]

Unfortunately, it seems to us that these so-called "philosophical" sentiments are foreign or uninteresting to some researchers. Such questions are sometimes regarded, we fear, as "not real linguistics" or "too conceptual." If this is true, the situation is not new. C. S. Pierce, calling for reflective evaluation of the explanatory adequacy of our theories, writes:

> There remains still another kind of power of observation which *ought* to be trained; and that is the power of observing the objects of our own creative fancy. . . . The highest kind of observation is the observation of systems, forms, and ideas.[2] (editors' emphasis)

We believe that the desire to determine the properties of our theories, and the explanatory depth achieved by them, i.e. the extent to which all the relevant phenomena have been explained, should be regarded not as an issue that is "just conceptual," but instead as *the central issue confronting theory construction*.

Of course, with Newton (1690),

> We are certainly not to relinquish evidence of experiments for the sake of dreams and vain fictions of our own devising; nor are we to recede from the analogy of Nature, which is wont to be simple and always consonant itself. . . .[3]

The question that then arises is: How do we proceed? More specifically, what shall we regard as "a genuine explanation" as opposed to "a restatement of a problem in other terms"? That is not an easy question to answer; there are no hard and fast criteria; there is no explanatory gauge that can measure the "degree" to which genuine explanation has been attained. But, the question we should ask is: To what extent have we explained anything? How do we ever know if we are on the right track?

In grappling with this very question, Einstein writes:

> Can we ever hope to find the right way? Nay, more, has this right way any existence outside our illusions? Can we hope to be guided safely by experience at all when *there exist theories (such as classical mechanics) which to a large extent do justice to experience, without getting to the root of the matter*? I answer without hesitation that there is, in my opinion, a right way, and that we are capable of finding it. Our experience hitherto justifies us in believing *that nature is the realization of the simplest conceivable mathematical ideas*.[4] (editors' emphasis)

Not only should each idea be "mathematical" (we assume meaning formally explicit) and the simplest conceivable, but in addition, understanding is maximized through the minimization of the number of "simplest conceivable mathematical ideas" postulated:

> Resolved to maximize our understanding, we find ourselves committed to a highly characteristic effort to minimize the *number* of theoretical premises required for explanation.[5] (editors' emphasis)

Thus, we seek to minimize each premise, and the number of them, thereby seeking to maximize explanation through deduction (not empirical "coverage" through stipulation). Importantly then, the data is not satisfactorily "covered" if it is covered by stipulation. Einstein thus speaks of:

the grand aim of all science, which is to cover the greatest possible number of empirical facts by logical deduction from the smallest possible number of hypotheses or axioms.[6]

And Feynman writes,

in the further development of science, we want more than just a formula. First we have an observation, then we have numbers, ... then we have a law which summarizes all the numbers. But the real glory of science is that we can find a way of thinking such that the law is evident.[7]

We concur with these perspectives regarding the vital importance of being reflective about the theories we have; of being concerned with explanation in general and the explanatory depth of our theories in particular. Crucial is a willingness to at least inquire into ways in which deeper explanation through minimization of posited axioms and deduction from them might be attained. Again, "We are certainly not to relinquish evidence of experiments for the sake of dreams and vain fictions of our own devising," yet concern with the explanatory depth of our theories must remain a central goal in linguistics no less than it is in the other sciences.

In this regard, it seems that Lappin et al. (2000: 668) misunderstand the motivation for the shift from the GB theory to the Minimalist Program. They write:

If linguists wish to use the practices followed in the natural sciences as a guide, then it would be reasonable to expect the catalyst for the transition from GB to the MP to be a significant body of results that follow directly from Minimalist principles, but are unavailable on any plausible version of GB theory.

One pervasive catalyst, in any field, for exploring minimization is the ongoing (we would hope) unwavering quest for deeper explanation through self-criticism of articulated theories, even holding the data constant. This quest for simplification and deduction is more than just consonant with "the practices followed in the natural sciences;" it constitutes their "grand aim" (Einstein) and "real glory" (Feynman). Our hunch, following Chomsky, is that so-called GB theory (using Einstein's terms) "to a large extent do[es] justice to experience, without getting to the root of the matter ..."

Again, empirical "coverage" (though obviously of great importance) is not the sole issue, rather how the theory "covers" the data, always a very difficult question to answer, must be posed, discussed, and addressed. Contra this perspective, Lappin et al. (2000: 667) write of the shift in interest from GB to Minimalism:

Still more remarkable is the widespread perception that a novel approach with no more "battle-tested results" to its credit (and far narrower cross-linguistic coverage) than its predecessor represents a conceptual breakthrough for generative grammar. . . .

We believe that asking certain questions, in particular "Why?," and trying to provide an answer, can indeed represent a "conceptual" breakthrough in any field.

The Minimalist conjecture is that we can get at, or closer to, the root of the matter by first asking; "Why do these GB principles, definitions, filters, and postulates, and not others, hold – if they in fact do hold?" The derivational approach, aspects of which we outline below, seeks to answer by "finding a way of thinking" (through appeal to an independently motivated, local generative procedure; i.e. the derivation) such that the laws of GB theory (to the extent that they are empirically correct) are evident.

2   Derivation and explanation in the Minimalist Program

As concerns linguistic explanation in particular, Reuland eloquently summarizes the shift from GB to the Minimalist Program as follows:

> Contentment with higher level stipulations has been replaced by pursuing the question of why they would hold.   (Reuland 2000: 848)

In our view, the question of why they would hold is tantamount to the question of whether, in Einstein's terms, they can be logically deduced from, "the smallest number of simplest conceivable mathematical ideas."

Chomsky's Minimalist Program is committed to this same "highly characteristic effort to minimize . . ." conjecturing that the language faculty

> provides no machinery beyond what is needed to satisfy minimal requirements of legibility and that it functions in as simple a way as possible.   (Chomsky 2000: 112–13)

Although there is "no machinery beyond what is needed to satisfy minimal requirements of legibility . . .", it is important to note that there is machinery, i.e. mechanisms that generate objects, not just laws that the objects obey. The idea that the generative mechanisms play a crucial role in explanation is not limited to linguistics. This mode of generative explanation is pursued in, for example, J. Epstein's conception of the explanatory power of Agent-based Computational Modeling in what he calls "Generative Social Science" (J. Epstein 1999; see also J. Epstein and Axtell 1996). As Epstein notes:

> the central idea is this: To the generativist, explaining the emergence [footnote deleted] of macroscopic societal regularities, such as norms or price equilibria, requires that one answer the following question: "How could the decentralized local interactions of heterogeneous autonomous agents [i.e. individuals; SDE/ TDS] generate the given regularity?"   (J. Epstein 1999: 41)

J. Epstein assumes that one has explained, in at least *one* sense of the notion "explanation," the macroscopic societal regularity, to the extent that one can

> Situate an initial population of autonomous heterogeneous agents in a relevant spatial environment; allow them to *interact according to simple local rules,* and thereby generate – or "grow" – the macroscopic regularity *from the bottom up* [footnote deleted]. (J. Epstein 1999: 42; editors' emphasis)

In short, J. Epstein asserts that "If you haven't grown it, you haven't explained it."

With the above in mind, let us return to some of the specific proposals that Chomsky makes regarding the Minimalist Program. At the heart of these are, among other things, the following minimizing, simplifying, and eliminative conditions (from Chomsky 2000: 113):

(A) The only linguistically significant levels are the interface levels.

(B) The *interpretability* condition: LIs [i.e. lexical items] have no features other than those interpreted at the interface, properties of sound and meaning.

(C) The inclusiveness condition: No new features are introduced by Chl [Chl refers to "the computational system of human language"].

(D) Relations that enter into Chl either (i) are imposed by legibility conditions, or (ii) fall out in some natural way from the computational process [footnote deleted].

There are a number of points to make regarding (A)–(D); we start with (D)ii.

2.1   The computational process

First, and most important for present purposes, there is a computational *process* (see (D)ii),[8] specifically, there is a mechanism (i.e. rules) for generating syntactic objects. Like Standard Theory, the MP includes locally constrained transformational rules. These operations are, however, preferable to the Standard Theory transformations, since in the Minimalist Program, there are only two transformational rules: singulary (Move) and generalized (Merge); and neither is construction specific, nor language specific, but each is instead, by hypothesis, universal. Moreover, we assume that these rules are "minimal"[9] (as proposed in Collins (this volume); see also Seely 2000) and similar (as proposed in Kitahara 1997), each of the form: "A concatenated with B yields {A, B}." This is an attractive, arguably irreducible axiom of a generative theory of syntactic knowledge, seeking to explain the central object of inquiry – the creative aspect of language – by appeal to a finite, minimal, universal (recursive) system characterizing knowledge over an infinite domain. Notice that the "construction-specific" transformational rules of the Standard Theory might have done justice to the phenomena, but, if explanation is the concern, they indeed seemed not to get to the root of the matter. The same is true of, for example, construction-specific phrase structure rules, which to a large extent yielded empirical "coverage." Asking (and addressing) the question of *how* the facts were covered, led to the abandonment of such construction-specific mechanisms, a highly significant shift in our understanding of the nature of the syntactic component of the human language faculty.

2.2   Was GB nonderivational?

The Minimalist Program's appeal to rules and the proposed constraints on their iterative recursive application (e.g., the cycle) purportedly constitutes a radical departure from the Government and Binding (GB) "rule-free" approach. GB, as contrasted with the Standard Theory, is traditionally assumed to be representational, characterized as a "virtually rule-free system" (Chomsky 1986: 93). But "virtually rule free" isn't "rule free." Indeed, GB theory did have rules, including, for example, Move-alpha and whatever generated structures that could comply with (or violate) the X-bar schema. In addition, there were Case assignment rules, and other feature assignment mechanisms, which had the property of applying only in government configurations. Government was an elegant intermodular unifying relation, but it was nonetheless unexplained: government was defined on already-built-up trees, with no answer to the question "Why does government, and not some other definable relation, hold?" Here we see two unattractive, related aspects of the theory. First, by appeal to D-structure (DS), a *level* of representation, complex "sentential" structures are first completely assembled, all at once. Then, and only then, are relations expressible, and since the structure has already been entirely built (by virtue of the role and function of DS) the only way to express relations is to nonexplanatorily define them on the already-built representation. In fact, all relations were defined on already-built (macroscopic) trees. There was no apparent alternative in a virtually rule-free system. This left no way of explaining relations.

   In addition, representational concepts like chains, and traces, seem to us to be disguised derivational constructs, to the extent that they in fact encode into output representations the history of the derivation (for related discussion see Epstein and Seely (this volume), and Hornstein and Uriagereka (this volume)). If so, even leaving empirical matters aside,[10] our hunch is that if such constructs do justice to experience (and we don't think they do), they don't get to the root of the matter. Thus, for example, Chomsky (1981) states that a typical A-chain "in an obvious sense, represents the derivational history of this [i.e. the moved] NP by successive applications of move-alpha . . ." And similarly, Chomsky (1986: 95) regards "a chain [as] the S-structure reflection of a 'history of move-ment'." Within the GB framework, nothing "should", nor could, be deduced directly from (the accidental) properties of the amorphous rule "Move anything anywhere optionally" as it blindly applies in any one of an infinite number of ways that it logically could. As a result of this approach, the idiosyncratic properties of successive rule application must be *encoded* so that the output representation (to which necessarily descriptive, representational constructs apply) "in an obvious sense represents the derivational history." Herein lies the motivation for trace theory and for representational chains. The derivation (successive rule application) is in fact recognized as vitally important, but direct appeal to the derivation is "forbidden" in a "rule-free" system so that the output representations must include constructs needed to encode derivational history – since it is clearly relevant.

At the same time, this (encoding) postulate "chain" increases the types of "syntactic objects" postulated so as to include not only syntactic categories/constituents, but also more complex objects, namely chains. (And, in fact, if we adopt a simplified, minimized, arguably ineliminable, definition of syntactic object, chains are prohibited; a chain is, unlike e.g., a DP, not a syntactic constituent.[11]) If then they do indeed encode properties of the derivation, and their definition (thus needlessly) extends the class of syntactic objects, the question of their eliminability should, at least, arise.

As concerns one kind of chain, in this case a type of head chain, an arguably striking illustration of Einstein's idea of being able to do justice to experience without getting to the root of the matter is reflected in the following:

> It is generally possible to formulate the desired result in terms of outputs. In the head movement case, for example [a case of raising from N-toV followed by [$_V$ N+V], raising to Infl]) one can appeal to the plausible assumption that the trace is a copy, so the intermediate V-trace includes within it a record of the local N→V raising. But surely this is the wrong move. The relevant chains at LF are (N, t_N) and (V, t_V), and in these the locality relation satisfied by successive raising has been lost. . . . These seem to be fundamental properties of language, which should be captured, not obscured by coding tricks, which are always available. A fully derivational approach both captures them straightforwardly and suggests that they should be pervasive, as seems to be the case.   (Chomsky 1995: 224)

Within GB theory, it seems that rules remain ineliminable, although they can be largely, but perhaps not entirely, hidden through representational encoding devices, such as chains, which needlessly enrich the class of syntactic objects, without getting to the root of the matter.[12]

Importantly, then, GB, a so-called "representational" theory, is, in our view, a kind of derivational theory since there are transformational rules (virtually rule free is not rule free). Moreover, there are traces and chains, which are "lookback" notations whereby the empirically crucial derivation that produced the representation is encoded (see Epstein and Seely (1999), (forthcoming) for detailed discussion).

2.3   Which type of derivational theory is preferable?

If we are on the right track, then such so-called "representational" theories are, in fact, just one kind of derivational theory. The question then is not: "Which is preferable, derivational or representational theory?" but rather "Which type of derivational theory is preferable?" The options would seem to be these: (i) a derivational theory that seeks to empirically and explanatorily exploit the arguably ineliminable rules and derivation itself. Or, (ii) a derivational theory that instead implicitly incorporates rules and derivations, but does not (or cannot) appeal to them and instead encodes derivational history in macroscopic, molecular, representations, by (for example) defining chains on them.

Our hunch is that the latter approach underlies the postulation of complex derivation-encoding objects such as chains, while forcing us to constrain output representations with unexplained laws (filters and principles), and definitions (e.g., Government, Minimal Domain, etc.) as defined upon macrostructure levels of representation, assembled instantaneously.

We do not think that the answer to the question of which derivational theory is preferable is obvious or clear, but we do think that the question is of fundamental importance, directly addressing the formal properties of human linguistic knowledge representation. If this is indeed a question, it concerns all analyses. Imagine being told by someone in another field, "Well, there remains, it would seem, always two different ways of implementing things." Obviously, the critical response should be, "That's really crucial, and you should seek to show either that they are equivalent, or that there is a difference, and what the difference is, empirically, and with respect to explanatory depth" (see Brody (this volume) for important discussion of this point; and for a rather different perspective than ours.) The usual assumption is that empirical coverage and explanatory depth are at odds. We disagree in that empirical "coverage" is illusory, to the extent that the data are "covered" by stipulation. All analysts should then be interested. Have I formulated my analysis in one way or another, and do I have evidence for either? The question seems to us unavoidable: What is the architecture of the system? How does it work? What is the evidence for doing it one way vs. another? One crucial "difference" seems to us to be at least partially related to the central concern of explanatory depth, even holding the data constant. The laws/higher level stipulations/macroscopic regularities might be deducible from the simplest conceivable mathematical mechanisms, such as recursive application of rules like A+B => {A, B}. It is certainly always worth exploring the idea that it is empirically and explanatorily preferable to cover the facts, or better, yet more of the facts, with fewer stipulations.

2.4   *Explanation through representational minimization*

Let us now continue our consideration of the minimizing conditions mentioned above, turning to (A)–(C), repeated here:

(A)   The only linguistically significant levels are the interface levels.

(B)   The interpretability condition: LIs [i.e. lexical items] have no features other than those interpreted at the interface, properties of sound and meaning.

(C)   The inclusiveness condition: No new features are introduced by Chl.

As concerns (B), it imposes a severe limitation on the class of lexical features, which constitute the atomic elements upon which the operations of

Chl compute. Thus lexical representations are severely impoverished. Furthermore, under the Inclusiveness condition (C), nonexplanatory representational encodings like subscripts, superscripts, bar-levels, and star marking are no longer an option, but are instead explicitly prohibited. For example, Kitahara (1999) (see also Kitahara, this volume) represents perhaps the "classic" illustration of Inclusiveness in action, seeking to eliminate the "suspect" star-feature invoked in the analysis of Chomsky and Lasnik (1993). In a similar vein, Epstein and Seely (1999; forthcoming) argue, that given, in addition to (A)–(D), a restrictive definition of "syntactic object"/"syntactic category" (as provided in Chomsky 1995), chains too are prohibited by Inclusiveness (see also Hornstein 1998), an arguably welcome result if, as a matter of fact, "a chain . . . [is the] . . . S-structure reflection of a 'history of movement'" and is moreover a representational reflection which, we believe, engenders empirical difficulties in at least the case of A-chains. This brings us to (A), the issue of levels.

Obviously, (A) represents another form of representational impoverishment. If S-structure is eliminated, chains and (what are, in a certain sense) nonexplanatory filters (e.g., the Case Filter) on representations can no longer be defined on S-structure representations. That, too, is a welcome, if not daunting, result. Moreover, as noted, with the elimination of an initiating "all-at-once" level like DS, perhaps we will not be compelled to nonexplanatorily define relations on already-built-up trees, but might instead explain syntactic relations – a central goal of an explanatory theory of syntax (see, for example, Epstein 1999 and Epstein et al. 1998).

The elimination of levels might be further advanced by seeking to eliminate not just D- and S-structure, but also PF and LF as well (as in Epstein et al. 1998; Epstein and Seely 1999, forthcoming; and Uriagereka 1999). Chomsky, moreover, characterizes his phase-based analysis as level eliminating as well:

> In this conception there is no LF: rather, the computation maps LA to <PHON, SEM> piece-by-piece cyclically. There are, therefore, no LF properties and no interpretation of LF, strictly speaking, though sigma and phi interpret units that are part of something like LF in a non-cyclic conception. (Chomsky 2001: 4)

2.5 Summary

To sum up, we believe that we all "must become philosophical and must enter upon a thorough criticism of the theory's own foundations" (Whitehead). This willingness to first carefully examine "the objects of our own creative fancy" (Pierce) and then to criticize them, and be "discontent with higher level stipulation" (Reuland), underlies the highly characteristic effort to increase explanatory depth by minimizing theoretical apparatus (Nash, as noted above, and, of course, Chomsky's Minimalist Program). Minimization-through-derivation, as discussed here, asks "Can we explain the laws by finding 'a way of thinking such that the laws are evident'?" (Feynman). Can we grow or generate the macroscopic ("sentential/syntactic") regularities from the bottom up? (J. Epstein). These are the very kinds of questions, all regarding deduction and explanation, which we think it is never wrong to ask (and always counter-productive to denounce), that each paper in this volume seeks to explore, in one way or another, and, in some cases, with productive disagreement regarding the role of derivation in explanation.

3   The articles

This volume contains a collection of articles by leading researchers, each of which investigates aspects of the fundamental questions raised above. All papers are concerned with explanation, consonant with Reuland's summary of the shift from GB to Minimalism within which "Contentment with higher level stipulations has been replaced by pursuing the question of why they would hold;" and all assume some form of minimization. The majority develop a derivational approach, Brody's contribution being an important exception. As for the more specific proposals raised above, a few (all too brief) comments on the papers are in order.

One central research goal, as specified in section 2 above, is to deduce as much as possible from the arguably necessary (but cf. Brody) syntactic structure-building machinery; i.e. the universal and minimal rules and their mode of recursive application. What is to be avoided, among other things, on this view is defining relations on already-built-up trees, such definitions being, in our view, nonexplanatory. Kayne and Zwart, for example, don't define binding-theoretic domains on trees but rather attempt to account for con-straints on the binding of Y by X, under the assumption that X and Y are first-merged as sisters (the simplest rule-created relation) and then X undergoes independently constrained movement. Thus, Kayne, "adopting the derivational perspective of Chomsky's recent work, [explores] the idea that antecedent-pronoun relations should be rethought in movement terms, including what we think of as Condition B and Condition C effects." This represents a signi-ficant shift from defining binding-theoretic domains on trees to seeking an explanation of them in terms of independently motivated, and seemingly ineliminable, apparatus (movement theory) and a highly simplified version of certain referential relations (posited to hold under sisterhood, as created by Merge when X and Y are concatenated by a single rule application). In a related paper, Zwart seeks to account for both local and nonlocal binding relations under a similarly derivational approach.

Various forms of minimization were reviewed above, including the minim-ization of levels (at most the interface levels are posited), minimization of lex-ical items (the interpretability condition: no features other than those interpreted at the interface), and the minimization of syntactic objects (the inclusiveness condition: no new features are introduced by Chl). Collins provides a classic form of representational minimization, attempting to eliminate phrasal category labels entirely, and argues that "as representations are simplified (e.g., labels are eliminated), it becomes necessary to articulate the precise nature of syntactic derivations (e.g., minimize search, the Locus Principle, etc.)."

With respect to Inclusiveness, Hornstein and Uriagereka argue that "[The] 'loss of information' scenario [i.e. where information is available at one point in the derivation but not at another] fits poorly into models which make use of enriched representational codings (including traces, indices, and similar elements) because whatever information may have been lost in the course of the derivation can be [arguably incorrectly] reconstructed through some abstract [and sometimes Inclusiveness-violating] coding." And Zwart, as part of his development of a derivational approach to binding phenomena, argues that "with each new operation Merge, the element merging to the structure acquires additional features which are interpreted at LF, but no trace or chain is created, and no information can be gathered from these entities."

Similarly, Kitahara, "under the framework of Epstein et al. 1998, . . . articulates how . . . mechanisms of scrambling interact with the interpretive procedures applying in the course of a derivation." And McCloskey "argues that the form of the complementizer in Irish A'-binding constructions depends not on the mechanism of Specifier Head agreement (as has been widely assumed), but rather is sensitive to the mode of introduction of the specifier material (whether it is introduced by Merge or by Move)." Thus, mere inspection of the representational output is predictively insufficient.

Richards "develop[s] an approach to the derivation that generates the material at the root of the tree first, and adds new material to the bottom of the existing structure," and explores "the surprising prediction that under certain circumstances, A' movement should share with A-movement the property of being unable to skip an intervening A-position."

Torrego seeks to account "for cross-linguistic variation involving subject-to-subject raising over an Experiencer," arguing that "the analysis must be couched in a framework of derivational economy that imposes strict derivationality. . . ." Thus, the Minimal Link Condition arguably must be a movement constraint, not an S-structure filter.

Frampton and Gutmann "argue that an optimal derivational system, at least from a computational point of view, is a system that generates only objects that are well-formed and satisfy conditions imposed by the interface systems." Further, "we demand that the computational system be crash-proof. That is, that no filters are imposed on the end products of derivations. . . ."

Epstein and Seely, also pursuing minimization, argue that Spell Out applies inside each transformational rule application, and that "this conception of Spell Out allows for the elimination of: levels, special categorial phases, lookahead, lookback, and simultaneous rule application (as well as "principles" like the EPP)."

Pursuing an important alternative view, Brody argues that "no pure derivational theory of narrow syntax exists." And further, it is argued that "the derivational explanation of the asymmetry of the notion of c-command . . . like other explanations of c-command (and also like other derivational explanations) is not successful."

To conclude this introduction, each author's abstract is presented, in alphabetical order.

Michael Brody: "On the Status of Representations and Derivations" (Chapter one)

I discuss the point here that current mixed theories of syntax that involve both derivations and representations are redundant and in principle less restrictive than their pure representational or pure derivational counterparts. Next I show that no pure derivational theory of narrow syntax exists. To be minimally adequate, derivational theories must be mixed, hence the arguments against mixed theories apply to these too. In addition to this, I argue that everything else being equal, and with no additional stipulations added, current derivational theories with the rule of move are less restrictive than representational theories with the concept of chain. In the third section of the chapter I consider the derivational explanation of the asymmetry of the notion of c-command and conclude that this explanation, like other explanations of c-command (and also like other derivational explanations) is not successful. I suggest instead that we should eliminate c-command from the grammar and replace it by simpler interacting notions.

Chris Collins: "Eliminating Labels" (Chapter two)

In this chapter, I argue that it is possible to eliminate the labels of phrasal categories. I consider four areas where labels have been used in syntactic theory: X'-Theory, Selection, the Minimal Link Condition, and the PF Interface. In each case, I show that it is possible to capture the relevant generalizations without the use of phrasal category labels. This chapter illustrates the relationship between derivational and representational approaches to syntax. As representations are simplified (e.g., labels are eliminated), it becomes necessary to articulate the precise nature of syntactic derivations (e.g., minimize search, the Locus Principle, etc.).

Samuel David Epstein and T. Daniel Seely: "Rule Applications as Cycles in a Level-free Syntax" (Chapter three)

In a number of important recent papers, Chomsky postulates multiple, cyclic Spell Out, and seeks to explain (not stipulate) this central, derivational departure from the long-dominant Y-model. Since features are valued iteratively, i.e. derivationally, and since once valued, Spell Out cannot properly operate, Chomsky suggests that it follows that Spell Out must itself also apply iteratively. We reveal potential problems confronting this important explanation of cyclic Spell Out. We argue that the explanation can be maintained, while overcoming the problems noted, by "driving Spell Out inside each transformational rule application." We argue further that this conception of Spell Out allows for the elimination of: levels, special categorial phases, lookahead, lookback, and simultaneous rule application (as well as "principles" like the EPP). Although far from conclusive, this eliminative approach identifies (and pursues to some degree) what we believe to be the null hypothesis regarding the architecture of UG.

John Frampton and Sam Gutmann: "Crash-proof Syntax" (Chapter four)

The Minimalist Program is guided by the idea that the syntactic system of the language faculty is designed to optimally meet design specifications imposed by the interface systems. In this chapter we argue that an optimal derivational system, at least from a computational point of view, is a system that generates only objects that are well formed and satisfy conditions imposed by the interface systems. We explore the feasibility of constructing such a system, one in which there is no notion of "crashing derivations." We also argue that both the interface conditions and the derivational system which is designed to satisfy them are real, and in this sense we expect to find a pervasive redundancy in linguistic explanation. We demand that the computational system be crash-proof, that is, that no filters are imposed on the end products of derivations, and that no global filters (e.g. "comparison of derivations") assign status to derivations as a whole. By exploring the properties of a crash-proof system, we hope to clarify the boundary between the derivational system and the interface conditions, and to make progress in understanding both.

Norbert Hornstein and Juan Uriagereka: "Reprojections" (Chapter five)

This chapter explores the possibility that projected labels may change in the course of the derivation (hence the name *reprojection*). Label changes do not alter phrasal geometry, and in that sense are not transformational processes; however, representational dependencies are altered via reprojection in such a way that, for instance, head–specifier relations are redefined. The main consequence of this is that it provides a natural syntax for binary quantifiers, in much the same way that transitive verbs take their arguments within their (extended) projection. Interestingly, it is these quantifiers which induce islands for various LF dependencies across them. In our terms this follows from the fact that, after reprojection, a putative LF dependency would have to be across a non-complement branch. Unary quantifiers need not reproject in order to meet their syntactic/semantic demands, and hence do not induce LF islands of this sort. The chapter extends these results to other, less obvious domains.

Richard S. Kayne: *"Pronouns and their Antecedents"* (Chapter six)

Adopting the derivational perspective of Chomsky's recent work, I explore the idea that antecedent–pronoun relations should be rethought in movement terms, including what we think of as Condition B and Condition C effects. This allows me to capture the compelling similarity between Condition C and the prohibition against downward movement, and to dispense with the notion of "accidental coreference" in Lasnik's sense. All instances of "intended coreference/binding" involve a movement relation. In the spirit of the Lebeaux/ Chomsky proposals concerning Condition A, I argue that neither Condition B nor Condition C is a primitive of UG. The effects of both follow, in a derivational perspective, from basic properties of pronouns and basic properties of movement. What underlies Condition B effects underlies the existence of reflexives. The movement approach explored, which leads to some use of sideward movement, has consequences for circularity effects, for reconstruction effects, and for backwards pronominalization.

Hisatsugu Kitahara: *"Scrambling, Case, and Interpretability"* (Chapter seven)

Saito (1992) examines a number of binding phenomena involving scrambling and proposes that the binding theory applies not solely at LF, but at some pre-LF-level as well. In this paper, I elaborate Saito's proposal under the framework of Epstein et al. (1998). I first specify the mechanisms of scrambling in Japanese, adopting certain aspects of the probe-goal system (Chomsky 2000, 2001). I then articulate how these mechanisms of scrambling interact with the interpretive procedures applying in the course of a derivation.

James McCloskey: *"Resumption, Successive Cyclicity, and the Locality of Operations"* (Chapter eight)

This chapter is concerned with the mechanisms by which "long" A'-binding relations are constructed, and in particular with the role of intermediate positions in constructing those relations. The main empirical issue it grapples with is the way in which in Irish the form of C varies according to:

(i)   whether or not a clause hosts an instance of A'-binding;
(ii) what kind of A'-binding (binding of a trace or binding of a resumptive pronoun) it hosts.

The paper shows that long A'-binding can involve "mixed chains," some of whose links are created by movement, and some of which are created by merge of a binding operator in the specifier of CP.

It also argues that the form of the complementizer in Irish A'-binding constructions depends not on the mechanism of specifier–head agreement (as has been widely assumed), but rather is sensitive to the mode of introduction of the specifier material (whether it is introduced by Merge or by Move). The core characteristic of the system that emerges is its locally blind character. Choices are made at intermediate positions with no "foresight" about what the consequences for semantic interpretation will be. Locality is more highly valued than ease of interpretation.

Norvin Richards: "Very Local A' Movement in a Root-first Derivation (Chapter nine)

Richards (1999), following Phillips (1996, to appear), developed an approach to the derivation that generates the material at the root of the tree first, and adds new material to the bottom of the existing structure. The approach made the surprising prediction that under certain circumstances, A' movement should share with A-movement the property of being unable to skip an intervening A-position. In this paper I try to show that the prediction is true in a range of cases, under circumstances largely predicted by the theory.

Esther Torrego: "Arguments for a Derivational Approach to Syntactic Relations Based on Clitics" (Chapter ten)

A well-known complication concerning the data studied for subject-to-subject raising over an Experiencer is the grammatical source of cross-linguistic variation. Concentrating on Romance in the area of clitics, I show how certain aspects of the particulars of dative Case influence this variation for the languages considered. The analysis must be couched in a framework of derivational economy that imposes strict derivationality of the sort argued by Epstein and Seely (1999). Relevant comparison between languages of the French type and of the Spanish type attributes a range of grammatical differences between the two groups to a general property of "doubling" clitics, and the range of clitics that license *pro*.

Jan-Wouter Zwart: "Issues Relating to a Derivational Theory of Binding" (Chapter eleven)

The derivational approach to syntactic relations (DASR, Epstein et al. 1998), adopted here, implies (in its strongest form) that syntactic relations between α and β exist iff α and β are merged as sisters at some point in the derivation. In the spirit of DASR, Kayne (this volume) proposes that coreference results from the circumstance that the antecedent and the pronoun are merged as sisters, after which the antecedent moves up to the appropriate Case and theta-positions. This paper adopts the general outlook, but argues that Kayne's proposal applies to local anaphor binding only, not to nonlocal coreference/bound variable anaphora. The approach assumes that a reflexive pronoun is the marked Spell Out of an abstract category (bundle of features) PRONOUN, which acquires the feature [+coreferential (with α)] iff it is merged with α in a sisterhood configuration. Since the antecedent moves away from the PRO-NOUN via A-movement, the fact that the locality conditions on binding and A-movement coincide is accounted for.

Acknowledgments

For extremely helpful written comments we thank Pam Beddor, Joshua Epstein, Mark Hale, Richard Lewis, Elaine McNulty, and Jason Stanley.

Notes

1   Whitehead (1925) as cited in Carl Caither and A. Gavazos-Gaither, eds., (2000) *Scientifically Speaking*, Bristol: Institute of Physics, p. 305.
2   From C. S. Pierce, Chapter 5, "Training in Reasoning," in *Reasoning and the Logic of Things*, ed. K. L. Ketner, Cambridge, MA: Harvard University Press 1992, pp. 186–7.
3   As cited by E. Sober, *Core Questions in Philosophy*, New York: Macmillan 1991, p. 279.
4   Albert Einstein (1934) "On the method of theoretical physics." Delivered at Oxford, June 10, 1933. In *Ideas and Opinions*, New York: Bonanza Books 1954, p. 274.
5   From L. K. Nash (1963) *The Nature of the Natural Sciences*, Boston, MA: Little, Brown, p. 173.
6   Albert Einstein, *Ideas and Opinions*, New York: Bonanza Books 1954, p. 282.
7   See R. P. Feynman, R. B. Leighton, and M. Sands, *The Feynman Lectures on Physics*, vol. 1, chapter 26, p. 3, Reading, MA: Addison-Wesley 1963 (as cited in Freidin and Vergnaud's very insightful "Exquisite connections: some remarks on the evolution of linguistic theory." MS, Princeton, NJ, 2001, p. 22).
8   Notice that (D) constitutes a disjunctive, hence suspect, definition of the absolutely central notion "syntactic relation." See Epstein (2000) for discussion. Importantly, we believe that contra D(i) the bare Output conditions cannot "impose" relations, and (thus) the relations are, by hypothesis, only those created by the generative procedure (Epstein et al. (1998), S. D. Epstein (1999), Epstein and Seely (1999, forthcoming), a procedure which precisely relates categories by combining them (recursively). Chomsky's "optimal solution" question, we believe, is then whether the relations created by the generative procedure, are "used for" interface inter-pretation, as appears to be true of, e.g., c-command, hypothesized to be used both for the "purpose" of phonetic linearization, under Kayne's (1994) LCA, and for semantic/"LF" interpretation as well. See John Frampton and Sam Gutmann (this volume) who "argue that both the interface conditions and the derivational system which is designed to satisfy them are real, and in this sense we expect to find a pervasive redundancy in linguistic explanation."
9   See Chomsky (1994). As for labels, in the sense of Chomsky (1994), see the label-free program of Collins (this volume); and see also Seely (2000).

10   For an interesting recent debate see Hornstein (1998), Brody (1999), Hornstein (2000), Brody (2001).
11   See Hornstein (1998) and Epstein and Seely (1999; forthcoming).
12   See Hornstein (1998), Epstein and Seely (1999; forthcoming), and Lasnik (1999) for arguments that justice to experience is in fact not achieved through certain chain analyses, which these authors argue are empirically inadequate.

References

Brody, M. 1999. "Relating syntactic elements: Remarks on Norbert Hornstein's movement and chains." *Syntax: A Journal of Theoretical, Experimental and Interdisciplinary Research* 2.3: 210–26.

Brody, M. 2001. "One more time." *Syntax: A Journal of Theoretical, Experimental and Interdisciplinary Research* 4.2: 126–38.

Chomsky, N. 1981. *Lectures on Government and Binding*. Dordrecht: Foris.

Chomsky, N. 1986. *Knowledge of Language: Its Nature, Origin and Use*. New York: Praeger.

Chomsky, N. 1994. "Bare phrase structure." In G. Webelhuth, ed., *Government and Binding Theory and the Minimalist Program*. Oxford: Blackwell.

Chomsky, N. 1995. *The Minimalist Program*. Cambridge, MA: MIT Press.

Chomsky, N. 2000. "Minimalist inquiries." In R. Martin, D. Michaels, and J. Uriagereka, eds., *Step by Step: Essays on Minimalist Syntax in Honor of Howard Lasnik*. Cambridge MA: MIT Press.

Chomsky, N. 2001. "Beyond explanatory adequacy." MS, MIT, Cambridge, MA.

Chomsky, N. and H. Lasnik 1993. "Principles and parameters theory." In *The Minimalist Program*. Cambridge, MA: MIT Press, 1995.

Epstein, J. 1999. "Agent-based computational models and generative social science." *Complexity*, 4(5), 41–60.

Epstein, J. and R. Axtell 1996. *Growing Artificial Societies: Social Science from the Bottom Up*. Cambridge, MA: MIT Press.

Epstein, S. D. 1999. "Un-principled syntax and the derivation of syntactic relations," in S. D. Epstein and N. Hornstein, eds., *Working Minimalism*, Cambridge, MA: MIT Press, 1999.

Epstein, S. D. 2000. "Disjunctive relations," MS, University of Michigan.

Epstein, S. D., E. Groat, R. Kawashima, and H. Kitahara 1998. *A Derivational Approach to Syntactic Relations*. Oxford: Oxford University Press.

Epstein, S. D. and N. Hornstein, eds. 1999. *Working Minimalism*. Cambridge, MA: MIT Press.

Epstein, S. D. and T. D. Seely 1999. "SPEC-ifying the GF 'subject:' Eliminating A-chains and the EPP within a derivational model," MS, University of Michigan and Eastern Michigan University; paper also presented at the LSA Summer Institute (1999).

Epstein, S. D. and T. D. Seely (forthcoming) *Transformations and Derivations*. Cambridge: Cambridge University Press.

Hornstein, N. 1998. "Movement and chains," *Syntax: A Journal of Theoretical, Experimental and Interdisciplinary Research* 1.2: 99–128.

Hornstein, N. 2000. "On A-chains: A reply to Brody," *Syntax; A Journal of Theoretical, Experimental and Interdisciplinary Research* 3.2: 129–43.

Kayne, R. 1994. *The Antisymmetry of Syntax*. Cambridge, MA: MIT Press.

Kitahara, H. 1997. *Elementary Operations and Optimal Derivations*, LI monograph #31, Cambridge, MA: MIT Press.

Kitahara, H. 1999. "Eliminating * as a feature (of traces)," in S. Epstein and N. Hornstein, eds., *Working Minimalism*, Cambridge, MA: MIT Press.

Lappin, S., R. Levine and D. Johnson 2000. "The structure of unscientific revolutions," *Natural Language and Linguistic Theory* 18(3), 665–71.

Lasnik, H. 1999. "Chains of arguments," in S. Epstein and N. Hornstein eds., *Working Minimalism*, Cambridge, MA: MIT Press.

Phillips, Colin 1996. "Order and structure." PhD dissertation, MIT, Boston, MA.

Phillips, Colin (to appear) "Linear order and constituency." *Linguistic Inquiry*.

Reuland, E. 2000. "Revolution, discovery and an elementary principle of logic." *Natural Language and Linguistic Theory* 18(4), 848.

Richards, Norvin 1999. "Dependency formation and directionality of tree construction." *MITWPL 34: Papers on Morphology and Syntax, Cycle Two*, ed. Vivian Lin, Cornelia Krause, Benjamin Bruening, and Karlos Arregi. Cambridge, MA: MIT Working Papers in Linguistics.

Saito, Mamoru 1992. "Long-distance scrambling in Japanese." *Journal of East Asian Linguistics* 1: 69–118.

Seely, T. D. 2000. "On projection-free syntax," MS, Eastern Michigan University.

Uriagereka, J. 1999. "Multiple spellout," in S. Epstein and N. Hornstein eds., *Working Minimalism*, Cambridge, MA: MIT Press.

Chapter one

On the Status of Representations and Derivations

Michael Brody

1 Representations and derivations – the status of the mixed theory

1.1 Restrictiveness and duplication

As set out in earlier work, elegant syntax (ES) differs from the minimalist framework in several important respects.[1] I shall elaborate here some remarks made earlier on those features of this approach that relate to the so-called representational–derivational issue. I argued that since chain and move express the same type of relation, a theory that contains both concepts is redundant, and, therefore, at least in the setting of ES, wrong.[2] As has been also noted repeatedly, the issue is more general: there is a redundancy built into the architecture of theories that assume that both representations and derivations play a role in the competence theory of narrow syntax.[3]

Let us note first that a general conceptual argument from simplicity in favour of a pure (representational or derivational) theory against a mixed one is weak or nonexistent. This is because it is in principle possible that derivational and representational principles are both necessary in syntax and that they hold in different domains, and/or are distinguished also by other independently needed principles and properties – i.e. cluster in a modular fashion. Such clustering of properties with chains in one module and move in another does not seem to obtain in narrow syntax (the lexicon to LF-interface mapping), but this does not seem to be a necessary state of affairs, but rather an empirical fact about language. It may be that in wider domains, like the theory of mind, for example, both derivational and representational components will be necessary. The important point here is that the argument from redundancy against mixed theories of narrow syntax, to be discussed below, is not purely conceptual but is ultimately empirically based.[4]

Consider then representations and derivations in narrow syntax.[5] In principle there are two possibilities here (ignoring now logically possible but apparently nonexistent mixed situations that involve both possibilities in a modular fashion). Either derivational and representational accounts of the lexicon to LF relation are (a) empirically distinguishable, or (b) they are not. Although it may have been sometimes argued that both of these situations obtain, it is obvious that these two states of affairs are incompatible.

I return to (b) in the next subsection. Let us consider first the situation where we take (I think correctly, see section 1.2 below) the representational and the derivational theory to be empirically distinguishable. When the argument against the mixed theory was initially put forward there were essentially no attempts to construct analyses that relied on the existence of both derivations and representations. Given the lack of such arguments one obviously opts for either a fully derivational or a fully representational theory on general grounds of restrictiveness.

While there may now be some contributions in the literature that postulate both representations/chains and derivations/move and exploit one or another assumed (typically stipulated) difference between these pairs, as far as I am aware there are essentially no strong arguments for postulating both concept-pairs as part of narrow syntax.[6] Nobody has attempted to show that the results achieved in the less restrictive framework, that apparently involves systematic duplications (a property that is strange even in a minimalist setting, let alone ES), cannot be restated in a nonmixed system that avoids redundancy and lack of restrictiveness. There are also no attempts to argue that the assumed advantages outweigh the considerable burden of weakening the grammar. It is clear that even if focused arguments existed for the claim that both derivations and representations must exist side by side within the competence system of the language faculty and largely duplicate each other, these would have to be treated with extreme caution, since they would amount to a proposal to adopt a less restrictive grammar.[7] Everything else being equal, there are clearly more analytical possibilities in a theory that has both representations and derivations with differing properties than in a system that only has one of these concepts.

I shall refer to these considerations as the argument from restrictiveness against the mixed theory of narrow syntax. Let me summarize this argument. Suppose that representations/chains on the one hand and derivations/move on the other have different properties. (This seems to be the case.) Then it's an empirical question which notion(-sets) are the right ones. Having both would weaken the theory in the sense of increasing the analytic options available (see note 7), hence very strong arguments would be needed to maintain that both concept-sets are part of the competence theory of syntax. No strong argument appears to exist. Further, in addition to the problem of the unmotivated lack of restrictiveness, we would also have the problem of the unmotivated systematic (representational–derivational) duplications.

1.2   Principles of I-language

Suppose then, as is sometimes suggested, that arguments for a mixed theory are lacking because the issue they would address is effectively meaningless.

Representations and derivations are just notational variants, they are simply different approaches to expressing the same notions and the same generalizations. Suppose that there were no empirical differences to distinguish the derivational and the representational views.

But on such an assumption a mixed theory like standard minimalism only becomes more strange. Putting aside the uninteresting case where notational variance means synonymy – two names for the same concept – let us look at the situation where we take derivation/move and representation/chain to be two different aspects of, or two different ways of looking at, the same phenomena. Consider first a situation in physics that might be somewhat similar. The famous double slit experiment of quantum theory can be interpreted either in terms of probability waves or in terms of a particle being able to traverse multiple trajectories before hitting a target.[8] The two interpretations apparently do not result in distinguishable empirical predictions. (This is the case now, and may or may not remain so in the future). Assuming this fact, it would be a strange theory that postulates both multiple trajectories and probability waves, say mapping one into the other. It would be much like a theory whose ontology is committed to two entities, the evening star and the morning star, in the context of the assumption that ultimately they are empirically indistinguishable. The standard minimalist framework mapping derivations into representations appears to be equally curious – especially so when viewed from the perspective of ES, which rules out in principle the option of attributing syntactic redundancy to the effect of selection or to evolutionary accidents.[9]

To repeat, on the assumption that representation/chain and derivation/move are just notational variants (i.e. no empirical evidence distinguishes them), they are either just different names for the same notions or perhaps different but (at least currently) not empirically distinguishable notions. So one could suggest that the choice between them is not real, that one of them is just a way of looking at the other. In such a situation it may be reasonable to look for some deeper notions that subsume the two competing ones. But it seems mistaken to conclude from the assumption that, say, move captures the properties of chain, that both chain and move are part of the grammar. If we talk about (some module of) I-language, and say that y is part of it, hence a real object and furthermore that x is just an aspect of y, a way of looking at or treating y, this does not then seem to entail postulating x as a distinct element of the mind. Further evidence would be necessary for that, but by hypothesis this would be unavailable if the two notions cannot be distinguished empirically. I shall refer to this consideration below as the argument from I-language ontology. So this argument is meant to establish that the mixed theory cannot be defended even on the (empirically dubious) grounds of derivations and representations being notational variants. But the main argument against mixed theories remains the consideration based on restrictiveness and duplication: there is relatively little evidence for distinguishing derivations and representations, and not surprisingly there is essentially no serious evidence for adopting both.

2   Representations or derivations

2.1   *Derivational theories and weak representationality*

Suppose then that the rejection of mixed derivational–representational theories, mainly on grounds of empirically and conceptually unmotivated lack of restrictiveness, is correct. Next comes the related but distinct and secondary issue of whether syntactic theory is better thought of as purely derivational (PDT) or purely representational (PRT). By a PRT of narrow syntax (or LF) I understand a system that generates the interface level in the mathematical sense of generation. This consists of a set of constraints or principles that determine well-formedness. We could assume that, essentially as in the standard minimalist framework, these constraints can only include bare output conditions and a definition of possible LF structures (that bare output conditions constrain further).

Such a structural definition could, for example, run along the following lines: a representation (tree) consists exclusively of nodes ($n_1, \ldots, n_n$) and the immediate domination relation such that each node (except the root) must be immediately dominated by some other unique node (ensuring the connectedness of the tree). (This sketchy definition is not intended as an actual proposal, but simply as an indication of the form a representational definition of LF could take. Under various theories, various elaborations will be necessary and various aspects of this definition may follow from elsewhere. (See, for example, Brody (1997b, 2000a) and Abels (2000) for more extensive discussions of two versions of a particular approach along the above lines.)

We could proceed further by defining constituents recursively in terms of immediate domination. Alternatively, as suggested in note 5, we could take domination as the primitive notion and assume that x immediately dominates y iff x dominates y and there is no z such that x dominates z and z dominates y. A constituent will then be a subtree that contains every node a given node n reflexively dominates. (Note, however, that in the context of the theory in the works just cited, it may not be necessary to define constituents for the purposes of narrow syntax at all. If linking of chain members, binding, etc. are taken to be matters of interpretation – a natural and empirically motivated assumption – then constituents might be visible/created only in the interpretive components.)

I assume further, though not crucially, that the question of how to assemble as opposed to constrain (or generate, in the sense of "specify") the representation falls outside of the competence theory of grammar and is part of how the linguistic competence system is used – most plausibly it corresponds to the theory of parsing and sentence production.

A PDT is an ordered series of operations with input and output, where the input may only consist of terminals and the outputs of some other operations.[10] The following three-way distinction will be useful: (i) a derivational theory is nonrepresentational if the derivational operations create opaque objects whose internal elements and composition is not accessible to any further rule or operation; (ii) a derivational theory is weakly representational if derivational stages are transparent in the sense that material already assembled can be accessed by later principles (i.e. the derivational stages are representations); finally (iii) a derivational theory is strongly representational if it is weakly representational and there are constraints on the representations (weak sense) generated.

It is clear that derivational theories must be at least weakly representational. Take an object z, the result of merging x and y. At some later step move can only apply to y if z is a transparent rather than an opaque object since otherwise y would not be accessible or even visible for this operation. Notice that even if move is reduced to merge and an interpretive linking operation (as in the theory of distributed chains, Brody 1998b, 1999a), the same conclusion would still hold: the interpretive link between x and y could not be established if z was opaque. The derivational theory therefore is at the same time a (weakly) representational theory with multiple (weakly) representational stages instead of just one at the interface.[11]

So there can be no derivational theories that are fully nonrepresentational. The derivational theory will always be a mixed one to some extent. It would also seem to be almost necessarily a multirepresentational theory. One might think that this sort of weak representationality does not matter, since the spirit of the theory remains derivational. I can see two problems with this sort skepticism about the argument. First, weakly representational derivational theories are clearly mixed theories and the I-language ontology argument above in section 1.2 applies to them just as much as to any other empirically unmotivated mixed theory. The fact that all derivational theories must be mixed then appears to already provide a good reason for rejecting derivational theories of all kinds.

Secondly, consider the suggestion that weak representationality does not matter, because the crucial difference between the representational and derivational view is that the latter is not strongly representational, there are no representational constraints on the structures that the derivation assembles, hence these structures (although weakly representational) are still not levels of representation in some more important sense. But given that derivational theories are at least weakly representational, a derivational operation must have an input and an output both of which are at least weakly representational. Hence a derivational operation involves, or is equivalent to, a set of representation-pairs: a set of possible input–output pairs (in fact, representation n-tuples in the general case, since in principle there can be more than one input or output). The operation can thus equivalently be thought of as a member of a (partially?) ordered set of multirepresentational constraints. We can understand a weakly representational derivational theory as having an ordered set of such multirepresentational constraints.

It should be clear then, that the distinction between weakly and strongly representational derivational theory, despite appearances, does not really have to do with the derivational–representational distinction. What the distinction between weakly and strongly derivational theory really concerns is the question of whether there are constraints that are additional to those captured by the postulated derivational steps (whether we view these latter as representational or derivational constraints) and bare output conditions. Currently the restrictive working hypothesis of many linguists working in this domain is that there are no such additional constraints. But the answer to this question may be either negative or positive, both on the representational and on the derivational view.

Consider current "derivational" theory with the operation merge, some applications of which are a suboperation of move. The input of merge is any two well-formed representation WR and WR' (built from terminals and subtrees by merge) and the output WR" is WR augmented by WR' in a way that merge specifies. Thus in general merge is a tri-representational constraint. Where merge is a subpart of move, it applies to an element WR' of a tree WR and augments WR with a proper subpart of WR, WR'. What merge specifies is that WR and WR' will be sisters in WR" and furthermore WR" inherits its label from WR or WR' (in the case of move, always from WR for reasons independent of merge).

Thinking of the derivational approach as a multilevel representational theory, we see that this constraint is essentially equivalent to the requirement that at every level L a (sub)tree ST" is well formed iff (a) it immediately dominates two well-formed subtrees ST and ST' [whose correspondents are present at L−1] each composed of terminals and other subtrees (in the case of move, ST' is properly dominated by ST [at L−1]); and (b) ST" carries the label of ST or ST' (always ST in the case of move). Given this background, the question of whether there are any syntactic constraints that are additional to the structural definition of possible LF representations (whether in terms of merge and move or their representational equivalents, or in terms of different notions) has little to do with representationality or derivationality of the system. We expect, mostly on the grounds of the (at least partial) empirical explanatory success of theories heading in this direction, and on the basis of considerations of theoretical elegance, that there aren't any. But if there are, they can be stated either in derivational or representational terms. Note in particular that a constraint on a single representation can always be phrased as a bi- or tri-representational constraint with no restriction on the input(s), or with placing parts of the condition on the input as in fact happens in the case of merge and move. (Note in this connection also, that the square bracketed level statements above seem unnecessary, as expected from the viewpoint of the single level representational theory.)

Thus the essence of representationality appears to be weak representationality. Strong representationality does not seem to add a property that genuinely distinguishes between derivational and representational approaches. The distinction between weak and strong representationality in fact pertains only to the irrelevant, though otherwise important, issue of whether the elegant theory that assumes only a (hopefully trivial) structural statement and bare output conditions can be maintained. If it is true that the core concept of representationality is weak representationality, then of course, having shown that derivational theories must be weakly representational, the question of whether we should adopt derivational theories of narrow syntax again reduces to whether we should adopt mixed theories in this domain. As we have seen in the previous section, this we should probably not do.

2.2 *Restrictiveness again*

So current (apparently pure) derivational theory is equivalent to a restricted multirepresentational theory that has only such conditions on representations that can be stated as conditions that hold on two adjacent levels. As we have seen, it is in fact not clear that this really is a restriction with respect to a multilevel representational theory, since a single-level condition could be equivalent to a bi-level condition where the input may be any structure. The real difference between derivational and representational approaches is different. The representational theory is a single-level theory: all representations/ derivations except the "final" representation, LF, are eliminated – so conditions can only hold here. This is clearly one obvious way to constrain the multi-representational theory: assume the existence of only a single representation, the one corresponding to the final output of the derivational system. Henceforth I refer by representational theory unambiguously to the single-level representational approach. To emphasize the representational properties of derivational theories I shall use the term "multirepresentational."

The derivational approach constrains the multirepresentational theory differently, in a way that does not resolve the problems of the mixed theory. The derivational representational duplication now translates as the duplication between the final representation and the relevant aspects of all representations generated that carry the same information. Sisterhood and projection is duplicated at multiple levels by the effects of merge and chain by those of move.[12] The derivational theory ignores the problems of duplication and lack of restrictiveness, but suggests a different restriction. In this approach constraints like merge and move (which, as we have seen, are effectively equivalent to multilevel representational constraints) are individuated and are crucially required to operate in a sequential manner.

Perhaps there are aspects in which the sequential derivational theory is more restrictive than the unilevel representational theory in an empirically motivated way. As far as I know, this has never been argued and there is little to indicate that this might be the case. On the other hand, there is immediate evidence of this type for the unilevel representational theory. It is more restrictive than existing derivational approaches since it disallows bleeding relations, which do not seem to occur in narrow syntax. In particular the effects of the cycle follow automatically from the representational nature of the theory. But the cycle (unlike an inviolable extension condition that current derivational approaches reject) is just an additional stipulation under the derivational system.

If there really were derivational components in syntax we would expect bleeding relations to occur with some regularity, and if syntax was fully derivational, as is frequently suggested, bleeding relations should be commonplace. Derivational systems are eminently suitable to express the situation where one operation bleeds another rule or constraint. Consider cases where lack of bleeding of some constraint C can be detected as the fact that ungrammatical sentences (ruled out by C on one derivation) do not become grammatical on a different one where the context for C would not arise. Take for example the well-known fact that the wh-island or the subject island constraint cannot be bled by a derivation that involves movement before the relevant configuration is created, as e.g. in (1) and (2):

(1)   a.   What did you wonder Mary bought (what) when ==>
        b.   *What did you wonder when Mary bought (what) (when)

(2)   a.   Who was bought [a picture of (who)] ==>
        b.   *Who was [a picture of (who)] bought ([a picture of (who)])

   To deal with the descriptive problems, the usual restrictive assumption added to derivational framework has for a long time been the idea of the cycle in various incarnations. The derivations in (1) and (2) do not obey the cycle: cyclic application of all rules and constraints removes this empirical problem together with other similar ones. The solution is less than satisfactory if proposed as an explanation of the lack of bleeding in derivational frameworks. While the cycle may be a simple and attractive construct, nevertheless it is an additional stipulation that (as first observed in a somewhat different framework by Freidin 1978) appears to be unnecessary on the representational view. Until the cycle is independently motivated, the representational theory has the advantage of being more restrictive than the derivational theory in an empirically motivated way. The derivational approach can achieve the same degree of restrictiveness and empirical adequacy only by invoking an additional descriptive stipulation.[13]

   Epstein et al. (1998) proposed that the cycle is a consequence of an appropriately defined notion of c-command, together with a PF ordering requirement. The intuitive idea is that a relation based on c-command must be defined between all terminals of the tree – to make possible the exhaustive ordering of the terminals at PF by Kayne's (1994) Linear Correspondence Axiom (LCA) – and c-command is defined in terms of merge (as holding in a particular way between the merged categories, see section 3.1 below). In a countercyclic operation applying to A, A will not therefore have this c-command-based relation established with higher nodes in the tree. Such operations will thus be impossible.

   As noted in Brody (1997a), the account based on PF ordering does not rule out, however, all violations of the cycle. Since traces are invisible at PF and therefore do not need to be ordered, countercyclic movement or merger of A followed by cyclic raising of A is still incorrectly allowed. The approach allows also lowering rules if followed by cyclic raising – highlighting another aspect in which the derivational theory is less restrictive than the representational.

   In the representational theory chains are neutral with respect to lowering, raising, and round trip (lowering followed by raising into the same position) derivations. These distinctions by now rather clearly seem empirically unmotivated. Although they could be stipulatively grafted onto a representational theory, the basic concepts of this approach, unlike that of the derivational theory, do not naturally provide for these unnecessary distinctions.

The reliance of Epstein et al.'s explanation of the cycle on the LCA is also questionable. The status of the LCA as an external stipulation on an otherwise overgenerating derivational system raises the same issues as the cycle. Surely we should prefer a theory in which the basic building blocks of hierarchical relations simply did not permit the types of structures that in standard frameworks we need the LCA to rule out. Brody (1997b, 2000a) presents a theory with this property, and recently Kayne also discussed the problematic nature of the externally stipulated LCA and argued for a partly similar approach (Kayne 2000).

In addition to these considerations there is an even more crucial problem with deriving the cycle from (an appropriately constructed) c-command: the notion of c-command has a complexity presented by its asymmetrical nature, so it is probably even more problematic than the cycle that it is called for to explain. See Brody (1997b, 2000a) and below, especially note 18.

3   C-command

3.1   *Derivational definition*

Epstein pointed out in an influential paper (1995) – see also Epstein et al. (1998) – that in the cyclic derivational framework of the minimalist approach, c-command can be defined as in (3):[14]

(3)   x c-commands all and only the terms of a category y with which x was paired by merge or by move in the course of the derivation

He compared (3) with Reinhart's representational definition, which I restate in (4):

(4)   x c-commands y iff
    a.   the first branching node dominating x dominates y; and
    b.   x does not dominate y; and
    c.   x does not equal y.

Epstein claimed that the derivational definition in (3) answers certain questions concerning properties of the relation that are "unanswerable given the representational definition of c-command" (p. 19 in the MS). Before looking at this claim, notice that (4) can be made more easily comparable to (3) if it is restated as (5) in a form parallel to (3):[15]

(5)   x c-commands all and only the terms of its sister

He suggests that (3) explains that (a) x appears to c-command whatever the *first* (and not fifth, nth etc.) branching node dominating x dominates, since "this is the projected node created by pairing of x and y . . ." Furthermore x does not c-command (b) the first branching node dominating x, (c) nodes dominated by x and (d) x itself – in each case the reason being that x was not paired with the category in question by merge or move during the derivation.

But the derivational definition in (3) appears to give us neither more nor less insight into why these properties characterize c-command than the representational definition in (5). We can say without any loss (or gain) in understanding that x appears to c-command whatever the *first* (and not fifth, nth etc.) branching node dominating x dominates, since "this is the node that dominates (all and only) the terms of x and those of its sister y." Similarly instead of saying that x does not c-command itself, the nodes dominating it and the nodes it dominates because x was not paired with these, we can say without any apparent loss of insight that x does not c-command these because these are not its sisters (since all and only sisters are paired).

The insight these alternative definitions give is limited. In the case of the representational version we might ask why sisterhood is relevant. Additionally we don't know why x c-commands the terms of its sister rather than, conversely, x's terms c-command x's sister. Or why does not x only c-command its sister or why all x's terms don't c-command all the terms of x's sister. The same questions arise for the derivational statement: here we may ask why derivational pairing is relevant – notice that pairing is not identical to c-command but only enters its definition. The other questions just asked in connection with the representational version also arise here: why a paired category c-commands the terms of its pair rather than conversely, or symmetrically (i.e. why x does not only c-command its pair or why terms of x do not c-command terms of x's pair).

It is important to see that if the derivational account of c-command is to be taken as evidence in a strict sense for a derivational view, then the question of why derivational pairing is relevant to c-command cannot be answered by saying that derivational pairing is the only mechanism that establishes (purely) syntactic relations. The existence of derivations cannot be presupposed in an argument that wishes to establish precisely that. So this way of answering would beg the question: does the pairing relation have to be derivational?

Epstein suggests also that the fact that c-command makes reference to branching can be explained in a framework where "Structure Building (Merge and Move) consists of Pairing, hence it invariably generates binary *branching*." Again, this point is in fact neutral with respect to the issue of whether syntax should be constructed as a representational or derivational system. The assumption that pairing by merge and move is always binary is an additional assumption – there is nothing in the notion of concatenation that would force this operation to always be binary. The syntactic concatenation could in principle operate on any number of elements. This would allow also the unary operation alongside the binary, ternary etc. options. But just as the concatenation operation can be restricted to be binary, correspondingly, the branching of trees can be restricted to the binary option, ensuring the same result in representational terms: the elimination of nonbranching nodes (along with the elimination of other n-ary branching for n not = 2).

Additionally, Epstein argues that the representational definition of c-command is inconsistent with the independently motivated hypothesis of the invisibility of intermediate projections.[16] He considers the example of the category that is the sister to a VP-internal VP-spec subject – I will refer to this as V'. If V' is invisible for the computation of c-command relations then the elements contained in it (the verb and its complement) will c-command the subject and also the categories the subject contains. This is undesirable. On the other hand, Epstein suggests that the situation is different if c-command relations are determined derivationally by (3). Then even under the assumption that the intermediate projection V' can ultimately neither c-command nor be c-commanded (i.e. if its c-command relations established by (3) are eventually eliminated), the subject will still asymmetrically c-command the verb and its complement as required by Kayne's LCA. Notice that if V' is fully visible to c-command relations then the subject and V' will symmetrically c-command each other, creating problems for the antisymmetry hypothesis.

Given the assumption of antisymmetry, it seems necessary to assume that V' or more generally intermediate projections (or lower adjunction segments) are visible for the computation of c-command relation, but cannot themselves c-command or be commanded. There is nothing, however, in this state of affairs that would be "incompatible" with a representational view.

Consider instead the weaker claim that this behavior of intermediate projections can be naturally attributed to the assumption that at the point in the derivation where a category becomes an intermediate projection (i.e. once it projects further), its c-command relations become invisible (it neither c-commands nor can it be c-commanded) but nevertheless during the earlier stage of the derivation it has already participated in determining c-command by other nodes (it counts for the calculation of c-command by these).

The problem with this line of argument is that the interpretation of "becoming invisible" is not antecedently given, it is not any more natural to understand invisibility as entailing only the loss of ability to c-command and be c-commanded than to understand it as the loss of any c-command related role (including the role in the calculation of c-command relations between other nodes). Thus again the advantage of the derivational approach is only apparent. The statement that intermediate nodes participate in the calculation of c-command relations by other nodes but they do not participate in c-command relations themselves is not improved upon by saying that this latter property arises at a point in a derivation where the nodes become intermediate nodes/project further.[17]

3.2 Derivational explanation?

The various definitions of c-command – as Epstein notes in connection with his cyclic derivational version – do not explain why c-command exists, they just state its properties. The question remains why certain – or perhaps all – syntactic relations are restricted by c-command. Why cannot categories establish the relation with any other category in the tree? And if the set categories with which a given element can establish a (relevant) relation is to be restricted, why is it restricted precisely in the way the definition of c-command states, rather than in one of the infinitely many other imaginable ways?

Epstein offered an explanation within the cyclic derivational framework he adopted. This is based on two assumptions, which he refers to as (a) the first law/the unconnected tree law and (b) the law of pre-existence. The unconnected tree law states that a syntactic relation can only hold between elements that are members of the same tree and excludes relations between elements of unconnected trees. "Derivationally construed," as in (6), it disallows relations between elements that at any point in the derivation were members of different unconnected subtrees.

(6)   [Epstein's (27)] T_1 can enter into c-command (perhaps more generally, *syntactic*) relation with T_2 only if there exists *no derivational point* at which:
      (i) T_1 is a term of K_1 (not = T_1) and
      (ii) T_2 is a term of K_2 (not = T_2) and
      (iii)   there is no K_3 such that K_1 and K_2 are terms of K_3.

Given the cycle, the condition in (6) prevents sideways c-command between two elements x and y. In all such configurations cyclicity allows only derivations in which two unconnected subtrees have been formed at some stage that properly contain x and y respectively.[18]

Notice that "derivationally construed" actually adds another assumption to the unconnected tree law, namely that lack of (c-command) relation at any derivational level freezes and cannot be overridden later:

(7)   If there was no (c-command) relation at any given point in the derivation between terms x, y (both already merged into some subtree) there cannot be a relation later.

Statement (7) still allows x to have a relation to (c-command) y where y c-commands x, since in such a configuration no unconnected subtrees that contain both x and y have been formed.[19] Epstein excludes this configuration by his principle of derivational "pre-existence" (8), which disallows x c-commanding y on the grounds that y was not present when x was introduced.

(8)   x cannot bear a relation to y when y is nonexistent.

Given the assumption that the lack of a relation at a derivational point cannot be remedied at a later stage, i.e. (7), (8) entails the exclusion of what we might call upward or reverse c-command.

On closer examination, the condition in (6) does not actually explain, however, the impossibility of sideways relations. The intuitive content of the condition is that two categories unconnected at any point in the derivation cannot enter into a (c-command) relation. But in fact all merged/moved categories were unconnected before merger, all can still c-command the appropriate nodes. In order to allow categories to c-command at all, it is necessary to add the stipulation in (6i,ii) that "K not = T," i.e. that the top node of an unconnected tree does not count as an unconnected element. But this means that "K not = T" in fact just encodes the difference between c-command and lack of it. In other words, it encodes the difference between the c-command domain of x being the local dominating node of x (K = T) and a nonlocal dominating node of x (K not = T) not constituting such a domain. So instead of an explanation we have only another way of stating the c-command configuration.

Epstein comments on the "K not = T" restriction by noting about the top nodes (to be related by merge/move) of the unconnected trees, i.e. about K_1 K_2, that "each equals a root node, neither has undergone Merge or Move, hence each is (like a lexical entry) not 'yet' a participant in syntactic relations."[20, 21] In other words, the two instances of the "K not = T" stipulation in (6i) and (6ii) can be exchanged for an additional fourth subclause as in (6'):[22]

(6') T_1 can enter into c-command (perhaps more generally, *syntactic*) relation with T_2 only if there exists *no derivational point* at which:
    (i) T_1 is a term of K_1 and
    (ii) T_2 is a term of K_2 and
    (iii) there is no K_3 such that K_1 and K_2 are terms of K_3 and
    (iv) merge/move has already applied to T_1 and T_2.

The intuition (6') appears to express is that two terms that are integrated into some subtree by merge/move cannot form a relation if at any point in the derivation *after they have been so integrated* they are unconnected, i.e. they are members of distinct subtrees. With the addition of (6'iv), (6') states that if applying merge/move to two elements x, y does not result in a subtree of which both are terms, then x does not c-command y, that is, either x or y must have been merged with some tree that included the other. (Invert the conditional: if x c-commands y then merge/move applying to x and y must have resulted in a subtree that includes both.)

The explanation of the definition in (3) involves then breaking it up into two parts: x c-commands y if neither of the following two situations obtains: (a) there is no derivational point at which x, y have been integrated into unconnected structures and (b) there is no derivational point at which x is present/integrated but y is not. Clearly, we can bring the two parts of the account (6') and (8) together again, since in both cases what is crucial is that there is a derivational point at which a (sub)tree exists into which x is integrated but y is not. But whether or not we make this improvement, the account provides no evidence for derivations, since it can again be easily restated in representational terms.

Instead of referring to a derivational point at which there is a (sub)tree into which x is integrated but y is not, we can say that x cannot c-command y if in the single syntactic representation there is a subtree which properly contains (i.e. contains but is not equal to) x but not y. Instead of rationalizing that all derivational stages must be checked for x–y connection and, where no c-command holds, there was one at which x was in a (sub)tree that did not contain y, we can presume that all subtrees in the representation must be checked for x–y connection and we have no c-command where we find one in which they are unconnected. (Note also that the representational version is in fact preferable, if the bottom-to-top derivation and the cycle have no independent motivation (see Brody 1997a and the text above), since the derivational account needs to assume these. Furthermore, the easy translatability of the account into noncyclic representational terms provides some additional evidence against these constructs.) But until we have an explanation of why a relation cannot be established at a later derivational stage that connects the relevant subtrees that were unconnected earlier (or, in representational terms, why the connection must hold in all subtrees), it will remain at the very least debatable for both the representational and the derivational versions to what extent the account explains and not just rephrases Reinhart's definition.

In contrast to the clear exposition of the nonexplanatory nature of the definition in (3) in Epstein's paper, this definition is itself sometimes taken to provide a sufficient explanation of c-command. Thus, for example, Groat (1995) states that while c-command is arbitrary as a representational definition, "it is explainable as a property of the derivation." Take a configuration like (9), where Z c-commands A B C, A,B does not c-command Z:

(9) $Z+[_C \ A \ B]$

According to Groat this "follows straightforwardly if the relations formed by [merge] are in fact properties of the operation. Z is merged, hence Z is in relation with $[_C \ A \ B]$. A B were not merged with Z, hence they are not in relation with Z."

But again, we need to decide if merge/move applies to trees or to categories. If the former, then in (9) Z merges with C, hence Z does not c-command A and B. If the latter, then say $[_Z \ D \ E]$ merges with $[_C \ A \ B]$, and D and E are incorrectly predicted to c-command A and B. In neither case do we get the desired result. We can, of course, stipulate c-command again, by saying, for example, that it is always a category that merges with a tree.

3.3   Domination

The core of the c-command problem is the arbitrary asymmetric conjunction in its definition: x c-commands y iff the following two conditions of somewhat different nature obtain: (a) there is a z that immediately dominates x, and (b) z dominates y. It is crucial, but unexplained, that the two subclauses make use of different notions of domination. None of the attempted explanations, some of which I reviewed in the previous section, are able to explain this asymmetry.[23] Consider a different approach (Brody 1997b, 1999a). Instead of trying to explain the strange properties of c-command, let us assume that no such strange properties exist because, despite appearances, no notion of c-command is part of syntax or more generally of the grammar. Cases where c-command appears to be useful are cases of accidental interplay between two (in principle unrelated) notions, one of which is domination.

How about the other notion? In standard frameworks this must sometimes be the specifier–head relation and sometimes the head–complement relation. I shall only consider here the specifier–head relation because in the ES representation provided by mirror theory (Brody 1997b, 1999b, 2000a) the head–complement relation reduces to domination. (In mirror theory heads and the associated "projected" phrases are not distinguished in the syntactic representation, hence c-command by a head H reduces to domination by H.)

Consider a typical condition that refers to c-command like, for example, principle C of the binding theory. Suppose that spec–head agreement has the effect of the head inheriting/sharing the referential/thematic features of its specifier. Then instead of requiring that an R-expression not be c-commanded by a coreferential category we can prohibit the configuration where the R-expression is dominated by an Agr node carrying the same reference.

Similarly, the requirement that each chain member c-command the next can be straightforwardly restated in terms of domination. Again I ignore head chains here, since in mirror theory their members will be in a strict domination relation with each other. Consider chains that are constructed on potentially larger structures (phrasal chains in standard terms). Assume that the members of these chains always occupy spec positions. Let us think of the heads associated via spec–head relations with the spec positions occupied by the chain members as themselves constituting a chain, call it r(estricted)-chain. (Note that an r-chain is a chain whose members are heads, but it has nothing to do with the head chains expressing the head–chain/movement relation. In mirror theory head chains in this latter sense reduce to morphology and do not exist narrow syntax internally.) It is the domination relation that must hold then between members of r-chains. Additionally and independently we require that r-chain members must have identical or nondistinct specifiers. This is natural since the heads participating in the chain are by virtue of that fact at least in some respects identical, so they will naturally require identical, or at least nondistinct (see Brody 1997b, 1998b), specs.[24]

4   Summary

The representational framework seems more restricted than the derivational one in that there are many derivations for a single representation, but not conversely. I argued on the empirical grounds of bleeding relations that some of the derivations need to be eliminated to reach descriptive adequacy. Additional asumptions are necessary in the derivational framework, which are not entailed by the hypothesis that syntax is derivational. As we have seen, the corresponding problems do not arise in the representational framework where the correct consequences follow directly from the representational nature of the system. Additionally I provided arguments against mixed derivational–representational theories of the kind where derivations and representations essentially duplicate each other's work. I showed that no observationally adequate pure derivational theory can exist, that on closer examination derivational theories are mixed theories with derivational–representational duplications, hence arguments against mixed theories hold also against apparently pure derivational theories.

In the second part of the paper I argued that the derivational explanation of the asymmetry in c-command is unsuccessful, hence no argument for a derivational approach can be based on it. I suggested that the explanation may be so difficult to find because this complex notion is epiphenomenal only and does not exist within the grammar. I put forward an alternative approach, developed in more detail elsewhere,[25] according to which syntactic principles thought to refer to c-command refer to simple domination instead. Other independently necessary principles of spec–head agreement ensure that reference to domination, instead of c-command, is sufficient.

Note finally that derivational explanations tend to assume that merge is a conceptually necessary part of the competence theory of syntax, and argue that given its inevitability, it should be taken as a basic concept that makes various other assumptions unnecessary. All that seems really unavoidable, however, is that consequence of merge, that lexical items must be related in some way, so that they form a (connected) syntactic representation. Other properties of merge, like its derivational (sequential) nature, the fact that it relates sisters directly, and also its projection and labeling properties, seem to be stipulative and arbitrary. Although many linguists are used to the notion of merge as an unanalyzed primitive, at least sequentiality, projection and labeling are curious additions to some basic relation R between lexical items, and together they appear to form a strange and arbitrary package. Furthermore these properties of R seem to be unnecessary and eliminable. They are in fact eliminated in mirror theory, the approach to LF hierarchical structure that ES subsumes.

Acknowledgments

I am grateful to Noam Chomsky for a series of detailed and helpful e-mail exchanges relating to some of the points discussed. I'd like to thank also Klaus Abels, David Pesetsky, Sam Epstein, Daniel Seely, and Michal Starke for comments that I hope resulted in clarifications. As usual, no agreement on anything or transfer of responsibility is implied. Earlier prepublication versions of this manuscript appeared in University College London Working Papers (UCLWP), 12 and in Israel Association of Theoretical Linguistics (IATL), 8 (Tel Aviv University).

Notes

1   Brody (1997a,b, 1998a,b). Although in these works I referred to the framework of elegant syntax as perfect syntax, the operative sense of perfection was invariably that of theoretical elegance. Hence the change of terminology.
2   Brody (1995, 1997a,b, 1998b). As has been noted before, in Brody (1995), the argument against mixed theories (which include both the pure derivational and

the pure representational alternatives) and the argument for the representation option (as opposed to the derivational one) are clearly distinguished. A certain amount of confusion has been generated in subsequent literature by not always keeping these two points distinct.

3   See esp. Brody (1995, 2000a). For more recent discussions of the "architectural" duplication see Epstein et al. (1998) and Starke (2000). See also Hornstein (1999, 2000) and Brody (2000b, 2000c), among other related matters, for a discussion of a somewhat curious position that retains the architectural redundancy but wishes to eliminate the chain–move duplication. Hornstein (1999) also argues for eliminating chains rather than move, but on the basis of flawed arguments (Brody 2000b). He attempts unsuccessfully to defend one of these in Hornstein 1999. See Brody (2000c).

4   A possible argument against the approach I'm taking here might be that it focuses narrowly on LF. When we take the full theory of expressions generated by the grammar this seems to include a derivational component: a mapping from narrow syntax to PF. Therefore, one could argue, the overall theory of grammar would be simpler if the theory of the lexicon–LF relation was also derivational. But we seem to know too little about Spell Out for this argument to carry much force. First, it is not clear that the Spell Out component is indeed derivational (i.e. sequential) and not just a one-step mapping. Secondly, even if they are derivational, we do not know if the principles of Spell Out are different or similar to those of narrow syntax. The general idea of syntax being a generative and Spell Out an interpretive component would not make it unexpected that Spell Out principles have a different cluster of properties from the principles of narrow syntax. If this is the case that would make at least the intuitive simple version of the simplicity argument inapplicable. More complex versions – like, for example, that the same principles apply differently in the two domains (the differences being due to the different properties of the elements to which they apply) – may still hold. But again we seem to know too little about Spell Out to make any such point with more confidence than its opposite.

5   It is sometimes suggested that a representational approach simply translates a derivational approach and with the cost of involving richer set theoretical assumptions. It is not clear how the richness of the set theory involved is relevant to what is an empirical issue: which system is instantiated in the mind of the speaker. This is an empirical matter to which both empirical considerations and conceptual considerations of sharpening the concepts involved may be relevant, but the mathematical properties of the object postulated to exist will have to be whatever empirical research (with concepts adequate for the task) determines them to be. Once the set theoretical point is eliminated from the picture, as I think it should be, it is clear that a priori we do not know if the derivational theory is a (perhaps misleading) translation of the representational approach or conversely.

Recursivity of LF structures is also sometimes cited as entailing derivationality, at least in spirit. Note, however, that we can define LF without employing rules that reapply to their output. LF could be structurally characterized, for example, by some relation R (e.g. immediate domination) that all nodes have to enter (with special clauses for roots and terminals). For more discussion see e.g. Brody (2000a). It is expected that in the framework of ES no narrow syntactic principles will refer to the notion of constituent. That is, it would not be necessary to define constituents for narrow syntax, but only for the interpretive modules. But in any case the notion of constituent would not necessarily have to be defined recursively in terms of immediate domination. If the primitive notion is domination, then a node together with every node it dominates is a constituent – and immediate domination can also be defined nonrecursively in terms of domination without intervention.

Remnant movement is also sometimes taken to provide evidence for derivations. In a derivational theory the context for a simple statement of the c-command relation between the element moved out from a constituent to be moved itself (the remnant) is destroyed by the later step of moving the remnant. The problem, however, does not seem to arise in a representational theory with copies, given the assumption that c-command of traces inside chain members, like anaphoric connections in general, have to hold only with respect of a single chain member. This corresponds to the fact that in a derivational approach c-command has to hold only at one step of the derivation. That is, with X forming a chain with a copy (indicated here by "t") inside the bracketed chain-forming remnant ("X extracted from the remnant"), X needs to c-command only one of the relevant copies ("t's") inside the members of the chain formed from the two bracketed remnants in (i):

(i)   [...t...].....X[...t...]

Another question raised by David Pesetsky (personal communication) about representationality and remnant movement concerns principles of Spell Out, in particular, what ensures that in (i) the copy in the position indicated by the first "t" is silent. Concentrating on two-member "overt" chains without resumption, this appears to follow from the cyclic derivational theory. Move involves copy and delete. If X remerges and deletes before the remnant does (as it must, given the cycle), the original position of X in the copied remnant will be empty.

Note first that cyclicity of syntax does not in fact follow; the same result is translatable to a grammar with a representational syntax, if Spell Out is cyclic. Spell Out might have the two rules of identity check of chain members (corresponding to the identity requirement of copy) and +silent marking of the lower member (corresponding to part of delete). If these apply cyclically then identity check for the remnant will cover also the +silent mark on the lower copy of X in the lower remnant in (i), hence the higher remnant will have silent X. But even cyclicity of Spell Out can also apparently quite straightforwardly be avoided if we assume that the identity requirement on chain members covers also the +silent marking quite generally, but only up to recoverability. Thus in a remnant chain, if one member properly contains a +silent element, so must the other. But in an ordinary nonremnant chain, where the lower member is silent marked, the requirement will not entail that the higher member is also silent, since this would violate recoverability.

6   Heycock (1995) was one early case where it was explicitly argued that both derivational and LF conditions are necessary. For critical discussion see Brody (1997b) and Fox (1999). To take a somewhat random choice from relatively recent work that assumes and attempts to argue for a mixed theory, take first Nunes (2000), who argues that Move should be decomposed into copy (C), merge (M), form chain (FC) and chain reduction (CR). In fact M is not different from the usual merge operation that puts together phrase structures, CR is a Spell Out issue and C need not be separate from selecting from the lexicon the same thing twice. (The difference between the relation linking the two pronouns in "He said he left" and "He was seen (he)" does not have to do with different lexical access, as is sometimes suggested.) It is plausible to attribute that to FC having applied (or being able to apply legitimately) to the two pronouns in the second but not in the first structure. So only FC remains. In other words, it is not clear that this approach really needs to be different from a representational account. It looks different, of course, for Nunes C applies as part of a derivation. That a derivation exists and that C is part of it are thus additional assumptions.

In support of the assumption of keeping copy and (re)selection from the lexicon distinct Nunes refers to Chomsky's (1995) argument from expletive construction where greater cost is assigned to move than to merge to rule out (i).

(i) *There seems a man to have left

The strength of this argument is questionable since (i) may be excluded by independent reasons: for example, that no lexical element, expletive or not, is ever permitted in the infinitival subject position that follows *seem*-type predicates. On accounts that exploit this fact, assigning different cost to different derivations would become irrelevant.

In support of the assumption that derivation exists, Nunes cites also the following contrast:

(ii)   "*Which book did you review this paper without reading?"
(iii) "Which book did you review without reading?"

This is supposed to motivate derivations on the grounds that *which book* moved sideward from an island in (iii) before it became an island and then to the front while a similar non-island-violating derivation is not possible in (ii). But there are no reasons why a largely similar alternative account could not be given in a representational vocabulary. In (ii) *which book* is separated from its trace (theta position) by an island. In (iii) it is not, since there is a trace in object position of the matrix clause. The trace in the island causes no violation if the wh-phrase needs only a single thematic trace to be subjacent to it (see e.g. Richards' (1997) principle of minimal compliance, a major and very interesting generalization of a proposal in Brody (1995), or this latter work for a somewhat different approach). All this seems straightforward, and makes no direct reference to parasitic chains. It is not clear why the derivational approach would be better. In fact for there to be an argument for derivations here, it would be necessary to argue that something along these representational lines can not be right, otherwise Nunes' account (and the derivational equipment it is supposed to motivate) is redundant and therefore undesirable.

Lechner (2000) proposes an interesting analysis of NP-comparatives, where an empty operator raises to an intermediate spec-C position and the AP moves into the matrix:

(iv)   Mary met [young-er men]$_i$ [$_{CP}$Op$_j$ than Peter met [$_{DegP}$ [$_{AP}$ young men] Deg t$_j$]]

He suggests an argument for a mixed theory based on the following observation: "empty operators in spec-CP of the than-XP [do] not interfere with AP-movement" (p. 16). He observes that the two APs should not form a chain for thematic/ semantic reasons, hence he suggests that these APs are linked by a move operation that applied countercyclically to avoid the island effect induced by the empty operator. Note that countercyclic operations seem to be (a) quite problematic (see section 2.2 below) and (b) they also seem to be beside the point if the relevant locality constraints (like on Lechner's assumptions of the thematic requirements) apply only to chains. Furthermore, no crossing problem will arise if the matrix AP and the empty operator are coindexed and the operator in turn is related to the whole degree phrase in the lower clause – as in other similar constructions analyzed in terms of empty operator movement since the late 1970s. Lechner provides arguments from principle C, etc., that the structure does not involve pure deletion only but movement/chain, but his evidence does not seem to distinguish between linking the AP to its matrix clause correspondent or linking it only to the operator at the edge of the embedded clause.

Pesetsky and Torrego (2000) provide an interesting and intricate new analysis of the *that*-t effect and various related matters. They argue for what they call "relativized extreme functionalism," which appears to be an approach essentially identical to Brody's (1997a) bare checking theory. (I think the colorful name they give is misleading: the issue involved in eliminating features that are in principle uninterpretable is one of restrictiveness and has little to do with functionalism.)

In bare checking theory all features must be interpreted in principle, but in a given sentence some occurrences of features may be in positions where their usual interpretation cannot be assigned to them, where interpreting them would not make sense. In such cases occurrences of features of type t (say *wh* for example) in position(s) where they cannot be interpreted will have to merge (presumably via the chain and the spec–head relation) with another feature of type t that is in a position where interpreting it would make semantic sense. Pesetsky and Torrego's approach is not completely identical to bare checking theory because they wish to retain the otherwise apparently dispensable operation of feature deletion (as it follows feature checking) in order to integrate into their system the anti-*that*-t effects in sentences with topicalization like:

(v)   Mary said *(that) John she liked

However it is not clear if such sentences should or can be integrated with other data they analyze. Anti-*that* trace effects constitute a much less clear class of facts than *that*-t effects. Maybe a pause in cases like (v), where the matrix verb does not select for *that*, suffices, suggesting perhaps an approach in terms of parsing. Pesetsky and Torrego attempt to extend their theory to cover such facts, but at the cost of a set of otherwise unnecessary and ad hoc assumptions that in turn question the claim that these facts have genuinely been "integrated." It is necessary to reengineer their notion of locality into a less appealing form specifically to cover this case; it is necessary to retain the otherwise unnecessary operation of feature deletion; and it is even necessary to adopt a gamma-marking type mechanism, essentially identical to that of Chomsky (1999), that distinguishes deletion of a feature from the feature being marked for deletion – the latter carried part way through the derivation.

It seems fair to say that even if we assume that the anti-*that*-t effects must be treated syntax internally, Pesetsky and Torrego have not successfully integrated these into their theory. Assuming that anti-*that*-t effects need to be treated differently, all dubious theoretical adjustments and innovations just mentioned can be dispensed with. The argument for derivations that they consider to have provided then disappears, together with the curious gamma-marking type distinction between marking for deletion at one derivational stage and deleting at a later one. (Gamma marking for deletion as in Chomsky (1999) and Pesetsky and Torrego (2000) is clearly undesirable, and it is also dispensable in general since the deletion operation itself is in fact unnecessary – see e.g. Brody (1997a) on this latter point.)

7   To make the point of restrictiveness more concrete, recall for example that (as noted in Brody 1997a), Chomsky (1995) proposes a representational definition in addition to the derivational system of interface assembly (in effect an additional definition) of what counts as a well-formed syntactic object (cf. also Brody 1998a for some discussion). Or take the additional distinction he makes between deletion

(interface invisibility only) and erasure (essentially invisibility also for Move), where erasure occurs only if this would not violate the representational duplicate definition of well-formed syntactic object. Such duplications that exploit the derivational–representational duplication and distinctions that in turn might build on these additional duplications should probably have no place in a restrictive system of syntax and are indeed excluded in principle by avoiding the less restrictive mixed theory that makes them possible in the first place.

8   Remotely – and at least here irrelevantly – resembling syntactic chains.

9   See Brody (1995, 1997a,b, 1998b, 1999a, 2000b) and Epstein et al. (1998) for more discussion of the redundancy issue and related matters.

10 Actual PDTs and PRTs may have other restrictions, relating, for example, to the number of branches of nodes, etc.

11 If chain members are linked interpretively and at a single interface level, and furthermore the status of z can switch from opaque during the derivation to transparent at LF, then the theory may not be multirepresentational, but would still be mixed. The same conclusion seems to hold also for the various older and more novel multiply dominated single-element theories of chains, since the multiple positions of the relevant category need (also) to be interpretively linked. (Incidentally, this fact might render syntactic multiple domination unnecessary.)

12 In fact I argued that neither categorial projection (Brody 1997b, 2000a), nor the chain relation (Brody 1998b, 1999a) should exist narrow syntax internally, but I put these matters aside here.

13 Note that the examples in the text are not simply cases analyzed representationally that are translatable derivationally without any gain or loss in understanding – something that often seems to be the case with putative arguments for derivations. The examples here illustrate the point that there are several derivations for a single representation, some of which need to be stipulatively exluded by some principle that is not entailed by the derivational nature of the grammar. So it does not matter, for example, if in (1b) *when* in the lower spec-C is in the (intermediate) trace position of *what* or that there are two positions available here, one for each wh-phrase. The pure derivational theory that contains no traces/copies (if it did, it would encode earlier stages of the derivation into later representations) will not exlude (1b) without some auxiliary assumptions that prohibit the countercyclic derivation.

Similarly in (2) it is not relevant that the subject island constraint apparently holds of subjects only. This is not a stipulation that is additional to what would be necessary to exlude the structure in a derivational framework. Derivationally, the assumption translates as the constraint holding only for extraction from subjects. This much is necessary so that the structure be excluded on the cyclic derivation, but does not suffice to rule out by itself the countercyclic derivation. On the representational approach, the representational statement of the subject island does not need to be similarly supplemented by (some equivalent of) the cycle.

Consider a different line of attack. On the representational approach we need to ensure that the trace/copy inside the subject is part of the chain that includes *who* in spec-C and the trace/copy inside the object. But again this is not an extra statement that would correspond to the stipulation of the cycle on the derivational view. If one A-position copy of *who* would be a trace and the other would not be, then the two copies of the subject-to-object chain of *pictures of who* would not satisfy the identity requirement on chain members that corresponds to the identity requirement of move, which is "copy (involving identity) and delete" on the derivational view. But properties of move in the derivational theory do not ensure the ungrammaticality of the countercyclic derivation, while given a representational approach, the corresponding properties of chain do.

14   Sections 3.1 and 3.2 correspond, with minor changes, to sections of Brody (1997b). For the purposes at hand "term" in (3) can be taken as a synonym of "constituent." Citations of and references to Epstein's work in these sections relate to Epstein (1995).

15   Or, if binary branching was not assumed then:

(5')   x c-commands all and only the terms of its sisters

Note that sisterhood is taken not to be reflexive in (5)/(5').

16   In Brody (1998a), I argued that the best hypothesis to explain the invisibility of intermediate projections (for chain theory) is that they do not exist. See also note 12 for references to a later and stronger hypothesis ("telescope") that subsumes this one.

17   The problem of intermediate projections does not arise in the framework of mirror theory referred to in note 12, where no categorial projection exists.

18   Note that presupposing the cycle in the explanation of c-command and c-command in the explanation of the cycle (see section 2.2 above), as in Epstein et al. (1998), makes the explanation of these notions circular in addition to the other problems discussed in the text.

19   More precisely, no two unconnected subtrees have been formed that respectively properly include x and y.

20   More precisely, K_1 and K_2 have not yet undergone merge or the merge part of move.

21   Notice that "syntactic relation" here must mean: not yet part of the tree, and not as before, c-command.

22   Again, read "merge part of move" for "move" in (6').

23   It is often suggested that c-command follows from the way semantics works but proponents of this view typically do not raise the question of why the semantics they assume has to work in the way that the strange asymmetry of the notion of c-command/scope comes into existence, why this relation must be what it is. So in effect such accounts often restate c-command in semantics but do not attempt to explain its surprising property. In fact as far as I am aware, all attempted explanations in syntax or semantics so far simply define c-command differently and stipulate the asymmetry differently rather than explain it.

24   In Brody (1999a), some empirical advantages of this view are sketched. Additionally, the substitution of domination for c-command may solve the antisymmetry problem of the well-motivated instances of c-command from the right (see Brody 1997b, 2000a; Brody and Szabolcsi 2000). The latter work discusses also the extension of this view, that semantic scope is similarly a matter of domination.

25   See Brody (1999a).

References

Abels, Klaus. 2000. "Move?" MS, University of Connecticut.

Brody, Michael. 1995. *Lexico-Logical Form: A Radically Minimalist Theory.* Cambridge, MA: MIT Press.

Brody, Michael. 1997a. "Perfect chains." In Liliane Haegeman (ed.), *Elements of Grammar.* Dordrecht: Kluwer, pp. 139–67.

Brody, Michael. 1997b. "Mirror theory." MS, University College London. (Still earlier short version in *UCL Working Papers in Linguistics*, 9, University College London.)

Brody, Michael. 1998a. "Projection and phrase structure." *Linguistic Inquiry* 29, 367–98.

Brody, Michael. 1998b. "The minimalist program and a perfect syntax." *Mind and Language* 13, 205–14.

Brody, Michael. 1999a. "Chains in perfect syntax." Paper presented at the GLOW workshop on "Technical aspects of movement", Potsdam, April 1999.

Brody, Michael. 1999b. "Word order, restructuring and mirror theory." In Peter Svenonious (ed.) *Proceedings of the Tromso VO–OV Workshop*. 27–43. Amsterdam: John Benjamins.

Brody, Michael 2000a. "Mirror theory: syntactic representation in perfect syntax." *Linguistic Inquiry* 31.1.

Brody, Michael. 2000b. "Relating syntactic elements." *Syntax* 2, 210–26.

Brody, Michael. 2000c. "One more time." To appear in *Syntax* 4, 126–38.

Brody, Michael and Anna Szabolcsi. 2000. "Overt scope: a case study in Hungarian." MS, New York University and University College London.

Chomsky, Noam. 1995. *The Minimalist Program*. Cambridge, MA: MIT Press.

Chomsky, Noam. 1999. "Derivation by phase." MS, Cambridge, MA: MIT Press.

Chomsky, Noam. 2000. "Minimalist inquiries: The framework." In Roger Martin et al., eds., *Step-by-step: Essays on Minimalist Syntax in Honor of Howard Lasnik*. Cambridge, MA: MIT Press.

Epstein, Samuel. 1995. "Un-principled syntax and the derivation of syntactic relations." MS, Harvard University. Published version in *Working Minimalism*. 1999. Cambridge, MA: MIT Press.

Epstein, Samuel, et al. 1998. *A Derivational Approach to Syntactic Relations*. Oxford: OUP.

Fiengo, Robert and Robert May. 1994. *Indices and Identity*. Cambridge, MA: MIT Press.

Fox, Daniel. 1999. "Reconstruction, binding theory and the interpretation of chains." *Linguistic Inquiry* 30, 157–96.

Freidin, Robert. 1978. "Cyclicity and the theory of grammar." *Linguistic Inquiry* 9, 519–49.

Groat, Eric. 1995. GLOW abstract.

Heycock, Caroline. 1995. "Asymmetries in reconstruction." *Linguistic Inquiry* 26, 547–70.

Hornstein, Norbert. 1999. "Movement and chains." *Syntax* 1, 99–127.

Hornstein, Norbert. 2000. "On A-chains: A reply to Brody." *Syntax* 3, 129–43.

Kayne, Richard. 1994. *Antisymmetry of Syntax*. Cambridge, MA: MIT Press.

Kayne, Richard. 2000. "Recent thoughts on antisymmetry." Paper presented at the Cortona Workshop on Antisymmetry, May 2000.

Kuno, Susumo. 1998. "Binding theory in the minimalist program." MS, Harvard University.

Lechner, Winfried. 2000. Class handouts, Blago Summer School, July–August 2000.

Nunes, Jairo. 2000. "Sideward movement." MS, University of Maryland.

Pesetsky, David and Esther Torrego. 2000. "T-to-C movement: Causes and consequences." In M. Kenstowicz, ed., *Ken Hale: A Life in Language*. Cambridge, MA: MIT Press.

Reuland, Eric. 1997. "Primitives of binding." Utrecht Institute of Linguistics, working paper.

Richards, Norwin. 1997. "What moves where in which language." Doctoral dissertation. Cambridge MA: MIT.

Safir, Ken. 1998. "Vehicle change and reconstruction in A'-chains." MS, Rutgers University, NJ.

Starke, Michal. 2000. GLOW abstract.

Chapter two

Eliminating Labels

Chris Collins

This somewhat speculative and exploratory paper will argue that the labels of phrasal categories (e.g., VP versus NP) are not needed in syntactic theory. In other words, no operation or condition may be defined that makes reference to VP versus NP. An immediate consequence of this proposal is that bar-levels, such as X' versus XP, are impossible to define. This paper can be seen as an extension of the program, begun in Chomsky's 1994 paper "Bare Phrase Structure," to derive X'-Theory from more basic principles.

Perhaps the earliest use of labels was in the statement of phrase structure rules (e.g., VP → V PP, S → NP VP, etc.). Restricting combinations of constituents using phrase structure rules is possible only if the constituents have labels. It is now largely assumed that the effects of phrase structure rules are subsumed under various subtheories: Theta-theory, Case theory, X'-Theory, and subcategorization. Thus one reason to postulate the existence of labels has disappeared (phrase structure rules). However, it is still necessary to investigate the various subtheories to see how labels play a role.

In order to approach the issue in a concrete way, consider the theory of phrase structure articulated in Chomsky (1995a, 1995b). In this theory, a VP such as (1a) has the structure given in (1b):

(1) a.   VP
            ╱   ╲
           V   X
     b.   {V, {V, X}}

The structure in (1b) is a result of the operation Merge(V, X). In (1b), X is the complement of V. V is a minimal projection. The constituent {V, {V, X}} in (1b) is a maximal projection. X is also a maximal projection, since it does not project any further (X may or may not dominate further constituents). In a theory without labels, the structures in (1a,b) would be replaced by the structures in (2a,b) below:

(2) a.
         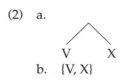
           V   X
     b.   {V, X}

Once again the structure in (2b) is the result of Merge(V, X). In these structures, there is no label. The only information that is represented is the fact that V and X are grouped together. Since there are no labels, there is no way to define whether any of the constituents is a maximal (XP) or nonminimal projection of a lexical item. In other words, in a theory with structures like (2a,b) it is not possible to state generalizations or formulate operations that refer to labels (like VP versus NP), or projection levels (like VP versus V').

In any theory of grammar, there will be a lexicon, a PF component and an LF component. In addition, there will be some operation (called Merge) that combines phrases and lexical items into larger phrases. This operation is a necessary part of any theory of human grammar. It allows us to explain how grammar makes "infinite use of finite means." In other words, given two constituents A and B, there must be some way to combine these into a larger constituent {A, B}. What is important to realize is that the notion of a label for {A, B} goes way beyond these elementary considerations, since in addition to the combination of A and B into one constituent, either A or B has to be designated as the label.

To put this in more concrete terms, consider (1) and (2) again. The question is whether the result of the operation Merge(V, X) is {V, X} or {V, {V, X}}. The fact that Merge(V, X) combines two elements into a larger phrase is a necessary part of any theory of human language. The assumption that {V, {V, X}} is formed rather than {V, X} (that a label is chosen), goes way beyond what is necessary for grammar to make "infinite use of finite means."

In Chomsky's analysis illustrated in (1b) bar-levels are not explicitly represented. However, Chomsky (1995b: 242) defines the notions of minimal, intermediate, and maximal projections: "A category that does not project any further is a maximal projection XP, and one that is not a projection at all is a minimal projection X; any other is an X', invisible at the interface and for computation." Chomsky also uses the notions of minimal, intermediate, and maximal projections in the explanation of certain principles, in particular, the Uniformity Condition (Chomsky 1995b: 253) and the ordering of a specifier and an intermediate projection (Chomsky 1995b: 336). In the theory given in (2), it is not even possible to define minimal, intermediate, and maximal projections (since there is no label that serves to project features).

I will try to avoid using the term "head" as much as possible, since it is a somewhat ambiguous term in syntactic theory. One use of the term "head" corresponds closely to the way I am using the term "label," which is defined by structures like (1). Note that I am not arguing against category labels like N, V, P, Adj for lexical categories. Every word has some categorial feature. Rather, I will be arguing that these categorial features do not project and therefore (nonlexical) phrases do not have labels.

In this chapter, I will defend structures like those in (2a,b). I will show how some of the phenomena that have been explained using labels can be explained in other ways. In section 1, I show that some of the basic properties of X'-Theory can be derived without labels. In section 2, I show that basic properties of selection (in particular, subcategorization) can be handled without labels. This crucially involves extending the notion of Minimality (Relativized

Minimality, the Minimal Link Condition) to subcategorization features. In section 3, I show that the Minimal Link Condition (MLC) makes implicit use of labels, and discuss how the MLC can be modified so as not to make reference to labels. In section 4, I briefly discuss the question of whether labels are needed at the PF interface. Section 5 is a summary.

Since virtually every syntactic analysis in the generative tradition makes use of labels on phrasal categories (either implicitly or explicitly), the task of eliminating labels from syntactic theory is enormous. This paper will only suggest an outline of what a theory without labels would look like.

The resulting label-free theory of syntax turns out to be much more derivational than a theory with labels. Labels are a part of a representation. Once they are formed, they persist throughout the derivation.

In a highly derivational theory, all syntactic generalizations must be derived from the interaction of economy conditions, the properties of individual lexical items (e.g., X has an uninterpretable feature F, X needs two arguments), and interface conditions (bare output conditions, or legibility conditions).

1   Basic properties of X'-Theory

In this section, I will show how some of the basic properties of X'-Theory can be derived in a theory without labels. The basic properties of X' Theory are illustrated below (see Jackendoff 1977 for an early systematic treatment; see also Fukui 2001 for a clear historical overview):

(3)   XP

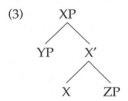

First, every phrase (XP, YP, ZP) has a label. Second, a lexical item X may have a complement and a specifier (it may be possible for there to be more than one specifier). Third, the complement and the specifier are maximal projections.

I would like to put forth the following hypothesis:

(4)   The generalizations of X'-Theory can be reduced to statements about derivational syntactic relations and economy conditions.

The syntactic relations are (at least) the following:

(5)   a.   Theta(X, Y)   X assigns a theta-role to Y
      b.   EPP(X, Y)   Y satisfies the EPP feature of X
      c.   Agree(X, Y)   X matches Y, and Y values X
      d.   Subcat(X, Y)   X subcategorizes for Y

Theta(X, Y) holds between X and Y when Y is assigned a theta-role by X. For example, in "John rolled the ball," "roll" assigns a theme theta-role to "the ball" (a maximal projection). EPP(X, Y) holds between X and Y when Y satisfies the EPP requirement of X. In English, the EPP forces Infl to have a specifier (whether or not Infl is finite). Agree(X, Y) holds between X and Y when X matches Y and Y values X. For example, the interpretable phi-features of a DP value the unvalued phi-features of Infl (which are deleted at Spell Out). Subcat(X, Y) holds between X and Y when X subcategorizes for Y. For example, D subcategorizes for an NP, so we have the relation Subcat(D, NP). I will return to a more articulated theory of subcategorization in section 2.

There may be other local syntactic relations that play a role in projecting phrase structure, but those in (5) are sufficient for our purposes. I will assume that these syntactic relations play a role in the syntax in the manner described in Chomsky (2000). Consider first Merge (we return to Agree in sections 2 and 3). When A and B are merged, a feature F of one of the merged elements must be satisfied for the merge operation to take place. This feature F is called the selector (which is analogous to the probe in the Agree relation). In other words, Merge satisfies Last Resort (see also Collins 1997: 66 and especially Watanabe 1996: 142). For example, suppose that the expletive "there" is to be merged into Spec IP. This operation is licensed by the presence of the EPP feature of Infl which selects "there." Similarly, if a DP is merged with a verb, this is licensed by the presence of a theta-role that the verb has to assign. In other words, it is the theta-role of the verb that selects the DP.

Chomsky furthermore proposes that if two categories X and Y are merged, the category that projects is the one that contains the selector for Merge. For example, if "there" and I′ merge, I′ projects. If V and DP merge, V projects. In this way, the label of a constituent is entirely predictable, and therefore it does not have to be represented. I do not adopt this analysis, since it assumes the existence of labels.

Given these background assumptions (the set of syntactic relations in (5), and the theory of Merge), let us return now to the basic properties of X′-Theory. First, consider the fact that a lexical item can have a complement and a specifier. If the lexical item X has a syntactic property that needs to be satisfied, it will select an element Y to form {X, Y}. Y is what we call the complement. The notion of complement has no other significance. If X has an additional property, it selects an element Z to form {Z, {X, Y}}. The position that Z occupies is the closest possible position to X (given the fact that Y has already been merged to X). Z is what we call the specifier. The notion of specifier has no other significance.[1]

Consider now the principle of X′-Theory that the complement and the specifier must be maximal projections. This principle blocks the following type of structure: [$_{XP}$ X Z′]. A number of structures that are blocked by this principle of X′-Theory are the following: [$_{CP}$ Comp Infl′], [$_{I′}$ Infl V′], [$_{VP}$ V Comp′].

In the structure [$_{XP}$ X Z′], a nonmaximal projection Z′ is the complement of X. In the framework of Bare Phrase Structure (Chomsky 1995a), it is not possible to have [$_{XP}$ X Z′]. The reason is that the complement of X is a ZP by definition, since Z does not project any further. Since this analysis assumes the existence of labels, I do not adopt it.

A different way of looking at the constraint against [$_{XP}$ X Z'] is the following: if Z only projects to the Z' level, this means that Z has some probe/selector that has not been satisfied. Furthermore, since Z' is the complement of X, Z's probe/selector will never be satisfied. In order to formalize these intuitions, we will make use of Chomsky's (2000: 132) condition on lexical access, which I will call the Locus Principle (the following condition is a slightly modified version of Chomsky's condition; see also Frampton and Gutmann 1999: 7; 2000: 8):

(6)   Let X be a lexical item that has one or more probe/selectors. Suppose X is chosen from the lexical array and introduced into the derivation. Then the probe/selectors of X must be satisfied before any new unsaturated lexical items are chosen from the lexical array. Let us call X the locus of the derivation.

A lexical item is *saturated* if it does not contain any probe/selectors.[2] A lexical item that contains at least one probe or selector is *unsaturated*. In other words, the determiner "the" is unsaturated, since it subcategorizes for an NP (see section 2 below for more on subcategorization). Other elements that are unsaturated include the verb "destroy" (which assigns an agent and theme theta-role), the finite complementizer "that" (which subcategorizes for a finite Infl), the infinitival "to" (which subcategorizes for a VP), etc.

Consider a concrete case discussed in Chomsky (2000: 138), whose analysis I essentially adopt. We would like to block the combination of a complementizer (such as "that") with Infl', forming the constituent [$_{CP}$ Comp Infl']. Our goal is to block this combination without reference to the notion of maximal projection (or, more generally, to the notion of label).

Consider the following derivation. I will assume that the lexical items are copied out of the lexicon and put in a lexical array (LA) (following Chomsky 2000: 100, although see Collins 1997 for critical discussion of the Numeration). Lexical items are chosen from the lexical array and put into a workspace, where they can play a role in the derivation:

(7)   a.   Choose "John" from the lexical array.
       b.   Choose "arrive" from the lexical array.
       c.   Merge(John, arrive) = {John, arrive}, satisfying the theta-role of "arrive."
       d.   Choose "will" from the lexical array.
       e.   Merge(will, {John, arrive}) = {will, {John, arrive}}, satisfying the subcategorization feature of Infl "will."
       f.   Choose "that" from the lexical array.
       g.   Merge (that, {will, {John, arrive}}) = {that, {will, {John, arrive}}}, satisfying the subcategorization feature of Comp "that."

The problem with this derivation occurs at step (f). After step (e), Infl still has an EPP feature that needs to be satisfied. Therefore, the locus just after step (e) is Infl (which contains "will"). At step (f), the complementizer "that" is chosen from the lexical array. The Comp has a selector, which is its sub-categorization feature. Since two unsaturated lexical items occupy the workspace simultaneously, the derivation is ruled out by the Locus Principle.

Consider now a few other derivations that are blocked by the Locus Principle:

(8)   {{see, the}, man}
  a.   Choose "see" from the lexical array.
  b.   Choose "the" from the lexical array.
  c.   Merge(see, the) = {see, the}.
  d.   Choose "man" from the lexical array.
  e.   Merge({see, the}, man) = {{see, the}, man}.

This derivation is blocked at step (b), since "see" has a theta-role that has not yet been satisfied. Therefore, the Locus Principle derives the fact that in the string "see the man," "the" and "man" form a constituent.

(9)   {John, {will, {see, Mary}}}
  a.   Choose "see" from the lexical array.
  b.   Choose "Mary" from the lexical array.
  c.   Merge(see, Mary) = {see, Mary}.
  d.   Choose "will" from the lexical array.
  e.   Merge(will, {see, Mary}) = {will, {see, Mary}}.
  f.   Choose "John" from the lexical array.
  g.   Merge(John, {will, {see, Mary}}) = {John, {will, {see, Mary}}}.

The problem with this derivation is at step (d). Since "see" has not satisfied both of its theta-roles, it is impossible for "will" to be chosen from the lexical array. Therefore, the Locus Principle derives the VP Internal Subject Hypothesis.

We can extend the term "saturated" to constituents that are not lexical items. Suppose that Y (a phrase) contains a lexical item X that contains at least one probe or selector (that has not been satisfied internal to Y). Then we call Y unsaturated. For example, the constituent {PRO, {to, leave}} in the sentence "I tried to leave" is saturated. However, the constituent {to, leave} is unsaturated since the EPP feature of "to" needs to be satisfied. Similarly, the constituent {give, {to, John}} is unsaturated, since the theme theta-role of "give" needs to be assigned.

What about structural Case? I claim that constituents such as {the, man} are saturated. Certainly, {the, man} has an unvalued Case feature that needs to be valued and deleted. The reason that this Case feature does not render {the, man} unsaturated is that the Case feature of {the, man} is not an attractor (in the sense of Chomsky 1995b) or a probe/selector (in the sense of Chomsky 2000). In fact, Chomsky (2000) argues that the function of Case is to make a goal active (not to act as a probe).[3]

The notion of saturated constituent (in the label-free theory) is similar to the X'-Theory notion of maximal projection. For example, the generalization that the complement of X must be a maximal projection can be restated as the generalization that the complement of X must be a saturated constituent. In fact, Koopman and Sportiche (1991: 215) state just this condition: "No category takes as a complement a syntactic category corresponding to a non-saturated predicate."

Since the notion of maximal projection does not exist in a label-free theory, it is impossible to define m-command (see Chomsky 1995b: 35). It is, however, possible to define c-command. X c-commands Y iff Y is contained in the sister of X (see Chomsky 2000: 116; see also Seely 2000 for an extensive discussion of c-command in a label-free theory).

Another property of X'-Theory is the possibility of adjunction. It is impossible to define adjunction in a theory without labels. This is made particularly clear in the theory of Chomsky (1995a, 1995b: 248), where adjunction structures are defined as follows:

(10) $L = \{<H(K), H(K)>, \{\alpha, K\}\}.$

In this structure, α is adjoined to K yielding L. Now note that this definition requires the label $<H(K), H(K)>$. If L had no label, adjunction would be impossible to define in this way. The empirical facts that have been analyzed with adjunction (for example, those of Kayne 1994) need to be given alternative accounts, a task which I will not take up in this paper for lack of space.

It is obvious that the notion of label and the notion of locus are closely related. For example, if a word X with a probe/selector is merged with a constituent Y to form {X, Y}, then X is the label in a theory with labels and X is the locus in a theory without labels. The major difference between a label and a locus is that there is only one locus at a particular point in a derivation, but there are many labels; each constituent has a different label.

Another related difference concerns the amount of search that must be done in a derivation. Suppose at a given step in the derivation A, B and C have been formed (and they have not yet been merged to each other). The next step in the derivation can be one of the following: choose a lexical item from the lexical array, merge two elements (satisfying a selector), or establish an Agree relation (satisfying a probe). In order to apply Merge or Agree, a probe/selector must be found. Chomsky (2000: 132, 134) proposes that the probe/selector must be found in the label of A, B, or C. Chomsky argues that this restriction follows because the search for probe/selector must be minimized, and restricting the search to the label of some syntactic object limits the search. If there are three elements A, B, and C, we search the labels to find a probe/selector. But this involves search, since each of A, B, and C have labels. The size of the search increases with the number of elements in the workspace. For example, suppose that a DP, a CP, and a VP occupy the workspace (assuming a theory with labels). Suppose furthermore that VP is unsaturated, so that V still has a feature to satisfy. In order to find a probe or a selector, the labels of each of these three constituents must be examined.

Does the Locus Principle eliminate search? The Locus Principle presupposes a kind of memory in the derivation (the locus). In order to apply an operation, we look at the locus to find a probe/selector. I make the further stipulation that the locus is identifiable in the workspace with no search. Rather, *the locus is the lexical element from which all search takes place (search to find a goal, search to find a constituent to Merge or Move, search to find a new locus)*. To extend the metaphor, the locus is the bench in the workspace on which all the actual work is done.

In the context of the issue of derivational versus representational approaches to syntax, a locus is much more of a derivational notion than a label. A label, once created, remains in existence for the rest of the derivation as part of the representation that is continually being built. A label is accessible throughout the derivation and at the interfaces. A locus is ephemeral; once exhausted, it ceases to be the locus.

The Locus Principle can be seen as a particular example of "As Soon As Possible" (ASAP) (see Yang 1997; Collins 2001; Ura 1996: 41). If it is possible for a feature of the locus to be satisfied, then it must be. Whether other economy conditions apply to accessing the lexical array (or the lexicon) is a topic that needs to be investigated.

2 Selection

The selection of a constituent Y by a lexical item X is an area where labels and projections have been traditionally used. In order to approach the topic of selection, we need to make a distinction between several different types of selection.

First, there is what is called s-selection (see Grimshaw 1981; Pesetsky 1982). This arises when the relation between a lexical item and its complement is semantic in nature. Consider the following examples:

(11) a. John asked what time it was.
      b. John asked the time.

(12) a. John wondered what time it was.
      b. *John wondered the time.

Pesetsky (1982: 193) assumes that the Canonical Structural Realization (CSR) of propositions, questions, and exclamations is DP or CP. Both the verb "ask" and the verb "wonder" s-select a question. In (11a) this is realized as a CP, and in (11b) the embedded question is realized as a DP. Pesetsky argues that "wonder" s-selects for a question, but does not assign accusative Case. There-fore, the complement of "wonder" cannot be a concealed question, since the DP complement would receive no Case (see (12b)).

What seems to be clear is that s-selection is not selection for some property of the label of the XP complement. In other words, we cannot say that the verb "ask" s-selects for a Q complementizer in (11a). The reason is that in (11b), there is no complementizer and there is still s-selection for a question. There-fore, s-selection does not require labels.

There are also cases of selection that are not obviously reduced to s-selection. These are cases traditionally grouped under the name "subcategorization" (or c-selection). I am assuming that subcategorization cannot be reduced entirely to s-selection (see Grimshaw 1981, 1991; Pesetsky 1982; Chomsky 1986; Sag and Pollard 1989; Chomsky and Lasnik 1993; and Odijk 1997 for discussion of the issue). I should point out that if it turned out that all cases of subcategorization (see (13) below) could reduce to s-selection, there would be even less of a need for labels, since I have just shown that s-selection does not make reference to labels.

Consider the following examples (in each case, I underline the lexical item which has a subcategorization requirement), where the subcategorization frames are given on the right:

(13) a. I <u>told</u> on John   "tell" [__PP$_{on}$]
      b. <u>the</u> destruction/*destroy   "the" [__ NP]
      c. I <u>will</u> go to the store   "will" [__ VP]
      d. I <u>have</u> eat-en the food   "have" [__ VP$_{en}$]
      e. <u>that</u> John will leave   "that" [__ IP$_{fin}$]
      f. <u>too</u> happy to leave   "too" [__ CP$_{inf}$]
      g. <u>so</u> happy that I will leave   "so" [__ CP$_{fin}$]^4

The above cases are diverse, but all represent some type of selection. In (13a), the verb "tell" selects a PP whose label is the particular preposition "on." There are many cases of this nature where a lexical item selects for some particular lexical item in its complement. In (13b) a determiner selects for a following NP. It is impossible for the determiner to be followed by a VP. It is difficult to see how this fact could be attributed to semantics, since both the VP "destroy" (true of events) and the NP "destruction" (true of events) are semantically predicates of events. Note that I am not drawing any distinction between selection by a lexical category (13a) and selection by a functional category (13b–g).^{5}

There are essentially two (empirically equivalent) theories of subcategorization that have been used in generative grammar to capture these dependencies. In one theory, a lexical item subcategorizes for an XP with certain properties (14a). In the other theory, a lexical item subcategorizes for a particular feature or lexical item (14b). These two theories are illustrated below:

(14) a. tell: [__PP$_{on}$]
      b. tell: [__ on]

In (14a), the subcategorization frame specifies that the verb "tell" requires a PP sister with the features of the lexical item "on." The lexical item that the PP can inherit features from is "on" (since P is the label of the PP). This approach relies on the following assumption:

(15) The subcategorization requirements of H are satisfied under sisterhood.

The subcategorization frames in (13) reflect the "sisterhood" theory of subcategorization.

In (14b), the subcategorization frame specifies that the verb "tell" requires a particular lexical item "on" in the following constituent. This lexical item is guaranteed to be the label of the following constituent by the following principle (modified from Baltin 1989):

(16)   Subcategorization is always for the label (in other words, the head).

Both of the theories above (14a,b) rely on the notion of label. Without labels and projections, we have to make sure that when "tell" takes a constituent as a complement, the complement contains "on" in a position that is not too deeply embedded. To clarify what is at issue consider the following diagram:

(17)

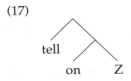

The question is, if there is no label, how are the selectional properties of "tell" satisfied in (17)? The central intuition that I want to pursue is that the local relationship found between a lexical item X and the selected item Y (a feature or lexical item) is fundamentally similar to the local relation existing between a moved element and its trace.[6]

I will implement this idea using Chomsky's (2000, 2001) theory of Agree. In this theory, Agree holds between a feature of a lexical item (the probe P) and the feature that it matches (the goal G). The Agree relation is subject to several conditions. First, the probe must be identical to the goal in features (like number). Second, the probe must c-command the goal. Third, there is a locality relation between the probe and the goal. I will call this relation Minimality, and I adopt Chomsky's (2000: 122) formulation (I will return to some further aspects of Minimality in section 3):

(18)   **Minimality**
       Let P be a probe and G be a matching goal. Then P and G satisfy
       minimality if there is no G' matching P such that P asymmetrically
       c-commands G' and G' asymmetrically c-commands G.

Consider the following example of agreement in an expletive construction:

(19)   there are people in the room
            probe = phi-features of Infl
            goal = phi-features of "people"

The probe matches the goal, and there is no other set of matching phi-features intervening between the probe and the goal. Therefore, the phi-features of "people" value the unvalued phi-features of Infl under matching. I follow Chomsky (2000: 124) in assuming that what matters for Minimality is identity of features (like number), not feature value (like singular or plural).

Given Chomsky's theory of Agree, we can now formulate our theory of subcategorization. I will call the relation Subcat. I will make the following assumptions. First, following Baltin (1989), the subcategorization frame of a lexical item X is of the form [__Y], where Y is some feature or lexical item (e.g., +/−V, +/−N, Infl$_{fin}$, "on", etc.). Second, I will assume that the subcategorization feature of X needs to be satisfied. It is unclear whether a subcategorization feature of X needs to be valued. Third, the satisfaction of a subcategorization feature takes place under identity. Fourth, if Subcat(X,Y) (where Y satisfies a subcategorization feature of X), then X c-commands Y. Fifth, the satisfaction of the subcategorization feature of X must obey Minimality.

In addition, I will make the following assumption about how Minimality applies to subcategorization for lexical categories:

(20)   If X selects Y (where Y is a lexical category),
       then *X Z Y
       where Z intervenes between X and Y, and Z is any lexical category
       (+/−V, +/−N)

I assume that Z intervenes between X and Y if X asymmetrically c-commands Z and Y, and Z asymmetrically c-commands Y (in other words, Z is closer to X than Y is).[7] This locality condition has the result that subcategorization for a lexical feature is blocked by any other lexical feature. In (17), the probe is [__on], which is the subcategorization feature of "tell." This feature is satisfied by the lexical item "on," which is contained in the sister of "tell" (in other words, the relation Subcat(tell, on) is established). Since no lexical category intervenes between "tell" and "on," Minimality is satisfied (this account will be revised in section 2.2).

In the following example, "the" subcategorizes for a N category:

(21)   a.   {the, destruction}
       b.   *{the, destroy}
       c.   *{the, {destroy, {the, city}}}
       d.   *{the, {destroy, cities}}

In (21b), "the" subcategorizes for N, but is only followed by a verb. In (21c), "the" is followed by both the verb "destroy" and the noun "city." However, "destroy" intervenes between "the" and "city," and so "city" cannot satisfy the subcategorization feature of "the" (by Minimality). The extremely local nature of subcategorization (as opposed to agreement for phi-features) follows from the fact that any lexical category (+/−N, +/−V) can block subcategorization for any other lexical category.[8] In (21d), "destroy" does not asymmetrically c-command "cities," so "cities" should be able to satisfy the subcategorization feature of "the." One way to handle this example would be to postulate the presence of a null determiner preceding "cities" so that the structure would be {Det, cities}. If this were the correct structure, "destroy" would asymmetrically c-command "cities," blocking Subcat(the, cities). I will return to an alternative in section 2.2 below.

Consider now an example, where a functional projection does not block subcategorization (modified from Rothstein 1991b: 103):

(22) a. John looks happy.
      b. John looks too happy to leave.

The verb "look" subcategorizes for an Adj, which is shown in (22a). This subcategorization property is satisfied in (22b), even though "too" intervenes between the verb "look" and the adjective "happy." The reason is that "too" has no lexical categorial features (+/−N, +/−V), and so the subcategorization relation is not blocked by Minimality.[9]

We have so far considered cases of subcategorization for a lexical feature (+/−N, +/−V). There is evidence that shows that Minimality also constrains cases of subcategorization for a nonlexical feature. Consider the following example:

(23) *It is important that to say John is nice.
      "It is important that someone say that John is nice."

I assume that "that" subcategorizes for a finite Infl (see (7) above). It is impossible for the finite Infl (of the most embedded clause) to satisfy the subcategorization feature of "that," since the nonfinite Infl intervenes.

My theory of subcategorization makes it possible to account for certain cases of long-distance subcategorization. The subjunctive in English may provide one example (Mark Baltin, personal communication; Liliane Haegeman, personal communication; see also Grimshaw 1991):

(24) Bill demanded that John leave.

In this example, the verb "demand" requires a subjunctive Infl. We can assume that there is a special modal M (a lexical item), that embodies this subjunctive force. Therefore, "demand" has the following subcategorization frame [__M]. The example in (24) can be represented as follows:

(25) demand   that   M
      [__ M]

It is fairly clear that there is no additional M intervening between "demand" and M, therefore Minimality (18) is obeyed (note that the condition in (20) is not relevant here, since M is not a lexical category).[10]

My theory of subcategorization makes the prediction that a lexical item H should be able to subcategorize for the specifier of its complement. I will not investigate this particular prediction for lack of space (although see Kayne 1994: 154, fn. 8).

Let us turn now to a slightly different type of example where Minimality eliminates the need for labels (or headedness). Babby (1987) gives extensive evidence that in Old Russian (OR), the numeral "five" was the head (or label) of the structure "five bottles." On the other hand, in Modern Russian (MR), the noun "bottles" is the head (or label) of "five bottles." For example, Babby (1987: 105) gives the following contrast:

(26)   a.   ta   pjat'   butylok (*Old Russian*)
            that:NOM-SG-FEM   five:NOM-SG-FEM   bottles:GEN-PL
            "those five bottles"

     b.   te   pjat'   butylok (*Modern Russian*)
            those:NOM-PL   five:NOM   bottles:GEN-PL
            "those five bottles"

Babby notes that the demonstrative agrees in number with the numeral in Old Russian, but not in Modern Russian. This seems to indicate that in Old Russian, the numeral is actually the head of the construction, since according to Babby (1987: 102) "modifers agree in gender and number with the head of the NP."

We can recast Babby's results in our framework as follows: in both Modern Russian and Old Russian "five" contains a selector that drives the formation of the constituent {five, bottles}. In Old Russian, "five" has inherent gender and number features. In Modern Russian, "five" does not have inherent gender and number features. Because of this, agreement between the demonstrative and the noun is blocked by the numeral in Old Russian, but not Modern Russian.

2.1   Subcategorization and Merge

One further question is how the above theory of subcategorization fits in with Chomsky's (2000) theory of Merge. As pointed out earlier, Chomsky assumes that if two elements A and B are merged, a feature F of one of the elements must be satisfied. Chomsky calls this feature the selector.

Under Chomsky's analysis, it is natural to assume that the subcategorization features discussed above (see (13)) motivate Merge. In other words, they are selectors for Merge. Consider "tell on John." Suppose that during the course of the derivation we have formed two syntactic objects:

(27)   SO1:   "tell" (with the subcategorization feature [__on])
       SO2:   {on, John}

Let us assume that the subcategorization feature [__on] in SO1 matches the lexical item "on" in SO2. The question is what now motivates the merging of SO1 and SO2. I propose the following condition:

(28)   Let X (a lexical item) be in SO1, and let Y (a lexical item or feature) be in SO2, where SO1 and SO2 are two independent syntactic objects (lexical

items or phrases). If X and Y enter into a Subcat relation, then Merge (SO1, SO2).

Given this condition, since the subcategorization feature in SO1 matches the lexical item "on" in SO2 of (27), SO1 and SO2 can merge.

Are all Merge operations motivated by subcategorization features? The answer to this question is entirely unclear, and depends on a much more articulated theory of subcategorization. In particular, the question is whether in a simple transitive such as "John saw Mary," "see" has a subcategorization feature. The standard analysis (since Pesetsky 1982) is that "see" has a Case assigning feature, and a theta-role, but that there is no subcategorization feature. If this analysis is correct, then it follows that not all Merge operations are motivated by subcategorization features. Alternatively, in cases such as "John saw Mary" there may be a generalized subcategorization feature (similar to an EPP feature) that is satisfied when "see" and "Mary" merge.

2.2   Accessibility

Consider once again the stage in the derivation illustrated in (27). One problem with the condition in (28) is that since SO1 and SO2 have not yet been combined into a single syntactic object, "tell" does not c-command "on" (which is contained in {on, John}). Therefore it is unclear how search for a feature matching the subcategorization feature contained in SO1 will proceed.

It seems that the principle in (28) needs to be augmented with the following notion of accessibility (suggested to me by Hiroyku Ura; see Collins and Ura (2001)):

(29)   **Accessibility Condition**
A lexical item X (and the features it contains) is accessible without search to a syntactic operation OP if X contained the probe/selector for the last operation in the derivation.

Now consider once again the stage in the derivation illustrated by (27). Since the lexical item "on" in the phrase {on, John} contained the probe/selector for the last operation (Agree(phi$_{on}$, phi$_{John}$), which valued the Case features of "John"), "on" is accessible when "tell" and {on, John} are merged.

While the Accessibility Condition is needed on purely conceptual grounds, it also allows some cases that are difficult for Minimality in (20) to be handled easily. Consider first the problem of determiner selection in Dutch partitive constructions (see Van Riemsdijk 1998):

(30)   a.   het   vijfde   glas   wijn   (het/*de glas)
            the   fifth   glass wine

       b.   *de   vijfde   glas   wijn   (de/*het wijn)
            the   fifth   glass wine

In Dutch, neuter nouns take the definite determiner "het" and nonneuter nouns take the definite determiner "de." I assume that "het" subcategorizes for a N[neuter]. Ignoring the numeral "fifth," I assume that N1 and N2 in a direct partitive construction are sisters (see Van Riemsdijk 1998: 39), and that N2 is an argument of N1 in some extended sense. Therefore, we can represent the partitive construction schematically as follows:

(31)   {Det, {N1, N2}}

Now the question is how to determine whether Det agrees with N1 or N2. If the above structure is correct, then the determiner should be able to agree with either N1 or N2 according to Minimality (20) (since neither N1 nor N2 asymmetrically c-commands the other).

One possibility would be to abandon the structure in (31) in favor of a branching structure such as {Det, {N1, {X, N2}}}. This structure more closely reflects the English translation "the glass of wine." Since N1 is closer to Det than N2, the agreement facts follow without the modification to Minimality given in (20).

However, it is worthwhile to investigate how to obtain the correct agreement facts given the structure in (31). Note that when the Det and {N1, N2} are merged, N1 is accessible by the Accessibility Condition (29). Therefore, N1 satisfies the subcategorization feature of Det and not N2. A similar explanation rules out the ungrammatical (21d) above (*{the, {destroy, cities}}).

Consider lastly the difficult case of adjectives:

(32)   a.   {the, {smart, {student, {of, physics}}}}
       b.   {the, {{very, smart}, {student, {of, physics}}}}

In example (32a), "the" subcategorizes for an N. The problem is that the adjective "smart" intervenes between "the" and "student." Therefore, by Minimality (20), the relation between "the" and "student" should be blocked, and the example should be unacceptable. The example in (32b) does not have a similar problem, since "smart" no longer c-commands "student." This suggests that one way to deal with (32a) is to assume that prenominal adjectives are always branching categories (see Rubin 1996 for arguments for this assumption).

However, another approach would be to maintain in (32a) that the adjective "smart" is not branching, and to investigate whether the Accessibilty Condition (29) solves the above problem.

First, let us suppose that the adjective is the specifier of a head X, and that X has nominal features. This X might be a light n (the equivalent of Chomsky's light verb v). Then the correct structure of adjectival modification will be as follows:

(33)   {the, {smart, {X, {student, {of, physics}}}}}

When X is the locus, {student, {of, physics}} is merged as the complement of X, and "smart" is merged as the specifier of X. Then when "the" becomes the locus, X is accessible by the Accessibility Condition (29). At this point the subcategorization features of "the" are satisfied by X.

3   The Minimal Link Condition

In this section, I will show that the Minimal Link Condition (MLC) makes implicit reference to labels, and show how labels can be eliminated from its formulation.

One straightforward way to state the MLC is as follows (see Chomsky 1995b: 297, 2000: 122; see also Rizzi 1990):

(34)   Let P be a probe. Then the goal G is the closest feature that can enter into an agreement relation with P.

In this formulation, "closest feature" means that P c-commands G and there is no G′ such that P asymmetrically c-commands G′ and G′ asymmetrically c-commands G. In a label-free theory, this condition faces the following problem. Suppose that a lexical item H has an uninterpretable feature P (probe), and that there are two (branching) XPs c-commanded by H. This is illustrated as follows:

(35)   H[P]   [$_{XP1}$ ... X1 ...]   [$_{XP2}$ ... X2 ...]

Suppose that features matching the probe are located both in the lexical item X1 (the goal G1) and in the lexical item X2 (the goal G2). Then in a theory without labels, neither one of the features (G1 or G2) is closer than the other to H (since neither X1 nor X2 c-commands the other). In a theory with labels, we could say that the features G1 project up to the XP1 level, and the features of G2 project up to the XP2 level. Since XP1 c-commands XP2, the features G1 of XP1 will be the closest to H.

Now, given these considerations, consider the following structure:

(36)   C[+wh] you wonder [[which man] C[+wh] [stole the money why]]

Our goal is to block agreement between the matrix Comp[+wh] and the wh-phrase "why." In a theory with labels, it might be possible to propose that the wh-feature of "which" projects ("percolates") up to the level of the DP [$_{DP}$ which man]. Since the DP [$_{DP}$ which man] c-commands "why," the MLC would block agreement between the matrix Comp and "why." In a theory without labels, things are not as straightforward. Since "which" of {which, man} does not c-command "why," agreement between the matrix Comp and "why" cannot be blocked by the MLC.

There are other reasons to be suspicious of the standard projection/percolation analysis. Consider the following example:

(37)   C[+wh] you wonder [[which man's daughter] C[+wh] [stole the money why]]

Agreement of the matrix Comp and "why" is impossible in this case. It is highly implausible to appeal to projection of the [+wh] feature from "which" to the constituent [DP which man's daughter], since "which" is not even the label of the whole constituent.

How can the MLC be made consistent with a label-free theory? I will assume that it is not "which man" that blocks agreement between the matrix Comp and "why" in (36), rather it is the [+wh] feature of the embedded Comp that blocks agreement. Schematically, the following relation is blocked:

(38)   *C[+wh]   C[+wh]   why

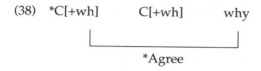

*Agree

In effect, we are saying that the Minimal Link Condition is stated purely in terms of the features involved, with no reliance on projections at all. This condition blocks both (36) and (37) without appealing to projection of a [+wh] feature in a DP. I summarize this discussion with the following condition:

(39)   **Minimality**
       Let X (a lexical item) contain a probe P. Let G be a matching goal. Then Agree(P,G) is established only if there is no feature F (a probe or a goal) matching P, such that P asymmetrically c-commands F and F asymmetrically c-commands G.[11]

This Minimality condition is identical to that found in Chomsky (2000: 122). The only difference is that it explicitly recognizes that an Agree relation can be blocked by either the features of an intervening probe or goal.

An alternative label-free analysis of sentences like (36) and (37) can be given in terms of the Phase Impenetrability Condition (PIC) of Chomsky (2000: 108). I will not attempt a comparison of (39) and the PIC for reasons of space.

Consider now the example of superraising:

(40)   *The man₁ seems that it was told t₁ that Mary left.
       "It seems that the man was told that Mary left."

This example shows that it is impossible to raise the constituent {the, man} from the object position of "told" to the matrix subject position. Assuming movement is contingent on Agree (see Chomsky 2000), we must prevent agreement between the matrix Infl and {the, man} in the following configuration:

(41)   Infl seems that it [Infl was] told the man that Mary left.

Minimality, as stated in (39), blocks agreement. The matrix Infl c-commands "it" (a nonbranching pronoun), and "it" c-commands {the, man}. Therefore, "it" (which has phi-features), blocks agreement between the matrix Infl and {the, man}.

One respect in which this analysis of superraising may appear to be unsatisfactory is that it relies on the expletive being nonbranching (so that "it" c-commands {the, man}). Suppose hypothetically that there were a language with a branching expletive (for example, the branching expletive might be the constituent {it, it}). Then the phi-features of the expletive would not block agreement between the matrix Infl and {the, man}. This seems counterintuitive. Similarly, we want branching categories in general in Spec Infl to block raising. Therefore, I propose the following alternative. Suppose that what blocks agreement in (41) between the matrix Infl and the constituent {the, man} is not "it," but rather the embedded Infl (which also has phi-features, agreeing with "it"). In other words, agreement is being prevented in the following configuration:

(42)   Infl   Infl   {the, man}

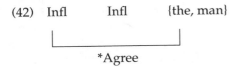

*Agree

The configuration is nearly identical to that found in (38), except Comp is replaced by Infl. This analysis presupposes that when "it" and the embedded Infl enter into an agreement relation, the phi-features of the embedded Infl are valued but are not deleted (they must still be around to block agreement). This is a departure from the assumptions in Chomsky (1995b, 2000, 2001). However, we can justify it in the following way. Normally, the phi-features of Infl are uninterpretable. However, suppose that when an Agree relation is established between a set of interpretable phi-features (in {the, man}) and uninterpretable phi-features (in Infl), the relation established is sufficient to anchor the uninterpretable phi-features, thus rendering them interpretable at LF. Or, to put it another way, each set of phi-features becomes an occurrence (see Chomsky 2000: 116) of a single interpretable set of phi-features.[12] This minimal change to the theory seems to be necessitated on the label-free approach, given such empirical issues as superraising.

In summary, I have shown that the Minimal Link Condition implicitly relies on the notion of a label and have suggested one possible way of modifiying the Minimal Link Condition so that it is label free. This modification has widespread implications which I have only begun to investigate in this paper.

4   Labels at the PF interface

In the above sections I addressed the question of whether labels are needed internal to the syntactic derivation, leaving aside the question of whether labels are needed at the PF interface. In this section, I will address the question of whether labels are needed for the application of the rules of phrasal phonology.

The label-free approach to phrase structure makes certain predictions about the phonology–syntax interface. One prediction is that we will not find phonological phrasing rules that make reference to VP versus NP (or NP versus PP, etc.). This prediction seems to be borne out. Inkelas and Zec (1995: 537) state: "Certain other aspects of the syntactic constituency, such as syntactic category or the morphological specifications of terminal elements, appear to be irrelevant for the purposes of phonology and, in a sufficiently constrained theory, the phonological component should not be able to access them." On the other hand, on the label-free approach, phonological phrasing should be able to make reference to the lexical category/functional category distinction, the clitic/nonclitic distinction and prosodic branching. These predictions are borne out (see Zec and Inkelas 1990 for a number of examples).

The label-free approach to syntax also seems to make the prediction that phonological rules cannot make reference to X′ versus XP (e.g., an X′ will be treated differently from an XP). This prediction contradicts the usual practice in the phonological phrasing literature of making reference to maximal projections (see Zec and Inkelas 1990: 377; Truckenbrodt 1999: 228). I will assume (perhaps erroneously) that in fact it is an accurate generalization that maximal projections enter into phonological phrasing. The question is how this can be captured without labels.

Let us suppose that phonological phrasing rules make reference to the notion of *saturated constituent*, which is similar to the notion of maximal projection (see section 1). Unfortunately, this conception seems to yield a computational nightmare. Suppose that phonological phrasing takes place as part of Spell Out, and that Spell Out occurs at a single point in the derivation (as in Chomsky 1995b). Now suppose that a syntactic structure enters the phonological component, with no labels. We cannot say that each constituent is marked as being saturated or not, since that would be a form of label, which is disallowed in the theory of this paper. Therefore, the phonological phrasing rules must calculate for every phrase whether or not that phrase is saturated. This calculation is difficult for two reasons. First, it demands that all the syntactic relations (such as theta-role assignment and agreement for phi-features) be accessible to the phonological rules. Second, since the constituents have no labels, it would require quite a bit of search to verify if some constituent is unsaturated. These problems result from the fact that concept of saturation is a derivational notion. The notion of saturation plays a role internal to the syntactic computation, and so seems irrelevant once the phonological component has been entered. Given these problems, I would like to propose the following solution.

Suppose that at the point in the derivation where a lexical item finally becomes saturated, the phrase (which is the entire workspace at that point in the derivation) is passed onto the phonological component. In other words, Spell Out occurs every time a lexical item is saturated (multiple Spell Out). The phonological string X corresponding to this saturated constituent is then marked as a potential phonological phrase (see Chomsky 2000: 131; 2001; and Uriagereka 1999: 299 for similar theories). Whether or not X ends up being a phonological phrase depends on the parametric choices of the particular language.

I should emphasize that the above considerations argue for the following conclusion: the phenomenon of phonological phrasing can only be accounted for in a label-free theory if there is multiple Spell Out. A label-free theory would also be consistent where syntactic units other than saturated constituents are sent to Spell Out (for example, the phases of Chomsky 2000, 2001).

5   Conclusion

The main point of this paper is to suggest that it may be possible to eliminate labels in the minimalist framework. In other words, the operation Merge(V, X) yields (43b) rather than (43a).

(43)   a.   Merge(V, X) = {V, {V, X}}
      b.   Merge(V, X) = {V, X}

In a theory where Merge is defined as in (43b), it is not possible to state generalizations or formulate operations that refer to labels (like VP versus NP), or bar-levels (like VP versus V').

I have discussed the following areas where labels have been used:

(44)   a.   X'-Theory
      b.   Selection
      c.   Minimal Link Condition
      d.   PF Interface

I have found that in each of these cases, it is possible to explain the generalizations without making reference to labels. In a theory without labels, it is necessary to be very specific about the elementary syntactic relations given below:

(45)   a.   Theta(X, Y)   X assigns a theta-role to Y
      b.   EPP(X, Y)   Y satisfies the EPP feature of X
      c.   Agree(X, Y)   X matches Y, and Y values X
      d.   Subcat(X, Y)   X subcategorizes for Y

If there were some theory of any one of these relations that crucially made use of the concepts of X'-theory (such as labels, bar-levels, feature projection, or percolation of any sort), that theory would be unacceptable. For example, consider a theory where we postulate that V assigns a theme role but V' assigns a goal role. This (simple) theory of thematic roles would be disallowed, since it makes reference to V' (an intermediate projection). The theory developed in this paper places a heavy burden on the precise statements of syntactic relations in (45).

I have assumed that derivations are governed by economy conditions, such as Minimality and other conditions that minimize the search needed to carry out an operation (see Chomsky 2000). Postulating such conditions is quite natural in a label-free theory. As representations are simplified, it is to be expected that derivational constraints (e.g., minimize search, the Locus Principle, the Accessibility Condition, etc.) will become more articulated. It is important to note that all of these conditions are extremely local in character (in the sense of Collins 1997; Ura 1995; and Chomsky 2000).

To the extent that it is possible to eliminate labels from the theory of syntax, the central assumptions of the Minimalist Program receive strong support. Syntactic structure is the result of the interaction of the properties of lexical items (containing probe/selectors) and economy conditions, constrained by bare output conditions. Future minimalist research should be oriented towards systematic evaluations of all the fundamental concepts of syntactic theory, including such notions as constituent structure, c-command (see Epstein 1999; Seely 2000), dominance, Agree, Merge, parts of speech, theta-roles, etc.

Acknowledgments

I would like to thank Mark Baltin, John Bowers, Rob Chametzky, Noam Chomsky, Yoshi Dobashi, Sam Epstein and Howard Lasnik, Daniel Seely, and Hiroyuki Ura for many helpful discussions. I have benefited greatly from the opportunity to present the ideas in this paper at the First International Symposium on Linguistics, Lyon (1999), the Landelijke Onderzoekschool Taalwetenschap (LOT) Summer School, Utrecht (1998), Instituto Universitario Ortega y Gasset, Madrid (1998), and the Cornell Colloquium series (1998).

Notes

1   I put aside the possibility of ternary branching, which can be ruled out by economy considerations (see Collins 1997: 77).
2   I use the term *saturated* in roughly the same way as Speas (1990: 110). See also Fukui (2001) for related ideas about the relation between phrase structure and "feature discharge."
3   See Seely (2000) for discussion of this issue. See also Frampton and Gutmann (2000: 20) for a related issue.
4   On degree clauses see Rothstein (1991a). Rothstein makes the point that subcategorization cannot be reduced to theta-role assignment.
5   A form of subcategorization that I will not discuss here is quirky or lexical Case (see Babby 1987: 95, 116). See Watanabe (1996: 142) for some other clear cases of subcategorization. The relatively large cross-linguistic variation in the subcategorization requirements of lexical items suggests strongly that subcategorization cannot reduce completely to s-selection.
6   For similar approaches, see Koopman (1994: 289) and Svenonious (1994a,b). Both of these researchers make use of labels in various ways.
7   In formulating Minimality, I have benefited from discussions with Daniel Seely (see also Seely 2000).
8   In the label-free theory, the "DP Hypothesis" (see Bernstein 2001) can be recast as the hypothesis that D contains probe/selectors, and that these resemble (in some interesting way) the probe/selectors of Infl.
9   A similar case could be D subcategorizing for N over Num (number or numeral). Similarly, the complementizer "that" subcategorizes for finite T over Agrs, in the split Infl framework.

10   I also assume that the complementizer "that" in (24) subcategorizes for a finite Infl, which implies that the subjunctive Infl is finite. The presence of the modal M explains the lack of subject–verb agreement in the subjunctive.

11   This condition will not block standard superiority examples, such as "What did which girl eat?" The reason is that in the underlying structure [Comp [[which girl] eat what]], "which" does not c-command "what" and therefore does not intervene between Comp and "what."

12   See also Frampton and Gutmann (2000) on "feature sharing." Note, the analysis of superraising in (42) is not consistent with the deletion of uinterpretable features at the phase level (see Chomsky 2001).

References

Babby, L. H. 1987. "Case, prequantifiers, and discontinuous agreement in Russian." *Natural Language and Linguistic Theory* 5: 91–138.

Baltin, M. 1989. "Heads and projections." In M. Baltin and A. Kroch, eds., *Alternative Conceptions of Phrase Structure*. Chicago: University of Chicago Press, pp. 1–16.

Bernstein, J. B. 2001. "The DP hypothesis: identifying clausal properties in the nominal domain." In M. Baltin and C. Collins, eds., *The Handbook of Contemporary Syntactic Theory*. Oxford: Blackwell, pp. 536–61.

Chomsky, N. 1986. *Knowledge of Language*. New York: Praeger.

Chomsky, N. 1995a. "Bare phrase structure." In G. Webelhuth ed., *Government and Binding Theory and the Minimalist Program*. Oxford: Blackwell, pp. 383–439.

Chomsky, N. 1995b. *The Minimalist Program*. Cambridge, MA: MIT Press.

Chomsky, N. 2000. "Minimalist inquiries." In R. Martin et al., eds., *Step by Step*. Cambridge, MA: MIT Press, pp. 89–155.

Chomsky, N. 2001. "Derivation by phase." In Michael Kenstowicz, ed., *Ken Hale: a Life in Language*. Cambridge, MA: MIT Press, pp. 1–52.

Chomsky, N. and H. Lasnik. 1993. "Principles and parameters theory." In J. Jacob et al., eds., *Syntax: An International Handbook of Contemporary Research*. Berlin: Walter de Gruyter, pp. 506–69.

Collins, C. 1997. *Local Economy*. Cambridge, MA: MIT Press.

Collins, C. 2001. "Economy conditions in syntax." In M. Baltin and C. Collins, eds., *The Handbook of Contemporary Syntactic Theory*. Oxford: Blackwell, pp. 45–61.

Collins, C. and H. Ura. 2001. "Accessibility." MS, Cornell University and Kwansei Gakuin University.

Epstein, S. D. 1999. "Un-principled syntax: the derivation of syntactic relations." In S. D. Epstein and N. Hornstein, eds., *Working Minimalism*. Cambridge, MA: MIT Press, pp. 317–45.

Frampton, J. and S. Gutmann. 1999. "Cyclic computation, a computationally efficient minimalist syntax." *Syntax* 2.1: 1–27.

Frampton, J. and S. Gutmann. 2000. "Agreement is feature sharing." MS, Northeastern University, Boston, MA.

Fukui, N. 2001. "Phrase structure." In M. Baltin and C. Collins, eds., *The Handbook of Contemporary Syntactic Theory*. Oxford: Blackwell, pp. 374–406.

Grimshaw, J. 1981. "Form, function, and the language acquisition device." In C. L. Baker and J. McCarthy, eds., *The Logical Problem of Language Acquisition*. Cambridge, MA: MIT Press.

Grimshaw, J. 1991. "Extended projection." MS, Brandeis University, Waltham, MA.

Inkelas, S. and D. Zec 1995. "Syntax-phonology interface." In J. A. Goldsmith, ed., *The Handbook of Phonological Theory*. Oxford: Blackwell, pp. 535–49.

Jackendoff, R. 1977. "X'-Syntax: a study of phrase structure." Cambridge, MA: MIT Press.

Kayne, R. 1994. *The Antisymmetry of Syntax*. Cambridge, MA: MIT Press.

Koopman, H. 1994. "Licensing heads." In D. Lightfoot and N. Hornstein, eds., *Verb Movement*. Cambridge: Cambridge University Press, pp. 261–96.

Koopman, H. and D. Sportiche 1991. "The position of subjects." *Lingua* 85: 211–58.

Odijk, J. 1997. "C-Selection and s-selection." *Linguistics Inquiry* 28: 365–71.

Pesetsky, D. 1982. "Paths and categories." Doctoral dissertation, MIT, Cambridge, MA.

Rizzi, L. 1990. *Relativized Minimality*. Cambridge, MA: MIT Press.

Rothstein, S. D. 1991a. "Syntactic licensing and subcategorization." In *Syntax and Semantics*, Vol. 25. San Diego: Academic Press, pp. 139–57.

Rothstein, S. D. 1991b. "Heads, projections and category determination." In K. Leffel and D. Bouchard, eds., *Views on Phrase Structure*, Dordrecht: Kluwer Academic Publishers, pp. 97–112.

Rubin, E. J. 1996. "The transparent syntax and semantics of modifiers." West Coast Conference on Formal Linguistics, 15.

Sag, I. and C. Pollard 1989. "Subcategorization and head-driven phrase structure." In M. Baltin and A. Kroch, eds., *Alternative Conceptions of Phrase Structure*. Chicago: University of Chicago Press, pp. 139–81.

Seely, T. D. 2000. "On projection-free syntax." MS, Eastern Michigan University.

Speas, M. 1990. *Phrase Structure in Natural Language*. Dordrecht: Kluwer.

Svenonius, P. 1994a. C-Selection as feature checking. *Studia Linguistica* 48.2: 133–55.

Svenonius, P. 1994b. "Dependent nexus." PhD dissertation, University of California, Santa Cruz.

Truckenbrodt, H. 1999. "On the relation between syntactic phrases and phonological phrases." *Linguistic Inquiry* 30: 219–55.

Ura, H. 1995. "Towards a theory of 'strictly derivational' economy conditions." *MIT Working Papers in Linguistics* 27: 243–67.

Ura, H. 1996. "Multiple feature-checking: a theory of grammatical function splitting." Doctoral dissertation, MIT, Cambridge, MA.

Uriagereka, J. 1999. "Multiple Spell Out." In S. D. Epstein and N. Hornstein, eds., *Working Minimalism*. Cambridge, MA: MIT Press, pp. 251–82.

van Riemsdijk, H. 1998. "Categorial feature magnetism: the endocentricity and distribution of projection." *Journal of Comparative Germanic Linguistics* 2: 1–48.

Watanabe, A. 1996. *Case Absorption and Wh-Agreement*. Dordrecht: Kluwer.

Yang, C. 1997. "Minimal computation: derivation of syntactic structures." MS, MIT, Cambridge, MA.

Zec, D. and S. Inkelas 1990. "Prosodically constrained syntax." In S. Inkelas and D. Zec, eds., *The Phonology–Syntax Connection*. Stanford, CA: Center for the Study of Language and Information.

Chapter three

Rule Applications as Cycles in a Level-free Syntax

Samuel David Epstein and T. Daniel Seely

1   Introduction: the role of Minimalist method

Minimalism can be characterized as the specification of a method of inquiry under which it is hoped that explanatory adequacy will be advanced – explanatory adequacy in both the general scientific sense and the linguistic-specific sense (of explaining how humans develop knowledge of language).[1] A well-known assumption of Minimalist syntactic inquiry is that sound and meaning are ineliminable, and correspondingly the two interface levels of PF and LF, and only these, are postulated. Certain legibility conditions for these interface levels are hypothesized, including the arguably natural conditions that every element appearing in a PF representation must have a phonetic interpretation and every element in an LF representation must have a semantic interpretation.

Lexical items, each composed of a bundle of features, also seem ineliminable. Some features of lexical items are illegitimate at one or the other interface. For instance, certain features have no LF interpretation but do have a PF interpretation; and the structural Case feature borne by N is an important instance of this. The pronoun *him* seems synonymous with *he*, although their PF interpretations are distinct, as evidenced by their different pronunciations. Thus, given the legibility condition that only LF-interpretable features can appear in an LF representation, it follows that there must be some mechanism by which the LF-uninterpretable Case feature of an N (DP) is removed before an LF representation is generated. The mechanism is assumed to be syntactic (*he* vs. *him* being distributionally determined); in other words, in certain "licensing configurations" the Case feature can be removed, yielding an LF legitimate Case-free DP.

This is an oversimplified, but (we hope) illustrative review of how a milestone in the development of an explanatory theory of syntax, namely Chomsky's eliminative explanation of the Case Filter and its reduction to independently motivated apparatus, is facilitated by the Minimalist method. Lying at the heart of this method is the identification of the legibility conditions, and determination of what might constitute an optimal "solution" to them. Proceeding in this manner allows one to identify what represents a departure from optimal assumptions, thereby identifying topics for further investigation. As Chomsky (2001a: 2, "Derivation by phase," henceforth DBP) writes:

> the Strong Minimalist Thesis sets an appropriate standard for true explanation; anything that falls short is to that extent descriptive, introducing mechanisms that would not be found in a "more perfect" system satisfying only legibility conditions.

Thus, Minimalist method first seeks to determine "in the abstract" what would constitute an optimal solution. With this in mind, the data is then analyzed and we seek to construct an analysis evincing as little departure from these assumptions as is possible, the ideal being no departure from these assumptions at all.

This is precisely how DBP proceeds. On the basis of just the legibility conditions, feature interpretability at the interfaces, and feature valuation, DBP argues that Spell Out must be cyclic. Not wanting to *stipulate* the cycle in this derivational system, DBP seeks to *explain* why there is cyclic Spell Out (i.e. more than one application of Spell Out in a derivation), arguing that this central departure from the Y-model architecture "follows naturally from examination of feature interpretability" (DBP, p. 5). The explanation of cyclicity (what we call Chomsky's "general" argument) hypothesizes that such cyclicity follows from the generative on-line derivational process of feature valuation and legibility. Importantly, this argument, guided by Minimalist method, provides in effect the "target" for the empirical analysis. The analyses proposed in DBP are designed to conform to the general argument that Spell Out must be cyclic. The general argument then raises a question that centrally concerns DBP: "If it follows naturally that Spell Out must indeed be cyclic, which particular categories undergo cyclic Spell Out?" And DBP argues that the categories that undergo cyclic Spell Out, i.e. the "phases," are *v*P and CP. Thus, on the one hand, there is the general argument in DBP that there must be cyclic Spell Out; and, on the other hand, there is the specific argument(s) that cyclic Spell Out proceeds via *v*P and CP phases, and hence that there is derivation by phase.

In what follows, we will suggest that the general, methodologically guided argument seeking to explain the existence of cyclic Spell Out in DBP is problematic; a detailed presentation of what we take to be the problem is given in section 2. The basic empirical problem is that Spell Out does not have the required information to operate properly before or after feature valuation; i.e. neither the prevaluation nor postvaluation representation is sufficient; hence it can't operate at all. As a result the DBP general argument that iterative feature valuation naturally induces iterative (i.e. cyclic) Spell Out cannot be maintained. We will then suggest possible approaches to the problem. In our view, the most natural approach overcomes the problem confronting the timing of cyclic Spell Out in DBP by assuming that Spell Out is derivational and applies to the output of every transformational rule application (as in the level-eliminating system of Epstein et al. 1998, and Epstein and Seely 1999, forthcoming). Applying Spell Out in this manner seems conceptually optimal in that it requires no account of why some categories get spelled out cyclically, i.e. constitute phases (a central concern of DBP), while others do not. In short, spelling out at each transformational rule application not only readily overcomes the precise problem in DBP we reveal, but is also "natural" in requiring no new mechanisms beyond those already postulated in a derivational system. This model incorporates ordered transformational rule application but eliminates levels of representation in the standard sense, instead placing them or their effects "inside" transformational rule application. Moreover, the architecturally suspect, empirically problematic, and computationally inefficient mechanisms of lookahead, as well as lookback (each discussed explicitly below), are rendered unnecessary precisely because the interfaces are reached by each transformational rule application. We suggest that putting Spell Out "inside" transformational rule application is not only the null hypothesis, but may represent the only way to maintain the DBP *explanation* of cyclicity as following naturally from feature valuation and interpretability.

Overall, we seek to eliminate all levels, and thus overcome a problem confronting the application of Spell Out in DBP, which requires appeal to an unspecified lookback algorithm, which is needed to find the previously unvalued form of a now valued feature. We seek to solve the ordering problems inducing lookback Spell Out (and also lookahead) by "bringing the interfaces to each rule application," so that lookback and lookahead are not necessary. This, in turn, simplifies the model to include *no* levels, and seeks to deepen explanation by moving one step closer to relocating within the independently motivated, universalized rules of Merge, Move/Attract, and Agree all GB principles, filters, and stipulated definitions of relations on representation.

2   DBP's general argument for cyclic Spell Out

This section presents important background material regarding the feature system and the nature of feature valuation assumed in DBP (subsection 2.1). Subsection 2.2 presents the general DBP argument seeking to explain the existence of cyclic Spell Out, and then reveals a possible problem with it.[2]

2.1   Background: The DBP feature system

Fundamental to the Minimalist Program is the assumption that there are lexical items, each consisting of three types of features: semantic, phonological, and formal. The formal features, which play a central role in the analyses of DBP, include Case, EPP, the phi-features of the functional categories T and *v*, and the phi-features of the lexical categories N and V. Some of these formal features are LF-interpretable – for example, the phi-features of N; while others are not – for example, the Case and EPP features. In earlier stages of the development of "feature checking" in Minimalism, interpretability is assumed to be an inherent property of features. Thus, in Chomsky (1995, chapter 4) "Categories and Transformations" (CT) and in Chomsky (2000) "Minimalist Inquiries" (MI), Case is not, but the phi-features of N are, LF-interpretable. In DBP, on the other hand, the notions interpretable and uninterpretable play no direct role in the statement of syntactic operations; they are replaced, in a manner that we make clear below (section 3), with "valued" and "unvalued."

The following generalizations regarding interpretability and feature value, which figure crucially in the general argument explaining cyclic Spell Out, hold:

(1)   a.   It is (naturally) assumed that unvalued lexical features are illegible (and hence uninterpretable) at both PF and LF, and thus any expression containing such features will fail to converge.

      b.   Valuation, however, is a necessary but not sufficient condition for LF convergence. The Case feature of a DP/N, for example, may be valued by the operation Agree, but a valued Case feature is by hypothesis still not interpretable at LF, rather it is interpretable only at PF – this is the nature of structural case. In fact, all unvalued features that can be valued by a syntactic operation (i.e. the Case feature, the phi-features of T and v, and the EPP feature) are ultimately unuseable at LF; either they are by hypothesis LF-uninterpretable (as is true for the Case feature and the EPP feature) or else they are LF-interpretable and so can appear in a convergent LF representation but yield "gibberish." Such is arguably true with the valued phi-features of T; the phi-features themselves (e.g., the feature [singular-number]) are LF-interpretable, but the complex consisting of T and its valued phi-features is LF-anomalous, hence "convergent gibberish." Note, however, that some valued features are PF-interpretable; for example, Case and the phi-features of T.[3]

According to the DBP analysis, some formal features enter a derivation with a value (e.g. the phi-features of N), and all such features are interpretable at LF. Some formal features enter a derivation without a value (e.g. Case, EPP, and the phi-features of T and v).[4] The syntactic operations Agree and Move (may) assign values (under the appropriate circumstances) to unvalued features. The now-valued formal features are never useable to LF (they yield either LF nonconvergence or gibberish), but they may be perfectly interpretable to PF (depending on the feature).

Why does DBP seem to have both the valued vs. unvalued distinction and the interpretable vs. uninterpretable distinction? We answer the question in greater detail in section 3, but the answer relevant to immediate concerns is this: Spell Out can have access to valued and unvalued without having to know anything about whether the valued or unvalued feature is LF-interpretable. This is a desirable result since Spell Out (arguably) has no direct access to the LF interface and so in fact cannot know if a feature is LF-interpretable. Importantly, lookahead to the interface levels in DPB is, through the notion valuation, thereby avoided. Spell Out can make what turn out to be crucial derivation-internal decisions, namely to Spell Out all and only features that *will* or *would* be uninterpretable[5] at the later LF level, but it can do so just by seeing whether or not the feature *now*, derivation-internally, has a value.

2.2   The general DBP argument that Spell Out must be strongly cyclic

Notice, first, that from (1a) above, it follows that unvalued features must be valued (if an expression initially containing these unvalued features is ever to converge). Indeed, unvalued features drive the syntactic operations Move and Agree, both of which result in valuation (thus, the valuation operations conform to "Last Resort"). An unvalued feature of X renders X "active," and only active elements may participate in syntactic operations. Move and Agree are thus purposeful; they apply for a reason, and the reason is to value unvalued formal features; syntactic operations have the "goal" of generating objects that are legible to the interfaces.

From (1b), it follows that those formal features that are valued by a syntactic operation must be "stripped away" from the narrow syntax. These syntactically valued features must not make their way to LF; if they do, then the expression containing them will either fail to converge (for Case and/or EPP features) or else will converge as gibberish (as is arguably true for an LF representation containing valued phi-features of T). Since Spell Out is the operation that removes features from the narrow syntax, it thus follows from DBP that *at least one* application of Spell Out is necessary. If there were no Spell Out, then virtually all expressions would fail to converge (or else would converge as gibberish).

DBP makes the further argument that Spell Out is cyclic (i.e. it occurs more than once in the course of a single derivation), and that this need not be stipulated, but rather, by the general argument it "follows naturally from examination of feature interpretability . . ." DBP thus has the important goal of not stipulating but rather of explaining the existence of cyclic Spell Out. With the important background and detail on feature valuation and interpretability in place, let us now examine this argument, turning thereafter (section 3) to a possible problem with it.

First of all, according to DBP, Spell Out removes (what amount to) LF-uninterpretable features from a syntactic object K. Thus, after Agree applies between T and N in (2), valuing the Case feature of N and the phi-features of T,

(2)   T be a man outside

Spell Out removes, among other things, the LF-uninterpretable Case feature of *man*, and the phi-features of T, sending the residue to the narrow syntax *en route* to LF. Spell Out, then, must "know" what to Spell Out. The question is: how does it know? How does Spell Out know which features are

LF-(un)interpretable given that Spell Out is a non-"semantic" operation applying derivation-internally before the LF interface is reached?
   DBP answers:

(3)   The natural principle is that the uninterpretable features, and only these,
      enter the derivation without values, and are distinguished from interpretable
      features by virtue of this property.   (DBP, p. 5; editors' emphasis)

Note, then, that DBP effectively replaces the notions interpretable/
uninterpretable with valued/unvalued, questions concerning which we will
consider in some detail below. Notice also that the distinction between interpretable and uninterpretable made in (3) rests on feature status upon entering
the derivation, but Spell Out applies after (potentially long after) entry, as we
will discuss shortly.
   The question that now arises is: "When does Spell Out apply in the course
of a derivation?" Crucially, to actually spell out before valuation is problematic. As DBP notes, this is "too early" since unvalued features are in fact
PF-uninterpretable (as well as LF-uninterpretable) and thus spelling out an
expression containing such unvalued features will fail to converge.[6] Thus,
Spell Out cannot apply before valuation.
   The other option is for Spell Out to apply after valuation. However, DBP
claims that this too is problematic. Spelling out after valuation is "too late"
since the distinction between LF-interpretable and LF-uninterpretable is "lost"
immediately after valuation:

(4)   The operation Spell Out removes LF-uninterpretable material from the
      syntactic object K and transfers K to the phonological component. It must
      therefore be able to determine which syntactic features are uninterpretable,
      hence to be removed. Prior to application of Agree, these are distinguished
      from interpretable features by lack of specification of value. *After applica-*
      tion of Agree, the distinction is lost.   (DBP, p. 5; editors' emphasis)

The basic point here is clear enough. DBP assumes that Spell Out cannot know
in a direct way what is and is not semantically interpretable. Spell Out is not
itself "semantic" and has no access to the LF interface. It cannot look at a
derivation-internal representation, consult the LF bare output conditions,
determine what is interpretable at LF, and then go back inside the derivation
to Spell Out the LF-uninterpretable features present in the current representation. But the right result can be obtained in an indirect way, and in conformity
with Inclusiveness, by assuming featural underspecification. Spell Out can see
the valued vs. unvalued distinction, and since valued/unvalued is linked to
LF-interpretable/uninterpretable in the right way, Spell Out can "know" what
to strip away to the phonology. Spell Out *does* have access to valued and
unvalued. However, once a feature is valued, then, for Spell Out, the distinction between LF-interpretable and LF-uninterpretable is lost.
   To sum up, DBP argues that Spell Out before valuation is too early, but after
valuation is too late. But this is precisely the crux of DBP's general argument:

that it follows from basic assumptions that Spell Out must apply cyclically. Recall that this is argued to "follow naturally;" and hence cyclic Spell Out, the central architectural innovation in the MI/DBP abandonment of the Y-model, is not stipulated. The crucial passage is given below in its entirety:

(5) The operation Spell Out removes LF-uninterpretable material from the syntactic object K and transfers K to the phonological component. It must therefore be able to determine which syntactic features are uninterpretable, hence to be removed. Prior to application of Agree, these are distinguished from interpretable features by lack of specification of value. *AFTER application of Agree, the distinction is lost*. To operate without reconstructing the derivation, *Spell Out must therefore apply SHORTLY AFTER the uninterpretable features have been assigned values* (if they have not been assigned values at this point, the derivation will crash, with uninterpretable features at the interface). Spell Out must be strongly cyclic (as assumed in MI). The conclusion, which follows naturally from examination of feature interpretability, has other desirable consequences. (DBP, p. 5; editors' emphasis)

The idea seems to be that features are being valued iteratively (since the derivation is assumed to proceed "bottom-up," Chomsky 1993), and once they are valued, Spell Out cannot operate in the requisite fashion. Thus, Spell Out must also operate iteratively.

3   The problem with the general argument that Spell Out must be strongly cyclic

The argument, as stated in (5), that cyclic Spell Out "follows naturally from examination of feature interpretability" seems to us to contain a logical contradiction. Simply put: if it is true that "after application of Agree [i.e. value-assignment, SDE/TDS] the distinction is lost," then it does not follow that "Spell Out must therefore apply *shortly* after the uninterpretable features have been assigned values." If after valuation is too late, then shortly after is too late as well. Spelling out shortly after value-assignment provides no solution to the central problem at hand, since as soon as a feature is valued, Spell Out will not have the information required to operate. Yet it is this very on-line derivational valuation process that constitutes the explanatory argument that Spell Out must apply cyclically, since the distinction upon which Spell Out operates is lost quickly, as the derivation proceeds. To illustrate the problem, consider again (2), repeated here:

(2) T be a man outside.

Suppose that Agree has applied, valuing (among other things) the phi-features of T. Suppose that Spell Out applies immediately after Agree. Looking just at the object (i.e. the single representation) in (2), what Spell Out now sees are valued features. And after valuation (shortly after or otherwise), the phi-features of T have the same status as the phi-features of N; they are valued features, and, therefore, Spell Out will not be able to distinguish them; i.e. it will not know that N's phi-features should not be spelled out, but that T's should be. Indeed, after valuation (even shortly after), it is not obvious that Spell Out could operate at all since, "without reconstructing the derivation" (see (5)); i.e. by looking just at the object in (2), Spell Out has no means of knowing what to actually Spell Out. More specifically, without derivational lookback, it has no means of knowing which of the valued features that it now sees were, at an earlier derivational point, unvalued. And without derivational lookahead to the interfaces, Spell Out cannot know what is or isn't interpretable at the not-yet-reached interfaces LF and PF.

Notice that the logical problem raised above could potentially be resolved if there *were* some form of derivational lookback.[7] Spell Out could be designed to Spell Out only those features that were valued in the course of the derivation; and to determine this, Spell Out would need access to the derivation itself (and not just the current syntactic representation). In section 5, we consider this potential resolution to the problem in some detail. First, however, we will examine more closely DBP's introduction of the notion "valuation" and further clarify the problematic nature of the general argument for cyclic Spell Out, and we will then, in section 4, present a possible solution to this problem, one which appeals to fundamental properties of the derivation itself.

Cyclic Spell Out, in the general sense, means that the transference of features to PF occurs not just once but more than once during the derivation; and furthermore that it occurs bottom-up in the course of the derivation. Thus, rather than the standard Y-model as in (6)

$$
\begin{array}{c}
\text{PF} \\
/ \\
\text{Spell Out} \\
/
\end{array}
$$

(6)   Lexicon → syntactic operations

$$
\begin{array}{c}
\backslash \\
\text{LF}
\end{array}
$$

we have (something like) the model in (7)

$$
\begin{array}{ccc}
\text{PF} & \text{PF} & \\
/ & / & \text{. . . etc.} \\
\text{Spell Out} & \text{Spell Out} & \\
/ & / &
\end{array}
$$

(7)   Lexicon → syntactic operations -----------------------> LF

DBP abandons the long-standing Y-model in favor of a model more like that in Epstein et al. (1998), Epstein and Seely (1999, forthcoming) and Uriagereka (1999), to the extent that cyclic Spell Out is hypothesized.

Recall now the key step in the DBP argument seeking to explain such cyclic Spell Out:

(8)   Prior to application of Agree, these [i.e. LF-uninterpretable features] are distinguished from interpretable features by lack of specification of value. After application of Agree, the distinction is lost. To operate without reconstructing the derivation, Spell Out must therefore apply shortly after the uninterpretable features have been assigned values. . . .

One question that we raised earlier, and will examine now in more detail, is this: Why is a distinction made between an interpretable/uninterpretable feature vs. a valued/unvalued feature? Why does DBP introduce the concept "valued/unvalued;" why not maintain the analyses from CT and MI postulating just and only "interpretable/uninterpretable"?

The answer, we believe, is twofold. First, the introduction of the notion "valued/unvalued" can be seen perhaps as a response to a problem raised by Epstein et al. (1998), concerning the entire Minimalist theory of transformational rule application. Specifically, the problem is how a syntactic operation can be triggered by the uninterpretability of a feature at the LF interface *before* the LF interface is reached. Adapting the Epstein et al. observation to Spell Out in DBP, we can ask: How can Spell Out know that a feature is not interpretable to the LF interface when Spell Out is not at the LF interface and furthermore has no direct access to the LF interface? The valued/unvalued distinction, on the surface at least, solves this problem. Spell Out in fact does not know which features are LF-(un)interpretable. All it sees (focusing on formal features for present concerns) are features that have or do not have a value, and that is sufficient if, as we saw above, "all unvalued features are LF-uninterpretable/unuseable."

And there is an additional possible reason for DBP's introduction of "valued/unvalued." If we have just interpretable and uninterpretable, as in CT and MI, then we need feature deletion followed, in some cases, by feature erasure, and, as DBP itself notes, this is undesirable, creating an architectural paradox.[8] In the CT and MI frameworks, there are cases where a feature is deleted but still accessible to the syntax. In some cases, this deleted feature is then erased, which means that it is eliminated entirely and hence absent at the LF interface. The valued/unvalued distinction of DBP, along with not applying Spell Out immediately,[9] gets the effect of the CT/MI deletion-erasure mechanisms in, perhaps, a more elegant way. In DBP, certain formal features enter the derivation without a value. A syntactic operation, like Agree, results in the valuation of the feature. The feature is not yet spelled out, and hence the valued feature can, and crucially does, participate in later syntactic operations. This is just what happens in DBP in example (9), for instance:

(9)   [C [$_{TP}$ T seem [EXPL to have been [caught several fish]]]]
       (= DBP example (18a), p. 17)

Here the participle *caught* Matches the direct object (*several*) *fish*, and Agree
applies, valuing the number and gender features of the participle. These now-
valued phi-features of the participle, crucially, are not spelled out at this point
in the derivation but rather remain until the matrix TP. When the derivation
subsequently reaches this TP, there is Agreement between T and the participle
due precisely to the still-present, although earlier valued, number and gender
features of the participle. Since these features still remain they can and do
Match T, which, in turn, values the NOM Case feature of the participle, as is
necessary for convergence.

But this clarification of the motivation for "valued/unvalued" makes the
problem with the DBP argument for cyclic Spell Out all the more salient. Spell
Out can detect only valued/unvalued; it can't detect (LF) interpretable/
uninterpretable. Thus, Spell Out is analogous to a device that is designed to
detect color (say, red vs. blue); but can in no way detect heat (say, hot from
cold). But imagine that red is always hot and blue is always cold. In that
case, we, as observers outside the device, can say that since it can distinguish
red from blue, then it can effectively sort hot from cold without in fact being
heat sensitive. Unvalued features are always PF- and LF-uninterpretable; and
syntactically valued features are always LF-uninterpretable.[10] So we can say
that Spell Out can distinguish LF-interpretable from LF-uninterpretable without being "semantically-sensitive."

The problem, however, is that after a feature has been valued, what Spell
Out sees is a valued feature (just as our analogous device above would see
just red if the color changed from blue to red and the device looked in after the
color change). And for Spell Out a valued feature is a valued feature; Spell Out
cannot tell anything about whether the valued feature is LF-interpretable:
recall, "after valuation the distinction is lost." And if the distinction is lost after
valuation, then the distinction is *necessarily* lost "shortly after" valuation as
well. Thus, the central DBP argument seeking to explain cyclicity is apparently
problematic.

Note further that the problem is not "conceptual" (whatever that ever means).
Rather it is entirely empirical, concerning nothing other than the generative
capacity of all grammars given this proposed architecture of universal grammar. Indeed, it is not clear how any convergent derivation can be generated by
this system since Spell Out cannot operate in the requisite way before or after
valuation. So, in order to generate convergent derivations, when can Spell Out
apply?

4   A derivational approach to the problem of cyclic Spell Out

It is not sufficient for Spell Out to operate upon only the representation before
valuation. Nor does it suffice for it to operate upon only the representation
appearing after valuation. Crucially, then,

(10)   There is no single representation upon which Spell Out can operate in an empirically adequate manner.[11]

Thus, Spell Out must examine multiple representations, i.e.:

(11)   Spell Out must itself be a derivation-sensitive operation, not a purely representational one.

Minimally, it examines two, and no more than two, representations. Which two? The null hypothesis is that it can examine only the input to a given transformational rule application (in which a feature is unvalued) and the output of that same transformational rule application (in which the feature is now valued). Crucially, this requires no new mechanisms (such as phases and phase level lookback, to be discussed in section 5). Universal grammar already incorporates independently motivated mechanisms each with a "before" and an "after," namely transformational rules consisting precisely of a structural description (a "before"), specifying the input to the transformational rule application, and a structural change (the "after"), specifying the output of the transformational rule application. Thus, we propose that Spell Out operates on all and only those formal features that appear without a value in the input to a rule being applied, but appear in the output of that rule application with the "previously" unvalued feature now valued. If no single representation is sufficient, the minimal "phase" is optimally a single transformational rule application[12] – requiring no stipulated privileged phasal categories such as *v*P and CP, and requiring no new mechanisms at all.

   Consider, for example, (2), repeated below, focusing for illustration on just the phi-features of T:

(2)   T be a man outside.

Under the Probe–Goal analysis, the structural description of the operation Agree applying to T and *man* includes the unvalued phi-features of T. The structural change of this operation includes the now valued phi-features of T. If Spell Out can see both the input to and output of Agree, it can see the "process" whereby an unvalued feature became valued, and then can spell out just these features, as desired. Notice again that the input to and output of a single transformational rule application seems to be the minimal set of objects that Spell Out can inspect. Thus, our central proposal is that Spell Out operates "inside" transformational rule application. This comports with the theory proposed in Epstein (1994, 1999), Epstein et al. (1998), and Epstein and Seely (1999, forthcoming), which seeks to explain syntactic relations, syntactic filters, and, more generally, macrostructure tree properties, as expressed by GB Principles, by appeal to independently motivated properties of local transformational rule application, within a level-free model in which the interfaces are reached at each transformational output.

   Importantly, this seems consonant with the "last resort" theory of movement, lying at the heart of the Minimalist goal of explaining transformational rule application in terms of optimal solutions to the bare output conditions imposed by the interfaces. That is to say, every rule application must value features, which, if unvalued, induce crash at the interface. What is the most efficient way to determine that features have been valued by each transformational rule application? Suppose every transformational output is evaluated by PF (and LF), whose very legibility conditions each transformational rule application seeks to satisfy as best as is (locally) possible. Notice that, as a result, we eliminate not just D-structure and S-structure, as in Chomsky (1993); but PF and LF too are eliminated as levels of representation in the standard sense (as in Epstein et al. 1998, and Chomsky 2001b, as will be discussed below). Applying Spell Out in this manner seems conceptually optimal in that it requires no account of why some categories get spelled out cyclically, i.e. constitute phases (a central concern of DBP) while others do not. In short, spelling out each transformational output not only readily overcomes the precise DBP "before and after" problem we reveal, but is also "natural" in requiring no new mechanisms beyond those already postulated in a derivational system. This model incorporates ordered transformational rule application but eliminates levels of representation in the standard sense, instead placing them or their effects "inside" transformational rule application. Moreover, lookahead is rendered unnecessary, precisely because the interfaces are reached by each transformational rule application.

4.1   A single representation?

Recall that section 4 began with the assertion that there is no single representation upon which Spell Out can operate in an empirically adequate manner. However, it might be counter-argued that there is a single representation, i.e. a single syntactic object, upon which Spell Out could operate correctly. Consider (12):

(12)   John was arrested John

Suppose the occurrence of *John* in Spec-TP contains a valued case feature, whereas the occurrence in direct object position bears unvalued case. Then, as long as Spell Out knows that this is the "same feature," Spell Out could see in this single representation both the valued and unvalued Case feature, and hence know to spell it out. No derivational lookback would seem to be required under this view. We have two points to make regarding this roughly "chain-based" approach.

   First, it has been argued that there are no traces/copies, from which it follows that a representation like (12) would simply not exist. It has been noted, for instance, that copies/traces are encodings of previous derivational stages. And, as Epstein et al. (1998) argue, such encodings are necessitated in the rule-free, derivation-free GB theory, precisely because we need to know where a category has been in the course of the derivation but are not allowed to refer to the derivation in this rule-free approach. Within the Minimalist framework, in which iterative transformational rule application (i.e. the derivation) is reified, the possibility of the elimination of traces/copies arises; indeed, the elimination of traces/copies is just what is suggested in Epstein et al. (1998).[13] On different grounds, Epstein and Seely (1999, forthcoming) argue against A-traces in examining successive cyclic A-movement in English; and Lasnik (1999) argues against A-traces based on nonreconstruction phenomena with A-movement. The central point is that if these arguments are on the right track, and there are no traces/copies, then a representation like (12) is not possible.

Second, suppose instead that there is a copy/trace, as in (12). The question that now emerges is: can the copy/trace have an unvalued Case feature, after the Case feature of the mover has been valued? We believe the answer is "no." Recall that under copy theory as identity there is in (12) only one DP *John*. There are, however, two occurrences of this *single* DP in the representation. Since there is but one DP in the representation and since that one DP is a bundle of features, each feature having one and only one value, it cannot be that one occurrence of a DP has a valued feature while the identical DP (in another position) has that same feature unvalued.[14] So it follows, even with traces/copies, that a representation like (12) is not possible, i.e. where the Case feature of the mover *John* is valued but the Case feature of the copy/trace is unvalued. This, in turns, supports our conclusion that Spell Out can't operate on a single representation.

5   Phasal Spell Out

We have just proposed that:

(13)   a.   No single representation will suffice; and

      b.   appeal to the derivation is therefore necessary; and, optimally, the only aspect of the derivation that needs to be inspected is inside single transformational rule applications, minimizing lookback, and eliminating lookahead.

This is tantamount to the claim that each transformational rule application constitutes a "phase," which we believe to be the null hypothesis. Like Epstein et al. (1998), Epstein and Seely (1999, forthcoming), and Uriagereka (1999), Chomsky (2000, 2001a, and 2001b) abandons the Y-model's single split to PF and LF in which interface interpretation applies only after all transformational rules have applied. For example, Chomsky (2001b): 4, "Beyond explanatory adequacy," henceforth BEA most recently characterizes his cyclic Spell Out approach as level-free, writing that

(14)   in this conception there is no LF: rather, the computation maps LA to <PHON, SEM> piece-by-piece cyclically. There are, therefore, no LF

properties and no interpretation of LF, strictly speaking, though sigma and phi interpret units that are part of something like LF in a non-cyclic conception.

Call the relevant units "phases." It remains to determine what the phrases are, and exactly how the operations work.

The difference between our proposal, which we believe to be the null hypothesis, and Chomsky's, concerns the size of the phase. For Chomsky, the phases are the specific categories *v*P and CP. In what follows we will discuss three ways in which this diverges from our null hypothesis, engendering what we take to be nonoptimal solutions to the output conditions. Furthermore, we note possible empirical problems with *v*P and CP as phases, in addition to problems confronting the quest to explain why CP and *v*P in particular are the only phases.

5.1   Why vP and CP?

The specification of particular phase level categories runs the risk of stipulation. As discussed at length in Epstein and Seely (1999, forthcoming), the specification of *v*P and CP as phases is potentially problematic. Chomsky (MI, DBP, BEA) attempts to motivate *v*P and CP as phases on the grounds that they are relatively independent at the interface. But, leaving aside potential unclarities concerning the notion "relatively independent," an important additional question is: How can we know that they are relatively independent *at the interface* if Spell Out applies *before* the interface is reached, and without access to interface properties? It is a potential architectural paradox to hypothesize that *v*P and CP are spelled out *cyclically, internal to the narrow syntax* by virture of them having the property of being, "later," relatively independent *at the interface*.

The other notion invoked to explain why *v*P and CP are phases is the concept "propositional." However, it seems to us that there are *v*Ps that are nonpropositional; for instance, *who bought what* and *everyone bought something*. Prior to movement these *v*Ps exhibit vacuous quantification; subsequent to movement they are open "sentences" which, internal to the *v*P, contain free variables. The same is true for the embedded CP in, for example, *who do you think that John likes?* Further, in the other direction, there are propositions that are arguably neither *v*Ps nor CPs; for example, the small clause in *I consider [John smart]*. Another question is: Why should a propositional element, where "propositional" is a semantic notion, be spelled out to PF; why should PF care about the propositional content of what is spelled out?

A third specification of phase is a category within which all theta-roles borne by the head are discharged. But this seems to allow raising TPs, passive, and unaccusative *v*Ps to be phases since all relevant theta-roles are in fact discharged, but this does not seem to be the desired result. Thus, the concern here is that *v*P and CP are stipulated as phases (moreover, see Epstein and Seely 1999, forthcoming) for extensive discussion of empirical problems with this stipulation regarding phases, involving Merge-over-Move and short passives).

Yet another possible problem is that these phases constitute special, privileged points in the derivation, which seem to us somewhat like the reintroduction of levels which MI, CT, BEA, Epstein et al. (1998), and Uriagereka (1999) all seek to eliminate.

5.2   Global lookback?

As we pointed out in section 4, one way to resolve the logical problem with Spell Out that we revealed is to assume derivational lookback. DBP does assume such lookback, but attempts to limit it to the phase level. Thus, DBP (p. 12), states that:

(15)   The valued uninterpretable features can be detected with only *limited inspection of the derivation* if earlier stages of the cycle can be "forgotten" – in phase terms, if earlier phases need not be inspected.   (editors' emphasis)

The important point here is that "inspection of the derivation" *is* required. Two questions emerge at once: why is it required? And, what exactly is the algorithm for inspection of the derivation?

   Consider, for illustration, (16):

(16)   I wonder what John will buy.

First-merge yields:

(17)   buy what

where *what* has an unvalued Case feature. The following further Merges then occur:

(18)   a.   v + [buy what]
         b.   John + [v [buy what]]

Next, *what* shifts to the outer spec of vP. At this point in the derivation (i.e. in this syntactic object), the Case feature of *what* is valued by phi complete *v*:

(19)   what + [John [v [buy what-copy]]]

Under copy theory, it is assumed that the Case feature on the *identical* copy is also valued, otherwise movement would never yield convergence. Valuing the trace/copy's feature is necessitated under the assumption that the copy is featurally identical with the mover (although these occurrences are positionally distinct; in other words, if, in the representation (19), *what* and *what*-copy are the same thing, then there is only one Case feature to value; and if *it* is valued, it is valued (for extensive discussion of this issue, see Epstein and Seely 1999, forthcoming; see also Nunes 1999 for important related discussion). Indeed, if the trace/copy's Case feature (somehow) remained unvalued, then movement for Case checking would fail to result in satisfaction of the bare output conditions, undermining the entire theory of movement/transformations. So, it is a general feature of the theory of movement, and its relation to the satisfaction of bare output conditions, that the trace/copy must be valued.

Next, *will* (T) is merged in; and thereafter *John* is attracted to spec of T:

(20)   John will what John-copy *v* [buy what-copy]

C now merges in, and C attracts the closest occurrence of *what* (occupying the outer spec of *v*P):

(21)   what John will what-copy John-copy *v* [buy what-copy]

Crucially, this is the position in which *what* is to be spelled out. However, as we saw in section 4, the current representation (i.e. (21)) provides insufficient information for Spell Out to operate correctly: the features of *what* and all its copies are valued and once valuation applies, it is too late for Spell Out to operate (without reconstructing the derivation). Again, as we noted in section 4, it is not clear why Spell Out would even try to operate at all here, since there is nothing offensive to spell out (or problematic) in the current representation. The issue of why Spell Out operates at all is empirically crucial, and pervasive. But suppose, for the sake of argument, that Spell Out has a "problem" of some sort, and knows that it must spell out something now, but all the features are valued so it can't. What is Spell Out to do? This is, we believe, the DBP argument for derivational lookback (i.e. "limited inspection of the derivation," p. 12). Spell Out detects the valued features on *what* and its occurrences and (for some reason) begins to engage in derivational lookback, seeking to find an earlier point in the derivation in which the Case feature of *what* was unvalued. If that unvalued feature can be found (in representations (17), (18), or (19)), Spell Out can "see" that the feature changed from unvalued to valued, and that information suffices to instruct Spell Out to spell out the Case feature of *what*. So, this seems to be why DBP assumes that derivational lookback is required.

The remaining question is: how does derivational lookback operate exactly? What is the algorithm? We're not sure. But the important point is, in the above derivation, when we constructed (21) (i.e. the final stage), Spell Out has to find a representation (i.e. a derivational stage) at which *what* still has an unvalued case feature; i.e. it has to find either (17) or (18), in each of which *what*'s case feature *is* unvalued. Moreover, Spell Out must have some means of determining that the valued case feature on *what* in the representation (21) is "the same" Case feature as the unvalued one in the syntactic object that was generated at an earlier stage in the derivation. Why the search is initiated, and how this search and determination of feature "identity" is to be formalized, and the extent to which it can be made computationally efficient, is beyond the scope of this chapter; but these constitute crucial questions for the DBP analysis, we think. However, since wh-movement is itself unbounded, e.g.:

(22)   What did Fred say that Bill said that Fred said that Bill said . . . that John will buy?

Notice that at best, it would seem that lookback would have to be indefinitely far. So, it is not clear that "inspection of the derivation" is indeed "limited" under the derivation by phase approach.

   In fact, the situation might be worse. Consider just one iteration of Spec-CP to Spec-CP movement:

(23)   What did Bill say that John will buy?

Again, for *what* to be spelled out at this point, the current representation (i.e. (23)), is insufficient (since the Case feature on each occurrence of *what* is valued). Thus, for some reason, Spell Out is compelled to look back to find a previous stage of the derivation that contains the corresponding Case feature on *what* unvalued. The previous derivational stages (syntactic objects) containing this unvalued form of the Case feature of *what*, however, are all internal to the most deeply embedded *v*P since, recall, it is in the outer Spec of this *v*P (early in the derivation) that the Case feature of *what* becomes valued. Thus, for derivational lookback to find a syntactic object with an unvalued case feature on *what*, it must look back to the derivational stage (*v*P; or points generated before that). Notice, however, that this is in fact impossible under DBP's (see also MI) Phase Impenetrability Condition (henceforth PIC):

(24)   The domain of H is not accessible to operations outside HP [HP a strong phase]; only H and its *edge* are accessible to such operations.

It is assumed in DBP that "optimally all operations are subject to the same conditions," and thus that Spell Out, which is an operation, is subject to the PIC. Thus, when *what* reaches the matrix Spec-CP and is to be spelled out, the most deeply embedded *v*P has already been spelled out, and thus is, under the PIC, the principle at the heart of the derivation by phase approach, inaccessible.[15] In a nutshell, before valuation is too early, after is too late, so you have to see "both," but, under the PIC, you can't. Overall, this represents a potentially serious problem with interphasal valuation.

   Intraphasal valuation may also be problematic in a different sense. Consider, for instance, the standard analysis of unbounded successive cyclic A-movement:

(25)   [$_A$ John seems to be certain to seem to be certain . . . to be arrested]

In this case, Spell Out would, at the point marked A, be operating within a single phase (none of the intermediate TPs are phases). Now, suppose that each movement of *John* (assuming that *John* has moved successive cyclically) is valuing an EPP feature on the intermediate Ts, as has been proposed (in, for example, CT; see also BEA). In the single CP, all the Ts, including the most deeply embedded T, are valued. This single representation is thus insufficient for Spell Out to operate on. Again, for some empirically crucial reason, Spell Out starts to look back. It is going to have to find a representation at which the most deeply embedded T was unvalued. But, its valuation happened "a long time ago;" in fact, given that A-movement is unbounded it can happen indefinitely "far back." The point we are getting at is that depending on the actual algorithm for looking back, and the order in which previous stages are to be inspected, limiting lookback to within-phase-lookback, under which earlier stages can be "forgotten," isn't necessarily computationally efficient. The lookback needed, even though limited to a single phase, could still be unbounded since there is recursion within phases.[16]

Pursuing the matter further, notice that for the Case feature of *John* in (25), the most efficient way to locate the unvalued Case feature quickly is to

(26)   Inspect the immediately preceding stage of the derivation.

By looking back just this far, Spell Out can see that *John*'s Case feature was unvalued, and hence is now to be spelled out. However, if this is the general algorithm, then to find the unvalued EPP feature on the most deeply embedded T, can, in certain cases, require an indefinite number of steps.

If EPP is not feature checking (see, for example, Chomsky 2000 and Lasnik 2001) then the illustration above is invalid. However, if, as Lasnik (and others) argue, EPP is in fact "configurational," then it seems to us to undermine the entire Minimalist theory of movement based on feature interpretability at the interfaces. More generally, "configurational" requirements represent a retreat to the stipulation of molecular tree properties and the failure to deduce molecular tree properties from atomic structure of lexical features, and their mode of attraction and repulsion. It amounts to the reincorporation of phrase structure rules and/or principles of GB, precisely the type of principle that gave rise to the quest for Minimalist explanation, which prohibits such postulates. Stating that "there must be a category here" if true, constitutes nothing more than a description.

5.3   *Simultaneity?*

It is perhaps in response to the "before" and "after" valuation problem discussed here[17] that BEA seeks to eliminate "time" within the phase. The basic idea seems to be that if before is too early and after is too late, then eliminate "time" by having all feature valuation transformations apply at once within the phase. As stated in BEA (p. 22):

(27)   Again, it is "as if" all operations are applying simultaneously at the phase level . . .

We should begin by noting that it is not entirely clear to us what precisely is meant by simultaneous rule application here, nor why it is "as if" operations apply simultaneously (as opposed to actually applying simultaneously). Thus, the discussion below is tentative. But, for purposes of discussion, we (naturally) assume that

(28) If the operations OP1, OP2 are applied simultaneously to a given syntactic object X, then X must meet the structural description of both OP1 and OP2. Furthermore, OP1 and OP2 apply to X without any ordering (or "time") between their application; and thus with no intermediate representation ever generated by the application of one OP, but not yet the other.

We now have a number of points regarding simultaneous rule application.

First, simultaneity does not seem compatible with Earliness, yet Earliness is advocated in DBP and BEA. In fact, DBP (p. 15), states that:

(29) As discussed in MI and sources cited, there is mounting evidence that the design of FL reduces computational complexity ... One indication that it may be true is that principles that introduce computational complexity have repeatedly been shown to be empirically false. One such principle, Procrastinate, is not even formulable if the overt/covert distinction collapses: purely "covert" Agree is just part of the single narrow-syntactic cycle. With the motivation for Procrastinate gone, considerations of efficient computation would lead us to expect something like the opposite: perform computations as quickly as possible, the Earliness Principle of Pesetsky (1989).

We adopt the position in DBP that delay is computationally inefficient. But simultaneous rule application represents a type of delay. Rather than applying an operation O1 at point P1 of a derivation, the syntax "waits" until a phase level is reached, at which point a set of operations (including O1), whose structural descriptions are all met, apply simultaneously.

A related point is that simultaneous rule application seems nonderivational. For example, a theory seeking to explain syntactic relations (as in Epstein 1994, 1999; Epstein et al. 1998) in terms of the step-by-step derivation cannot be maintained since the iterative steps of the derivation are necessarily eliminated under simultaneity. Thus, the syntactic relations that Chomsky characterizes as "free" run the risk of becoming costly. More generally, if simultaneous rule application is allowed, the question arises as to when it is allowed, and why. Unrestricted simultaneous rule application amounts to the elimination of ("Minimalist") derivation altogether, and a return to a GB-type representational theory.

Second, assuming that Merge (for some reason) is not subject to simultaneity, (rather, only feature valuation operations are), we would seem to have two cycles: Merge on the one hand and valuation on the other. Our goal is to have just a single cycle.[18]

Another problem concerning simultaneous rule application within the phase arises if, as in MI and DBP, there exists empirically motivated explicit rule ordering within a single phase. Such within-phase ordering in fact plays a crucial role in DBP and MI, in properly deriving the following case, which occupies a central role under the elimination of the Case Filter at S-structure:

(30)   There seems there-copy to be a man outside.

In the bottom-up step-by-step derivation of DBP and MI, the following point is reached:

(31)   [to be a man outside]

Under the Merge-over-Move analysis, since *there* is present in the Numeration, and visible to Merge, it must be merged *at this point*, yielding:

(32)   [there to be a man outside]

Subsequent step-by-step rule applications apply, still all within the same single phase, since there is no *v*P nor CP yet generated, producing:

(33)   T seems [there to be a man outside]

Now crucially, the idea within MI and DBP is that the matrix phi-complete T searches a Matching Goal. The *previously inserted "there"* is now the closest matching Goal, and therefore *there* is attracted to matrix spec TP, but *a* man is not, yielding the correct predictions:

(34)   a.   [CP [TP there seems [there-copy to be a man outside]
      b.   *[CP [TP A man seems [there to be a man-copy outside]

Recall, this all occurs within a single phase, the matrix CP. The success of the MI and DBP analyses thus rests on the explicit order of application of rules within a single phase.

(35)   Within the matrix CP phase (the only phase present), *there* had to be introduced before matrix T undertook Attraction, so that when matrix T attracted, *there* was already in place, and closer to *there* than is *a man*.

The prevention of such superraising thus rests on rule ordering within a single phase. Under simultaneous rule application within the phase, this central account is lost. We thus tentatively reject simultaneity as the solution to the "before and after" problem confronting Spell Out.

6   Summary

DBP (and also BEA) seeks to *explain*, not stipulate, why there is multiple, cyclic Spell Out, arguing that it "follows naturally from examination of feature interpretability" (DBP, p. 5). Since features are valued iteratively in the course of the derivation, and since, once valued, Spell Out cannot properly operate, it is said to follow that Spell Out must "shadow" the iterative valuation process and thus must itself apply iteratively (i.e. "shortly after" each feature valuation). Feature valuation itself is invoked, arguably, because the derivation-internal, nonsemantic operation Spell Out has no direct access to the LF interface and so cannot know if a feature must be spelled out to PF *now* because it *will* be uninterpretable at LF later. Crucially, lookahead to the interfaces is thereby avoided.

DBP also seems to seek to eliminate "lookback:"

(36) *After* application of Agree, the distinction is lost. *To operate without reconstructing the derivation*, Spell Out must therefore apply *shortly after* the uninterpretable features have been assigned values.

So, suppose there is no lookahead and no lookback. Suppose further that after application of Agree is too late, but before is too early. Then, we have argued, Spelling-out *shortly after* value assignment provides no solution to the entirely empirical problem, since as soon as a feature is valued, the distinction Spell Out operates upon is lost. But recall that it is this very on-line iterative derivational valuation process that constitutes the basis of the DBP (and BEA) attempt to explain why Spell Out must apply cyclically, this cyclic application constituting the crucial departure from the Y-model.

We thus conclude that this attempt to explain cyclicity is problematic, and, importantly, it leaves unclear when Spell Out can possibly operate at all.

Our remaining arguments can then be summarized as follows:

1. We have sought to maintain Chomsky's explanation for cyclicity by applying Spell Out neither before nor after valuation, since each is empirically problematic, but instead by applying Spell Out "inside" the very valuation (transformational) operation itself. This is tantamount to construing each single rule application as a "phase."

2. This is consonant with the derivational approach seeking to deduce principles, filters, and syntactic relations from the properties of simple, local, independently motivated transformational rule application. If correct, the study at hand is interesting since Spell Out, being neither a principle, nor a filter, nor a relation, is similarly "driven inside the rule."

3. Simultaneous rule application (as proposed in BEA) is rejected as the solution to the "before and after" problem. We note that simultaneous rule application is nonderivational and engenders empirical problems while raising issues of which operations are and are not simultaneous, and why.

With Spell Out located "within" the rule:

4. Levels are eliminated. Instead, interpretation by the interfaces applies to each syntactic object generated by the computational system.

5. Reaching the interfaces at each stage comports best with "last resort;" if derivation-internal operations must each increase legitimacy at the interface (the entire theory of movement), this is best enforced (without lookahead or lookback) by having the interfaces immediately evaluate the operation itself.

6. Under our analysis, there is no *lookahead*. Spell Out does not need to consult the interfaces in order to determine what is to be spelled out.

7. Under our analysis, there is no *lookback* (beyond the input–output of a single rule application) to find an earlier stage when the now valued feature was unvalued. We noted empirical problems concerning lookback (to what can't be seen given the PIC) as well as cases of unbounded lookback. More centrally, it is not clear what ever induces lookback to initiate a search for unvalued features in the first place, since valued features in the current representation are inoffensive to Spell Out. Nor is the precise lookback procedure specified. Specifically, it is not clear in what order previous stages of derivation are examined, nor why. Perhaps the most important point about lookback is that if the theory allows it, why not maintain the Y-model, lacking cyclic Spell Out, perform all transformations, then lookback and Spell Out features accordingly? For myriad reasons, this seems to be the wrong approach.

8. There is no need for an independent account of which categories are phases (e.g. CP and *v*P) and which are not, and why. All syntactic objects are phases, and as in 4 above, each syntactic object undergoes interface (PF/LF) interpretation.

Finally, we have argued along the way that:

9. Formulating the EPP as a "configurational principle" is barred under Minimalist assumptions (see Epstein and Seely 1999, forthcoming) since it is a representational macro-tree description, demanding explanation in terms of lexical features and their mode of combination.

Our proposals constitute what we believe to be the specification of the null hypothesis regarding the organization of a "multiple splits" derivation-based model of UG lacking levels altogether. Our analyses are far from conclusive, but, we hope, contribute to the ongoing and (we think) exciting attempts to explicitly identify and seek explanatory maximization in formulating the theory of the biologically determined aspects of human knowledge of language, as begun and continued in Chomsky's routinely pioneering work.

Acknowledgments

For detailed and insightful written comments, we would like to thank Justin Fitzpatrick, Sam Gutmann, Mark Hale, and Hisa Kitahara. Thanks also to Joshua Epstein, Zeljko Boscovic, Beverley Goodman, and Esther Torrego for valuable discussion. Finally, we thank the audience at the 2001 Landelijke Onderzoekschool Taalwetenschap (LOT, Netherlands Graduate School of Linguistics) Summer School at the University of Utrecht.

Notes

1   This is a substantially revised version of a paper originally written in June 2000 (entitled "Cyclic spell out in 'derivation by phase' "). We are indebted to Noam Chomsky for extensive discussion of this earlier version of the paper, which was written and distributed before the appearance of Chomsky (2001b), "Beyond explanatory adequacy," aspects of which we address below.

2   In section 5, we will consider a similar argument, from Chomsky (2001b), for cyclic Spell Out.

3   Note further that some features, like the purported EPP feature, are apparently not PF-interpretable, and hence not interpreted at all. This raises the issue of the unsatisfying "uniqueness" of the EPP feature; unlike all other syntactically valued formal features, the EPP feature is never interpreted by LF nor by PF, which may suggest that it does not "exist," as is claimed in Epstein and Seely (1999). We will address the EPP in greater detail in sections 4 and 5 below.

4   Note that it has been argued recently (see, for example, Lasnik 2001) that EPP may not be a feature but rather a "configurational requirement." See section 5 below for discussion of, and skepticism regarding, this view.

5   By "uninterpretable" here we mean features that cause either LF crash or yield LF gibberish. Technically, it is not that Spell Out spells out all and only LF uninterpretables in the strict sense; rather it spells out all and only those features that are "unuseable" to LF in the sense specified in (1b) above.

6   For instance, if Spell Out transfers the unvalued Case feature of *man* in (2) to the phonology, the result is fine for LF (the Case feature is not present in the object that is seen at LF and thus cannot cause LF crash) but since that Case feature has not yet been valued, and unvalued features cause crash (see (1a) above), then spelling out to PF before valuation invariably induces PF crash.

7   We consider the issue of derivational lookback in DBP in detail in section 5. Derivational lookback, to the phase level, is (crucially) assumed in DBP. But the matter is not entirely straightforward; for example, DBP (p. 5) states that "To operate *without reconstructing the derivation*, Spell Out must therefore apply shorter after the uninterpretable features have been assigned values . . ." "Without reconstructing the derivation . . ." might suggest that there is no derivational lookback. We will argue that this quote is perhaps best interpreted as "Without reconstructing *the entire* derivation . . ." Thus, there is lookback, but it is limited (to the phase). See section 5 below for further discussion.

8   Thus, footnote 7 of DBP: "and without recourse to some such device as the distinction between erasure and deletion, invoked in Chomsky (1995) to deal with a paradox of EST-based systems with a single position for Spell Out: the 'overt' part of the narrow-syntactic computation eliminates uninterpretable features, but they have to remain until the stage of Spell Out of the full syntactic object, because of their phonetic reflexes."

9   As we will note in more detail in section 5, phasal Spell Out in DBP entails that Spell Out is in fact delayed until the phase (i.e. vP/CP) is reached. At this point, our focus is still on the general argument for the existence of cyclic Spell Out,

rather than the more specific argument that the actual units to be spelled out are
vP and CP.

10   More precisely, they are "unuseable" (see note 5 above).

11   (10) holds under the (standard) view that if a feature F of a mover is valued, then
the feature F of the occurrences of the mover are also valued, i.e. under copy
theory as identity. We consider this matter in some detail in section 4.1 below.

12   Note that Chomsky (2001b: 14) argues that "It follows that phases should be as
small as possible, to minimize memory for S-O [i.e. Spell Out]...." See section 5
below for further discussion.

13   See particularly, Epstein et al. (1998: 153, 175).

14   See Nunes (1999) for important discussion of this, and related, issues; see also Epstein
and Seely (1999, forthcoming) for extensive discussion of copy theory as identity.

15   It is also perhaps noteworthy that under the PIC, the residue of Spell Out, i.e. what
remains after Spell Out, is itself not a constituent; e.g. [vP Spec [v' v ...]] is not a
syntactic category, i.e. a head and its Spec(s) do not form a constituent.

16   We would like to thank Sam Gutmann for very helpful discussion of this issue.

17   And in Epstein and Seely (2000).

18   Note that BEA (p. 4) argues that "the best case is that there is a single cycle only."

References

Chomsky, N. 1993. "A Minimalist Program for linguistic theory," in K. Hale and S. J.
Keyser, eds., *The View from Building 20: Essays in Linguistics in Honor of Sylvain
Bromberger*. Cambridge, MA: MIT Press. (Also appears as chapter 3 of Chomsky
1995.)

Chomsky, N. 1995. *The Minimalist Program*. Cambridge, MA: MIT Press.

Chomsky, N. 2000. "Minimalist inquiries: the framework," in R. Martin, D. Michaels,
and J. Uriagereka, eds., *Step by Step: Essays on Minimalist Syntax in Honor of Howard
Lasnik*. Cambridge, MA: MIT Press.

Chomsky, N. 2001a. "Derivation by phase," in Michael Kenstowicz, ed., *Ken Hale: a Life
in Language*. Cambridge, MA: MIT Press.

Chomsky, N. 2001b. "Beyond explanatory adequacy," MS, MIT, Cambridge, MA. A
revised version to appear in A. Belletti, ed., *Structures and Beyond: Current Issues in
the Theory of Language*, submitted to Oxford University Press.

Epstein, S. D. 1994. "The derivation of syntactic relations," MS, Harvard University.

Epstein, S. D. 1999. "Un-principled syntax and the derivation of syntactic relations,"
in S. D. Epstein and N. Hornstein, eds., *Working Minimalism*. Cambridge, MA: MIT
Press, 1999.

Epstein, S. D., E. Groat, R. Kawashima, and H. Kitahara. 1998. *A Derivational Approach
to Syntactic Relations*. Oxford: Oxford University Press.

Epstein, S. D. and N. Hornstein, eds., 1999. *Working Minimalism*. Cambridge, MA: MIT
Press.

Epstein, S. D. and T. D. Seely. 1999. "SPEC-ifying the GB 'subject:' eliminating A-
chains and the EPP within a derivational model," MS, University of Michigan and
Eastern Michigan University; paper also presented at the LSA Summer Institute
(1999).

Epstein, S. D. and T. D. Seely. 2000. "Cyclic Spell Out in 'derivation by phase,'" MS,
University of Michigan and Eastern Michigan University.

Epstein, S. D. and T. D. Seely (forthcoming) *Transformations and Derivations*. Cambridge:
Cambridge University Press.

Lasnik, H. 1999. "Chains of arguments," in S. D. Epstein and N. Hornstein, eds., *Working Minimalism*. Cambridge, MA: MIT Press, 1999.

Lasnik, H. 2001. "A Note on the EPP," *Linguistic Inquiry* 32, 2: 356–61.

Nunes, J. 1999. "Linearization of chains and phonetic realization of chain links," in S. D. Epstein and N. Hornstein, eds., *Working Minimalism*. Cambridge, MA: MIT Press, 1999.

Pesetsky, D. 1989. "Language particular processes and the Earliness Principle," paper presented at the GLOW colloquium, Utrecht, The Netherlands.

Uriagereka, J. 1999. "Multiple Spell Out," in S. D. Epstein and N. Hornstein, eds., *Working Minimalism*. Cambridge, MA: MIT Press, 1999.

Chapter four

Crash-proof Syntax[1]

John Frampton and Sam Gutmann

The Minimalist Program is guided by the idea that the syntactic system of the language faculty is designed to optimally meet design specifications imposed by the interface systems. In this chapter we argue that an optimal derivational system, at least from a computational point of view, is a system that generates only objects that are well-formed and satisfy conditions imposed by the interface systems. We explore the feasibility of constructing such a system, one in which there is no notion of "crashing derivations." We also argue that both the interface conditions and the derivational system which is designed to satisfy them are real, and in this sense we expect to find a pervasive redundancy in linguistic explanation. We demand that the computational system be crash-proof. That is, that no filters are imposed on the end products of derivations, and no global filters (e.g. "comparison of derivations") assign status to derivations as a whole. By exploring the properties of a crash-proof system, we hope to clarify the boundary between the derivational system and the interface conditions, and to make progress in understanding both.

1 Filters versus constrained operations

We start by trying to make clear the contrast between generative systems that rely on extensive overgeneration and filtering on the one hand, and systems which rely on the generative algorithms themselves to produce well-formed outputs on the other. In its pure form, we can state the contrast roughly as follows.

Free generation and filtering: Syntactic representations (or derivations) are freely generated. An extensive system of filters assigns status to these representations or to the derivations which produced them.[2]

Highly constrained generation: Precisely constrained operations iterate to derive a class of representations which are well-formed and interpretable by the interface systems. Output filters play no direct role in the generation process.

Of course, posing the contrast like this sharply overstates the differences that actually exist between current proposals. A representational theory must specify the algorithm that "freely generates" its representations, at least if it claims to remain within the framework of *generative* grammar.[3] And derivational theories standardly employ some filters that apply to the final representations produced by the generative process.[4] Here are three examples of output filters which have played a prominent role in derivational syntax:

1. If a derivation produces a final representation which violates the Θ-Criterion, it is up to a filter (or the interpretive system itself) to mark it deviant.
2. If the final representation produced by a derivation contains uninterpretable (or unvalued) features, the derivation "crashes." Even strict derivationalists who argue that the final representation of a derivation has no special status employ this filter. See for example Epstein and Seely (1999).
3. The device of "comparison of derivations" is a filter that determines the deviance (or non-economy) of an entire derivation.

   The recent trend in derivational syntax has been toward a system of tightly constrained local operations (steps in derivations) and a corresponding reduction in the role of filters applying to terminal representations. We believe that this development has led to real advances in understanding the nature of the syntactic computation. The goal of this paper is to explain "the crash-proof program:" what it is, what questions it allows us to address, and what view it embodies of the relationship between the syntactic computational system and the interfaces that this system connects. We illustrate this trend with the three examples given above.

1. In Chomsky (2000, "Minimalist inquiries," henceforth MI) and (2001, "Derivation by phase," henceforth DBP), the Θ-Criterion is partially incorporated into the definition of selection and merger. It operates as a derivational constraint. Only arguments can be introduced in θ-positions, and only non-arguments can be introduced in non-θ-positions. In Frampton and Gutmann (1999, "Cyclic Computation," henceforth CC) the Θ-Criterion is completely eliminated as a filter on outputs (see section 5 below).[5] Heads merge with their arguments at the point they enter the derivation.[5] The terminal representations of derivations therefore satisfy the Θ-Criterion tautologically. Note that this organization of the derivation is incompatible with a theory in which subjects are not VP-internal.

    The Θ-Criterion has vanished as a filter. Its statement remains as a fact both about the way the syntactic computation works as well as how the interpretive system works. The design of the grammar has aligned the computational system with the requirements of the interpretive system. This is an example of the pervasive redundancy referred to earlier.

2. Uninterpretable (or unvalued) features drive agreement operations, which take place in order to eliminate these features. Thus the filter (1) plays a particularly important role in minimalist syntax:

(1)   *terminal representations with uninterpretable features

Even here, however, the trend toward replacing filters with constraints on operations is evident. In MI/DBP, for example, agreement operations are triggered by a probe, which is always the head of the object constructed so far. Consider, for example:

(2)   [T [SUBJ v [V . . .]]]

In (2), the probe is T, which contains unvalued ϕ-features. The derivation cannot continue until T values its unvalued ϕ-features. If it cannot do so, the derivation immediately fails. Uninterpretable features on probes must be eliminated before the current representation is extended by merger with a new head that selects it. Thus uninterpretable features on probes impose constraints on derivations. We view uninterpretable (unvalued) ϕ-features on probes and the derivational constraint that they must be eliminated immediately as the device employed by narrow syntax to satisfy an interface requirement, the formation of chains (see section 7 below). Note that uninterpretable ϕ-features never reach the interpretive system, so on this view they never cause (1) to act as a filter.

Crucially, this requirement of immediate elimination/valuation does not apply to case features. Case features on nominals do not probe. They are valued when the nominal agrees with certain probes. But the failure of one probe to value a nominal's case feature doesn't mean that a subsequent probe won't succeed. Thus the filter (1) can be replaced, in standard Minimalist syntax, by the Case Filter:

(3)   *terminal representations with unvalued case features

This filter is not local. Case features need not be valued immediately after they are introduced, but only eventually. (In DBP, this filter can be replaced by the requirement that a case feature be valued before the end of the phase after the phase in which it is introduced.) We discuss the Case Filter in detail in section 6.

3.   Comparison of derivations was used to account for:

(4)   *There seems a man to be here.

There have been several attempts to explain (4) without recourse to comparison of derivations. See, for example, CC and Collins (1997). Discussion of comparison of derivations has led to expanded consideration of what importance, if any, should be assigned to the construction of computationally simple syntactic theories, and to what extent computational and aesthetic simplicity are compatible. In MI/DBP in fact, Chomsky succeeds in accounting for (4) without recourse to comparison of derivations, though crucially relying on an initial choice of the array of lexical items (a "numeration") which the derivation uses. The ranking of the rules of combination was stipulated to be such that if a numeration contained *there*, the operation inserting *there* takes place in preference to any movement. Starting with the numeration which consists of the same lexical items as (4), this produces:

(5)   There seems to be a man here.

Starting with the same numeration, except omitting *there*, yields:

(6)   A man seems to be here.

Note that in this system, (4) is simply underivable, not excluded by a filter. The introduction of numerations, however, is precisely the kind of device that we are seeking to eliminate from the grammar. Numerations are freely generated and most are doomed from the start. Only the subsequent attempts at using a numeration to generate a derivation determine whether that numeration can yield a well-formed result. Developing a crash-proof syntax must therefore eliminate reliance on initial lexical arrays as a mechanism for solving syntactic problems. See CC for a numeration-free syntax, in particular one that provides an account of (4).[6]

Comparison of derivations made it necessary to distinguish between derivations that crash and those that converge syntactically, but to which the semantic system is unable to assign a coherent interpretation. The later derivations were said "to converge to gibberish." The distinction was needed in order to establish the set of derivations which a convergent derivation was compared with. In a theory without comparisons, this distinction plays no role in the syntax, and may be difficult to make, though in principle it might still exist: derivations that "converge to gibberish" violate conditions of the interfaces, while "crashing" derivations violate formal filters which are part of the syntax. In the crash-proof syntax we envision, there are no formal filters in the syntax. Every derivation converges. If such a syntax is possible, it will then make sense to try to extend the crash-proof program and determine the extent to which "convergent gibberish" at the output can be avoided by further constraining the derivational system.

Another way that recent proposals have moved in the direction of crash-proof syntax is in the treatment of case features. In early feature-checking treatments, nominals were introduced into the derivation with a valued structural case feature (nominative, accusative, . . .), and ultimately checked by a case-assigning head. There was the possibility that the checker would clash with the nominal's case feature, causing the derivation to fail. The move to unvalued structural case features that are valued only when checked eliminates the possibility of case clash. The consequence is to eliminate a source of an ultimate crash which cannot be detected locally.

2   Crash-proof syntax and computational efficiency

A syntax *with* crashes can include derivations of arbitrary length that are already doomed to crash at a very early point. Consider a derivation that begins:

(7)   it to be believed Max to be happy

In a theory that relies on excluding (7) via the Case Filter, it is not possible to determine efficiently that (7) could not be part of a well-formed sentence. Derivations can continue from (7) and proceed indefinitely, futilely, never detecting the fatal flaw already present in (7), until the question of convergence arises at the interface. For example:

(8)   *It was expected to seem to be believed Max to be happy.

A crash-proof theory must establish that (7) is already ill-formed, so that the deviance is not a question of an ultimate "crash" when the interface is reached. (We will show below how this is accomplished.) A system which is not crash-proof is therefore computationally inefficient. As usual, arguments that one system is inferior to another because the first lacks some property of computational efficiency that the other possesses are inconclusive. The connection between core competence and the performance algorithms that generate and analyze utterances is perpetually obscure. But to the extent that the performance algorithms are built on competence, a theory that permits long-doomed derivations is implausible.

3   Redundancy

We return to the discussion of the Θ-Criterion, which requires that all θ-roles are assigned, and all arguments have been assigned θ-roles. Before MI/DBP, the interface system filtered out representations which violated the Θ-Criterion. In the MI/DBP system, the Θ-Criterion is imposed derivationally (see (6) of DBP). But the interface system still requires that the representations it is presented with satisfy the Θ-Criterion. Thus there is apparently a redundancy in the theory. One might want to argue that this demonstrates that the Θ-Criterion should not be imposed derivationally. Instead, we now want to argue that redundancy of this type is correct, and pervasive, and what we should expect from the minimalist perspective.

   There are other fundamental requirements imposed by the interfaces. We will regard the Case Filter as a requirement of the output interfaces: nominals must bear valued case features. Another fundamental requirement we take to be the Chain Condition (as viewed in Frampton and Gutmann 2000, "Agreement is feature sharing," henceforth AFS), which we discuss in section 7.

One possibility is that these (and other) requirements imposed by the interface systems on representations are all there is to language. One is then forced to the position that heuristics, properties of the performance systems, do the job of more or less efficiently generating representations that meet these conditions.

But there is strong evidence against this scenario. The discovery of powerful explanatory derivational principles, e.g. the mechanism of feature checking, make it appear that the algorithm which governs the generation of successful representations is a central part of the language faculty. This derivational algorithm and the set of interface requirements are essentially redundant. The structures generated by the derivational system are essentially the ones that satisfy the interface requirements. But this redundancy doesn't make the algorithm any less real, or the interface conditions any less real. Optimality Theory systematically confuses this issue, by automatically assuming that the principles which impact the design of a cognitive computational system are themselves the principles of computation. To make clear why the distinction is crucial, consider another biological question: do animals copulate to reproduce, or because sex is fun?

How should we explain *why* animals copulate? One answer might be that animals copulate in order to propagate the species. A second might be that they are driven to it because of certain biologically endowed "sex drives." These are rather different answers. The first leads to an externalist inquiry into population dynamics. The second leads to an internalist inquiry into the nature of sex drives. A little reflection shows that the second answer is much the better one, at least to the question that was asked. The first addresses the question of why it is that animals are endowed with sex drives, not the question of why they copulate. A lesson of the Darwinian revolution in thinking about biological systems is that it is important to be clear about the distinction between questions of why it is that organisms are designed the way they are and questions of how organisms function.

Population dynamics will not tolerate organisms that do not successfully reproduce themselves. The biological endowments of organisms ensure that they have properties which meet the demands of population dynamics. Returning to our case, language-external mandates (which we must discover) constrain the language faculty. But we must also study the computational properties of the language faculty that ensure that these demands are met.

We have arrived at the standard position of the Minimalist Program. The interfaces impose conditions, and the language faculty is designed to satisfy them (that is, to generate structures satisfying them) in some optimal way. Redundancy is inherent in this position.

4 Optimal design

What does "optimal" mean? In the early Minimalist Program, optimality was related to "economy" conditions. For example, if two derivations yielded end products with the same interpretation, then only the shorter derivation's product was well-formed. It is important here to distinguish two uses of "economical." An algorithm which yields results using as few steps as possible is efficient and might be called economical. This is the kind of efficiency we have already discussed. Ruling out (7) as ill-formed is more efficient than ruling out all the continuations of (7) after they terminate. But an algorithm which includes an "economy condition" filtering out all derivations which are not shortest possible will almost certainly be computationally complex. A math teacher who gave students the task of not only proving certain theorems but proving that their proofs were the shortest possible would be giving students an enormously difficult problem. The teacher would surely have to wait a long time for the homework to be turned in if the students were forced to resort to exhaustive search.

There are, of course, no a priori grounds for supposing that "optimal" is equivalent to computationally efficient. But the restriction to efficient derivational theories has been a successful research strategy. The investigation of a crash-proof derivational system is a further step in this program. A derivational system is optimal to the extent that the end products of its derivations meet the interface requirements, with the need for filtering out defective products kept to a minimum. Plausibly, another requirement of optimality is that the derivational system generates a wide range of structures, though it is almost certainly too much to expect that it generates everything permitted by the constraints of the interfaces. There will likely be semantically perfect structures which cannot be generated by the narrow syntax. The first desideratum is what we call crash-proof syntax. The second is that the derivational system maximally exploit the opportunities which the interfaces offer, which we could call "rich generative capacity."

5   Crash-proof selection

We have tried to argue why a crash-proof derivational system, as an optimal solution to the design problem posed by interface requirements, is conceptually desirable. In the remainder of this chapter we turn to some of the specific mechanisms required to achieve a crash-proof system, and some of the problems. Below, we will look at the Case Filter, and the Chain Condition of AFS. We start with the question of how the derivational system can enforce the correct order of mergers, without generating incorrect structures with unmet selectional requirements that must be marked deviant by postderivation filters.

To take the simplest possible example, consider the derivation of *men arrived*, which we can take to be formed from the three heads *men*, *arrive*, and Past. We discuss this example in detail because (a footnote in) DBP contains an argument against the possibility of a crash-proof syntax using essentially this example. In the DBP system, merger of X and Y is permitted as long as X selects Y. Applied to this example, the DBP argument is that a derivation in which Past selects *arrive* before *arrive* selects *man* will inevitably crash because, by cyclicity, *arrive* will never get a chance to select its required argument.

The proposal in CC for how the computation is organized avoids this difficulty. In this system, a derivation is a series of cycles. Each cycle is triggered by the introduction of a new head. Certain features of that head, called the pivot, must be satisfied before a new cycle is undertaken. First every selectional feature of the pivot must be satisfied by merger with phrases headed by previous pivots. After the selectional needs of the pivot are satisfied, certain "attracting features" of the pivot must be satisfied by agreement. The first head to be introduced must be *men*, which does not select anything. Only a head which does not select can start the derivation. The head Past cannot be introduced next because Past selects a V and no V has been introduced yet. Thus *arrive* must be introduced next. When *arrive* is introduced it must select an N, and immediately merges with *men*, which was previously introduced. Since *arrive* has no attracting features, the cycle is complete. The next cycle starts with the introduction of the pivot Past, which selects a V and hence merges with the previously formed *arrive men*. Finally, the attracting features on Past (which are unvalued ϕ-features, say) are satisfied by agreement, which happens to involve movement in this case.

The way that CC organizes the series of cycles that constitute a derivation overcomes the difficulty which led to possible crashes in the DBP system. The heads are introduced automatically in the right order, and no crash caused by incorrect order of selection is possible.[7]

We now turn to two other challenges to the possibility of crash-free syntax, the Case Filter and the Chain Condition of AFS.

6   The Case Filter

The early GB Case Filter became the Visibility Condition, which became the filter demanding that uninterpretable features must be eliminated, which next became the filter demanding that unvalued features must receive a value. But although these efforts to embed the Case Filter in a system of greater generality have played a major role in the development of the Minimalist Program, case features still have properties that separate them from all the other formal features that figure in syntactic operations. In the framework of Attract and the strict cyclicity of current derivational theories, case features are the only unvalued (uninterpretable) features that do not trigger Agreement/Move operations.[8] Further, they are not valued in the cycle (understood as in CC, described above) in which they are introduced.

Any number of raising tense heads can occur without an intervening case-assigning T or v, so valuation of case features can be postponed indefinitely. Four raising heads in (9) intervene between the position in which *Max* first appears in the derivation and the position to which it moves when it is assigned case.

(9)   Max is likely to appear to be believed to be foolish.

The standard claim is:

(10)   If case features remain unvalued at the end of a derivation, then the derivation crashes at the LF interface.

The corresponding end product is deviant. This version of the Case Filter plays an important role in most Minimalist grammars. Crash-proof syntax must show how the derivational system achieves the effects of the Case Filter with only local operations.

There are, first of all, apparent exceptions to (10). Many languages have some mechanism of "default case assignment." Its character is always absolute last resort. Icelandic default nominative assignment is familiar from the attention that dative experiencer verbs in Icelandic have received in recent years. A typical gloss would look like:

(11)   we believe them(dat) to like horses(nom)

Here, *horses* does not have its unvalued structural case feature valued by any case-assigner, but surfaces as nominative in the fully acceptable (11).

The simplest account of the last resort character of default case assignment is that it is not part of the syntax at all, but supplied in the mapping from syntax to morphology. This mapping would fix the morphological case features of nouns on the basis of association with particular categories of "case-assigning" functional heads, when such association had been established syntactically. If case features are not fixed in this way (i.e. structurally) or directly selected (i.e. inherently) then the mapping resorts to whatever language-particular default devices are available. The syntactic computation itself is blind to morphological case features.

Under this view, the Case Filter is not connected to the interface between syntax and LF. (For similar suggestions see Epstein 2000, introduction and references there.) The language of the PF interface is something close to a language of "motor instructions." The Case Filter cannot even be stated in this language. So the Case Filter is not a PF-interface condition, either. We leave the Case Filter as a morphological condition:

(12)   Nominals must reach the morphological component with a case feature.

This feature can be assigned structurally, inherently, or by a default mechanism.

If this is true, it cuts against our thesis that the filters that shape the design of the grammar are conditions on the interface between language itself and language-external systems. The Minimalist idea must be extended to filters based on interfaces between language-internal subsystems. A suggestion for how a language-internal interface could be thought about in Minimalist terms is to suppose a multi-stage development of language. Whatever characteristics one stage acquires in optimally solving the design problems it faces would become a kind of interface condition for further development of the language faculty. In this instance, conditions at the true PF interface might lead to conditions at the phonology/morphology interface, which in turn would lead to the Case Filter, at the morphology/syntax interface.

But this is speculation. The bottom line is that although progress has been made in understanding the role and nature of the Case Filter from a Minimalist perspective, it remains only dimly understood at this point. If default case assignment were freely available as a morphological operation that can provide case to nominals that have failed to acquire it derivationally, then the Case Filter would not have any effect on the design of the derivational system. It must be that default case assignment is limited in some way, so that the Case Filter does have an effect on the design of the derivational system and yields products satisfying some (poorly understood) requirement on the connection between sound and meaning.

In spite of this uncertainty about the status and character of the Case Filter, we adopt (12). The "crash-proof program" we have embarked on therefore demands that we show how the derivational system conspires (i.e. is designed) to generate structures that satisfy this condition.

Consider again the example in (7), at the point:

(13)   [T [be [believed [Max to be happy]]]]

Inserting *it* to value the unvalued features of T is a fatal mistake. A crash-proof syntax must ensure that this choice is never made. It is not enough to permit it, knowing that the Case Filter will mark the end product of the derivation as deviant.

The solution is straightforward. The Agree operation is viewed algorithmically, as a search undertaken by the probe, T in this instance. The search proceeds top-down and succeeds when it reaches *Max*. (We are leaving aside the potential complication of partial agreement with the participle first.) Then T agrees with *Max*, which entails movement in this case. Insertion of *it* is never a possibility.

What is the status of the representation underlying (14) in this system?

(14)   *It is believed Max to be happy.

It is simply underivable. (Recall the discussion of (4) for an earlier example of a surface form that is simply underivable, as opposed to derivable but starred by some filter.) One could add that if it did reach the interface it would violate the Case Filter, and that the operations of syntax have therefore been designed to prevent it from being derived in the first place. This is an example of what we called pervasive redundancy: the Case Filter would not tolerate (14), and the rules of syntax prevent its derivation. The rules of syntax, in this case the rules for how probes find goals, never refer to the Case Filter. But the rules have "been designed" so that they generate structures which satisfy it.

We need to compare (13) with:

(15)   [T [be [believed [that Max is happy]]]]

In (15), we must ensure that the top-down search by the probe T for an agreeing nominal must fail. In recent work (e.g. CC and MI) the notion of inactivity has been used: *Max* is inactive in (15) because it has no unvalued features; that is, its case feature has already been valued. The top-down search ends when any nominal, active or inactive, is encountered. This is simply an operational statement of the minimal link condition.

The notion of inactivity is only useful if it can refer to case features on nominals. Our decision above to make the Case Filter a morphological condition makes it unnatural to allow a valued versus unvalued distinction in case features to play any role in the syntactic computation. In the system developed in AFS, case features are specifically excluded from the syntax, so no notion of activity can be appealed to. In that system, the top-down search undertaken by T in (15) ends when it encounters a C. The search does not proceed into the complement of a C. This recalls the old Tensed S Condition, and is argued for on independent grounds in AFS.

Whether by Inactivity or by C-complement Opacity, the top-down search undertaken by T in (15) fails, and the features of T can only be valued by merger with an expletive *it*. We have the desired contrast: in (13), *it* cannot be inserted, and in (15), *it* must be inserted. (CC and AFS also contain an analogous account, derived from Frampton 1996, which depends on assuming that expletive insertion is a last resort.)

Next consider another example where deviance might be ascribed to a violation of the Case Filter:

(16)   *Max to be here

In a crash-proof theory, (16) is derivable and well-formed. Although *Max* in (16) is not in a configuration that will permit case assignment, we take the status of (16) to be the same as the status of the examples in (17):

(17)   a.   that Max is here
       b.   for Max to be here
       c.   PRO to be here

None of the examples in (17) have case assignment problems. In (17c), null case is assigned to PRO. All three representations are interpretable, although they do not have the interpretations of main clauses. The same is true of (16).

What about the standard idea that some verbs "do not assign case"? Consider:

(18)   *We hope miracles.

Note that in a system in which accusative case is assigned by a functional verb v that bears unvalued ϕ-features, (18) is actually:

(19)   ... v hope miracles

The content of *"hope* does not assign case" is that *hope* is not selected by a version of v that bears unvalued ϕ-features and assigns accusative case. But once selection is implicated anyway, the straightforward account of (18) is that *hope* does not select a nominal. This is apparently right; (20) has no unvalued case features.

(20)   *Miracles were hoped.

In the same way, if *hope* does not select raising T, then we successfully predict both (21a) and (21b):

(21)   a.   *We hoped Max to be here.
       b.   *Max was hoped to be here.
       c.   It is hoped that Max will be here.

We cannot exclude (21b) by appealing to failure of case assignment. There are no semantic problems, as can be seen by (21c). Only the selectional restriction predicts (21b).

There are other verbs for which neither the selectional nor the case feature account seems to suffice, e.g. *think*:

(22)   a.   *We thought Max to be a fool.
       b.   Max was thought to be a fool.
       c.   We thought Max a fool.
       d.   *Max was thought a fool.

Our goal has only been to show the plausibility of a derivational system in which there is no reliance on the Case Filter, and we leave the matter here.

7   The Chain Condition

AFS implements the agreement operation carried out between two heads (which in DBP is taken to be the valuation of an unvalued feature of the probe) as coalescence of two features, so that the two heads come to *share* a common feature. It will be a valued feature if one of the coalescing features is valued. A chain is the set of heads sharing a particular feature. For the sake of simplicity, we focus here on chains involving ϕ-agreement and case, excluding *wh*-chains and head movement. Certain heads, called TE-heads (temporal-event heads), play a special role in the case system. They are the heads that assign structural case: finite T, and v (at least). A precise version of the Chain Condition in the AFS system would require an extended discussion of the entire feature set involved in the case system. It suffices for our purpose here to consider one of its implications.

(23)   Interpretable case chains contain at most one TE-head.

Consider (24a), for example. Omitting movement, we display the relevant heads in (24b).

(24)   a.   We believe Max to love Mary.
     b.   [T [we v_1 [believe [T_r [Max v_2 [love Mary]]]]]]

Here v_1 and v_2 are functional verbs, and T_r is raising (i.e. infinitival) tense. There are three chains in (24): $\{v_2, \text{Mary}\}$, $\{v_1, T_r, \text{Max}\}$, and $\{T, \text{we}\}$. Each chain contains one TE-head.

We want now to examine what properties of the syntactic system and lexical items ensure that chains will not violate (23). The crash-proof program demands that the system does not generate violations of the interface conditions. As mentioned above, in AFS there is no notion of inactivity. This view of agreement, combined with the Chain Condition, yields an explanation of Burzio's Generalization: A functional verb v that assigns accusative case must select a subject. Suppose, to the contrary, that the lexicon contained a TE-head v that assigned accusative case but did not select a subject. A derivation might reach the point:

(25)   [T [v [grow tomatoes]]]

Here, v agrees with *tomatoes* and the chain $\{v, \text{tomatoes}\}$ has formed. Now T probes to value its unvalued features and T agrees with *tomatoes*. Remember that there is no inactivity. One chain, $\{T, v, \text{tomatoes}\}$, is formed, violating the Chain Condition. If, instead, v had been a head that assigns accusative case and selects a subject, we might have:

(26)   [T [Max v [grow tomatoes]]]

Now when the probe T does a top-down search, it stops when it reaches *Max*. Two well-formed chains result: $\{T, \text{Max}\}$ and $\{v, \text{tomatoes}\}$. The subject prevents the formation of a chain which is destined to violate an interface condition.

We therefore view Burzio's Generalization as a statement about the selectional properties of certain functional elements. It is a generalization that holds because the system adapts itself to prevent the generation of derivations which fail at the interface. Note carefully the distinction we are making. Burzio's Generalization is not a filter which has the effect of excluding derivations which contain lexical items of a certain type. It is a property of certain lexical items which has the effect of avoiding violations of an interface filter, the Chain Condition. This account illustrates well the theme of the present paper. The Chain Condition is a design specification, plausibly imposed by the LF interface, which requires interpretable structures. The condition is partially implemented by the absence from the lexicon of unsuitable versions of v. The result is that derivations cannot produce these kinds of violations of the Chain Condition.

Here is another example where the Chain Condition of AFS has an impact on the selectional properties of lexical items. Consider:

(27)   [T [be [believed [Earth is round]]]]

Suppose that the sentential complement *Earth is round* is a TP, as opposed to a CP. When the matrix T probes, it will agree with *Earth*. The resulting chain will involve two TE-heads, both the matrix and embedded T (which previously agreed with *Earth*). Thus the Chain Condition is violated. If, however, *believe* does not select tensed T, but does select C, then the crashing derivation is avoided. As discussed earlier, the opacity of C-complements prevents T from agreeing with *Earth* in:

(28)   [T [be [believed [C [Earth is round]]]]]

In (28), the derivation continues successfully with the insertion of expletive *it* to value the unvalued features of T. So we conclude that *believe* cannot select T. Now consider:

(29)   We believe Earth is round.

This might satisfy the Chain Condition even if the sentential complement in (29) is a TP. But (29) with a TP complement is underivable, because of the selectional properties of *believe*. Here we have a (minor) example of a sentence which apparently meets all interface conditions but which cannot be derived by the syntactic system which has been designed to implement the interface conditions. As noted above, it is too much to expect that the syntax will take complete advantage of the possibilities left open by the fundamental constraints of the interfaces.

8   Conclusion

In this chapter we have explored the possibility of constructing a derivational syntax which is crash-proof, that is, a system whose derivations are all well-formed. Thus we hope to dispense with filters that apply at the end of derivations. We can then obtain a neat separation. Because we demand that the derivational system produce only well-formed derivations, principles that appear to filter the end products of derivations must be viewed as outside the derivational system. They must be requirements of the interface systems. Thus we have a glimmer of how we can make "[p]rogress in understanding [the interface systems] . . . hand-in-hand with progress in discovering the language systems that interact with them" (MI). Take the Case Filter. If we can make an argument that the grammar is designed in such a way that it conspires to produce representations which satisfy the Case Filter, we learn something both about the properties of the computational system and about why it is constructed the way it is. Without a "crash-proof perspective," no such conclusion can be drawn. If output conditions can be freely viewed as part of the computational system itself, we learn nothing about the properties of that system.

Notes

1   We thank Cedric Boeckx, Noam Chomsky, Sam Epstein, Gil Rappaport, Daniel Seeley, and Charles Yang for comments and criticisms.
2   We make a distinction between *filters* and *constraints*. We understand the latter to mean *derivational* constraints. They influence the course of derivation by affecting the possible operations which can apply at each step in the derivation. Filters have no effect on the step-by-step course of a derivation. Their effect is only to evaluate representations that have been produced by derivations.
3   This algorithm is subject to the usual criteria that are used to decide between one theory and another. Are some algorithms for "free generation" better than others?
4   In earlier theories, e.g. GB, filters applied at intermediate levels of representation as well.
5   No operations can intervene before these mergers are complete.
6   Numerations act as an "expletive flag," determining whether or not a sentence (or a phase) will be an expletive construction. In CC, expletive constructions are forced when certain nonspecific nominals are merged in. There, nominals lack features required to agree with T and expletives supply them.
7   In recent work, Chomsky (class lectures) has refined this criticism of the crash-proof program. The argument goes like this. There is no syntactic terminal corresponding to the verb *arrive*. There is a root ARRIVE, which forms a verbal complex when selected by a "small v" and a nominal complex when selected by a "small n." *Max arrived*, for example, starts out with a vP, [v [ARRIVE Max]], while *the arrival* starts out with an nP, [n ARRIVE]. The force of the example comes from the fact that ARRIVE itself has no selectional requirements. Chomsky points out that the CC view of selection has no way to distinguish ill-formed [v ARRIVE] from well-formed [n ARRIVE].

This critique misses its mark. In a crash-proof syntax, at the end of each cycle, either the syntax recognizes that the structure is ill-formed, or there is some well-formed continuation. Assuming, as we did in CC, that violations of c-selection were syntactically ill-formed, a theory in which verb roots are not syntactic terminals, but v-root complexes, does require a modification of the theory of selection implicit in the CC proposal. But the modification is straightforward. It is applied in the cycle in which the "verb root" (i.e. the v-root complex) is formed. At the end of the v cycle, selection correctly recognizes that [v ARRIVE] is ill-formed. On the other hand, in a theory in which violations of c-selection are not considered ill-formed by the narrow syntax, which is what Chomsky proposes in recent work, crash-proof syntax has no responsibility to recognize the eventual interpretive deviance in the semantic component of [v ARRIVE]. Either way, the criticism does not challenge the crash-proof program.
8   According to some analyses, wh-features also have this property. But the proper analysis of wh-features is far from settled.

References

Chomsky, Noam. 2000. Minimalist inquiries: the framework. In *Step by Step: Essays on Minimalist Syntax in Honor of Howard Lasnik*, eds. Martin Rogers, David Michaels and Juan Uriagereka. Cambridge, MA: MIT Press.
Chomsky, Noam. 2001. "Derivation by phase." In Ken Hale, *A Life in Language*, ed. Michael Kenstowicz. Cambridge, MA: MIT Press.

Collins, Chris. 1997. *Local Economy*. Cambridge, MA: MIT Press.

Epstein, Samuel David. 2000. *Essays in Syntactic Theory*. London and New York: Routledge.

Epstein, Samuel David and T. Daniel Seely. 1999. "SPEC-ifying the GF 'subject;' eliminating A-Chains and the EPP with a derivational model," MS, University of Michigan and Eastern Michigan University.

Frampton, John. 1996. "Expletive insertion," In Chris Wilder, Hans-Martin Gärtner, and Manfred Bierwisch, eds., *The Role of Economy Principles in Linguistic Theory*. Berlin: Akademie Verlag.

Frampton, John and Sam Gutmann. 1999. "Cyclic computation, a computationally efficient minimalist syntax." *Syntax* 2.1: 1–27.

Frampton, John and Sam Gutmann. 2000. "Agreement is feature sharing." MS, Northeastern University. (Available at *www.math.neu.edu/ling*)

Chapter five

Reprojections

Norbert Hornstein and Juan Uriagereka

1 Introduction

It is hard to decide whether a proposal should be couched in derivational or representational terms, or some combination of the two. The best kind of argument for derivations involves the need for representations whose information is required piecemeal – being vital at one point and unwanted at another. In such cases, one would favor analyses that involve partial representations whose properties are not conserved as the derivation unfolds. This "loss of information" scenario fits poorly into models which make use of enriched representational codings (including traces, indices, and similar elements) because whatever information may have been lost in the course of the derivation can be reconstructed through some abstract coding.

What follows offers a candidate "loss of information" phenomenon. It is expressed within one particular interpretation of the Minimalist Program which drastically reduces notational options (Chomsky 1995, 1999, 2000). We argue that losing information has a natural Minimalist interpretation and intriguing semantic and syntactic empirical consequences. So far as we can see, the mechanism we explore, *reprojection*, can be replicated in purely representational terms only at the cost of added, otherwise unnecessary, notational machinery. Hence if reprojection should prove to occur grammatically, it would argue that grammars are (at least in part) derivational systems.

The basic idea concerns the merging mechanism in (1), which results in some labeling:

(1) X ⇔ Y

Following Chomsky (1995) we may code that label as in (2), where L is the label:[1]

(2) {L {X, Y}}

A key issue is whether L is identical to X or to Y. The options are:

(3) a.   X (Formally: {X, {X, Y}}   b.   Y (Formally: {Y, {X, Y}})
     / \   / \
     X Y   X Y

It is natural to assume that what determines the choice in (3) are the properties of X and Y. For instance, if X is a verb and Y is a DP, then X will project; if X is a DP and Y is a v', then v will project. Collins (this volume) suggests that this reasoning, appropriately extended, can deduce what label any given object will bear. Suppose this is true. A question remains: might a phrase-marker's label *change* in the course of a derivation?[2] Were this possible, and (3b) but not (3a) reached the interpretive component, we would have a nice argument for derivations.

2   Basic mechanics

Although we want to keep the discussion at a deliberatively intuitive level – so that an informal idea of reprojection can be grasped by the reader – it ought to be clarified that reprojection is strictly speaking not an operation in itself. Rather, it simply signals the fact that, in the course of the derivation, different operations have taken place between two categories X and Y, such that at some stage it is sound to consider their mother a YP, whereas at some other stage, instead, their mother is seen by the system as an XP.[3] Schematically:

(4) a.   YP   b. XPi
     / \   / \
     XPi Y' ====REPROJECTION====>   X'i YP
       / \   / \
      Y . . . ti . . .   Y . . . ti . . .

What is derivational is a system that behaves this way, identifying a given "geometrical" entity as a YP and later on as an XP (the very same "geometrical" entity).

Next consider a formal problem for reprojection. There are two reasons to prevent reprojections involving heads and their specifier. First, for specifiers derived by movement reprojection will result in improper or nonuniform chains, as can be seen in (4). The chain (XPi, ti) in (4a) becomes (4b) after reprojection. If the intended chain is still (XPi, ti), it will be improper (the first link dominates but does not c-command the last); if the chain in question is now (X'i, ti), it will be nonuniform in the sense of (5) (Chomsky 1995: 253):

(5)   A chain is uniform with regard to phrase structure status.

In (4b), given a chain (X'i, ti), the first link is not a maximal projection, the last one is.

A second problem for reprojection is that it alters checking configurations. Thus XP in (4a) is in the checking domain of Y, while in (4b) YP is in the checking domain of X.

These possible objections reflect a representational bias. A changing checking domain in (4) could reflect the fact that Y's checking domain (vis-à-vis XP) is relevant only *at some derivational time* Dt, while at some later point Dt', instead, the checking domain of X (vis-à-vis YP) is what is relevant. As for the first objection concerning chain uniformity, it is possible that the chains involved in (4) are read by the interfaces *prior to* their becoming either nonuniform or improper.[4]

Note that should reprojection take place, it must do so late in the derivation, in fact only in the LF component; otherwise the altered command relations would yield PF linearizations which are "backwards," according to Kayne's (1994) mapping of c-command to precedence (the Linear Correspondence Axiom). In particular, the new specifier after reprojection would have to precede the rest of the structure.[5] In this paper we will assume that the above worries can be met. Specifically, we assume that (i) covert reprojection does alter checking relations (notably for Case and agreement), but after these relations have already been exploited in overt syntax; and (ii) chains are interpreted by the system before reprojection, assuming on-line interpretation by phases (Epstein et al. 1998; Chomsky 1999; Uriagereka 1999).

The focus of this chapter is to show that allowing reprojection provides us with a novel perspective on some peculiar syntactic and semantic properties of quantifiers. The gist of the idea comes from the observation in Larson and Segal (1995) that binary quantifiers like *most* behave much like transitive verbs in that they take "ordered" arguments (thematic arguments in the verbal case, and a restriction and a scope in the case of a quantifer). If this is so, and provided that verbs "take" their arguments in familiar syntactic ways (within extended verbal projections), it is reasonable to ask whether quantifiers too "take" their arguments in familiar syntactic ways. To illustrate, consider a sentence like (6):

(6)   Most people love children.

Here the quantificational argument *people* (the restriction) is in a standard syntactic relation with regards to the quantifier *most* (as its complement). In contrast, the quantificational argument *love children* (the matrix) is not a syntactic dependent of this quantifier; rather, *most children* is in construction with the relevant IP (as its specifier), within customary assumptions. This is not what we want semantically, if we require basic compositional relations to be expressed in terms of basic syntactic dependencies.

Now suppose reprojection is possible. Then nothing prevents the quantifier *most* from handling its argumental requirements after the Case and agreement requirements of IP have been met. At that stage in the derivation (i.e. covertly), (7b) is what we obtain from (7a):

(7) a.

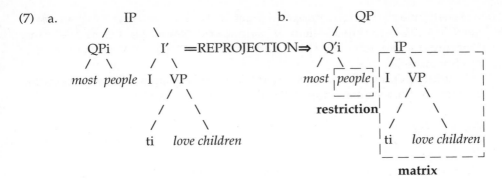

Now *most* is in construction with its restriction and matrix, as in (7b). The dependency with the restriction has not changed after reprojection, as desired, since it was adequate from the start; but the dependency with the matrix is now appropriate: the IP is a dependent of *most people*.

In order to extend that reasoning from subject quantifiers to others we clearly need some form of Quantifier Raising. For the purposes of reprojection, any of the theories in the literature will do. There could be a separate rule of QR (as in Fox 1995; Reinhart 1995), a targeted quantificational displacement to check specific morphology (as in Beghelli 1995), or some piggy-backing on already existing A-movement (as in Kitahara 1992; Hornstein 1995). In all instances there would be some target X which would take the rest of the structure (prior to QR) in its domain, and would fall in the quantifier domain after reprojection:

(8) a.

XP
/ \
QPi   X'   =REPROJECTION⇒
/ \   / \
most people X   YP
/ \
/...ti...\

b.

QP
/ \
Q'i   XP
/ \   / \
most ⌐people⌐ X   YP
└─ ─ ─┘ / \
restriction /...ti...\

matrix

So for instance, X would be *v* or T for A-movement theories of QR; and some designated Q phrase for A'-movement theories. A technical difficulty arises for standard QR theories if they involve adjunction, as it is not clear what it means to say that an adjunct reprojects a mere "segment" of the adjunction site (see section 7 below).[6]

3 An important prediction

The present proposal has an interesting consequence. Intuitively: what was a "complement branch" in (7a) becomes a "noncomplement branch" in (7b).

In what follows we will bring this fact to bear on a very complex set of facts involving so-called "quantifier-induced" islands, known at least since Linebarger (1980) (see Den Diken and Szabolcsi 1999 for a recent summary of the literature).

Basically put, whenever we try to establish an LF relation between positions X and Y in (9) across a binary QP, unacceptability ensues.

(9)   ... [X ... [QP ... [Y ...]...]...]...
                      Z

The very same type of relation of grammar is possible if it takes place in overt syntax:

(10)   a.   *Nobody* gave **most children** *a red cent.*
       b.   *Nobody* gave two children *a red cent.*
       c.   What did *nobody* give **most children** *t*?

In (10a) we try to relate *nobody* and the polarity item *a red cent*, across the binary quantifier *most children*, which induces an intervention effect. We bold-face quantifiers that induce LF islands to distinguish them from those, like *two children* in (10b), which do not. That the island arises only at LF is shown by the acceptable (10c), where the wh-element overtly moves across the blocking quantifier.

Our proposal is that reprojection induces an island in (10a), but not in (10b) or (10c). The reason for the first of these desiderata has already been explained: *most* has semantic demands that are met assuming reprojection. Importantly, those demands are not active until late in the derivation (intuitively after QR), or else (10c) would also be prevented in terms of whatever our island condition is. In turn, it must be the case that (10b) induces no reprojection, even at LF. We discuss in more detail in section 9 how unary quantifiers need not, and thus do not, invoke a reprojection process, as their semantics does not involve the two arguments that make reprojection relevant to begin with. If that is the case, we do not expect an island in (10b), prior to or after Spell Out.

There are three separate issues involved in quantifier-induced (QI) islands: (i) the reasons the island arises; (ii) the constructions that test them; and (iii) the quantifiers that create them.

This chapter does not concentrate on why the LF island arises. Arguably it relates to a version of Huang's Condition on Extraction Domains (CED).[7] Relations across noncomplements are impossible, and after reprojection the relevant domains are specifiers, not complements. In Hornstein and Uriagereka (1999) we show how this follows from an interpretive procedure in which chains are interpreted before split constructions are resolved. However, we lack the space to go into this here.

As regards the second question, QI islands manifest themselves in "split" constructions, which involve a quantificational expression that attempts to establish a relation with another element, typically an indefinite. We saw in (10) a canonical split construction: a relation between a downward-entailing quantifier and a negative polarity item (NPI). Other such constructions analyzed in the literature include the "what . . . for" split of Germanic and Slavic languages, partial wh-movement, the wh-movement of pure adjuncts, and possibly also some instances of multiple questions (see Honcoop 1998 and Pesetsky 2000 for much relevant discussion; and Szabolcsi and Zwarts 1993 for the original classifications).

As for the third question, the set of elements that create QI islands is hard to characterize. We consider this next.

4   QI island inducers

The easy part of the story is this: binary quantification induces islands at LF. This is as we expect, if binary quantification requires reprojection, and LF islands are tied to this. But things are more complex. Binary quantification appears at first glance neither necessary nor sufficient to induce an LF island. Thus, negation induces them, but does not seem to involve binary quantification; in contrast, some strong quantifiers which might take two arguments do not induce LF islands. Part of our goal here is to show that this early, pessimistic conclusion is in fact too hasty.

Consider the latter apparent counterexample first. To clarify how we establish whether a determiner is a valid candidate for inducing binary quantification, we must evaluate whether it is "symmetric." A determiner is symmetric if, when introducing a subject NP predicate X for a VP predicate Y, switching X and Y does not affect truth conditions. For instance, compare:

(11)   a.   Most Basques are Spaniards. ←/→ Most Spaniards are Basques.
       b.   Some Basques are Spaniards. ↔ Some Spaniards are Basques.

Most is obviously not symmetric, whereas *some* is. Symmetric quantifiers can be analyzed in unary fashion: after QR we can take their single argument to be their scope, their restriction being undetermined. Nonsymmetric quantifiers cannot be so analyzed, and require the customary two arguments. In fact, the quantifier is binary in that the truth conditions of the proposition it introduces are computed by compositionally relating the determiner, first to its restriction, and next (together with what it relates to in the previous instance) to the matrix. If we were to change these basic orderings we would get the same absence of reversability that we find in a normal sentence, when the first argument of the verb (its direct object) is interpreted as its second argument (its subject). It is no more true that most Spaniards are Basque than it is that Spaniards understand Basques, although it is true that most Basques are Spaniards, just as it is true that Basques understand Spaniards.

All weak quantifiers (the ones possible in environments that induce "definiteness effects," such as existential contexts) are symmetric in their standard readings. But not all strong quantifiers are asymmetric. In particular, quantifiers that are individual- or group-denoting are normally symmetric:

(12) a. The sun is the center of the universe. ↔ The center of the universe is the sun.
(Cf. *There is the sun in the universe.)
  b. Marilyn was the center of the universe. ↔ The center of the universe was Marilyn.
(Cf. *There was Marilyn in Hollywood.)

(13) a. (The) MGM stars were the best paid. ↔ The best paid were (the) MGM stars.
(Cf. *There were (the) MGM stars in Hollywood. [Out with generic interpretation.])
  b. The Marx Brothers were the best paid. ↔ The best paid were the Marx Brothers.
(Cf. *There were the Marx Brothers in Hollywood.)

Although none of the elements above are possible in existential contexts, they are clearly reversible. This is not at all surprising for names like *Marilyn* or *The Marx Brothers*, since there is no obvious sense in which these are quantificational expressions with two arguments. However, even corresponding individual-denoting, clearly quantificational definite descriptions or generic expressions are symmetric.

The good news for us is that those very expressions that are clearly symmetric do not induce LF islands. Thus observe:

(14) *Nobody* gave the sun/Marilyn/(the) MGM actors/the Marx Brothers *any credit*.

There is no difficulty relating an NPI to its licenser across names, definite descriptions, or generic expressions. We expect this result if these elements do not reproject, as they are symmetric and hence not binary. On the other hand, at least definite descriptions and generic expressions can be shown not to act symmetrically in some contexts. For instance:

(15) (The) Spaniards are (*the) NATO members. ↔ (The) NATO members are (*the) Spaniards.

Nonetheless, it is not obvious that this affects their capacity to induce LF islands:

(16) *Nobody* ever gives (the) Spaniards *any credit*.

In short, the first descriptive difficulty we face is this. By our own criteria, the nonsymmetric expressions in (15) should reproject, all other things being equal; as a consequence they should induce LF islands. But they do not. Hence they cannot reproject, in spite of having nonsymmetric properties.

There is also a second descriptive difficulty, the converse of the first. Consider (17):

(17) a. Why do you think that this is easy?
      b. Why don't you think that this is easy?

(18) a. What did you think this is t?
      b. What didn't you think this is t?

Example (17a) has two readings, depending on whether *why* modifies the matrix or the embedded clause. (17b), in contrast, is restricted to a matrix interpretation. It seems as if the negative element induces an intervention effect; that the effect arises in the covert component only is at least arguable, on the basis of the fact that the examples in (18) are both fine, and they clearly involve displacement of an argument from the lower clause.

We do not wish to enter a controversy here as to whether the problem just seen concerns a pre-/post-Spell Out asymmetry or rather with the distinction between pure adjuncts (17) vs. arguments; in fact, the latter is very dubious since, strictly, what we have extracted in (18) is not an argument, but a predicate. Regardless, the reason we raise these sorts of examples, first discussed in terms of intervention effects by Szabolcsi and Zwarts (1993), is because we do not know how to test the intervention properties of a negative element by way of a negative polarity item, as the negative element itself would irrelevantly license the polarity item in question.

In what follows, we assume that Szabolcsi and Zwart's cases of intervention (1993) are continous with those that interest us. The assumption is not evident. Many relevant cases are acceptable given the right presuppositions (see Kroch 1989), which contrasts with the simple unacceptability of split constructions in the contexts thus far discussed. It is then possible that negative islands should be handled differently. In fact, it is not clear that a *why* operator involves a "split" construction to begin with, in contrast with *what* or *who* operators – in the sense of relating to a covert part under the scope of an intervening quantifier.[8] We will sidestep both issues, however, to see where things lead if we do in fact assume a unified treatment. Then the puzzle we have created for ourselves is this: why should a negative operator induce an LF island if there is no clear sense in which this operator needs the two arguments that motivate reprojection? We address that, and the first descriptive difficulty noted above, in the sections that follow.

5   LF islands without binary quantification?

Observe how an embedded reading for *why* is unacceptable:

(19) a. *Why* did **few people** think that this was *easy*?
      b. *Why* did you **deny** that this was *easy*?
      c. *Why* did **exactly ten people** say that this was *easy*?
      d. *Why* did **TEN people** say that this was *easy*?
      e. *Why* **DID** some people say that this was *easy*?

We might try to relate (19a) to the negative instances seen in the previous section (17), arguing that *few* and similar downward-entailing elements can be analyzed in terms of a negative followed by a positive version: in this instance, *not many*. It is certainly true that some languages do not have the lexical equivalent of *few*, and must express that notion in terms of elements with the semantic import of *not many*; if that is taken as an argument for limited lexical decomposition – on the basis of some cross-linguistic interpretive uniformity – then abstractly (19a) would reduce to some form of (17b). Something similar might be relevant for (19b), the example involving some surface version of *assert not*.

But even radical decompositionalists will have trouble finding a suitable candidate for *exactly ten* in (19c). A semantically equivalent element is *no more than, and no less than, ten*, but we know of no language in which *exactly ten*, or a version along the lines in (19d), with emphasis in the determiner, is disallowed. In the absence of such a language, it is unclear how to make a lexical decomposition argument, on the basis of interlinguistic uniformity.[9]

Example (19d) suggests a different way out of the impasse. Note, first, that a sentence such as (19e) is bad as well if we want to interpret *why* across the emphatic element *DID*. No suitable negative decomposition exists for this expression, for an emphatic assertion is in no way a negation. However, negatives and emphatic elements have been shown to share the same syntax (Laka 1990), an insight that goes back to Klima (1964). It is possible that what unifies the examples above is Laka's Γ category, which is supposed to code an operator which either changes the pragmatically expected truth value of a sentence (normally positive, thus turning it to negative) or alternatively reaffirms that expected truth value (confirming the positive assumption). Suppose this is the correct approach.

Why should the syntax of Γ induce reprojection? To examine this question in detail, we must separate standard instances of relations across unmarked negation – in English the clitic element *n't* – from focused examples involving the nonclitic element *not*, or stress in the auxiliary. Under the latter circumstances, a much more complex set of generalizations obtain:

(20)   a.   What do you not think is easy?
       b.   What DON'T you think is easy?

As Paul Portner points out (personal communication), (20a) involves a peculiar reading whereby the focused negative associates with the wh-element; a paraphrase of this reading would be: "of what do you not think that it is easy?", or, in other words, "what stands out as an exception among the things of which you have the thought that they are easy?" (20b) has that reading, plus one more, paraphrased as a rhetorical question: "is there *anything* you do not think is easy?" In this reading the focused negative has widest scope, and associates to the entire clause. Although we ultimately think that focus is also amenable to a reprojection treatment, especially if understood in the LF terms advocated in Herburger (2000), we set focus aside for now.

Concentrating on the standard readings of negative questions, a further distinction must be made. Consider two scenarios. In the first one, you are assumed to *hold* a belief about something not being easy, say trigonometry or calculus, but the questioner doesn't exactly know which. Call that the *positive* scenario. In a second one, which we will call *negative*, you are assumed not to hold a belief about something being easy, although that is, in itself, a perfectly reasonable belief to have – for example, that geometry is easy. In fact, suppose you believe no particular thing simply because you don't know a word of math, more generally, hence cannot reasonably have a belief about one of its parts. In this instance the questioner knows that you *lack* a given belief, and would like to specify the general contents of that belief that you happen not to have (perhaps they did not hear part of the conversation, where it was mentioned that the missing belief involved math).

As it turns out, Spanish distinguishes between those two possible readings in terms of the mood of the embedded clause. Observe this, first, in the affirmative:

(21) a. No creo   que esto sea facil.   [*positive*]
         Not believe.I that this be easy

     b. No creo   que esto es facil   [*negative*]
         Not think.I that this is easy

We have tried to keep the glosses apart by using two different English verbs to express each thought: *think* for the negative scenario (which goes together with indicative in the embedded clause) and *believe* for the positive scenario (which selects embedded subjunctive).

Here is then the interesting contrast:

(22) a.   Que no crees   que sea facil?   [*positive*]
             what not believe.you that be easy

     b. ??? Que no crees   que es facil?   [*negative*]
             what not think.you that is easy

For some reason, the question out of the embedded clause in the context we have called negative is significantly degraded. The problem is not in its semantics, as the paraphrase in (23) indicates:

(23) a. Que es lo que no crees   que es facil?   [*negative*]
         what is it that not think you that is easy

     b. Que es [lo [Op que [pro no crees [que pro es facil]]]]

In this instance there is no extraction from the embedded clause, and instead a resumptive, null (subject) pronoun associates to a relative wh-operator; the real question happens in the main clause. Pronominal resumption is much harder in instances of bona fide questions, as in (22b), which accounts for the degradation of that example *if it involves overt movement across some island*.[10]

The grammaticality of these sorts of questions in Spanish is easy to test because of the overt morphological realization of mood, but if one can carefully control for the different meanings involved in each scenario, a relatively strong contrast emerges in English as well, suggesting that in this language too there is some kind of island that the wh-question is forced to move through in the negative scenario.

Importantly, Spanish is just like English with regards to adjunct movement:

(24) a. Por que no   crees   que sea facil la matematica?   [*positive*]
          why   not believe you that be easy the mathematics

      b. Por que no   crees   que es facil la matematica?   [*negative*]
          why   not think you that is easy the mathematics

These are fine questions with different presuppositions; they are, however, inquiries regarding your reasons for believing/thinking something (or not, in (25b)), and certainly not about the reasons for math being difficult (or not, in (24a)). That must mean that, aside from the fact that the negative context involves an island already in overt syntax (thus the deviance of (22b)), even the positive context involves a blockage effect at LF (hence (22a) is perfect, but a corresponding long-distance question in (24a) is not). We interpret the blockage as a QI island – if *why* enters into a covert, split relation – in the hope that we can show how it follows from reprojection.

This is all to say, first of all, that we must set aside the extraction in the negative context, as it involves a sort of island that arises earlier in the course of the derivation, hence falls outside the scope of this paper. Presumably this island concerns the paratactic analysis of indicative clauses, but we have nothing to say about this here. The important thing is that the positive context patterns just as expected: no island for overt movement, but an island for covert relations. Moreover, there is something peculiar about what we are calling the positive context: in form, it is obviously negative as well – after all, the negative operator is pronounced in the matrix, not the embedded clause.

We try to show that LF islands across negation arise only when the negative operator stands in some kind of syntactic relation, in a sense to be discussed, with the clause where the split construction originates. A reprojection analysis of this situation is not implausible, and could extend to other instances of Γ. If so, there may be no LF islands without binary quantification, and hence reprojection.

6   Binary quantifiers with no associated LF islands?

The first descriptive difficulty we raised in section 5 concerned the fact that quantifiers with corresponding individual or group denotations do not induce LF islands, despite the fact that they are strong, as are binary quantifiers. Interestingly, these nonbinary strong elements are known to occasionally bypass familiar definiteness effects related to pleonastic association:

(25)   a.   Who can play Hamlet? Well, there's Olivier . . .
     b.   What can we use for a prop? There's always the table . . .

These contexts are obviously exemplary or presentational, and this clearly affects the definiteness effect. Nonetheless, binary quantifiers proper are not welcome in this context, whatever its characterization:

(26)   a.   Who can play Hamlet? #Oh, there's everyone . . .
     b.   What can we use for a prop? #There's really most things in the gym . . .

In turn, true existentials (controlling for exemplarity) are bad if they involve names or definites:

(27)   a.   #There's Olivier on stage.
     b.   #There's the table you got me for a prop on stage.

This must mean two things. First, that regardless of the existential nature of the expression, association between a binary quantifier and a pleonastic is bad (26); second, that nonbinary strong quantifiers are impossible in a purely existential context (27), but otherwise allow association to a pleonastic (25). We return to the first of these conclusions in section 7. As for the second, it may bear on our first descriptive difficulty, and in particular its relation to the fact that at least definite descriptions are nonsymmetric, and yet we do not want them to reproject. The key is to assume a notion of presuppositionality aside from the one involved in the shape of LF expressions (see Pietroski 1999).

In our terms, reprojection naturally articulates LF in terms of quantificational arguments, clearly separating a scope and a restriction for each relevant quantificational element. But there is nothing in our mechanism that precludes the possibility that certain expressions are *intrinsically* presuppositional, quite aside from the shape they obtain in the syntactic derivation, which contributes to what we may think of as their *syntactic* presuppositionality. Names are the first obvious case in point. *Marilyn Monroe* carries with it certain background assumptions about the individual rigidly bearing that name, which arguably do not make it into the syntax of an expression using that name, among other things because it seems as if this particular expression is not decomposable, or at least is not so trivially. Less obviously, an expression such as *the first megastar* would appear to presuppose its descriptive content (in satisfaction of Heim's (1982) Descriptive Content Condition). These expressions induce poorly understood conflicts in existential contexts, regardless of whether they are introduced by pleonastic *there*. We have nothing to say about this here, though see Zucchi (1995) for much relevant discussion. We will have something to say, however, about why association with *there* results in ungrammaticality for a binary quantifier, in fact regardless of whether the context is existential (26).

If names, definite descriptions, and similar individual- or group-denoting elements are intrinsically presuppositional, we need not say anything about their being syntactically presuppositional. This means they do not need to engage in reprojection, even if relevant expressions are nonsymmetrical. In other words, we assume that the symmetry of an expression inversely correlates with its presuppositionality: presuppositional expressions are not symmetric. However, it need not be the case that the presuppositionality should be syntactic, and if so, a mechanism like reprojection – for that matter any other rearrangement of LF properties – need not be significant for this class of strong elements.[11]

In the end, then, we maintain the reprojection generalization in (28):

(28)   *Reprojection Generalization*
        All and only binary quantifiers reproject.

Strong quantifiers that are intrinsically presuppositional are not binary, thus do not create QI islands, as desired. In turn, although negative operators do induce LF islands, we have suggested that these are amenable to a binary treatment, a matter that we return to in section 10.

7   A "definiteness effect" in nonexistential contexts

As we have seen, binary quantifiers induce definiteness effects (more precisely, are incompatible with pleonastics) in nonexistential contexts (26), where similarly strong, though nonbinary expressions do not (25). We have a suggestion as to why this should be, by way of a set of data that has not been discussed in relation to QI islands, and which puts them in a curious, new light.

Kim (1998) observes that, in Korean, certain direct objects can appear caseless, which he attributes to Noun-incorporation. Weak and strong determiners fare differently in this respect:

(29)   a.   Nwukwu wassni?
            someone came
        b.   *Motun salam wassni?
            All men came

Most crucially for our typology, names and definite descriptions align with weak determiners:

(30)   a.   Con wassni?
            John came
        b.   Ku salam wassni?
            the men came

The first reason why Kim's data are important is that the elements which appear caseless in Korean (and other East Asian languages) pattern with the elements that determine QI islands, although there is no intervention effect in the case phenomenon. This means that accounts of the QI islands that are designed to deal exclusively with the latter, in terms of the transformational problem, will not obviously extend beyond those paradigms, although an extension seems warranted if the relevant case phenomenology swings in tandem with QI islands. Secondly, Kim's specific account for the Korean paradigm has a significant bearing on the incompatibility of binary quantifiers with pleonastics.

Kim suggests that caseless nominals determine their Case visibility in terms of noun-incorporation, in the spirit of Baker (1988). In this way he explains why the phenomenon is restricted to underlying direct objects (normal direct objects and subjects of unaccusative verbs, as in (29), (30)). If this is the correct approach, the question to ask is why incorporation should be barred if a binary quantifier is involved (29b), not otherwise ((29a) and (30)).

We have already mentioned in passing (section 2) that adjunction structures may pose a problem for reprojection. Let us discuss this now, making familiar assumptions about adjunction:

(31)   a.   Adjunction: b.   Failed reprojection:

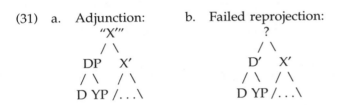

Adjunction of D to X forces the creation of a category *segment*, represented in between inverted commas in (31a). Plausibly, category segments must be labeled in terms of the category they are segments of, and thus cannot assume the label of the item that induced the projection (i.e., must have label X, not D). If so, reprojection would be banned in adjunction sites.

With that in mind, suppose a binary determiner were to incorporate in Korean. Assuming incorporation involves adjunction and adjunction disallows reprojection, the incorporated phrase cannot project. The derivation will thus either crash (if reprojection is demanded by convergence requirements) or converge with no intelligibility. In contrast, unary determiners face no such problem, as they do not involve reprojection to start with.

That part of the analysis accounts for Kim's facts in a straightforward way, but we would like to extend it to instances of nonexistential (expletive, binary determiner) association, which as we saw in the previous section are ungrammatical, unlike corresponding (expletive, unary determiner) associations. To set up our analysis, observe that if *every* or *most* in (26) must reproject, and *there* prevents them from so doing, then we would have a simple account for why binary elements like those are barred from being "associates" to an expletive.

Chomsky (1995: 156) argues that associates adjoin to the pleonastic at LF, thus making it inaccessible to interpretation. By parity of reasoning with the analysis of the Korean facts, the adjunction in question should prevent an associate from reprojecting, since the reprojection would face the same sorts of formal difficulties noted in (31), on general grounds. Again, that should be fine if the associate is unary, but results in semantic deviance – which speakers perceive – if it is binary. Thus this "definiteness effect" arises quite aside from the inherent presuppositional nature of the associates, which in nonexistential contexts should not matter. Assume it does not. We can explain the ungrammaticality of (26) if associates must raise to their expletive. For binary quantifiers, this will block reprojection and thereby result in a representation which prevents interpretation.

In recent years Chomsky has revamped his expletive replacement analysis, first in terms of feature adjunction (1995: 273ff.) and next in terms of the abstract process of Agree (2000: 103ff.). A feature adjunction analysis can be directly accommodated to the conclusions above, as this involves adjunction too. An Agree analysis can also be accommodated if the conclusions reached more generally in section 10 about the relevant relation hold in this instance as well.

8   Neg-Raising

Consider next what licenses the phenomenon of so-called Neg-Raising in a language like Spanish (responsible for the QI effect in our positive contexts). To show that no simple-minded syntactic analysis can account for relevant facts, consider the extension to our Spanish data in (32):

(32)   a.   (*Por que*) **no muchas personas** creen   que esto sea *facil.*
            why   not many   people   believe that this be easy

       b.   (*Por que*) **pocas   personas** creen   que esto sea *facil.*
            why   few   people   believe that this be easy

First note that a negative heading a subject (a kind of negative quantifier) licenses the Neg-Raising interpretation, which goes with the subjunctive mood in the embedded clause (32a). If negation had merely climbed from the embedded clause, it is unclear how it would end up inside the subject, in a position not commanding its putative origin. Moreover, the same Neg-Raising interpretation obtains for a lexical unit like *pocos* "few," which with the approximate meaning of "not many" is also capable of inducing subjunctive selection in the embedded clause plus an associated positive interpretation in the matrix. Again, if Neg-Raising is seen as cliticization of a negative from the embedded clause, we will need a morphology that allows the "late insertion" of *pocos* as the surface Spell Out of an abstract *NO MUCHOS*, as in (32a) (see Bosque 1980).

At the same time, some syntactic relation must hold between a negative element of some sort in the matrix and both subjunctive selection in the embedded clause and a positive interpretation for the matrix. For example, recall that quantificational expressions such as *exactly ten people*, which could be reasonably paraphrased as "no more than, and no less than, ten people" (as reasonably as we paraphrase *few people* as "not many people"), induce LF islands. Interestingly, they do not license subjunctive mood or a positive interpretation (33a), any more than emphasized expressions do which roughly have the same semantic import (*TEN* people, meaning "exactly ten," (33b)):

(33) a. (*Por que*) **exactamente diez personas** creen   que esto es/*sea *facil*?
          why   exactly   ten people   believe that this is/be   easy

      b. (*Por que*) **DIEZ personas** creen   que esto es/*sea *facil*?
          why   TEN people   believe that this is/be   *easy*?

      c. (*Por que*) **no mas de, ni menos de, diez personas** creen   que esto
          why   no more of nor less of   ten people   believe that this
          sea *facil*?
          be easy

In other words, although in terms of the entailments or implicatures that they license, *not many* should not be any more or less permissive than *no more than*, *and no less than, X*, it is just a fact that corresponding elements *few* and *exactly X* do not behave alike. What is more, the explicit *no mas de, ni menos de, X*, behaves like *pocas* "few" and unlike *exactamente X* "exactly X" (33c).

So some grammatical relation R must exist which codes the dependency between the (abstract) negative in the matrix and mood selection in the embedded clause. R must have two important consequences: semantically, it ought to license the positive interpretation; syntactically, it ought to induce an island for split constructions at LF. We will try to relate these two consequences in our analysis.

Minimally, R must code an interpretive dependency between the negative element and the embedded clause; the puzzle appears to be that the negative in point is not in construction with the embedded CP, at least not directly. Suppose, however, that R is just some valid, long-distance syntactic relation, perhaps of the Agree type in Chomsky's recent sense. Still, how do we ensure that this relation results in the positive interpretive effect and why should it induce an island at LF?

To answer those questions, let us consider the interpretation of Neg-Raising. Compare first:

(34) a. No cree   que esto sea facil.
          not believes that this be easy
          "He doesn't believe this to be easy."

      b. Cree   que esto no es facil.
          believes that this not be easy
          "He believes that this isn't easy."

A pure Neg-Raising analysis incorrectly expects synonymy between the two propositions in (34). But although they both can be used in the positive context that we mentioned, they do not mean the same thing. For example, if a witness says (34b) in a court of law concerning a given (different) individual on trial, this defendant can be assumed to hold, specifically, the belief that something isn't easy, according to the witness; in contrast, if the witness says (34a), no such strong commitment to the individual's beliefs is thereby invoked, although there is commitment about the defendant having some belief or other about the topic in question, that belief in fact *not* being that it is easy.[12]

A more accurate paraphrase for (34a) is (35), where the negative element is assigned wide scope with respect to the embedded clause and narrow scope with respect to the matrix predicate:

(35)   Cree   que no es (el caso) que esto sea facil.
       believes.he that not is the case that this be easy

Truth conditionally this is very similar in meaning to (34a), although we hasten to add that (35) has an added dimension that (34a) lacks: the paraphrase asserts something about him having a belief, whereas (34a) would seem to presuppose the belief part, while only concentrating on asserting the content of the belief, despite the grammatical form of the expression (starting "he doesn't believe . . .").

Let's put that added dimension to the side until section 10, concentrating on something else. Compare these examples:

(36)   a.   Pocas personas creen   que esto sea facil.
            few   people   believe that this be easy

       b.   No muchas personas creen   que esto sea facil.
            not many   people   believe that this be easy

       c.   Muchas personas creen   que esto no es facil.
            many   people   believe that this not is easy

       d.   Muchas personas creen   que no es el   caso que esto sea facil.
            many   people   believe that not is the case that this be easy.

Statement (36a) licenses Neg-Raising and (36b) is a paraphrase with similar characteristics, syntactically and semantically. (36c) is the deceptive paraphrase we have rejected, for (36a) or (36b), while (36d) is the more appropriate paraphrase with the negative in between matrix and embedded clauses. The question is how we get the negative element inside the subject to negate "all the way down."

At some level, that question is related to the one arising in (37):

(37)   a.   Poca gente ha   venido.
            few people have come

       b.   No mucha gente   ha   venido.
            not many   people have come

       c.   Mucha gente   no ha   venido.
            many people not have come

Example (37a) is equivalent to one reading of (37c) in much the same way that (36a) is to (36d), a fact that has generated much discussion.[13] Minimally, some relation of grammar exists between the surface negative inside the subject and the T position, where it can take scope. In fact, we know that the relation in question can even be pleonastic in nature, as in the "negative concord" witnessed in (38):

(38) a. Ninguen non veu.   (*Galician-Portuguese*)
          Nobody not came

      b. Personne n'est pas venu.   (*French*)
          Nobody   not-is not come

      c. Nimeni nu a   venit.   (*Romanian*)
          Nobody not has come

In all these instances the meaning expressed is that nobody came, rather than the opposite. These facts demonstrate that it is possible to relate T and a negative inside a subject, with the subject negative not having negative force – or the meaning of these sentences would be the opposite. Presumably all that the subject negative does is check some feature in the "real" negative in T. Assume this is the case regardless of whether the "real" negative in T has phonological content.

Suppose we then model relation R in terms of the more local one holding uncontroversially in (38), between a "real" negative in T and a pleonastic negative in subject position, and arguably also in (37a), so that this sentence has the same import as (37c). If so, the only difference between (37a) and an instance involving Neg-Raising, such as (36a), would be that in the latter the "real" negative in T does not negate "its own clause," but agrees into the lower T, which is where its negative import is manifested. We need this to allow a negative concord interpretation of Neg-Raising, as in (39):

(39)
a. Ninguno non puede conoscer al   Fijo sino por el   Padre.
    no one   not can   know   the Son but by the Father
    "No one can get to know the Son but through the Father."
                                    (*Medieval Spanish*), (Bosque 1980)

b. Ninguen non cree   que conoza ao   fillo sinon po-lo pai.
    no one   not believes that knows to-the son but   by-the father
    "No one believes himself to know the son but through the father."
                                            (*Galician-Portuguese*)

In languages where negative concord is apparent, the "double negative" in the matrix clause has to somehow have "neg-raised" from the embedded one, where it exerts negative force.

To make the (in effect) long-distance negation work syntactically we must ensure that there exists some locality between the "real" negative in the matrix T, what Chomsky (2000) calls the *probe*, and the embedded T which manifests the subjunctive, its *goal*. That locality is present, as the two Ts in question manifest the phenomenon of *consecutio temporum*, whereby matrix and embedded tenses have to match, presumably an indication of agreement between the two.[14] That should relate also to how the agreement works semantically, in such a way that the negative in the matrix does not get to exert its negative weight there, but does in the lower clause instead. To address this semantic concern, we must propose a binary account of negation. We do that after we briefly discuss weak determiners.

9   The interpretation of weak determiners

Recall that we do not want unary determiners to reproject, thus we must assume they have a single argument, their scope. This can be achieved if an element like *many* in (40a) is adjoined to the nominal whose variable it binds:

(40)   a.   many men are confused.   b.   [[many]   [men]]
                                                                        NP   NP

Adjunction of X to Y inherits the structural relations between Y and the elements it commands (the reason adjunction is defined in terms of category "segments"). Thus if Y commands Z, X adjoined to Y will also command Z.[15] Then *many* in (40) should be able to relate to whatever *many men* does, after QR. In particular, the lexical materials to specify the open expression *men (x) & confused (x)* are in construction with *many x*, which thus binds the variables.

That method of scope taking is considerably simpler than the one studied before, which needs reprojections as relevant arguments must be ordered. Quantifiers which are possible in existential contexts (a weak reading) will generally get by with the simpler method, and thus will not induce QI islands. However, in principle these same quantifiers are also possible in contexts where only binary quantifiers are felicitous (a strong reading), and thus we should be able to give them a reprojection analysis, in which case they should induce an LF island. For instance:

(41)   I *didn't* expect **many men that you did** to have a new idea/*a damn idea*.

For reasons that do not concern us now, antecedent-contained deletion (ACD) contexts force a proportional reading of a quantifier like *many*; in that instance, *many* has the effect of blocking a split construction, a fact that we have not seen discussed in the literature.

That a determiner like *many* should be allowed to reproject is not inconsistent with its semantics. Although different presuppositionally, the expressions in (42b) and (42c) have identical truth conditions:

(42) a. Many men are confused.
  b. Many x [man(x) & confused(x)]
  c. [Many x : men(x)] confused(x)

10 A binary treatment for negation

Having seen our binary analysis of determiners that can also be analyzed in unary fashion, which is necessary for instances where they induce LF islands, we proceed to show how we can treat negation in a similar way. Consider first a unary analysis of negation which we can then relate to a binary treatment in much the same way as (42b) relates to (42c). Since as we saw that negation patterns in some instances with emphasis, and they both manifest different interpretive procedures for Laka's Γ, we will attempt a quantificational analysis for not just negation, but in fact any manifestation of Γ.

Note first that locutions such as (43), discussed in Torrego and Uriagereka (1995), show how propositions can stand in integral (i.e. "possessive") relations with such elements as *truth*:

(43) Actually, [that the earth is flat] has [some/a ring of/elements of truth] to it.

Suppose we make this simple fact relevant to a quantificational analysis of Γ, in that we take this grammatical formative as an operator of truth values. In other words:

(44) Γx [*has* ([*that the earth is flat*], x)]

We introduce *the earth is flat* with the overt marker *that* both because that is how the locution comes out in (43), and because we want to take the first argument of *has* as a closed expression. The second argument of *has* is a variable ranging over "truth" and "falsity," which speakers take propositions to have, often explicitly; assume also that even in simple negative or emphatic sentences (though not obviously in affirmative ones) there is an implicit verb *has*. The interpretive procedure for Γ is simple: by default, we take propositions uttered to have truth to them, at least according to their speaker; if Γ is specified as *no*, then we explicitly challenge that default assumption; if Γ is specified as *indeed* (or some relevant emphasis marker), then we somewhat tautologically confirm our default assumption.

That, so far, is a merely unary analysis of negation. We can produce a binary analysis:

(45) [Γx : *has* ([*that the earth is flat*], x)] *has* ([*that the earth is flat*], x)

In the restriction of the Γ operator we have placed the entire expression that reappears in its scope. The effect of this will not be unlike the one obtaining in a tautology like (46):

(46) a. Many men are men.
      b. Many x [man(x) & men(x)]
      c. [Many x : man(x)] man (x)

That is, of course, when Γ is specified emphatically; this goes nicely with the fact that emphasis does have a tautological character to it, which distinguishes it from its absence; indeed, the only natural way to interpret tautologies like (46a) is emphatically. If in contrast Γ is specified negatively, no tautology would ensue. The relevant semantics, in that instance, can be paraphrased this way: "Regarding the assumption that the earth is flat has truth, actually the earth is flat has falsity (for the speaker)."[16] In turn, the syntax treats Γ in such a way that it has two arguments, which happen to be identical.

What we have done so far looks somewhat artificial, especially the binary interpretation. But this is arguably no more or less artificial than interpreting a quantifier like *many* in binary fashion, as we did in (42c). To repeat, since (42b) has the same truth conditions, the grammar would not normally have to bother with the representationally more complex (42c), which entails reprojection. Similarly now, since (45) has the same truth conditions as (44), the grammar should not bother with the former, which is restricted to emphatic interpretations. Then again, we also saw in the previous section that in some instances, for some reason or other, the grammar is forced to go into the more cumbersome route of reprojection, which then results in a QI island. We want to suggest that the phenomenon of Neg-Raising can be interpreted as an instance in which the grammar is indeed forced to provide a binary interpretation of Γ, which results in a QI island, as desired.

Consider again (36), where we decided that the "real" negative in the matrix probes the lower T as its agreement goal. Remember also that we want the (abstract) negative not to exert negative weight on the matrix, but on the embedded clause. Suppose the negative element is a Γ specification in the matrix and the goal it agrees with is actually its scope; in this instance, crucially, that scope would not coincide with the restriction, which would be the material in Γ's domain:

(47) [Γx : *has* ([*that many people believe that this be easy*], x)] *has* ([*that this be easy*], x)

Example (47) is saying: "Regarding the assumption that many people believe it to have truth that this be easy has truth, actually that this be easy has falsity (for them)."[17]

If we put aside the fact that (47) is a proposition about the contents of the embedded clause, (47) is truth-conditionally equivalent to our paraphrase in (36d) (where no binary analysis is necessary for Γ). Interestingly, the true paraphrase in (47) actually accords better with Spanish speakers intuitions than (36d) does, as it has the "added dimension" we set aside in section 8. Thus (48b), which has the rough semantic content of (47), is the closest paraphrase of (48a) that one can think of:

(48) a. Pocas/no muchas personas creen que esto sea facil.
      b. Para muchas personas, no es (el caso/cierto) que esto sea facil.

English variants that give the appropriate flavor are as in (49):

(49) a. Few/not many people believe this to be easy.
      b. For many people, it is not (the case/true) that this is easy.

   Some important questions remain. First, what verbs allow this sort of mis-match between the two arguments of Γ? Intuitively, it is only verbs which can be somehow "ignored" in discourse, such as *believe* or *think*; thus *do you believe/ think that John is sick?* is not normally a question about whether you possess a thought or opinion, but rather about John's health according to you. Second, how does the pleonastic negative "inside" *few* or similar elements get to Γ? Arguably, it does not actually *get* anywhere, anymore in these instances than in similar contexts where we saw negative concord or negative force expressed via the implicit negative. All one has to assume is that Γ can be abstract and determine its interpretive specifications through concord. Third, how does Γ reach down to the proposition it takes as its scope? If agreement holds between Γ and the (head of) the relevant proposition, so long as this relation is local, (some feature in) the relevant proposition will be in the checking domain of Γ, long distance, as it were. And finally, how does Γ reproject? It would if we demand a binary interpretation for it, taking the element it agrees with as its abstract specifier.
   The latter needs clarification, since up to now we had seen instances of what we may think of as "naive" reprojection: an element X in the checking domain of Y turns this basic relation on its head and results in taking Y as its checking domain (specifier). Now we have extended our notions, in the spirit of Chomsky (1999): long-distance agreement results in a nonconfigurational, or cross-configurational, checking domain. In the "naive" instances X and Y are sisters; in these distant situations, they are not, though they are still local in some appropriate sense.[18] If we allow abstract reprojections of this sort, the category that Γ's goal projects should be the abstract specifier of Γ, and thus island conditions should obtain for it just as they obtain in the simpler instances. Schematically:

          ....AGREE............
(50) a. [Γ [creen que [esto T sea facil]]]
          PROBE   TP GOAL

      b. First argument of Γ (boldfaced): **[Γ [creen que [esto T sea facil]]]**
                                               TP

      c. Second argument of Γ (italicized): **[Γ [creen que** *[esto T sea facil]***]]**
                                                   TP←LF-island→

   The conclusion above is necessary on independent grounds if instances of A-dependency and expletive replacement can be resolved by Agree, as opposed to Move or Attract, as argued by Chomsky (1999). In other words, in order to implement our QR proposals in section 2 we noted how the quantificational element must be in a scope-gaining position; at that time we were assuming this to be movement, for ease of exposition. But if relevant elements do not move to their targets, only agree with them, then our entire mechanism has to be recast in terms of Agree. Similarly with expletive replacement, as already mentioned in section 7; if the definiteness effect is to be explained in terms of impossible reprojections, and expletive replacement is just a matter of Agree, then it must be that reprojections can be involved in the Agree relation.

To conclude, note that, although the phenomenon of Neg-Raising neatly illustrates an instance where a binary analysis of negation is profitable, there should be other instances where Γ reprojects, for entirely different reasons. Although we do not have space to provide an analysis of this here, we believe that this should be the approach given to QI islands associated to emphasis or precise quantifiers (which we take to involve a mark of emphasis as well). These sorts of elements will not involve the phenomenology of Neg-Raising (subjunctive licensing, strange truth-theoretic properties), but nonetheless will involve relatively similar mechanisms – which of course poses the question of when the grammar is generally forced to analyze Γ in binary fashion; we have nothing to say about this now.

11   Conclusions and further questions

This chapter has explored a syntax for binary quantification, in terms of a possibility that Bare Phrase Structures allow within the Minimalist Program. In essence, binary quantifiers are allowed to covertly reproject after meeting their syntactic requirements. As a result, the semantic arguments of a quantifier are also its natural syntactic dependents, in terms of domains of the sort already needed to account for the specifications of θ-theory earlier on in the derivation (in configurational terms).

Our proposal has immediate consequences for LF processes of the sort witnessed in split constructions. In this paper we have not provided a precise mechanism for why specifiers of reprojected categories should be islands, merely likening the situation to that obtaining more generally in overt syntax: transformations are not possible across specifiers (Huang's CED). In any case, the relevant islands would arise only in the LF component, as desired.

We then extended our logic to less obvious instances of reprojection (for quantifiers like *many* or Γ) and also showed how elements that should apparently reproject (as they are nonsymmetric) need not. The latter relates to our account of some definiteness effects that arise in non-existential contexts, by way of a set of facts from Korean that also involves reprojection but which has nothing to do with QI islands. The theoretical conclusion we reached is that no instance of adjunction (incorporation, expletive replacement) should allow reprojection.[19]

We have dealt with concrete representational mechanisms, assuming the grammar needs to invoke them only when necessary for interpretive purposes. So our argument must not be construed *against* a representational system, but rather *for* a derivational one. There is nothing contradictory about this. Any system that assumes categories like V or N, like all systems we know of do, is already representational. What is at issue for us is, if in addition to representational, the system must also be derivational. Unless we are wrong, or a representational mechanism can elegantly capture our generalizations, we have presented a reasonable argument for the derivational character of the system.

Acknowledgments

We thank participants in our seminars for questions and comments, as well as audiences at CUNY, Harvard, Osaka, Kanda, and USC, especially Joseph Aoun, Mark Baltin, Marcel Den Dikken, Richard Kayne, David Pesetsky, Barry Schein, and Anna Szabolcsi. Thanks also to Elena Herburger, Paul Pietroski, and Paul Portner for helpful discussion, and to Sam Epstein and Daniel Seely for their interest in this piece. This work was funded by NSF Grant BCS-9817569.

Notes

1   By a label L we simply understand the *type* of the expression in question, assuming this is important. Chomsky (1995) argues that among the simplest, set-theoretic relations between X and Y that one could consider to determine L's properties, identity is the one that does not create formal problems.

2   Even if labeling can be deduced from more basic mechanisms, this does not mean that labels are not real. The Moon can be explained through gravity acting on asteroids hitting the young Earth; yet the Moon exists, giving rise, for instance, to tides, crucial in life. It is important for us both that labeling be deduced and that labels exist. Without labeling being deduced it could not be true that they can change in the course of the derivation; just as a notion like "maximal projection" is relational and may change in terms of Bare Phrase Structure, so too may the notion "head of" change if we are correct. Without labels being real, though, it would not make any sense to ask what happens upon relabeling.

3   If reprojection were an operation it would overlap with Merge and in part with Move as well. However, reproject is nothing but mere project, which happens again as different interpretive demands of the elements that merge arise in the course of the derivation.

4   This is assuming that uniformity is actually required for chains; for an argument against this view, see Hornstein (2000). Throughout this discussion we are assuming that chains are formal objects of a representational sort that the system identifies if certain conditions are met; in other words, given this implementation, in this respect our system is not purely derivational. This is why we say that our results provide an argument for the existence of derivational aspects in the system, though not for the system being only derivational.

5   There ought to be an explanation for this in deeper terms (in some sense related to whether or not the mapping to LF prior to and after Spell Out is entirely uniform,

and, if not, whether this is intrinsic or extrinsic to the system). We will not go into this here.

6   If all processes may be involved in quantifier interpretation, it is good to see that reprojection could accommodate all of them regardless of their respective details. Although QR as adjunction ought not to involve reprojection, if adjunction involves category segments, it is possible that this sort of QR involves the introduction of vacuous targets, which could reproject.

7   Huang's condition is expressed in terms of an extraction domain being governed, which complements are, unlike noncomplements. Uriagereka (1999) derives these effects from derivational dynamics.

8   Perhaps *why* and similar operations relate directly to event variables, unlike operators binding variables that are arguments of theta-role predicates. It is conceivable that the former, and not the latter, constitutes a "split" construction.

9   See also section 8 for an argument that decomposition would be factually incorrect in this instance.

10   If (22b) and (23b) are true paraphrases, this fact is interesting in itself. In particular, one can get semantic binding across the relevant island so long as there is no movement. This seems prima facie inconsistent with an analysis in which the main problem with LF islands is only semantic.

11   At this point it is worth emphasizing that reprojection is not an operation, hence its presence or absence in the system cannot be trivially deduced from considerations about computational complexity.

12   English glosses (involving Exceptional Case Marking as the closest expression of an English subjunctive) show similar results.

13   For a thorough discussion and an extensive presentation of the relevant references and analyses, see Herburger (2000).

14   Of course, no such temporal agreement exists in standard complementation; see Hornstein (1992) for related discussion and a framework where these temporal dependencies can be coded, and Thompson (1995) for a Minimalist translation, and further extension.

15   This can be independently shown, given the fact that a verb raised to Tense, for instance, behaves as if it were in situ with regards to its arguments (the intuition behind Baker's (1988) Government Transparency Corollary).

16   Actually, nothing in the logical form in (45) includes the point of view of the speaker, but we assume that some mechanism does. See Etxepare (1997) on this general topic.

17   The same issue raised in note 16 about point of view arises in this instance as well, although the perspective in (47) has to be that of the subject. This suggests that point of view, however captured, may be sensitive to intervening subjects, perhaps necessarily in instances like the present one.

18   Thus, for instance, *consecutio temporum* does not take place between a given T and a T two clauses down, skipping the intermediate T.

19   There are many questions we leave for future research. Technically, we would like to see how reprojection affects reconstruction, and what its precise nature is, whether transformational or not. Empirically, we are concerned with an example pointed out to us by David Pesetsky:

(i)   *Why* do there seem to **most readers** [to be several wrinkles *left*]?
Cf.   *Why* do there seem to many readers [to be several wrinkles *left*]?

Superficially, Pesetsky's example is like all others in this paper, *why* not being able to modify into the embedded clause, across *most readers* (modification being possible across *many readers*). Importantly, however, we want *several wrinkles* to relate to the pleonastic *there*. How can it, if *most readers* induces an island at LF?

References

Baker, M. 1988. *Incorporation*. Chicago, IL: University of Chicago Press.
Beghelli, F. 1995. "The phrase structure of quantifier scope." PhD dissertation, University of California, Los Angeles.
Bosque, I. 1980. *Sobre la negacion*. Madrid: Catedra.
Chomsky, N. 1995. *The Minimalist Program*. Cambridge, MA: MIT Press.
Chomsky, N. 1999. "Derivation by phase." MS, MIT, Cambridge, MA.
Chomsky, N. 2000. "Minimalist inquiries." In R. Martin, D. Michaels, and J. Uriagereka, eds., *Step by Step: Minimalist Essays in Honor of Howard Lasnik*. Cambridge, MA: MIT Press.
Den Diken, M. and A. Szabolcsi. 1999. "Islands." In *State of the Article*, GLOT International 4, 6: 3–8.
Epstein, S., E. Groat, R. Kawashima, and H. Kitahara. 1998. *A Derivational Approach to Syntactic Relations*. Oxford: Oxford University Press.
Etxepare, R. 1997. "The syntax of illocutionary force." PhD thesis, University of Maryland, College Park.
Fox, D. 1995. "Economy and Scope." *Natural Language Semantics* 3: 283–341.
Heim, I. 1982. "The semantics of definite and indefinite noun phrases." PhD thesis, University of Massachusetts, Amherst.
Herburger, E. 2000. *What Counts*. Cambridge, MA: MIT Press.
Honcoop, M. 1998. "Excursions in dynamic binding." PhD thesis, Leiden.
Hornstein, N. 1992. *As Time Goes By*. Cambridge, MA: MIT Press.
Hornstein, N. 1995. *Logical Form*. Oxford: Blackwell Publishing.
Hornstein, N. 2000. *Move!* Oxford: Blackwell Publishing.
Hornstein N. and J. Uriagereka. 1999. "Labels and projection: a note on the syntax of quantifiers." University of Maryland Working Papers in Linguistics, 8: 249–70.
Kayne, R. 1994. *The Antisymmetry of Syntax*. Cambridge, MA: MIT Press.
Kim, K. 1998. "(Anti-)Connectivity." PhD thesis, Maryland.
Kitahara, H. 1992. "Checking theory and scope interpretation without Quantifier Raising." Harvard Working Papers in Linguistics, 1: 51–71.
Klima, E. S. 1964. "Negation in English," in J. A. Fodor and J. J. Katz, eds., *The Structure of Language*. Englewood Cliffs, NJ: Prentice-Hall.
Kroch, A. 1989. "Amount quantification, referentiality, and long wh-movement." MS, University of Pennsylvania, Philadelphia.
Laka, I. 1990. "Negation in syntax: on the nature of functional categories and projections." PhD dissertation, MIT, Cambridge, MA.
Larson, R. and G. Segal. 1995. *Knowledge of Meaning*. Cambridge, MA: MIT Press.
Linebarger, M. 1980. "The grammar of negative polarity." Doctoral dissertation, MIT, Cambridge, MA.
Pesetsky, D. 2000. *Phrasal Movement and Its Kin*. Cambridge, MA: MIT Press.
Pietroski, P. 1999. "Plural descriptions as existential quantifiers in an event analysis." University of Maryland Working Papers in Linguistics, 9: 323–42.
Reinhart, T. 1995. *Interface Strategies*. Research Institute for Language and Speech, Faculty of Arts, Utrecht University.
Szabolcsi, A. and F. Zwarts. 1993. "Weak islands and an algebraic semantics for scope-taking." *Natural Language Semantics* 1, 3: 235–84.

Thompson, E. 1995. "The syntax of tense." PhD dissertation, Maryland.

Torrego, E. and J. Uriagereka. 1995. "Parataxis." To appear in J. Uriagereka (forthcoming) *Derivations*. London: Routledge.

Uriagereka, J. 1999. "Multiple Spell Out." In S. Epstein and N. Hornstein, eds., *Working Minimalism*. Cambridge, MA: MIT Press.

Zucchi, A. 1995. "The ingredients of definiteness and the definiteness effect." *Natural Language Semantics* 3: 33–78.

Chapter six

Pronouns and their Antecedents

Richard S. Kayne

1 Introduction

The similarity between binding and movement played a role in discussions of trace theory in the early/mid-1970s, with an attempt then to think of movement (antecedent–trace relations) in binding terms (see Fiengo 1977: 53). Conversely, in the work of Lebeaux (1983) and Chomsky (1986: 175) in the early/mid-1980s, an attempt was made to rethink (part of) Condition A of the Binding Theory in terms of movement.

More recently, O'Neil (1995; 1997) and Hornstein (1999) have proposed reinterpreting (obligatory) control in movement terms, and Hornstein (2001) has further developed a movement approach to Condition A, and also indirectly to Condition B.

In this chapter, adopting the derivational perspective of Chomsky's (1995; 2000; 2001) recent work, I will explore the idea that binding should be rethought in movement terms even more generally, including what we think of as Condition C effects.

If the obvious similarity between Condition C and the prohibition against downward movement can successfully be expressed, then we can dispense with the notion of "accidental coreference," in the sense of Lasnik (1976: 13). (The term could be retained for cases of "mistaken identity.") All instances of "intended coreference/binding" will involve a movement relation.

In attempting to integrate into a movement perspective core Condition C effects involving pronoun and antecedent, and in attempting to dispense with the notion of "accidental coreference," this paper will go beyond what Hornstein (2001) has tried to accomplish (although the spirit is much the same). I will also take a very different tack from Hornstein (and from Burzio 1991) on Condition B, which I do not think is derivable as a side-effect of Condition A. I will argue that the opposite is in fact closer to the truth, i.e. that there is a sense in which Condition B (or what it follows from) is more basic than Condition A (more exactly, more basic than the existence of reflexives).

In the spirit of the Lebeaux/Chomsky proposals concerning Condition A, I will argue that neither Condition B nor Condition C is a primitive of UG. The effects of both will be argued to follow, in a derivational perspective, from basic properties of pronouns and basic properties of movement.

2   Clitic doubling

There will in addition be a difference in execution, compared with Hornstein (2001). Hornstein takes pronouns (in many cases) to reflect the spelling out of the trace of movement. But if one interprets movement as copy + deletion/nonpronunciation, as in Chomsky (1995: 202), this is not entirely natural.[1] Movement will leave a (typically unpronounced) copy of the full antecedent; to get from there to the pronunciation of a pronoun requires an additional mechanism (see Hornstein 2001: 178) that may not be consonant with Chomsky's (1995: 225) inclusiveness condition (if the pronominal is not part of the numeration) and in any event has a countercyclic character that I would like to avoid.

I will prefer to have the pronoun present in the numeration, and, more specifically, to have it derivationally form a constituent with its antecedent. In addition, I will take the position that clitic doubling and antecedent–pronoun relations should be unified more than they have been.

Clitic doubling involves a clitic pronoun and an associated DP that together correspond to a single theta-role:

(1)   Le doy un libro a Juan.   (Spanish: "him (dat.) I-give a book to J" = "I am giving a book to John")

On the other hand, antecedent–pronoun cases such as (2) involve two distinct theta-roles, one for the antecedent and a distinct one for the pronoun:

(2)   John thinks he's smart.

My proposal will be that that (very real) difference is nonetheless compatible with substantial unification.

I will adopt an approach to clitic doubling of the sort found in Kayne (1972: 90) and Uriagereka (1995: 81), in which clitic and double start-out/are merged together,[2] and are subsequently separated. Oversimplifying in various ways,[3] we have the following sort of derivation, for the French (interrogative) subject clitic doubling example in (3):

(3)   Cela est-il vrai? ("that is it true")

(4)   [cela il] est vrai → verb movement
      est_i [cela il] t_i vrai → movement of the double
      $cela_j$ est_i [t_j il] t_i vrai

In (4), movement of the double *cela* has the effect of bringing the double to a position leftward of the clitic *il*. In the Spanish example (1), the double *Juan* ends up to the right of the clitic *le*. I take this Spanish fact to reflect the preposing of VP (or some bigger projection, perhaps including all of *le doy un libro*) induced by the preposition *a*, much as in Kayne (2000a, chaps. 14, 15; 2001a). A possible (oversimplified) derivation would be:

(5) doy un libro [Juan le] $\rightarrow^4$
     [Juan le]$_i$ doy un libro t$_i$ $\rightarrow^5$
     Juan$_j$ [t$_j$ le]$_i$ doy un libro t$_i$ $\rightarrow$ merger of *a*
     a Juan$_j$ [t$_j$ le] doy un libro t$_i$ $\rightarrow$
     [[t$_j$ le] doy un libro t$_i$]$_k$ a Juan$_j$ t$_k$

3 Antecedent and pronoun

Generalizing this to (2), the proposal is for a derivation of (2) of this sort:

(6) thinks [John he] is smart $\rightarrow$
     John$_i$ thinks [t$_i$ he] is smart

From within the lower sentence, *John* moves into the theta-position of the matrix verb (and then raises further).

In this derivation, the double *John* moves from within the doubling constituent [*John he*] into a higher theta-position. The essential difference between this case and (5) is that in (5) (in the second movement step) the double *Juan* moves from within the doubling constituent [*Juan le*] into a higher non-theta-position.

Notice that although the derivation in (6) countenances movement (of *John*) into a theta-position, it does not assign two theta-roles to *John* – the lower theta-role is assigned, rather, to the larger constituent [*John he*] (conceivably also to the head *he*).

4 Control

Movement into a theta-position is also proposed by O'Neil (1995; 1997) and Hornstein (1999; 2001),[6] but since they do not start from a doubling structure, they also have to allow a given argument to bear more than one theta-role, which the proposal illustrated in (6) does not need to do. In the specific case of control, they have *John* in (7) bearing two theta-roles:

(7) John tried to solve the problem.

The above approach to (6), on the other hand, does not lead to that conclusion. Rather, it leads to the claim that there is a pronominal double in (7) that is not pronounced:

(8)   tried to [John PRO] solve the problem

PRO is now the counterpart of *he* in (6). The double *John* moves into the theta-position of *try*; it does not thereby get a second theta-role, since the subject theta-role of *solve* is born by [*John* PRO].

It is natural to think of Case in a similar fashion. In (6), the nominative Case determined within the embedded sentence is born by [t$_i$ *he*]. The double/antecedent *John* bears no Case at all within the embedding; it gets (nominative) Case in a derived position within the matrix.

This solves a severe problem for the O'Neil/Hornstein approach to control that has been noted by Mark Baltin (personal communication), namely that their assimilation of (obligatory) control to raising leads to the expectation that the kind of Case inheritance found with raising constructions will also be found with control, contrary to fact. More specifically, in a language like Icelandic, as discussed by Thráinsson (1986: 252), a raised subject generally (see Sigurðsson 1989: 96) carries along its quirky Case (if it has one), but a controller always shows a Case determined by the matrix predicate, never a Case determined by the embedded predicate. This is expected given (8) – the embedded quirky Case, if there is one, will go to [*John* PRO], not to *John* itself, so that *John* will show only the Case determined by the matrix. (A similar point holds for (6).)

5   Merge and Move

Movement into a theta-position, even if it does not imply that an argument can bear more than one theta-role, appears to lead to an unwanted asymmetry, if we compare

(9)   John thinks he's smart.

with

(10)   John thinks you're smart.

In (9), on the reading where *John* is the antecedent of *he*, the subject theta-position of *think* is filled by movement, whereas in (10) it is filled by simple merger. (That is also true of (9), on the reading where *John* is not the antecedent of *he*.)

The apparently disparate treatment of (9) and (10) can be resolved if all phrasal merger is taken to have something in common with movement. Even in the case where the phrase merged with the selector is not part of the syntactic object containing the selector, what is merged with the syntactic object headed by the selector can be thought of as a copy (see the suggestion by Chomsky mentioned in Bobaljik and Brown 1997: 349n.). The other copy (located within the "derivation space" (set of syntactic objects belonging to the derivation) but not within the syntactic object headed by the selector) is not pronounced.[7]

6   Condition C

Questions arise concerning the internal structure of the constituent [*John he*] that appears in (6). I assume, following Uriagereka (1995: 81), that *John* is in the highest Spec of that constituent, either as a result of movement from within or as a result of direct merger to that Spec. As for the pronoun, it might be a simple head and exhaust the remainder of the constituent; more likely, the post-Spec structure is more elaborate, as he suggests.

More centrally important to what follows is the following claim (see Chomsky's 2001: 13 Phase Impenetrability Condition and the earlier ban against movement of nonmaximal phrases):

(11)   Extraction of a phrase from within a doubling constituent like [*John he*] is limited to extraction of the Spec.

(Conceivably, in some languages, a pronoun can be extracted by head movement – but see notes 4 and 23.)

Consider now:

(12)   He thinks John is smart.

Given (11), (12) is not derivable from:

(13)   thinks John-he is smart

because the pronominal part of [*John he*] is not extractable (except perhaps by head movement, which would not suffice to get *he* into the subject theta-position of *think* as would be needed in (12)).

Nor is (12) derivable from a structure that would look like:

(14)   [John he] thinks is smart

by movement of *John* into the subject position of *is smart*. This is so, on the uncontroversial assumption that rightward movement to a non-c-commanding position is prohibited by UG.

If we now compare (12) and (15):

(15)   John thinks he is smart.

we see that from the present perspective (including (11)) the contrast between (15) and (12) is essentially that between upward movement (legitimate) and downward movement (illegitimate).[8] A parsimonious theory of UG should need to say about (15) vs. (12) little more than that.

It is usual, however, to think that (12) (more exactly, the reading of (12) in which *he* takes *John* as antecedent) has another potential source, if *he* can "accidentally" corefer with *John* (cf. Lasnik 1976). This possibility appears to be a reasonable one given sentences like:

(16)   He is smart.

in which *he* seems to have no linguistically characterizable antecedent, yet the sentence seems to have an interpretation.

I think it is essential, however, to attribute compelling importance to the way in which the contrast between (15) and (12) mimics the contrast between upward and downward movement. This parallel will be directly and simply expressed by UG only if there is no "accidental coreference:"

(17)   Antecedent–pronoun relations as in (one reading of) (15) REQUIRE movement out of a constituent of the form [*John-he*]. That is the ONLY way to express an antecedent–pronoun relation.[9]

(In effect, (17) says that the language faculty expresses antecedent–pronoun relations through a combination of a local Spec–non-Spec relation (internal to the doubling constituent, where the non-Spec is pronominal) and movement.)[10]

If there is no accidental coreference in the familiar sense, then, given (11), the ungrammaticality of (12) in the relevant reading reduces to the ban against rightward movement to a non-c-commanding position. Given this approach, the exclusion of (12) (in the relevant reading) does not actually depend on Condition C as we have come to know it. Put more strongly:

(18)   Condition C is superfluous, i.e. is not a primitive part of UG.

7   More on Condition C and on apparently antecedent-less pronouns

If there is no accidental coreference (since a pronoun's antecedent must be its own Spec), what should one say about (16)? I would like to suggest that (16), with an unstressed *he*, is unacceptable in isolation.[11] (With a stressed, deictic *he*, (16) is grammatical, presumably because it then includes an unpronounced demonstrative.) It is possible, of course, to have:

(19)   John is famous. He's smart, too.

I take *he* here to have an antecedent, namely *John*. When a pronoun successfully takes a phrase in a preceding sentence as its antecedent, the two sentences in question form a single syntactic entity, akin to coordination.[12] In other words, (19) reduces to, or is strongly similar to the following, in which *John* starts out as Spec of *he* (I return to the c-command question later):

(20)   John is famous, and he's smart, too.

Examples of a sort discussed by Hankamer and Sag (1976), such as:

(21)   Watch out! He's got a knife.

I take to be grammatical with an unstressed *he* only if there is an unpronounced demonstrative, i.e. (21) in its well-formed reading is akin to (22) (in which *that man* starts out as Spec of *he* and then moves to a nonthematic dislocated position – cf. in part the clitic doubling derivation in (5)):

(22)   Watch out! That man, he's got a knife.

Taking (21) to be equivalent to (22) (apart from the silent topic/dislocated phrase in (21)) is to treat (21) as being similar to German sentences with (well-attested) silent topics.

In discussing Condition C so far, I have only considered cases in which a pronoun c-commanded a potential antecedent. I have argued that the impossibility for a pronoun to take a DP that it c-commands as antecedent reduces to the ban on rightward movement to a non-c-commanding position, and does not require attributing Condition C as primitive to the language faculty.

The question arises as to whether other restrictions, e.g. on "epithets," that have sometimes been taken to fall under Condition C (see Lasnik and Stowell 1991: 709) can be understood in comparable fashion. This restriction is illustrated in:

(23)   Smith's wife thinks that the poor guy should drop out of school.

(24)   Smith thinks that the poor guy should drop out of school.

Taking *the poor guy* to be *Smith* is natural in (23), but not possible in (24). This looks like a distinction based on c-command, therefore is plausibly thought of as a subcase of Condition C, which would then prohibit epithets like *the poor guy* from taking a c-commanding antecedent, whether local or not. From this perspective the relevant reading of (24) would be excluded in exactly the same way as (25) is excluded with *Smith* as the antecedent of *he*:

(25)   He thinks that Smith should drop out of school.

However, in other environments, the two cases diverge somewhat:

(26)   He probably doesn't even realize that we're planning to fire Smith next week.

(27)   Smith probably doesn't even realize that we're planning to fire the poor
        guy next week.

With *he* dependent on *Smith*, (26) continues to be impossible, like (25). But (27)
with *the poor guy* dependent on *Smith* seems better than (24), and in particular better than the relevant reading of (26). (Comparable French examples
are discussed by Ruwet 1990, §7).[13] I conclude from this discrepancy that
the epithet–antecedent question should be kept partially separate from the
pronoun–antecedent question, and more specifically that (24) and (25) are
not excluded for identical reasons.
    Somewhat similar to (23) and (24) is:

(28)   Smith's wife thinks that Smith should drop out of school.

(29)   Smith thinks that Smith should drop out of school.

With the two *Smiths* intended to be the same person, (28), although not perfect,
is appreciably better than (29). Again, this looks like a c-command difference,
with *Smith* apparently required to be disjoint from any c-commanding phrase.
In the light of (26) vs. (27), though, we need to ask about:

(30)   Smith probably doesn't even realize that we're planning to fire Smith
        next week.

It seems to me that (30), while less possible in the intended interpretation than
(27), is nonetheless not quite as bad as (26), and similarly for:

(31)   He'll only have to act as if everybody finds Smith trustworthy.

(32)   Smith will only have to act as if everybody finds Smith trustworthy.

(33)   He'll only agree to help if you ask Dawkins yourself.

(34)   Dawkins will only agree to help if you ask Dawkins yourself.

With the intended coreference in question, (32) and (34) seem more possible
than (31) and (33). I tentatively conclude that the movement-based account
that I have been suggesting for (26) (excluded because *Smith* would have had
to move rightward and downward to a non-c-commanding position) should
not be expected to transpose simply to (29).[14]
    On the other hand, a contrast that does fall together with that between (26)
and (35):

(35)   Smith doesn't even realize that we're planning to fire him next week.

is this one, containing a version of quantifier stranding:

(36)   Fortunately, my students haven't all of them seen that film.

(37)   *Fortunately, they haven't all of my students seen that film.

Example (36) is possible in some varieties of English (not mine), but I doubt that (37) is. (36) can be derived from:

(38)   haven't all of [my students them] seen that film

by raising *my students* from within the doubling constituent up to a higher specifier position (a nonthematic one, in this case).[15]
   There is no parallel derivation for (37), for a combination of two reasons. First, from (38), the pronoun cannot raise to a higher Spec position, given (11). Second, since (rightward) lowering is not available, (39) is not a possible source:

(39)   [my students they] haven't all of seen that film

8   Strong crossover

Consider now an example of "strong crossover," in which *he* cannot take *John* as antecedent:

(40)   John he thinks she's in love with.

This works out as follows. For *he* to have *John* as antecedent, *he* and *John* must start out as a doubling constituent, i.e. a pronoun can be interpreted only via its filled Spec (and must therefore have one).[16] Yet starting from:

(41)   thinks she's in love with [John he]

he by itself could not move to matrix subject position, given (11); thus, there's an important element in common between (40) and (12), repeated here, as expected:

(42)   He thinks she's in love with John.

The only remaining option for the relevant reading of (40) would be to try to move [*John he*] as a whole in (41), yielding:

(43)   [John he]$_i$ thinks she's in love with t$_i$

and then to topicalize *John*. But (43) itself is ill-formed, parallel to the following (in which two theta-roles have been assigned to the same phrase):[17]

(44)   *He/*John thinks she's in love with

A short-distance topicalization example corresponding to (40) would be:

(45)   John he considers intelligent.

Again, given (11), *he* cannot by itself reach subject position starting from:

(46)   considers [John he] intelligent

Example (45) in the relevant interpretation could not be derived, either, from:

(47)   [John he] considers intelligent

by lowering *John* and then topicalizing it, since the lowering step would be impermissible. Nor is (45) derivable, starting from (46), via movement to subject theta-position of [*John he*], followed by topicalization/dislocation of *John*, parallel to the well-formed:

(48)   John, he's considered intelligent.

since I have maintained the prohibition against arguments ([*John he*] in (46)) receiving two theta-roles.

   Note, finally, that one could not start from (47) and, in an attempt to derive (45), simply topicalize/dislocate *John*, since that would leave the embedded small clause subject theta-position unfilled, i.e. the embedded subject theta-role would remain unassigned.

   Somewhat better than (45) in the relevant reading is:

(49)   ??John even HE considers intelligent.

(50)   ??John he HIMSELF considers intelligent.

The status of these does not seem to me to be appreciably different from that of:

(51)   ??Even HE considers John intelligent.

(52)   ??He HIMSELF considers John intelligent.

These two (and hence the previous two) may in part reduce to the question of:

(53)   His wife considers John intelligent.

which I return to later. (If so, (49) and (51) may require an unpronounced counterpart of HIMSELF. The expectation would then be that (49)–(52) should be impossible in languages that disallow (53).)

   Also better than (45) in the relevant reading is:

(54) ??John's wife he considers intelligent.

In this case, the nontopicalized version is worse:

(55) *He considers John's wife intelligent.

Example (54) falls in part under the discussion of (56) (see section 17).

(56) John's wife thinks he's intelligent.

In summary, strong crossover fits in directly to the movement-based reductive approach to Condition C set out in the previous two sections.

9   Condition B

There is a familiar contrast (in the relevant readings) between (57) and (58)/(59):

(57) John thinks he's smart.

(58) John thinks highly of him.

(59) John considers him intelligent.

Why are (58)/(59) not derivable in parallel fashion to (57), starting from, e.g.:

(60) thinks highly of [John him]

with movement of the double *John* to subject theta-position?
    From the standard nonmovement perspective on these, there are two kinds of answers that have been given. One is stated in terms of Chomsky's (1981: 188) Condition B. A second (which has something in common with Chomsky's (1981: 65) "avoid pronoun" proposal) is of the sort pursued in different ways by Reinhart (1983), Burzio (1991) and Hornstein (2001), namely that (58) and (59) are excluded as a consequence of the existence of the corresponding sentences with reflexives:

(61) John thinks highly of himself.

(62) John considers himself intelligent.

    Lasnik (1980) takes the independence of Condition B effects to be clear in part on the basis of overlapping reference effects (subsumed under Condition B in Chomsky and Lasnik 1993; Chomsky 1995: 97), e.g.:

(63)   ?We consider me intelligent.

The deviance of this example cannot be attributed to the existence of a parallel reflexive-containing sentence, given:

(64)   *We consider myself intelligent.

Lasnik's position might appear to be weakened to some extent by the fact that (63) is not completely unacceptable.[18]

It is consequently important to take into account a fact pointed out to me about ten years ago by Luigi Burzio, namely that in Italian the status of (63) is sharper with clitics than with nonclitics, e.g.:

(65)   ?Consideriamo me intelligente. ("we-consider me intelligent")

(66)   *Mi consideriamo intelligente. ("me we-consider intelligent")

When, as in (65), the (accusative) pronoun is not a clitic, the Italian example has approximately the status of the English one, whereas when the accusative pronoun is made a clitic, as in (66), the sentence is sharply out.

The ungrammaticality of (66) clearly supports (given the fact that there is no reflexive counterpart to it at all) the idea that there are Condition B effects that are independent of the existence of reflexives. The same facts hold in Italian if we reverse singular and plural (judgments from Guglielmo Cinque):

(67)   ?Considero noi intelligenti. ("I-consider us intelligent")

(68)   *Ci considero intelligenti. ("us I-consider intelligent")

With nonclitic *noi*, the sentence is intermediate in acceptability; with clitic *ci* it is sharply out. Similarly in the third person, in the relevant interpretation:

(69)   ?Considera loro intelligenti. ("he/she-considers them intelligent")

(70)   *Li considera intelligenti. ("them he/she-considers intelligent")

With nonclitic *loro*, overlapping reference is marginal; with clitic *li* it is impossible.

Why are these Condition B effects in Italian very sharp with clitics but not with nonclitics? A plausible proposal would be that the Condition B effect is dampened in (65)/(67)/(69) by the presence of extra morphological material, either overt (if the morpheme *-e*[19] of *me* is relevant, for example) or covert (if *me, noi* and *loro* in these examples are all accompanied by a covert (approximate) counterpart of English *self* (but without the possessive structure) or Italian *stesso* ("same")),[20] which allows Italian to dampen the Condition B effect, in some way partially akin to what will be suggested below for English overt *self* (with possessive structure). (Clitics would be incompatible with such extra morphological material.)[21]

In conclusion, then, the ungrammaticality of (66), (68), and (70) supports the independence of Condition B, leaving us with the question of how best to understand Condition B effects and especially with the question of why there should be such a condition in UG in the first place.

The second question is not usually asked by those who accept an independent Condition B. I will attempt to give a partial answer. It will have something in common with Lebeaux (1983: 726) and Chomsky's (1986: 175) idea that Condition A involves the application of movement that resembles overt clitic movement.[22] (I will address Condition A below.)

The proposal so far has been that the reading of (57) in which *he* takes *John* as antecedent must involve a derivation in which *John* and *he* start out together as part of one "doubling" constituent (which gets the theta-role of *smart*). *John* itself gets no theta-role within the lower sentence; its theta-role comes about as the result of its moving into the subject theta-position of *think*. If that were the whole story, (58) and (59) would be derivable in similar fashion, incorrectly.

Let me therefore add to this picture the idea that in moving from within the doubling constituent up to the position in which it gets its theta-role *John* must pass through an intermediate position. The required intermediate position will be available in (57) but not in (58) or (59).

One way to formulate this idea would be to say that *John*, in these derivations, must pass through an intermediate A′ position. The question why Condition B effects exist would then become the question why such successive cyclicity need hold.

A potentially attractive answer is to say that it is precisely because *John* originates within a doubling constituent. My proposal, more specifically, is that the crucial intermediate step is actually movement of the doubling constituent itself.

Assume, thinking of Romance clitic movement (and Icelandic object shift), that unstressed pronouns must invariably move.[23] Assume further that a pronoun heading a doubling constituent, e.g. the *he* of [*John he*], in moving, pied-pipes the whole doubling constituent, so that the crucial intermediate step is in effect induced by properties of pronouns.

I will remain vague about where [*John he*] moves to except for the following claim:

(71)   The pronoun (hence the doubling constituent) must move to a position above the subject theta-position (i.e. outside the thematic part of the structure).[24]

Put another way, the core idea is:

(72)   There is no appropriate licensing position for the pronoun within VP or between VP and the subject theta-position.

In (57), repeated here, [*John he*] starts out in the subject theta-position of the embedded sentence:

(73)   John thinks he's smart.

Given (71)/(72), movement of [*John he*] to the lower Spec-IP suffices. Subsequently, *John* itself will move up to the subject theta-position of *think*.

In (58), a variant of which is repeated here, there is, desirably, a problem:

(74)   John praises him.

In the reading in which *him* takes *John* as antecedent, there must be a doubling constituent [*John him*] that originates in the object theta-position. By virtue of (71)/(72), [*John him*] must raise to a position above the subject theta-position. But then *John* would be too high to be able to move into that subject theta-position, with the result that *John* would get no theta-role (and the subject theta-role would remain unassigned). Consequently, (74) is impossible in the intended reading.

There is another potential derivation of (74) that must be excluded, one in which *John* moves into the subject theta-position prior to the pronoun pied-piping the doubling constituent. Let me take this to be a locality effect (which needs to be made precise), with the DP in subject theta-position then interfering with movement past it of a doubling constituent containing a trace/copy of that same DP.

The derivation of (59), repeated here, raises a related question:

(75)   John considers him intelligent.

For a coreferential reading to be possible, [*John him*] would have to start out in the theta-positon of *intelligent* and then move to a higher intermediate position before *John* moves up into the subject theta-position of *consider*. If there were such a position available, the coreferential reading would be derivable, incorrectly. In this case, one could plausibly say that the small clause is too "small," i.e. that there is no available intermediate pronoun position within it. While possibly correct for small clauses, that kind of answer might not be sufficient for infinitives:

(76)   John considers him to be intelligent.

An alternative (or additional) proposal would be that "raising-to-object" must apply first and that once it does [*John him*] is too high in the structure for there to be any available intermediate position above it, yet below the subject theta-position of *consider*.[25]

In summary, Condition B is not a primitive of UG. Condition B effects come about because pronoun–antecedent relations involve movement from within a doubling consituent, and because that movement must find an intermediate landing site somewhere between the theta-position of the doubling constituent and the theta-position of the double. When those two positions are too close together to allow for the presence of the required intermediate position, we find what have come to be called Condition B effects.[26]

10   Why are there reflexives?

This question is not usually asked explicitly. Discussions of (the relation between Condition A and) Condition B often take the existence of reflexives for granted.[27] It is reasonable, instead, to take the existence of reflexives as a fact about UG that needs to be understood.

English tolerates perfectly well the familiar ambiguity of:

(77)   John thinks he's smart.

The pronoun *he* can take *John* as antecedent or not. (From the present perspective, *he* is part of [DP *he*], where DP is either *John* or some phrase other than *John* that is not visible – see the discussion of (16)–(22).) Why then should English (and UG, more generally) bother with having reflexives, with their complex syntax?

The existence of Condition B effects (reinterpreted here in terms of UG properties of pronouns and movement) provides an answer if we grant that UG needs to allow for the expression of sentences in which object and subject are coreferential. (Without reflexives, (74)–(76) would not be expressible (using a pronoun).)

11   English-type reflexives

Why does the addition of *self* make coreference available in the following?

(78)   John thinks highly of himself.

(79)   John considers himself intelligent.

The answer must be that *self* makes available an intermediate position for the pronoun that is not available in the absence of *self*. It may be that the structure is:

(80)   thinks highly of D^0 [John-he] ('s) self

such that Spec-DP counts as an intermediate pronoun position to which [*John he*] can raise prior to *John* raising to the subject theta-position of *think*. Put a bit less specifically, the presence of the noun *self* licenses a possessive-type DP structure (see Helke 1971; 1973) one of whose Specs fulfills the pronoun's need (so that [*John he*] has no need to raise to a position above the theta-position of *think*).[28]

If the needs of [*John he*] are met DP-internally in (80), then the c-command and locality requirements on the antecedents of reflexives (i.e. on the position to which *John* subsequently moves) do not follow directly from the present set of proposals. This is particularly clear from:

(81)   John wants me to photograph his dog/*himself.

(82)   I want John to photograph my dog/*myself.

John can move long-distance out of a doubling constituent [*John his*] that is the possessor of *dog*, but not of *self*, and similarly for [*I my*] in (82). *Self* also imposes much stricter c-command requirements:

(83)   John's sister likes his dog/*himself.

(84)   My sister likes my dog/*myself.

It may well be that Helke (1971; 1973) was correct to emphasize common properties of *self*-reflexives and idiomatic possessives:[29]

(85)   John blew his top.

These share the locality and c-command properties of *self*:

(86)   John doesn't want me to blow my/*his top.

(87)   John's sister blew her/*his top.

Alternatively, or in addition, the locality and c-command requirements on the antecedents of ordinary reflexives may be related to the following (see Burzio 1986: 112 on emphatic pronouns in French and Italian; also Jayaseelan 1997):

(88)   John wants me to do it myself/*himself.

(89)   John's sister fixed it herself/*himself.

I will not pursue these (important) questions here.[30]

12   *zich*-type reflexives

R. Huybregts pointed out in Pisa in 1979 that Dutch reflexive *zich* has pronominal as well as anaphoric properties, in particular that to a certain extent it displays antilocality effects of the Condition B type (for more recent discussion, see Veraart 1996). To a certain extent, Italian reflexive nonclitic *sé* shows Condition B effects, too (see Kayne 2000a: 149).

   If Dutch *zich*, Italian *sé* and similar elements in Scandinavian show such effects, then they should be analyzed as entering a doubling constituent subject to the movement requirements proposed above for ordinary pronouns. *Sé* et al. differ from ordinary pronouns, however, in needing a c-commanding antecedent and in needing their antecedent to be relatively local (but not systematically as local as in the case of English reflexives).

In the preceding section on English reflexives, I suggested (see (83), (84), (87), and (89)) that the fact that c-command must hold between antecedent and reflexive may not be a fact specific to what we normally think of as binding theory. In the case of *sé*-type elements, too, it would be desirable not to have to stipulate a c-command requirement.

To approach a solution, let us look at the locality facts. These *sé*-type elements (with various interesting differences among them) may generally not be separated from their antecedents by an indicative clause boundary. They can, on the other hand, often be embedded in an infinitive within which their antecedent is not found, and to a lesser extent in a subjunctive.

The fact that the antecedent–*sé* relation is sensitive to distinctions like indicative/subjunctive/infinitive recalls comparable distinctions found with certain more familiar kinds of movement, e.g., quantifier (*tout*/*rien* – "everything(all)"/"nothing") movement of the French type:[31]

(90)   Il a tout voulu refaire. ("he has all wanted to-redo")

(91)   ?Il a tout voulu qu'ils refassent. ("he has all wanted that they redo(subjunctive)")

(92)   *Il a tout dit qu'ils ont refait. ("he has all said that they have(indicative) redone")

This similarity between the antecedent–*sé* relation and the movement of *tout*/*rien* in turn recalls the fact that on the whole Italian *sé* prefers that its antecedent be a quantified phrase (see Kayne 2000a: 150 and especially my proposal there (p.146) that *sé* can have a plural antecedent only via the intermediary of a(n abstract) distributor (like *each*) and that that distributor is responsible for certain locality restrictions (with plural antecedents)).

What all of this suggests is that we should generalize the distributor idea even further:

(93)   The antecedent of *sé* must always be quantified; when there is no overt quantifier/distributor, there must be a covert one; c-command must hold, as with movement of *tout*/*rien*.

(94)   This is true even for singular antecedents (in which case the distributor is degenerate, distributing over a singleton).[32]

(95)   It is the relation between the distributor and *sé* that is sensitive to indicative vs. subjunctive vs. infinitive.

Thus an Italian sentence like:

(96) Gianni ha parlato di sé. ("John has spoken of *sé*")

will look like:

(97) Gianni ha *DB* parlato di sé.

where *DB* is the abstract (and, here, degenerate) *each*.

In addition to the relation between *DB* and *sé* to which I am attributing the locality effects, there is a relation between *DB* and the antecedent, here *Gianni*. Since a "floating" distributor must be c-commanded by its "antecedent:"

(98) Those numbers are each divisible by a different prime.

(99) *The sum of those numbers is each divisible by a different prime.

it follows, given that *DB* must c-command *sé*, that the antecedent of *sé* must c-command *sé*.

We can now say that *sé* is like ordinary pronouns in being part of a doubling constituent (which yields the Condition B type effects), but that its double is (unlike that of ordinary pronouns) necessarily a *DB* (whence the locality effect), which is in turn related to a DP (yielding the c-command effects), in ways that I will not explore any further here.[33]

13 Backwards pronominalization

So-called "backwards" pronominalization, as in (100), is not expected if movement respects the extension condition and if antecedent–pronoun relations must invariably be expressed by movement of the sort proposed here:

(100) His mother is angry at John.

Although this at first seems like an unwanted conclusion, given the acceptability of (100), things look different if one takes into account the fact that many languages allow sentences like (100) much less readily than English, or not at all.[34]

This fact suggests that the correct theory of UG will make backwards pronominalization harder to come by. Consider the following proposal: (100) is only derivable as a counterpart of the topicalization example (101):

(101) John his mother is angry at.

Example (101) has an acceptable "strict" reading (with a possible follow-up . . . *but she's not angry at his little sister*), but the imaginable "sloppy" reading is for me appreciably more difficult.[35]

The acceptability of (101) is itself a challenge. If we start, e.g., from:[36]

(102)   [John his] mother is angry at

we express correctly the relation between *John* and *his*, but we have no phrase capable of bearing the object theta-role of *angry at*. One possible analysis would be the following. (101) in the strict reading has covert structure that if overt would look like:

(103)   Somebody (who is) John his mother is really angry at.

with an analysis:

(104)   [somebody (who is) __] [John his] mother is angry at

in which the object theta-role of *angry at* is now borne by the (moved) topicalized phrase *somebody (who is)* __. *John* moves from within the doubling constituent contained within the subject phrase [*John his*] *mother* to the position indicated by "__" (see section 17), yielding:

(105)   [somebody (who is) John$_i$] [t$_i$ his] mother is angry at

Example (100) is then derived from a structure like (104) via leftward movement around the "topic" of everything that follows it.

At a first approximation, the expectation is, now, that backwards pronominalization should be unavailable in English in cases where topicalization is unavailable. This may account for a contrast mentioned by Jayaseelan (1991):

(106)   It was John's pride that saved him.

(107)   What saved him was John's pride.

him can take *John* as antecedent in the cleft (106) but not in the pseudo-cleft (107). (106) is to be analyzed like (105). The unacceptability of pseudo-cleft (107) can from the current perspective be related to the impossibility of topicalization seen in:

(108)   *John's pride what saved him was.

Coming back to the necessary comparative syntax question, languages that disallow backwards pronominalization may be languages that disallow leftward movement around a topic,[37] or else disallow empty resumptives/covert *somebody (who is)*, or both.

The unacceptability (weak crossover) of:

(109)   *His mother was angry at every little boy.

would then in part reduce to the deviance of *somebody who is every little boy*, and perhaps similarly for the sloppy reading of (100) or (101) (but I will not pursue the question here).

14   Epithets again

As noted in the discussion of (27), epithets don't show a consistently strong Condition C-like effect. Another example is:

(110)   Smith probably doesn't even appreciate the good things we've been saying about the idiot these days.

This contrasts with:

(111)   The idiot probably doesn't even appreciate the good things we've been saying about Smith these days.

Taking *Smith* as antecedent of *the idiot* seems quite a bit harder in (111) than in (110). Although a bit weaker, this contrast obviously recalls that holding if we replace *the idiot* here by *he/him*. It suggests that we take (111) to be a Condition C effect of the familiar sort, like:

(112)   He probably doesn't even appreciate the good things we've been saying about Smith these days.

Now I have proposed that (112) be thought of as involving the prohibition against rightward movement to a non-c-commanding position. For that idea to extend to (111), it must be the case that (110) derives from a doubling structure via upward movement, just like:

(113)   Smith probably doesn't even appreciate the good things we've been saying about him these days.

Just as (113) involves (leftward, upward) movement of *Smith* from within the doubling constituent [*Smith him*], so (110) must involve the same movement from within a doubling constituent of the form [*Smith the idiot*].[38] If we now say, generalizing the earlier proposal about pronouns, that epithets can take an antecedent ONLY via a derivation involving movement out of a doubling constituent,[39] (111) will be unavailable parallel to (112).

Recall that my account of Condition B effects in section 9 depended in part on the idea that unstressed pronouns have to move to a licensing position outside *v*P. If epithets are unlike pronouns in that respect, then, despite the similarity between (111) and (112), we should expect not to find Condition B effects with epithets. That this expectation may hold is shown by the approximately equal status of:

(114)   Smith would like the idiot to be reelected.

(115)   Smith would like the idiot's sister to be reelected.

The unacceptability of these and of (24) (as opposed to (110) and (27)) would then need a new account.

15 Condition C reconstruction effects

In the following, *he* cannot take *John* as antecedent

(116) How many pictures of John did he take (with his new camera)?

The same is true of:

(117) He took five pictures of John.

Condition C as usually interpreted can relate (116) to (117) by taking advantage of the fact that (116) strongly resembles (117) prior to wh-movement and at LF, as in Chomsky's (1995, chap. 3) discussion. Put another way, (116) can be excluded if Condition C applies at the appropriate point.

But that approach to (116) depends on the interpretation of Condition C as a kind of filter (see Lasnik 1976). The proposal I have been outlining has no Condition C, strictly speaking, and the way in which Condition C effects are obtained is not filter-like. Condition C effects come about, instead, because the antecedent (starting from within a doubling constituent) cannot reach certain positions relative to the pronoun. From this perspective, (116) is excluded in part parallel to (117) (the antecedent cannot move rightward to a non-c-commanding position), but now there is another question – why could (116) not be derived via the following?

(118) how many pictures of __ did [John he] take

with *John* moving to the position following *of*.

One might, of course, respond by noting that that would require leftward movement to a non-c-commanding position. While apparently to the point, that response would leave open the well-known cases in which wh-movement has opposite behavior:

(119) Which of the pictures that John took yesterday did he destroy today?

Here *he* can take *John* as antecedent.
There may be a link here to a proposal of Huang's (1993) concerning:

(120) *Mary is wondering how proud of herself John is.

His account was that wh-movement had to carry along a subject position associated with *how proud of herself* and that the presence of that subject prevented *herself* from taking *Mary* as antecedent. In my terms, this must be interpreted as a fact about (the impossibility of) movement of the double *Mary* in:

(121)   is wondering how DP$_{subject}$ proud of [Mary her] self John is . . .

up to the subject theta-position of *wonder*. This movement view is supported (although much more needs to be made precise) by the fact that wh-movement is also not possible here:

(122)   *Which girl have you been wondering how proud of __ John is?

Huang's account of (120) in terms of extra material obligatorily associated with *how proud of X* can be adapted to:

(123)   How proud of Mary is she?

in which *she* cannot take *Mary* as antecedent.
    Let me make a proposal (related to those of Kayne 2001b) in part inspired by Ross (1969) (in addition to Huang 1993), in part by the English:

(124)   He's real smart, John is.[40]

(125)   He's talked to I don't know how many people!

and in part by Gulli's (2000) work on the Italian:

(126)   E' andato a Parigi è andato. ("he-is gone to P he-is gone")

The proposal is that (123) has hidden structure (a bit more than what Huang postulated) resembling the almost possible (perhaps dialectal):

(127)   ?She's how proud of him is she?

In other words, (123) is impossible in the relevant reading because it would have to correspond to:

(128)   ?She's how proud of Mary is she?

which is impossible with *Mary* as antecedent of *she*, just as in:

(129)   She's proud of Mary.

which has no valid derivation that would include the needed [*Mary she*]. (A full account of (128) will have to make sure that there is no point in the derivation at which *Mary* precedes every *she*.)
    Returning to (116), the Condition C effect there will now follow if the structure is obligatorily of the (128) sort:

(130) ?He took how many pictures of you/John did he take?

Example (119) will be distinguishable from (116) if (119) need not have such hidden structure. There is, of course, the familiar and difficult question of what underlies the difference between (119) and (116). The adjunct vs. complement distinction adopted by Chomsky (1995: 204) does not seem quite right – see Nunes (2001: 320n.) and references cited there; also the fact that the relative in:

(131) The ones *(John bought yesterday) he resold today.

is obligatory, given the "head" *ones*. I leave this question open.

16 Further Condition C reconstruction effects

Consider now:

(132) . . . and ask me to help him John will.

(133) . . . and ask me to help John he will.

John cannot antecede *he* in (133). It may be that these apparent instances of VP-preposing should be analyzed as close relatives of (124), i.e. as:

(134) . . . and John will ask me to help him John will.

(135) . . . and he will ask me to help John he will.

the problem with the latter then being the *he . . . John* relation, as in (128).
A somewhat different type is:

(136) He seems to John's wife to be tired.

in which *he* cannot take *John* as antecedent, despite the availability of that interpretation in:

(137) It seems to John's wife that he's tired.

Why can *John* not move from within [*John he*] leftward to the possessor position prior to subject-to-subject raising? The answer may be that the source of *John seems to Mary to be tired* is closer to (138) than to (139):

(138) It seems (that) you're tired to Mary.

(139) It seems to Mary (that) you're tired.

The greater naturalness of the latter may be misleading; it disappears under preposition stranding:

(140)   ?Who did it seem (that) I was tired to?

(141)   ??Who did it seem to (that) I was tired?

If in (136) subject-to-subject raising applies to:

(142)   seems [X to be tired] to Y's wife

the unwanted interpretation will be avoided (as long as the final word order is determined after subject-to-subject raising, perhaps by factoring out infinitival *to* in the manner of Kayne 2000a, chapter 14).[41]

17   Sideward movement

The availability of (119) with *John* antecedent of *he* looks like that of:

(143)   The woman that John is talking to doesn't like him/the guy.

Given my analysis, in order for *John* to antecede *him*, *John* here must originate within a constituent [*John him*] (and similarly for [*John the guy*] – see section 14), and the derivation must involve "sideward" movement in the sense of Nunes (2001), Bobaljik and Brown (1997), and Hornstein (2001), on the expectation that overgeneration can be kept in check, as they discuss. (I must take such sideward movement to be limited to leftward movement.)[42]
   Somewhat like (143) is:

(144)   Every farmer who owns a donkey loves it.

It remains to be seen whether the double of *it* can be taken to be as simple as *a donkey* (for relevant discussion, see Sauerland 2000).

18   Circularity

Higginbotham and May (1981) and Higginbotham (1983: 405) discuss cases like:

(145)   His wife just saw her husband.

in which it cannot simultaneously hold that *his* takes *her husband* as antecedent and *her* takes *his wife* as antecedent. In present terms, this is due to the fact that if, for example, *her* is given *his wife* as antecedent, we need:

(146)   . . . [his wife her] husband

But then *his* needs as its double the minimal phrase containing *her* and *husband*, which, however, contains *his*, leading to a regress.
   Bach (1970) has:

(147)   The man who shows he deserves it will get the prize he desires.

This may escape the regress problem through relative clause "extraposition," e.g. the antecedent of *it* may be *the prize* (not including the relative).

19   "Transitivity of coreference"

Lasnik (1976: 11) discusses examples like:

(148)   The woman he loved told him that John was a jerk.

in which it is not possible for *he*, *him*, and *John* to all be coreferential. To avoid the complication of a "backwards pronominalization" configuration (see section 13), let me take a simpler (in certain respects) example:

(149)   He says John thinks he's smart.

The two *hes* are in a legitimate coreference configuration, as are *John* and the second *he*. "Transitivity of coreference" might lead one therefore to expect the sentence to be possible with all three coreferential, incorrectly.
   In present terms, we can have:

(150)   . . . [John he] is smart

followed by movement of *John* to the subject theta-position of *think*, but that leaves the initial *he* in (149) "out of the picture." The two *hes* could be related if a silent DP double of the second *he* moved to the Spec of the first *he*, but that would leave out *John*. As in note 36, we can have, with two essential movement steps:

(151)   John says he thinks he's smart.

but no automatic "transitivity of coreference" is expected under the present proposal.

20   Split antecedents and overlapping reference

The following example

(152)   John told Bill that they should leave.

might, thinking of (153), involve a relation with only one of the apparent antecedents:

(153)   John told me that they had decided that Bill would go first.

See Larson and Vassilieva (2001) (and alternatively, den Dikken et al. 2000). Sentences like:

(154)   I think we should leave.

will require a doubling constituent of the form [*I we*], given the Condition B effects discussed in section 9.

21   Conclusion

I have explored a movement-based approach to pronoun–antecedent relations that attributes Condition C and Condition B effects to properties of movement and that eliminates both as primitives of UG. The existence of reflexives is traceable back to Condition B. No use is made of "accidental coreference" in the sense of Lasnik (1976).

Acknowledgments

This paper originated in talks given at MIT and at UMass Amherst in October, 1997. The material was subsequently presented at the Universities of Geneva (April 1998), Florence and Padua (June 1998), Venice (May 1999), Pennsylvania (October 1999), SUNY Stony Brook (October 2000); also at LSRL, Penn State (April 1998), WCCFL/UCLA (February 2000) and the Comparative Germanic Syntax Conference, Groningen (May 2000). I am grateful to all those audiences for their helpful comments, and to Sam Epstein and Daniel Seely for their helpful comments on a first draft.

Notes

1   Cf. Cinque's (1990: 61) argument against taking clitics to be the spelling out of a trace, made on the basis of the nonlicensing of parasitic gaps by clitics; similarly,

cf. Hoekstra's (1999, section 3) argument against taking the pronoun in (Dutch and Frisian) left dislocation to be the spelling out of a trace.

2   Sportiche's (1995a; 1995b) approach to clitic doubling likewise has the pronoun in the numeration, but differs in having the pronoun merged into a sentential functional head position (with the double then moving to it). Whether his approach to clitic doubling (and his related recent ideas on determiners) could be unified with the antecedent–pronoun relation of (2) in a way parallel to the text proposal (i.e whether the movement-based proposal developed in this chapter could be recast in his terms) is left an open question.

3   For recent, more detailed discussion of the French complex inversion illustrated in (3), see Pollock (2000).

4   The movement of [*Juan le*] may accomplish what classic clitic movement is intended to accomplish.

5   The extraction of the double *Juan* here from within [*Juan le*] is intended to recall right dislocation (which does not involve rightward movement) – see Kayne (1994: 83) and especially Cecchetto (1999) and Villalba (1999).

6   Though it is rejected by Chomsky (2000, note 35).

7   This differs from Nunes (2001: 322), who has nonpronunciation depend on c-command.

8   This parallel was alluded to in Kayne (1994: 158). For recent discussion of the question of why downward movement is illegitimate, see Epstein (2001).

9   I assume that mistaken identity examples do not involve syntactically represented cases of antecedent and pronoun.

10   A point of similarity to Chomsky (1995: 211) is that no indices are needed.

11   This is similar to McCawley (1978: 178).

12   For a similar point, see Hoekstra (1999).

13   Another type of example from English is:

(i)   Smith is so unhappy that everybody I know wants to offer the poor guy a job.
(ii) Smith isn't unhappy enough yet for people to be willing to offer the poor guy a job.

14   For partially similar skepticism, see Chomsky (1981: 227). See also note 39 below.

15   Locality conditions must be at issue in an attempted remnant movement derivation of (ii):

(i)   ?My students should have been all of them congratulated.
(ii)   *All of them should have my students been congratulated.
       Note that in the right-dislocation example (see note 5):
(iii) ?They've seen that film, all of my students.

they is doubled by *all of my students*, not by *my students* alone.

16   The notion "start out" is oversimplified – see note 36 below, where it is suggested that the Spec of a pronoun can be filled by Move as well as by pure Merge.

17   The doubling constituent [*John he*] does move within the embedded sentence in the derivation of:

(i)   John thinks that he will be blamed.

followed by movement of *John* alone to the subject theta-position of *think*.

18   Although clearly worse, as expected, than:

(i)   Our doctor considers me intelligent.

On the other hand, it's not clear that (ii) is much better, with overlapping reference (see Chomsky 1973: 241), than (iii):

(ii)   The soldiers' wives insulted the officers.
(iii)   The soldiers insulted the officers.

19   On this morpheme, see Kayne (2000a, chapter 8).
20   On the use of *same* with reflexives in some languages, see Safir (1996).
21   See Kayne (1975, §2.6); as would be weak pronouns – see Cardinaletti and Starke (1995).
   It may be that covert morphemes of this sort also underlie children's Condition B "errors" (i.e. children have Condition B (or rather what underlies it) but have greater latitude than adults in the use of covert morphemes here). Such covert morphemes would, setting aside (50) and (52), be expected to leave intact Condition C effects, which seems correct – see Thornton and Wexler (1999: 31, 50, 106).
   The fact that children basically get things right with quantified antecedents (Thornton and Wexler 1999: 28) suggests a link with the fact that in local contexts Italian nonreflexive pronouns show a preference for nonquantified antecedents – Kayne (2000a: 150).
22   See also Pica (1987).
23   See Hestvik (1992). I take stressed pronouns to contain unstressed ones as a subpart, as alluded to in the discussion of (49) and (51).
   Thinking of Kayne (2000a, chap. 13), I take pronoun movement and the associated pied-piping to be overt. All languages such as English in which object pronouns are preceded by V must have a means of moving the verb sufficiently high (past the pronoun), either by phrasal or by head movement. Thus in:

(i)   John thinks Mary will praise him.

him directly reflects the position to which the doubling constituent moves (it is not likely that the pronoun moves anywhere by itself).
   The idea that English pronouns move differently from nonpronominal DPs is supported by well-known facts such as (see Maling 1976):

(ii)   I'll buy them/*the books all.
(iii)   I'll talk to them/*the kids all.

24   Cf. in part my (1994: 42) claim that clitics are never adjoined to V.
25   Movement of [*John him*] to a clitic-like position within the infinitive prior to "raising-to-object" must not be possible, perhaps because pronoun-driven movement must follow Case-driven. Relevant is whether the "raising-to-object" landing site is above or below the subject theta-position in the matrix.
26   In (i), *him* must reach a position above the subject theta one, and *John* must move into its theta-position after *'s mother* has moved out of subject theta-position (see below):

(i)   John's mother praises him a lot.

27   A notable exception is Pica and Snyder (1997).
28   Italian-type reflexives with *stesso* ("same"), which is not a noun, presumably achieve a similar effect somewhat differently – for relevant discussion, see Safir (1996).

Helke's proposal for possessive structure in English is very clearly supported by those varieties of English that have *hisself* and *theirselves,* and by the Amsterdam Dutch that has as a reflexive *z'n eigen* ("his own") with an empty noun (Postma 1997: 299–300). The independence of the pronominal part and *self* is further supported by those varieties of English (like mine) in which number needn't match, as in:

(i)   If someone buys themself a new car, . . .
(ii) ?We each bought ourself a different kind of car.

For a different view, see Zwart (this volume).
29   For recent discussion, see Postma (1997) and references cited there.
30   Except to note, adapting a suggestion of Daniel Seely's, that in the spirit of this paper, (i) should be derived from (ii):

(i)   John fixed it ((all) by) himself.
(ii) fixed it ((all) by) [John him] self

with *John* moving into the subject theta-position of *fix,* and similarly for Italian emphatic pronouns.
31   For recent detailed discussion, see Cinque (2001).
32   The differences in Italian between singular and plural antecedents of *sé* must now be rethought.
33   The fact that some instances of *sé*-type elements don't show antilocality of the Condition B sort (e.g. inherent reflexive *zich*; all instances, apparently, of German *sich*) remains to be understood. Discussion of Romance reflexive clitics is beyond the scope of this paper.
34   See Huang (1982) on Chinese, Craig (1977: 150) on Jacaltec, Allan et al. (1995: 473) on Danish; also Jayaseelan (1991: 76) on some speakers of Malayalam.
35   My English here is more restrictive than that of Lasnik and Stowell (1991: 697), who would apparently accept, with a sloppy reading:

(i)   John his mother is angry at, Bill his mother isn't.

36   I assume that *J* could not start in object theta-position, get Case, and then move to Spec of *he* (and then to topic), for reasons that need to be elucidated.
    In (i), I take *John* to move from Spec of the lower *he* to Spec of the higher *he* before moving to a theta-position:

(i)   John$_i$ thinks he$_i$'ll say he$_i$'s hungry.

Martha McGinnis (personal communication) has called my attention to the question of relativized minimality (Rizzi 1990) here, i.e. to the fact that there seems to be no effect. The most telling case is:

(ii) Mary's brother$_i$ knows that their father$_j$ thinks that he$_i$ should show him$_j$ more respect.

The lack of such an effect might be related to the question whether movement of the double to a higher theta-position can be interpreted as attraction.

37   Cf. the existence of languages that disallow right-dislocation, such as Haitian (Michel DeGraff, personal communication); perhaps similarly Haitian also disallows "heavy-NP shift" (see Dejean 1993) (despite being "VO"; this, like the existence of scrambling in "VO" Slavic, is relevant to Saito and Fukui 1998).

38   On the importance of *the/that*, see Aoun and Choueiri (2000: 34n.).

39   This generalization to epithets would not be readily available to Hornstein's (2001) pronoun-as-copy approach.

For me, it is essential that [*Smith the idiot*] be an available doubling constituent with *Smith* in Spec and hence extractable, but not the reverse. In:

(i)   That idiot Smith made another mistake.

that idiot is therefore expected not to be a constituent.

Presumably, constituents of the form [*Smith the idiot*] or [*Smith him*] can ONLY be interpreted in "antecedent"-epithet/pronoun fashion and require movement of *Smith*; in any event, their relation to apposition needs to be looked into. On the possibility that this treatment of epithets should be generalized to all nouns (with an appropriate determiner), see Ruwet (1982, chap. 7) and Lasnik and Stowell (1991: 708n.).

Phi-feature clash may underlie the fact that (ii) has no interpretation in which *I* takes *John* as antecedent:

(ii)   John thinks I'm smart.

but one needs to take into account English quotative contexts and the more extensive use of first- and second-person pronouns in Kannada – see Nadahalli (1998).

If the (marginal) acceptability of the proper name examples in (30), (32), and (34) groups them with (110), then [*Smith Smith*] must be a well-formed doubling constituent and the extra restrictions on ... *Smith* ... *Smith* ... as compared with ... *Smith* ... *he* ... would be due to another factor. In which case the (relatively) well-formed double proper name example (28) would be derived via a doubling constituent plus movement. The contrast between English and (the extra possibilities with proper names found in) Malayalam (see Jayaseelan 1991) remains to be understood.

40   As brought to my attention by Ian Roberts (personal communication), British English has:

(i)   He's real smart, is John.

supporting the approach to (124) suggested in Kayne (1994: 78).

41   If (i) really involves raising of the *seem* type, then I would propose a comparable analysis:

(i)   He strikes John's wife as being tired.

42   In a way that remains to be made precise – see Kayne (2000b) on the possibility that derivations are built from right to left (in addition to being built from bottom to top), using as a primitive "immediate precedence" (from which a limitation to one specifier per head might follow).

Thinking of Epstein (2001), it may be that sideward movement is impossible with instances of Attract, if movement of the double to a theta-position is not an instance of Attract (perhaps relevant to the fact that movement of the double violates islands freely – cf. some instances of resumptive pronouns in wh-constructions).

The contrast between (143) and (i) (with *him* bound by *many a man*):

(i)   *The woman that many a man has spoken to doesn't like him.

must be due to an orthogonal property of scope (for relevant recent discussion, see Bianchi 2001). In sentences like (ii), in the bound pronoun reading, the double can be *every young man* only if *every* is not interpreted until it reaches its scope position:

(ii)   Every young man thinks he's immortal.

The alternative is to treat *every* as Sportiche has treated *the* in recent work and to have the double be just *young man*.

Recall from note 36 that movement from a theta-position into the Spec of a doubling constituent should be precluded.

The fact that movement from the Spec of a doubling constituent does not (as far as I know) give rise to reconstruction effects would follow if all binding and scope-related reconstruction effects had to be analyzed approximately as in (128)/(130) – see Kayne 2001b.

References

Allan, R., P. Holmes and T. Lundskær-Nielsen. 1995. *Danish: A Comprehensive Grammar*. London: Routledge.

Aoun, J. and L. Choueiri. 2000. "Epithets." *Natural Language and Linguistic Inquiry* 18: 1–39.

Bach, E. 1970. "Problominalization." *Linguistic Inquiry* 1: 121–22.

Bianchi, V. 2001. "Antisymmetry and the leftness condition: leftness as anti-c-command." *Studia Linguistica* 55: 1–38.

Bobaljik, J. D. and S. Brown. 1997. "Interarboreal operations: head movement and the extension requirement." *Linguistic Inquiry* 28: 345–56.

Burzio, L. 1986. *Italian Syntax: A Government-Binding Approach*. Dordrecht: Reidel.

Burzio, L. 1991. "The morphological basis of anaphora." *Journal of Linguistics* 27: 81–105.

Cardinaletti, A. and M. Starke. 1995. "The tripartition of pronouns and its acquisition: principles B puzzles are ambiguity problems." In J. Beckman, ed., *Proceedings of NELS 25*, GLSA, University of Massachusetts, Amherst.

Cecchetto, C. 1999. "A comparative analysis of left and right dislocation in romance." *Studia Linguistica* 53: 40–67.

Chomsky, N. 1973. "Conditions on transformations." In S. R. Anderson and P. Kiparsky, eds., *A Festschrift for Morris Halle*. New York: Holt, Rinehart and Winston, 232–86.

Chomsky, N. 1981. *Lectures on Government and Binding*. Dordrecht: Foris.

Chomsky, N. 1986. *Knowledge of Language*. New York: Praeger.

Chomsky, N. 1995. *The Minimalist Program*. Cambridge, MA: MIT Press.

Chomsky, N. 2000. "Minimalist inquiries: the framework." In R. Martin, D. Michaels, and J. Uriagereka, eds., *Step by Step: Essays in Minimalist Syntax in Honor of Howard Lasnik*. Cambridge, MA: MIT Press, 89–155.

Chomsky, N. 2001. "Derivation by phase." In M. Kenstowicz, ed., *Ken Hale: A Life in Language*. Cambridge, MA: MIT Press, 1–52.

Chomsky, N. and H. Lasnik. 1993. "The theory of principles and parameters." In J. Jacobs, A. von Stechow, W. Sternefeld, and T. Vennemann, eds., *Syntax: An International Handbook of Contemporary Research*. Berlin: de Gruyter.

Cinque, G. 1990. *Types of A'-Dependencies*. Cambridge, MA: MIT Press.

Cinque, G. 2001. "Two types of quantifier climbing in French." MS, University of Venice.

Craig, C. G. 1977. *The Structure of Jacaltec*. Austin: University of Texas Press.

Dejean, Y. 1993. "Manifestations en créole haïtien du principe d'adjacence stricte." MS.

Dikken, M. den, A. Lipták, and Z. Zvolenszky. 2000. "On inclusive reference anaphora: new perpectives from Hungarian." MS, Graduate Center, CUNY and New York University.

Epstein, S. 2001. "Deriving the proper binding condition." MS, University of Michigan.

Fiengo, R. 1977. "On trace theory." *Linguistic Inquiry* 8: 35–61.

Gulli, A. 2000. "Reduplication in syntax." MS, New York University.

Hankamer, J. and I. Sag. 1976. "Deep and surface anaphora." *Linguistic Inquiry* 7: 391–428.

Helke, M. 1971. *The Grammar of English Reflexives*. Doctoral dissertation, MIT, Cambridge, MA.

Helke, M. 1973. "On reflexives in English." *Linguistics* 106: 5–23.

Hestvik, A. G. 1992. "LF movement of pronouns and antisubject orientation." *Linguistic Inquiry* 23: 557–94.

Higginbotham, J. 1983. "Logical form, binding and nominals." *Linguistic Inquiry* 14: 395–420.

Higginbotham, J. and R. May. 1981. "Crossing, markedness, pragmatics." In A. Belletti, L. Brandi, and L. Rizzi, eds., *Theory of Markedness in Generative Grammar. Proceedings of the 1979 GLOW Conference*, Scuola Normale Superiore, Pisa, 423–44.

Hoekstra, E. 1999. "On D-pronouns and the movement of topic features." In W. Abraham, ed., *Characteristic Properties of Spoken Vernaculars (Folia Linguistica)* 33: 59–74.

Hornstein, N. 1999. "Movement and control." *Linguistic Inquiry* 30: 69–96.

Hornstein, N. 2001. *Move! A Minimalist Theory of Construal*. Malden, MA and Oxford: Blackwell.

Huang, C.-T.J. 1982 "Logical relations in Chinese and the theory of grammar." Doctoral dissertation, MIT, Cambridge, MA.

Huang, C.-T.J. 1993. "Reconstruction and the structure of VP: some theoretical consequences." *Linguistic Inquiry* 24: 103–38.

Jayaseelan, K. A. 1991. "The pronominal system of Malayalam." *CIEFL Occasional Papers in Linguistics* 3: 68–107.

Jayaseelan, K. A. 1997. "Anaphors as pronouns." *Studia Linguistica* 51: 186–234.

Kayne, R. S. 1972. "Subject inversion in French interrogative." In J. Casagrande and B. Sacink, eds., *Generative Studies in Romance Languages*, Rowley, MA: Newbury House, pp. 70–126.

Kayne, R. S. 1975. *French Syntax: The Transformational Cycle*. Cambridge, MA: MIT Press.

Kayne, R. S. 1994. *The Antisymmetry of Syntax*. Cambridge, MA: MIT Press.

Kayne, R. S. 2000a. *Parameters and Universals*. New York: Oxford University Press.

Kayne, R. S. 2000b. "Recent thoughts on antisymmetry." Paper presented at the Antisymmetry Workshop, Cortona, Italy.

Kayne, R. S. 2001a. "Prepositions as probes." MS, New York University.

Kayne, R. S. 2001b. "Remnant movement, A-movement and reconstruction." Paper presented at the Asymmetry Conference, UQAM and at the Workshop on the Structural Mapping of Syntactic Configurations and its Interfaces with Phonology and Semantics, University of Florence.

Larson, R. and M. Vassilieva. 2001. "The semantics of plural pronouns." Paper presented at SALT 11, New York University.

Lasnik, H. 1976. "Remarks on coreference." *Linguistic Analysis* 2: 1–22.

Lasnik, H. 1980. "On two recent treatments of disjoint reference." *Journal of Linguistic Research* 1: 48–58.

Lasnik, H. and T. Stowell. 1991. "Weakest crossover." *Linguistic Inquiry* 22: 687–720.

Lebeaux, D. 1983. "A distributional difference between reciprocals and reflexives." *Linguistic Inquiry* 14: 723–30.

Maling, J. M. 1976. "Notes on quantifier postposing." *Linguistic Inquiry* 7: 708–18.

McCawley, J. D. 1978. "Where do noun phrases come from?" In R. A. Jacobs and P. S. Rosenbaum, eds., *Readings in English Transformational Grammar*. Waltham: Ginn, 166–83.

Nadahalli, J. 1998. "Aspects of Kannada grammar." Doctoral dissertation, New York University.

Nunes, J. 2001. "Sideward movement." *Linguistic Inquiry* 32: 303–44.

O'Neil, J. 1995. "Out of control." In J. N. Beckman, ed., *Proceedings of NELS 25*, GLSA, University of Massachusetts, Amherst, 361–71.

O'Neil, J. 1997. "Means of control: deriving the properties of PRO in the Minimalist Program." PhD dissertation, Harvard University.

Pica, P. 1987. "On the nature of the reflexivization cycle." In *Proceedings of NELS 17*, GLSA, University of Massachusetts, Amherst, 483–99.

Pica, P. and W. Snyder. 1997. "On the syntax and semantics of local anaphors." In A. M. di Sciullo, ed., *Projections and Interface Conditions*. Oxford: Oxford University Press.

Pollock, J.-Y. 2000. "Subject clitics, subject clitic inversion and complex inversion: generalizing remnant movement to the comp area." MS, Université de Picardie à Amiens (to appear in *syn.com*).

Postma, G. 1997. "Logical entailment and the possessive nature of reflexive pronouns." In H. Bennis, P. Pica, and J. Rooryck, eds., *Atomism and Binding*. Dordrecht: Foris, 295–322.

Reinhart, T. 1983. *Anaphora and Semantic Interpretation*. London: Croom Helm.

Rizzi, L. 1990. *Relativized Minimality*. Cambridge, MA: MIT Press.

Ross, J. R. 1969. "On the cyclic nature of English pronominalization." In D. A. Reibel and S. A. Schane, eds., *Modern Studies in English: Readings in Transformational Grammar*. Englewood Cliffs, NJ: Prentice-Hall, 187–200.

Ruwet, N. 1982. *Grammaire des insultes et autres études*. Paris: Editions du Seuil (English translation by John Goldsmith.).

Ruwet, N. 1990. "EN et Y: deux clitiques pronominaux antilogophoriques." *Langages* 97: 51–81.

Safir, K. 1996. "Semantic atoms of anaphora." *Natural Language and Linguistic Theory* 14: 545–89.

Saito, M. and N. Fukui. 1998. "Order in phrase structure and movement." *Linguistic Inquiry* 29: 439–74.

Sauerland, U. 2000. "The content of pronouns: evidence from focus." In T. Matthews and B. Jackson, eds., *The Proceedings of SALT 10*, CLC Publications, Cornell University, Ithaca, NY.

Sigurðsson, H. A. 1989. "Verbal syntax and case in Icelandic." Doctoral dissertation, University of Lund.

Sportiche, D. 1995a. "Clitic constructions." In L. Zaring and J. Rooryck, eds., *Phrase Structure and the Lexicon*. Dordrecht: Kluwer, 213–76.

Sportiche, Dominique 1995b. "Sketch of a reductionist approach to syntactic variation and dependencies." In H. Campos and P. Kempchinsky, eds., *Evolution and Revolution in Linguistic Theory*. Washington, DC: Georgetown University Press, 356–98.

Thornton, R. and K. Wexler. 1999. *Principle B, VP Ellipsis, and Interpretation in Child Grammar*. Cambridge, MA: MIT Press.

Thráinsson, H. 1986. "On auxiliaries, AUX and VPs in Icelandic." In L. Hellan and K. K. Christensen, eds., *Topics in Scandinavian Syntax*. Dordrecht: Reidel, 235–65.

Uriagereka, J. 1995. "Aspects of the syntax of clitic placement in Western Romance." *Linguistic Inquiry* 26: 79–123.

Veraart, F. 1996. "On the distribution of Dutch reflexives." *MIT Occasional Papers in Linguistics*, 10.

Villalba, X. 1999. "Right dislocation is not right dislocation." In O. Fullana and F. Roca, eds., *Studies on the Syntax of Central Romance Languages*: Proceedings of the III Symposium on the Syntax of Central Romance Languages, Universität de Girona, 227–41.

Zwart, J.-W. (this volume). "Issues relating to a derivational theory of binding."

Chapter seven

Scrambling, Case, and Interpretability

Hisatsugu Kitahara

1 Scrambling and binding relations

As is well known, Japanese allows OBJ (Object) to undergo scrambling to
the sentence-initial position, where scrambling is taken to be an instance of
movement (see among others, Saito 1985, 1989, 1992). Consider (1a, b):

(1) a. [Taroo-ga   sono hon-o   katta] (*koto*)
          Taroo-Nom that book-Acc bought (*fact*)
          "Taro bought that book"

     b. [sono hon-o   [Taroo-ga   *t* katta]] (*koto*)
          that book-Acc Taroo-Nom   bought (*koto*)

Under this movement approach, Saito (1992) argues that clause-internal scrambling can form an A-chain. Consider (2a, b):

(2) a. ?*[[otagai-no sensei]-ga   karera-o hihansita] (*koto*)
              e.o.-Gen   teacher-Nom they-Acc criticized (*fact*)
          "Each other's teachers criticized them"

     b. ?[karera-o [[otagai-no sensei]-ga   *t* hihansita]] (*koto*)
          they-Acc   e.o.-Gen   teacher-Nom   criticized   (*fact*)

In the deviant (2a), an anaphor *otagai* "each other" inside SUBJ (Subject) is
unbound; hence, Binding Condition A (BC-A) is violated. In the well-formed
(2b), OBJ is scrambled to the sentence-initial position, where OBJ binds the
anaphor inside SUBJ. The observed contrast suggests that clause-internal
scrambling can form an A-chain (whose head binds the anaphor inside SUBJ,
serving as its antecedent).

Saito further argues that clause-internal scrambling can, but need not, form
an A-chain. Consider (3a, b):

(3) a.   [karera-ga [otagai-no sensei]-o   hihansita] *(koto)*
      they-Nom e.o.-Gen   teacher-Acc criticized *(fact)*
      "They criticized each other's teachers"

   b.   [[otagai-no sensei]-o   [karera-ga *t* hihansita]] *(koto)*
      e.o.-Gen   teacher-Acc they-Nom   criticized *(fact)*

In the well-formed (3a), an anaphor inside OBJ is bound by SUBJ; hence, BC-A is satisfied. In the well-formed (3b), OBJ is scrambled to the sentence-initial position, where the anaphor inside scrambled OBJ is unbound. The nondeviant status of (3b) suggests that clause-internal scrambling need not form an A-chain (otherwise, a violation of BC-A would necessarily result in (3b)).

    Based on data such as (2b) and (3b), Saito (1992) proposes that scrambling is movement to a nonoperator, non-A-position, but the landing site of clause-internal scrambling can be reanalyzed as an A-position at LF.[1] The reanalysis of the landing site is determined by the timing of Case marking. Saito first assumes that a verb undergoes LF movement, but Case marking may occur either before or after LF verb movement (dispensing with the S-structure application of Case Filter). He then proposes that the landing site of clause-internal scrambling becomes part of an A-chain (serving as an antecedent for a lexical anaphor) if it is Case-marked by the raised V; otherwise, it undergoes deletion. Saito further argues that the reanalysis of the landing site follows from Chomsky's (1981, 1986) Chain Condition. Consider (4).

(4) If $C = (\alpha_1, \ldots, \alpha_n)$ is a maximal chain, then α_n occupies its unique θ-position and α_1 its unique Case-marked position.

Given (4), depending on the timing of Case marking (with respect to LF verb movement), clause-internal scrambling yields two distinct LF representations: one involves Case marking before LF verb movement; the other involves Case marking after LF verb movement. Under these assumptions, Saito assigns the following LF representations to (2b) and (3b), respectively:

(5) a.   [$_{IP}$ karera-o [[otagai-no sensei]-ga   [[$_{VP}$ t_{OBJ} t_V] V+INFL]]]
      they-Acc   e.o.-Gen   teacher-Nom

   b.   [$_{IP}$ Ø [karera-ga [[$_{VP}$ [otagai-no sensei]-o t_V] V+INFL]]]
      they-Nom   e.o.-Gen   teacher-Acc

In (5a) (assigned to (2b)), where Case marking occurs after LF verb movement, OBJ is Case-marked in the scrambled position. This position, therefore being part of an A-chain, remains at LF, serving as a binder for the anaphor inside SUBJ. In (5b) (assigned to (3b)), where Case marking occurs before LF verb movement, OBJ is Case-marked in situ. The scrambled position, therefore not being part of an A-chain, undergoes deletion (as indicated by Ø). In this LF representation, SUBJ binds the anaphor inside in situ OBJ.[2]

As shown above, Saito's (1992) analysis captures the nondeviant status of (2b) and (3b), articulating how clause-internal scrambling interacts with verb movement, chain formation, and Binding Theory. His analysis, however, confronts the following problem. Consider (6a, b):

(6) a. *[kare$_1$-ga [Masao$_1$-no hahaoya]-o aisiteiru] *(koto)*
         he-Nom Masao-Gen mother-Acc love   *(fact)*
         "He$_1$ loves Masao$_1$'s mother"

     b. ?*[Masao$_1$-no hahaoya]-o [kare$_1$-ga *t* aisiteiru]] *(koto)*
         Masao-Gen mother-Acc he-Nom love   *(fact)*

In the deviant (6a), an R-expression *Masao* inside OBJ is bound by SUBJ; hence, Binding Condition C (BC-C) is violated. In the deviant (6b), OBJ is scrambled to the sentence-initial position, where the R-expression inside scrambled OBJ is unbound; hence, a violation of BC-C should be circumvented, but (6b) still exhibits deviance (with the intended interpretation). The deviant status of (6b) poses a problem for Saito's reanalysis of scrambling sites. Consider the following two LF representations available to (6b):

(7) a. [$_{IP}$ Ø [kare$_1$-ga [[$_{VP}$ [Masao$_1$-no hahaoya]-o t_V] V+INFL]]]
         he-Nom   Masao-Gen mother-Acc

     b. [$_{IP}$ [Masao$_1$-no hahaoya]-o [kare$_1$-ga [[$_{VP}$ t_{OBJ} t_V] V+INFL]]]
         Masao-Gen mother-Acc he-Nom

In (7a), where Case marking occurs before LF verb movement, OBJ is Case-marked in situ. The scrambled position, therefore, not being part of an A-chain, undergoes deletion. In this LF representation, SUBJ binds the R-expression inside in situ OBJ, thereby inducing a violation of BC-C. In (7b), where Case marking occurs after LF verb movement, OBJ is Case-marked in the scrambled position. This position, therefore, being part of an A-chain, remains at LF. In this LF representation, SUBJ does not bind the R-expression inside scrambled OBJ; hence, a violation of BC-C should be circumvented. Given the deviant status of (6b), (7b) cannot be an LF representation of (6b).

Suppose that the scrambled position cannot be Case-marked. Then, (7b) won't be generated (as desired). But, under this assumption, the nondeviant status of (2b) will be a problem. That is, under Saito's analysis, the landing site of scrambling must be Case-marked in order to allow the coreferential interpretation of *karera* and *otagai* in (2b), but it must not be Case-marked in order to force the disjoint interpretation of *kare* and *Masao* in (6b).

Saito (1992) acknowledges (6b) as a problem for his analysis. To ensure the disjoint interpretation in question, he proposes that BC-C must apply not solely at LF, but at some pre-LF level as well. He suggests that a violation of BC-C cannot be circumvented if BC-C applies at D-structure (prior to the application of clause-internal scrambling) (cf. Van Riemsdijk and Williams 1981; Lebeaux 1988). But this "pre-LF level" analysis poses a problem for the conception of LF, adopted in *The Minimalist Program* (MP) (Chomsky 1995). Consider (8):

(8)   LF is the only level where syntactic relations are expressed for interpretation.

Under MP, the linguistic levels are taken to be only those that are assumed to be conceptually necessary, namely, Phonetic Form (PF) and Logical Form (LF). Assuming PF to be a representation in universal phonetics (with no indication of syntactic elements or relations among them), MP adopts (8), which is inconsistent with the "pre-LF level" application of BC-C.

Lebeaux (1995) tries to resolve this inconsistency. He proposes that Binding Conditions apply derivationally, but their results (e.g. a violation of BC-C) are marked and retained for LF. More specifically, under his proposal, (i) BC-C applies at every point of the derivation, (ii) a violation of BC-C is marked as *, and (iii) such information is retained for LF. This "*-marking" analysis seems to resolve the inconsistency between the "pre-LF level" analysis and the conception of LF (8), but in fact it is a notational mechanism encoding into LF representation earlier stages of the derivation (in particular, violations in those earlier stages). Under MP, this aspect of Lebeaux's analysis violates the Inclusiveness Condition (perhaps, the core guiding assumption of MP). Consider (9):

(9)   No new objects are added in the computation apart from rearrangement of lexical features.

Given that * is not a lexical feature, the "*-marking" analysis is an apparent violation of the Inclusiveness Condition.[3] Furthermore, Lebeaux's derivational application of Binding Conditions contradicts the conception of LF (8) if Binding Conditions are (as seems natural) taken to be part of interpretive procedures (in the sense of Chomsky and Lasnik 1993), which, by definition, apply only at LF.[4]

Given the preceding discussion, I conclude that the binding phenomena reviewed here constitute a serious problem. Adopting this conclusion, I would like to pursue a different path which elaborates Saito's (1992) proposal (that the Binding Theory applies not solely at LF, but at some pre-LF level as well) under the framework of Epstein et al. (1998). In what follows, I first specify the mechanisms of scrambling in Japanese, adopting certain aspects of the probe–goal system (Chomsky 2000, 2001). I then explore how these mechanisms of scrambling interact with the interpretive procedures, yielding the observed interpretations of (2b), (3b), and (6b). The paper is organized as follows: In section 2, I identify a crucial distinction within the probe–goal system, which implements the observed instances of scrambling. In section 3, adopting the framework of Epstein et al. (1998), I address the question of how the probe–goal system (which implements scrambling) interacts with the interpretive procedures (applying in the course of a derivation). In section 4, I provide a unified account of (2b), (3b), and (6b) under the strongly derivational model of syntax. In section 5, I point out that the proposed analysis captures one important aspect of long-distance scrambling in Japanese. In section 6, I summarize.

2 Specifying the mechanisms of scrambling

In this section, appealing to a crucial distinction within the probe–goal system (Chomsky 2000, 2001), I specify the mechanisms that implement the observed instances of scrambling. Let us first review the relevant aspects of the probe–goal system.

Chomsky (2000) proposes that lexical subarray LA_i contains exactly one C or v, determining clause or verb phrase. A syntactic object derived from LA_i is called a phase, and a derivation is generated in a "phase by phase" fashion. Under these assumptions, Chomsky formulates the Phase Impenetrability Condition (PIC). Consider (10):[5]

(10) In phase α with head H, the domain of H is not accessible to operations outside α; only H and its edge are accessible to such operations.

Now notice, under PIC, any movement out of α will depart from the edge of α (or H). Thus, in any derivation D involving the scrambling of OBJ to the sentence-initial position, OBJ must undergo Object Shift (OS) and occupy SPEC-v, prior to the completion of vP. As a result, the probing of T to SUBJ in D necessarily takes place in the following structure:

(11) $[_{TP} [_{vP} \text{OBJ-Acc} [_{v'} \text{SUBJ-Nom} [_{v'} [_{VP} t_{OBJ} \text{V}] v]]] \text{T}]$

There are three kinds of uninterpretable features in (11): (i) the ϕ-set of T, (ii) the EPP of T, and (iii) the Case of SUBJ. The ϕ-set of T is taken to be a probe that seeks to match the ϕ-set of SUBJ, but shifted OBJ intervenes between T and SUBJ. If the first matching ϕ-set of OBJ (occupying the position of OS) interferes with the further search of probe T, then the derivation will crash due to the failure of the probing of T to SUBJ, contrary to fact.

The same problem arises in English. Chomsky (2001) points out that there is no other way to derive (12) if PIC is correct:

(12) (guess) what$_{OBJ}$ [John$_{SUBJ}$ T $[_{vP} t'_{OBJ} [t_{SUBJ}$ read $t_{OBJ}]]]$

In (12), OBJ moves first to SPEC-v, then to SPEC-C, which means that T must be able to "bypass" the first matching OBJ (occupying the position of OS) to raise SUBJ to SPEC-T. Chomsky implements this "bypass" analysis as follows. He first assumes that the subsequent movement of OBJ from SPEC-v to SPEC-C, in effect, licenses the probe–goal relation between T and SUBJ. He then proposes (13), for the structure: $\alpha > \beta > \Gamma$ (where > is c-command, β and Γ match the probe α):

(13) The first matching β prevents Match of α and Γ only if β has phonological content.

Chomsky further assumes that the probe–goal relation is evaluated for (13) at the next strong phase level, meaning that (13) is no longer a constraint on the application of Agree/Move. He suggests that, optimally, the operation Agree/Move, like others, should apply freely. Under these assumptions, SUBJ is allowed to move to SPEC-T over shifted OBJ, and the probe–goal relation between T and SUBJ is evaluated for (13) after it is known whether the position of OS has become a trace (losing its phonological content). If OBJ has no phonological content in the position of OS (as in (12)), it does not prevent Match of T and SUBJ, under (13).

Interestingly, Chomsky's analysis of (12) (incorporating (13)) extends to the derivation D involving scrambling. Here, OBJ undergoes scrambling prior to the completion of CP; consequently, OBJ has no phonological content in the position of OS when the probe–goal relation between T and SUBJ is evaluated for (13). Following Chomsky (2001), I assume that Agree of T and SUBJ can take place in D (valuing the ϕ-set of T and the Case of SUBJ), provided that, in D, the position of OS becomes a trace (losing its phonological content), prior to the next strong phase level (namely, CP).

The next question is, then, whether the scrambling of OBJ (from the position of OS to the sentence-initial position) can take place under this probe–goal system. The relevant uninterpretable feature is the EPP of T. Like other selectional features, the EPP of T seeks XP to merge with TP. In MP, Chomsky assigns the following option to EPP, allowing multiple specifiers (in languages like Japanese). Consider (14) (adapted from Chomsky 1995):

(14)   EPP has an option of remaining active even after merger.

If the EPP of T exercises this option once, C_{HL} merges two XPs with TP. Adopting this proposal, let us ask whether C_{HL} can map (11) to (15):

(15) $[_{TP}$ OBJ-Acc [SUBJ-Nom $[[_{vP} t'_{OBJ} [t_{SUBJ} [[_{VP} t_{OBJ} V] v]]]$ T]]]

Suppose that the EPP of T exercises this option once. Then, we would expect that C_{HL} merges SUBJ and OBJ with TP, yielding multiple specifiers of T (as in (15)). Under the probe–goal system, Agree of T and SUBJ selects SUBJ as a candidate for such merger. Thus, the merger of SUBJ with TP is permitted. But what about OBJ? It seems that there is no means to select OBJ for such merger. Note that Match of T and OBJ does not induce Agree of T and OBJ because OBJ is inactive in the position of OS, and EPP alone is not sufficient to induce movement because EPP is not a matching feature. Thus, the merger of OBJ with TP – the scrambling of OBJ to the sentence-initial position – is blocked; (15) is not generable under current assumptions.

At this point, there are several ways to proceed. I would like to pursue the possibility that the probe–goal system provides a crucial distinction, which gives C_{HL} a means to select OBJ for this type of merger/movement. Let us examine A-movement and scrambling under current assumptions.

Under the probe–goal system, A-movement may be characterized as follows:

(16)   A-movement is an instance of Agree-driven movement which values uninterpretable features and satisfies EPP.

The guiding intuition is that agreement licenses movement. But notice, there is a prerequisite for agreement, namely, matching. Assuming that these two relations (namely, matching and agreement) are available, scrambling may be characterized as follows:

(17)   Scrambling is an instance of Match-driven movement (supplementing Agree) which satisfies only EPP.

Given (16) and (17), I suggest that both Match-driven and Agree-driven movement are permitted in languages like Japanese.[6] Note that, under current assumptions, Match-driven movement, if permitted, is restricted to a supplement to the operation Agree, because an "extra" matching relation is necessarily a byproduct of an agreement relation under the probe–goal system. In mapping (11) to (15), for example, it is Agree of T and SUBJ that uses its supplementary relation (namely, Match of T and OBJ) to select OBJ for the satisfaction of the EPP of T. More specifically, Agree of T and SUBJ selects SUBJ for first merger with TP, and Match of T and OBJ selects OBJ for second merger with TP. The precedence of Agree-driven movement over Match-driven movement arguably follows from the supplementary nature of the latter.

Let us then proceed with this suggestion, namely, both Match-driven and Agree-driven movement are permitted in Japanese, and scrambling is taken to be an instance of Match-driven movement.

3   A strongly derivational model of syntax

In this section, adopting the framework of Epstein et al. (1998), I address the question of how the probe–goal system (allowing Match-driven movement) interacts with the interpretive procedures (applying in the course of a derivation). Let us first review the relevant aspects of the strongly derivational model of syntax (outlined in Epstein et al. 1998).

Recall that, within MP, the syntactic component is understood to be derivational in that C_{HL} selects lexical items from a numeration and performs a partially ordered structure-building procedure by applying successive applications of concatenation. The operation concatenation is an elementary operation shared by Merge and Move (Kitahara 1994, 1997). Assuming this elementary operation to be a fundamental property of C_{HL}, Epstein (1994, 1999) proposes a derivational model of syntax under which syntactically significant relations (such as c-command) are derived from the way lexical items and phrases are concatenated by C_{HL}. That is, the operation concatenation (putting two categories together) naturally enough establishes a syntactic relation (between the two categories to which the operation applies).

Epstein et al. (1998) further examine a number of phenomena exhibiting syntactic relations that are necessary for interpretation but cannot be represented simultaneously at any single point of a derivation.[7] The presence of such syntactic relations poses a serious problem for the conception of LF (8). To resolve this problem, Epstein et al. assign the derivational approach further prominence. They propose that C_{HL} not only determines syntactic relations but also provides such information directly for the interface systems in the course of a derivation. Under this strongly derivational model of syntax, Binding Conditions are understood to be part of derivational interpretive procedures (applying in the course of a derivation) – a clear departure from the conception of LF (8).[8]

The derivational application of interpretive procedures requires further elaboration. In particular, it is necessary to determine exactly when the LF system interprets lexical items (LIs) in the course of a derivation. One possibility that I would like to pursue is stated in (18) (Kitahara 1999, 2000: 155):

(18)   The LF system interprets LIs as they become interpretable (losing LF-uninterpretable features) in the course of a derivation.

Suppose that Case is the only uninterpretable feature borne by NP.[9] Then, under (18), the LF system interprets NP as Spell Out deletes Case from NP. It is only the presence of Case that renders NP inaccessible to the LF system.[10] Given this assumption, the question comes down to the application of Spell Out.

In MP, it has been assumed that the uninterpretable features must be removed from the narrow syntax (allowing derivations to converge at LF) but left available for the PF component (yielding language-variant PF-manifestation). This assumption poses a problem if Spell Out applies at a single point of a derivation. Chomsky (2000: 131) states this contradictory property of feature-deletion as follows:

(19)   Pre-Spell Out, the probe must delete when checked but yet remain until Spell Out.

To resolve this problem, he suggests that deleted features are literally erased, but only after they are sent to the phonological component. In the subsequent work, Chomsky (2001) elaborates this point. He assumes that the uninterpretable features, and only these, enter the derivation without values, and are distinguished from interpretable features by virtue of this property. Given this assumption, it follows that the uninterpretable features must delete when valued; otherwise, they will be indistinguishable from interpretable features at LF. Chomsky, thus, concludes that Spell Out applies cyclically (cyclic Spell Out). Specifically, under his system, Spell Out applies "shortly after" the uninterpretable features have been assigned values. The notion "shortly after" is taken to be at the relevant strong-phase level.[11]

Epstein and Seely (2000) suggest that Chomsky's (2001) argument for the existence of cyclic Spell Out is problematic. They point out that, if the distinction between interpretable and uninterpretable features is lost after valuation, then the distinction is necessarily lost "shortly after" valuation as well. To resolve this problem, Epstein and Seely eliminate the notion "shortly after" and propose that Spell Out strips away those newly valued uninterpretable features during the process of valuation itself.

In this paper, following Epstein and Seely (2000), I assume that Spell Out strips away Case from the narrow syntax in the process of valuation. I also assume Chomsky's (2000, 2001) Case-valuation analysis, where Case is understood as a single undifferentiated feature, and PF-manifestation of Case depends on probe: Nominative (Nom) for T, Accusative (Acc) for v, and Genitive (Gen) for D.[12] From these assumptions, it follows that the LF system interprets NP as the Case of NP is valued (and deleted) in the course of a derivation.[13] Note that, under this proposed analysis, interpretation may occur after certain transformations apply, yet before other transformations apply. This is impossible under the standard Y-model of syntax, where interpretation is performed upon the unique LF representation generated only after all transformations apply.[14]

4   A derivational analysis of binding relations

In this section, adopting the probe–goal system (which implements scrambling) and the strongly derivational system (which interprets NP in the course of a derivation), I argue that the binding phenomena reviewed in section 1 follow from the interaction of these two systems. Let us examine (2a, b), (3a, b), and (6a, b) in detail.

Recall (2a, b) (repeated here), where scrambling provides the setting for coreferential interpretation of OBJ and the anaphor (inside SUBJ):

(2)   a.   ?*[[otagai-no sensei]-ga   karera-o hihansita] (*koto*)
                 e.o.-Gen   teacher-Nom they-Acc criticized (*fact*)
           "Each other's teachers criticized them"

      b.   ?[karera-o [[otagai-no sensei]-ga   *t* hihansita]] (*koto*)
              they-Acc e.o.-Gen   teacher-Nom   criticized   (*fact*)

First examine the relevant aspects of the derivation of (2a). Consider (20):

(20)   a.   [$_{vP}$ [otagai-no sensei]-ga   [[$_{VP}$ karera-o V] v]]
                    e.o.-Gen   teacher-Nom   they-Acc

       b.   [$_{TP}$ [otagai-no sensei]-ga [[$_{vP}$ t_{SUBJ} [[$_{VP}$ karera-o V] v]] T]]
                    e.o.-Gen   teacher-Nom   they-Acc

In (20a), Agree of v and OBJ values the Case of OBJ.[15] The anaphor inside SUBJ has already been valued; hence, the LF system is working on the anaphor, in particular, BC-A is searching for a c-commanding phrase for the anaphor. In (20b), Agree of T and SUBJ merges SUBJ with TP and values the Case of SUBJ. Notice, in this derivation, OBJ remains in situ (where OBJ does not c-command the anaphor); hence, there is no chance for BC-A to establish coreferential interpretation of OBJ and the anaphor.

Now examine the relevant aspects of the derivation of (2b). Consider (21):

(21) a. $[_{vP}$ karera-o $[[$otagai-no sensei$]$-ga $[[_{VP} t_{OBJ}$ V$]$ $v]]]$
          they-Acc   e.o.-Gen   teacher-Nom

     b. $[_{TP} [$otagai-no sensei$]$-ga $[[_{vP}$ karera-o $[t_{SUBJ} [[_{VP} t_{OBJ}$ V$]$ $v]]]$ T$]]$
              e.o.-Gen   teacher-Nom   they-Acc

     c. $[_{TP}$ karera-o $[[$otagai-no sensei$]$-ga $[[_{vP} t'_{OBJ} [t_{SUBJ} [[_{VP} t_{OBJ}$ V$]$ $v]]]$ T$]]]$
              they-Acc   e.o.-Gen   teacher-Nom

In (21a), Agree of v and OBJ merges OBJ with vP and values the Case of OBJ. At this point of the derivation, BC-A can and does interpret the anaphor as coreferential with OBJ. In (21b), Agree of T and SUBJ merges SUBJ with TP and values the Case of SUBJ. Suppose that the EPP of T remains active even after this merger of SUBJ with TP. Then, Agree of T and SUBJ appeals to its supplementary relation (namely, Match of T and OBJ) and merges OBJ with TP, yielding (21c). Under current assumptions, these two instances of merger have nothing to do with the already established coreferential interpretation of OBJ and the anaphor (though the second merger satisfies the EPP of T and leaves a trace in the position of OS).

Recall (3a, b) (repeated here), where scrambling does not interfere with the setting for coreferential interpretation of SUBJ and the anaphor (inside OBJ).

(3) a. [karera-ga [otagai-no sensei]-o   hihansita] (*koto*)
          they-Nom e.o.-Gen   teacher-Acc criticized (*fact*)
          "They criticized each other's teachers"

     b. [[otagai-no sensei]-o   [karera-ga t hihansita]] (*koto*)
              e.o.-Gen   teacher-Acc they-Nom   criticized   (*fact*)

First examine the relevant aspects of the derivation of (3a). Consider (22):

(22) a. $[_{vP}$ karera-ga $[[_{VP} [$otagai-no sensei$]$-o V$]$ $v]]$
          they-Nom   e.o.-Gen   teacher-Acc

     b. $[_{TP}$ karera-ga $[[_{vP} t_{SUBJ} [[_{VP} [$otagai-no sensei$]$-o V$]$ $v]]$ T$]]$
              they-Nom   e.o.-Gen   teacher-Acc

In (22a), Agree of v and OBJ values the Case of OBJ. The anaphor inside OBJ has already been valued; hence, the LF system is working on the anaphor, in particular, BC-A is searching for a c-commanding phrase for the anaphor. In

(22b), Agree of T and SUBJ merges SUBJ with TP and values the Case of SUBJ. At this point of the derivation, BC-A can and does interpret the anaphor as coreferential with SUBJ.

Now examine the relevant aspects of the derivation of (3b). Consider (23):

(23)   a. $[_{vP}$ [otagai-no sensei]-o   [karera-ga $[[_{VP} t_{OBJ}$ V] $v]]]$
            e.o.-Gen   teacher-Acc   they-Nom

    b. $[_{TP}$ karera-ga $[[_{vP}$ [otagai-no sensei]-o $[t_{SUBJ} [[_{VP} t_{OBJ}$ V] $v]]]$ T]]
            they-Nom   e.o.-Gen   teacher-Acc

    c. $[_{TP}$ [otagai-no sensei]-o   [karera-ga $[[_{vP} t'_{OBJ} [t_{SUBJ} [[_{VP} t_{OBJ}$ V] $v]]]$ T]]]
            e.o.-Gen   teacher-Acc they-Nom

In (23a), Agree of v and OBJ merges OBJ with vP and values the Case of OBJ. In (23b), Agree of T and SUBJ merges SUBJ with TP and values the Case of SUBJ. At this point of the derivation, BC-A can and does interpret the anaphor as coreferential with SUBJ. Suppose that the EPP of T remains active even after this merger of SUBJ with TP. Then, Agree of T and SUBJ appeals to its supplementary relation (namely, Match of T and OBJ) and merges OBJ with TP, yielding (23c). Under current assumptions, this second merger does not interfere with the already established coreferential interpretation of SUBJ and the anaphor.

Recall (6a, b) (repeated here), where scrambling does not interfere with the setting for disjoint interpretation of SUBJ and the R-expression (inside OBJ):

(6)   a.   *[kare$_1$-ga [Masao$_1$-no hahaoya]-o aisiteiru] (*koto*)
            he-Nom Masao-Gen mother-Acc love   (*fact*)
            "He$_1$ loves Masao$_1$'s mother"

    b.   ?*[Masao$_1$-no hahaoya]-o [kare$_1$-ga *t* aisiteiru]] (*koto*)
            Masao-Gen mother-Acc he-Nom   love   (*fact*)

First examine the relevant aspects of the derivation of (6a). Consider (24):

(24)   a. $[_{vP}$ kare-ga $[[_{VP}$ [Masao-no   hahaoya]-o V] $v]]$
            he-Nom   Masao-Gen mother-Acc

    b. $[_{TP}$ kare-ga $[[_{vP} t_{SUBJ} [[_{VP}$ [Masao-no   hahaoya]-o V] $v]]$ T]]
            he-Nom   Masao-Gen mother-Acc

In (24a), Agree of v and OBJ values the Case of OBJ. The R-expression inside SUBJ has already been valued; hence, the LF system is working on the R-expression, in particular, BC-C is interpreting the R-expression as disjoint from every c-commanding phrase.[16] In (24b), Agree of T and SUBJ merges SUBJ with TP and values the Case of SUBJ. At this point of the derivation, BC-C can and must interpret the R-expression as disjoint from SUBJ.

Now examine the relevant aspects of the derivation of (3b). Consider (25):

(25)   a.   [$_{v}$P [Masao-no   hahaoya]-o [kare-ga [[$_{VP}$ t_{OBJ} V] v]]]
            Masao-Gen mother-Acc   he-Nom

    b.   [$_{TP}$ kare-ga [[$_{v}$P [Masao-no   hahaoya]-o [t_{SUBJ} [[$_{VP}$ t_{OBJ} V] v]]] T]]
            he-Nom   Masao-Gen mother-Acc

    c.   [$_{TP}$ [Masao-no   hahaoya]-o [kare-ga [[$_{v}$P t'_{OBJ} [t_{SUBJ} [[$_{VP}$ t_{OBJ} V] v]]] T]]]
            Masao-Gen mother-Acc he-Nom

In (25a), Agree of v and OBJ merges OBJ with vP and values the Case of OBJ. In (25b), Agree of T and SUBJ merges SUBJ with TP and values the Case of SUBJ. At this point of the derivation, BC-C can and must interpret the R-expression as disjoint from SUBJ. Suppose that the EPP of T remains active even after this merger of SUBJ with TP. Then, Agree of T and SUBJ appeals to its supplementary relation (namely, Match of T and OBJ) and merges OBJ with TP, yielding (25c). Under current assumptions, this second merger does not interfere with the already established disjoint interpretation of SUBJ and the R-expression.

As demonstrated above, under the strongly derivational model of syntax (dispensing with the conception of LF (8)), the binding-theoretic problem (posed by (2b) and (6b)) is resolved derivationally. The proposed derivational analysis captures all the cases discussed in section 1, and does so without inducing a violation of the Inclusiveness Condition.[17]

5   Long-distance scrambling

In this section, I point out one immediate consequence of the proposed analysis, which involves long-distance scrambling. Japanese allows OBJ to undergo scrambling to the sentence-initial position out of an embedded clause, as in (26a, b).

(26)   a.   [Hanako-ga   [[Taroo-ga   sono hon-o   katta]   to]
            Hanako-Nom   Taroo-Nom that book-Acc bought that
            omotteiru] (*koto*)
            think   (*fact*)
            "Hanako thinks that Taro bought that book"

    b.   [sono hon-o   [Hanako-ga   [[Taroo-ga   *t* katta]   to]
            that book-Acc Hanako-Nom   Taroo-Nom   bought that
            omotteiru]] (*koto*)
            think   (*fact*)

It has been observed that long-distance scrambling neither provides nor interferes with the setting for the binding interpretation in the matrix clause. Now suppose, as argued in the preceding sections, the LF system interprets NP as the Case of NP is valued (and deleted) in the course of a derivation. Then this observation naturally follows, because long-distance scrambling is necessarily movement of already interpreted NP, whose Case was valued (and deleted) in the embedded clause. Consider data such as (27a, b), where this "semantically vacuous" aspect of long-distance scrambling is exhibited (see among others, Oka 1989; Saito 1989, 1992; Tada 1990):

(27) a. *[[otagai-no sensei]-ga   [[Hanako-ga   karera-o hihansita]
           e.g.-Gen teacher-Nom   Hanako-Nom they-Acc criticized
           to]   itta] (*koto*)
           that said (*fact*)
           "Each other's teachers said that Hanako criticized them"

      b. *[karera-o [[otagai-no sensei]-ga   [[Hanako-ga *t* hihansita]
           they-Acc e.g.-Gen teacher-Nom   Hanako-Nom criticized
           to]   itta]] (*koto*)
           that said (*fact*)

The deviant status of (27a, b) suggests that BC-A fails to establish coreferential interpretation of embedded OBJ and the anaphor inside matrix SUBJ. This failure of BC-A follows if OBJ was already interpreted when the Case of OBJ was valued (and deleted) in the embedded clause.[18]

6 Summary

In this paper, after the brief review of the binding-theoretic problem involving scrambling (posed by (2b) and (6b)), I pointed out the inconsistency between Saito's (1992) solution to this problem and the conception of LF (8) (adopted in MP). To resolve this inconsistency, I first specified the mechanisms of scrambling within the probe–goal system. Specifically, appealing to the distinction between matching and agreement, I proposed that scrambling is an instance of Match-driven movement. I then advanced the strongly derivational approach with the proposal that the LF system interprets NP as the Case of NP is valued (and deleted) in the course of a derivation. Under these proposals, I presented the derivational solution to the binding-theoretic problem. I demonstrated that the proposed derivational analysis resolves this problem (along with all other cases discussed in section 1) without inducing a violation of the Inclusiveness Condition. Finally, I pointed out that, under current assumptions, long-distance scrambling of NP is necessarily movement of already interpreted NP, whose Case was valued (and deleted) in the embedded clause; hence, the "semantically vacuous" aspect of long-distance scrambling follows without any stipulation.

Acknowledgments

I would like to thank Jun Abe, Noam Chomsky, Norbert Hornstein, Yasuo Ishii, Noriko Kawasaki, Ruriko Kawashima, Howard Lasnik, Roger Martin, Yoichi Miyamoto, Masayuki Oishi, T. Daniel Seely, and especially Samuel D. Epstein and Mamoru Saito for valuable comments and helpful discussion. Part of the material in this paper was presented at Tokyo Metropolitan University (5th Tokyo Area Circle of Linguistics Summer Conference), University of Konstanz (21st Deutsche Gesellschaft für Sprachwissenschaft Workshop), Nanzan University (2nd Generative Linguistics in the Old World Conference in Asia), Massachusetts Institute of Technology (the Ling-Lunch, Spring 2000), and University of Amsterdam (the LOT Winter School 2001). I am grateful to the participants for clarifying remarks. Also, special gratitude goes to the following two institutions where this research was conducted: the Institute of Cultural and Linguistic Studies at Keio University and the Department of Linguistics and Philosophy at Massachusetts Institute of Technology. An earlier version of part of this paper appeared in *Keio Studies in Theoretical Linguistics II*. The research reported here was supported in part by the J. William Fulbright Foreign Scholarship and the Matsushita International Foundation. I am grateful to each foundation for its generous support.

Notes

1 See also Webelhuth (1989), Mahajan (1990), Tada (1990), Nemoto (1993), and Miyagawa (1997).
2 Note that the Chain Condition, being a definition, fails to answer questions such as: Why is Case relevant for the determination of a chain at LF? In section 3, I develop a derivational analysis of Case and interpretability, which provides an arguably natural answer to this question.
3 Similarly, Chomsky and Lasnik's (1993) "*-marking" analysis of movement asymmetries (a descendant of Lasnik and Saito's (1984, 1992) "γ-marking" analysis) violates the Inclusiveness Condition. For detailed discussion of their analysis, see Kitahara (1999).
4 Chomsky and Lasnik (1993) propose the interpretive version of Binding Theory, under which the indexing and interpretive procedures are unified along with the Binding Conditions themselves. Consider (i) (where D is the relevant local domain):

(i) A. If α is an anaphor, interpret it as coreferential with some c-commanding phrase in D.

　　 B. If α is a pronominal, interpret it as disjoint from every c-commanding phrase in D.

　　 C. If α is an R-expression, interpret it as disjoint from every c-commanding phrase.

They assume that the interpretive version of Binding Theory applies solely at LF. In sections 3 and 4, departing from this assumption (more specifically, the conception of LF (8)), I will reformulate the interpretive version of Binding Theory under the framework of Epstein et al. (1998).

5   The edge is understood as the residue of H-bar, either SPECs or elements adjoined to HP (= α). For detailed discussion of PIC, see Chomsky (2000, 2001).

6   To some extent, the distinction between "Agree-driven" and "Match-driven" movement can be seen as the revival of the distinction between "forced" and "unforced" ϕ-agreement (in the sense of Fukui 1986 and Kuroda 1988).

7   Epstein et al. (1998) examine problematic cases such as (i) (see also Brody 1995).

(i)   Mary wondered [which claim [that pictures of herself disturbed Bill]] he made *t*

In (i), *herself* takes *Mary* as antecedent, and *he* cannot take *Bill* as antecedent. This interpretation of (i) imposes the following contradictory requirements on the minimization of the restriction in the operator position:

(ii)   The restriction in the operator position must be minimized in order to force the disjoint interpretation of *he* and *Bill*, but it must not be minimized in order to allow (a licit θ-theoretic representation of) the coreferential interpretation of *Mary* and *herself*.

Given that there is no way to both "minimize and not minimize" the restriction in the operator position, the syntactic relations required for the interpretation of (i) cannot be represented simultaneously at any single point of a derivation. See Epstein et al. (1998) for more detailed discussion of (i) and other problematic cases.

8   See Epstein and Seely (1999, 2000) for recent developments in the strongly derivational model.

9   In this paper, I discuss only A-chain properties of NP.

10   Following Chomsky (2000, 2001), I assume that features are accessed not selectively. This assumption is arguably simpler than its alternative that features are accessed selectively, since the latter increases the degree of operative complexity.

11   See also Uriagereka 1999, where he argues for multiple application of Spell Out, based on different grounds.

12   I am extending Chomsky's (2000, 2001) Case-valuation analysis to Genitive.

13   The proposed analysis can be seen as an elaboration of Epstein (1992), where he derives the "last resort" property of NP-movement from the assumption that NP becomes an LF object upon the satisfaction of its Case. See also Chomsky (1986) and Pesetsky (1989) for relevant discussion.

14   If NP receives a θ-theoretic interpretation when introduced into a derivation, then the valuation/deletion of Case may mean the completion of the derivational interpretive procedure of NP. The task of clarifying this θ-theoretic issue, however, requires further investigation.

15   Note that, under the probe–goal system, Agree can establish a Case-agreement relation between probe and goal without movement.

16   Following Lebeaux (1995), I assume that the disjoint interpretive procedure continues to operate throughout the derivation.

17   Suppose that Θ-theoretic interpretation is determined in the strict cyclic fashion, along the line suggested in note 14. Then, the notion "trace" may be dispensable – at least for A-type movement. For recent discussion of this issue, see Epstein et al. (1998), Epstein and Seely (1999, 2000), Hornstein (1998), and Lasnik (1999).

18   In section 2, I proposed that clause-internal scrambling is an instance of Match-driven movement, which is, in effect, a byproduct of the probing of the ϕ-set. Concerning long-distance scrambling, a number of questions arise: Is long-distance scrambling also an instance of Match-driven movement? If so, the probing of what feature makes available a supplementary matching relation for long-distance scrambling? Needless to say, these questions require further investigation.

References

Brody, Michael. 1995. *Lexico-Logical Form: A Radically Minimalist Theory*. Cambridge, MA: MIT Press.

Chomsky, Noam. 1981. *Lectures on Government and Binding*. Dordrecht: Foris.

Chomsky, Noam. 1986. *Knowledge of Language: Its Nature, Origin, and Use*. New York: Praeger.

Chomsky, Noam. 1995. *The Minimalist Program*. Cambridge, MA: MIT Press.

Chomsky, Noam. 2000. "Minimalist inquiries: The framework." In *Step By Step: Essays on Minimalist Syntax in Honor of Howard Lasnik*, eds. Roger Martin, David Michaels, and Juan Uriagereka, Cambridge, MA: MIT Press, pp. 89–155.

Chomsky, Noam. 2001. "Derivation By Phase," In *Ken Hale: A Life in Language*, ed. Michael Kenstowicz, Cambridge, MA: MIT Press, pp. 1–52.

Chomsky, Noam and Howard Lasnik. 1993. "The theory of principles and parameters." In *Syntax: An International Handbook of Contemporary Research*, eds. Joachim Jacobs, Arnim von Stechow, Wolfgang Sternefeld, and Theo Vennemann, Berlin: Walter de Gruyter, pp. 506–69. [Reprinted in *The Minimalist Program*, 13–127. Cambridge, MA: MIT Press, 1995.]

Epstein, Samuel D. 1992. "Derivational constraints on A'-chain formation." *Linguistic Inquiry* 23: 235–59.

Epstein, Samuel D. 1994. "The derivation of syntactic relations." MS, Harvard University.

Epstein, Samuel D. 1999. "Un-Principled syntax and the derivation of syntactic relations." In *Working Minimalism*, eds. Samuel D. Epstein and Norbert Hornstein, Cambridge, MA: MIT Press, pp. 317–45.

Epstein, Samuel D., Erich M. Groat, Ruriko Kawashima, and Hisatsugu Kitahara. 1998. *A Derivational Approach to Syntactic Relations*. New York: Oxford University Press.

Epstein, Samuel D. and T. Daniel Seely. 1999. "SPEC-cifying the GF 'subject;' eliminating A-chains and the EPP within a derivational model." MS, University of Michigan, Ann Arbor and Eastern Michigan University.

Epstein, Samuel D. and T. Daniel Seely. 2000. "Cyclic Spell Out in *Derivation By Phase*." MS, University of Michigan, Ann Arbor and Eastern Michigan University.

Fukui, Naoki. 1986. "A theory of category projection and its application." Doctoral dissertation, MIT, Cambridge, MA.

Hornstein, Norbert. 1998. "Movement and chains." *Syntax* 1: 99–127.

Kitahara, Hisatsugu. 1994. "Target α: a unified theory of movement and structure-building." Doctoral dissertation, Harvard University.

Kitahara, Hisatsugu. 1997. *Elementary Operations and Optimal Derivations*. Cambridge, MA: MIT Press.

Kitahara, Hisatsugu. 1999. "Eliminating * as a feature (of traces)." In *Working Minimalism*, eds. Samuel D. Epstein and Norbert Hornstein, Cambridge, MA: MIT Press, pp. 77–93.

Kitahara, Hisatsugu. 2000. "Two (or more) syntactic categories vs. multiple occurrences of one." *Syntax* 3: 151–8.

Kuroda, Shige-Yuki. 1988. "Whether we agree or not: a comparative syntax of English and Japanese." *Linguisticae Investigationes*, 12, 1–47.

Lasnik, Howard. 1999. "Chains of arguments." In *Working Minimalism*, eds. Samuel D. Epstein and Norbert Hornstein, Cambridge, MA: MIT Press, pp. 189–215.

Lasnik, Howard and Mamoru Saito. 1984. "On the nature of proper government." *Linguistic Inquiry* 15: 235–89.

Lasnik, Howard and Mamoru Saito. 1992. *Move α: Conditions on its Application and Output.* Cambridge, MA: MIT Press.

Lebeaux, David. 1988. "Language acquisition and the form of grammar." PhD dissertation, University of Massachusetts, Amherst.

Lebeaux, David. 1995. "Where does the binding theory apply?" *University of Maryland Working Papers in Linguistics* 3: 63–88.

Mahajan, Anoop. 1990. "The A/A′ distinction and movement theory." Doctoral dissertation, MIT, Cambridge, MA.

Miyagawa, Shigeru. 1997. "Against optional scrambling." *Linguistic Inquiry* 28: 1–25.

Nemoto, Naoko. 1993. "Chains and Case positions: a study from scrambling in Japanese." Doctoral dissertation, University of Connecticut, Storrs.

Oka, Toshifusa. 1989. "On the Spec of IP." MS, MIT, Cambridge, MA.

Pesetsky, David. 1989. "Language particular process and the earliness principle." MS, MIT, Cambridge, MA.

Saito, Mamoru. 1985. "Some asymmetries in Japanese and their theoretical implications." Doctoral dissertation, MIT, Cambridge, MA.

Saito, Mamoru. 1989. "Scrambling as semantically vacuous A′-movement." In *Alternative Conceptions of Phrase Structure*, eds. Mark Baltin and Anthony Kroch, Chicago, IL: University of Chicago Press, pp. 182–200.

Saito, Mamoru. 1992. "Long distance scrambling in Japanese." *Journal of East Asian Linguistics* 1: 69–118.

Tada, Hiroaki. 1990. "A/A′ partition in derivation." Doctoral dissertation, MIT, Cambridge, MA.

Uriagereka, Juan. 1999. "Multiple Spell Out." In *Working Minimalism*, eds. Samuel D. Epstein and Norbert Hornstein, Cambridge, MA: MIT Press, pp. 251–82.

van Riemsdijk, Henk and Edwin Williams. 1981. "NP-Structure." *The Linguistic Review* 1: 171–218.

Webelhuth, Gert. 1989. "Syntactic saturation phenomena and the modern Germanic languages," Doctoral dissertation, University of Massachusetts, Amherst.

Chapter eight

Resumption, Successive Cyclicity, and the Locality of Operations

James McCloskey

1 Background

I will be concerned in this chapter with the mechanisms by which apparently nonlocal A′-connections, such as in (1), are established:

(1) He's <u>the guy</u> that they said they thought they wanted to hire——.

If locality conditions are at the heart of syntax (as increasingly seems to be the case), then the existence of apparently unbounded dependencies like that in (1) represents an anomaly. Since Chomsky (1973) it has come to be widely believed that the apparently distant connection between antecedent and variable position in such cases is in fact mediated by a sequence of more local connections – on one interpretation at least, a sequence of relatively local movements accessing successively higher left-peripheral positions between the variable position and the ultimate binder of that variable position. In all variants of this core idea, the specifier position of CP is one of the crucial left-peripheral positions in establishing these connections (in many variants it is the only such position). Thus, the derivation of (1) can be schematized as in (2):

(2) XP_j [$_{CP}$ t_j C [$_{TP}$ ... [$_{CP}$ t_j C [$_{TP}$ ... t_j ...]]]]

This general line of analysis has gained widespread acceptance – in part because of the theory of island-hood that it underpins, in part because, beginning in the middle 1970s, languages were investigated which provided morphosyntactic confirmation, of one kind or another, for the core idea that seemingly long movements are compositions of more local operations. The relevant languages are ones in which the postulated intermediate movements leave detectable signs of their having applied.

Given what is now a 24-year accumulation of evidence of this type (see Chung 1998: 234ff. for a recent survey), it seems reasonable to conclude that among the things that we have discovered in recent times is that this is in fact how natural language works – movement is always at least this local. A much harder question is the question of what makes this true – what property of language-design determines that this is how things work.

The present chapter tries to say something about these questions. It returns for a closer and more detailed look at the relevant evidence from Irish, and reassesses that evidence in the light of some recent proposals. In particular, it describes some fairly intricate interactions between movement and resumption, tries to understand them, and tries to draw some larger conclusions from that interaction. The analysis ultimately offered draws on ideas about successive cyclicity developed in Chomsky (2000) and Chomsky (2001b).

2   The core pattern and some initial issues

Irish is among the languages which have figured in the debate about successive cyclicity.[1] The reason for this is that finite complementizers in the language vary in form in a way that is sensitive to the presence of A'-binding relationships which reach into the clause of which they are the head. This sensitivity makes available a diagnostic tool by which properties and relationships that are normally hard to detect are rendered more visible.

Finite complement clauses in Irish are normally introduced by the particle *go* (which happens to be combined with the past tense marker -*r* in (3)):

(3)   Creidim gu-r   inis sé bréag.
      I-believe go-[PAST] tell he lie
      "I believe that he told a lie."

But any finite clause out of which movement applies to an A'-position is introduced by a different particle – the one conventionally written *aL*, as illustrated in (4) and as exemplified in (5).[2]

(4) XP_i [$_{CP}$ *aL* ... [$_{CP}$ *aL* ... [$_{CP}$ *aL* ... t_j ...]]]]

(5)   a.   an t-ainm a hinnseadh dúinn a bhí _ ar an áit
            the name *aL* was-told   to-us *aL* was   on the place
            "the name that we were told was on the place"

      b.   cuid den   fhilíocht a chualaís   ag do   sheanmháthair
            some of-the poetry   *aL* heard [S2] by your grandmother
            á rá   a cheap   an sagart úd   _
            being-said *aL* composed the priest DEMON
            "some of the poetry that you heard your grandmother saying that
            that priest composed"

The distributional pattern seen in (4)/(5) has generally been seen as reflecting a series of local applications of wh-movement (one per CP). The particle *aL*, on this view, is a member of the category C, whose form registers an application of wh-movement into its specifier position. On this interpretation, we have direct morphosyntactic evidence that "long movement" is more local than it initially appeared to be.

The core question, though, is this: from what properties of the theory of grammar, or of the grammar of Irish, does it follow that derivations must be shaped in this way? The original answer to this question was attractive in many ways:

- wh-phrases must ultimately end up in the highest specifier of CP position of an A'-dependency (to guarantee interpretability or to meet selectional requirements). But:
- Locality constraints require that movement not cross a CP-boundary. Therefore:
- Movement must proceed from Spec-CP to Spec-CP.
- Because the moved phrase must "pause" in Spec-CP, a specifier–head relation is established between the moved phrase and the head C.
- In virtue of this relation, the moved phrase in Spec-CP deposits a mark on the head C – a mark without morphophonological consequences in English, but which in Irish forces C to be realized as *aL*.

Note the direction of explanation here – *because* movement applies, the C head must bear a certain mark which (in Irish) has morphophonological consequences. A core presupposition of this mode of explanation is that movement of a phrase α to position γ is freely available unless blocked by some principle. Wh-phrases move to the closest Spec-CP position because they can. This conception, though, is at odds with the idea that movement is forced by properties of a head (the principle of Last Resort). According to this view, what one really wants to say for a simple case like (6):

(6)   an fhilíocht <u>a</u> chum   sí   _
      the poetry   *aL* composed she
      "the poetry that she composed"

is that a property of the head C (realized in Irish as the morphophonological bundle *aL*) forces movement (McCloskey 2001). The problem that has always seemed to dog this view, however, is the problem of the intermediate positions – why, or in virtue of what mechanisms, do the features required to force movement appear on intermediate C-positions in cases such as (4)/(5)?

One class of responses to this dilemma has been to hold that what drives the intermediate movements are "pseudo" wh-features – movement-driving features optionally present on C, or optionally added at the left edge of "phases" (Chomsky 2000). The need to postulate these features has been thought disquieting, though, since their presence is required neither by lexical requirements (in fact, they arguably violate lexical requirements of the verb which governs them), nor by considerations of interpretability. In fact, once again the presence of such features, and their associated phrases, in intermediate positions seems to make the business of building a semantic interpretation more difficult. To the extent that they can be argued to trigger interpretative processes (directly or indirectly), those processes need to apply at the top of the construction, not in intermediate positions.

This perceived dilemma has provoked a number of responses in the recent literature. One of the more interesting recent discussions is Heck and Müller (2000). The idea here is that theoretical devices made available within Optimality Theory permit one to eliminate appeal to "pseudo" wh-features. If Last Resort is a violable constraint in the sense of Optimality Theory, then derivations in which it is violated may be grammatical if they do better at satisfying constraints which are more highly ranked. More specifically, Heck and Müller build a system in which derivations violating Last Resort at intermediate stages in the derivation (at the edge of a phase) can satisfy a higher ranked constraint known as Phase Balance and as a consequence be well-formed. Phase Balance is defined as in (7):

(7)   Phases must be balanced: If *P* is a phase candidate, then for every feature *f* in the numeration there must be a distinct potentially available checker for *f*.

Crudely put, what this constraint does is to force a rough check at the completion of a phase (say at the completion of CP) to determine if the derivation has a chance of completing successfully or not. An attempt is made to pair unchecked features (in the numeration or in already assembled syntactic objects) with elements that could check those features. Potential checking elements must be in accessible positions (not, for instance, buried within completed phases). In the case at hand, if a wh-phrase has raised to the specifier of CP in the just-completed phase, it will be accessible and can be counted as a potential checker for remaining wh-features. If, however, the wh-phrase has not raised, it will be invisible to the operation which checks if Phase Balance is satisfied, and a violation of the constraint will be registered (assuming that there is a C somewhere in the derivation which bears a wh-feature needing to be checked).

There will thus be derivations in which Phase Balance is satisfied (because wh-movement has made a potential checking element accessible), but in which Last Resort is violated (because the movement which leads to the satisfaction of Phase Balance is not itself driven by featural properties of the attracting C). Given the logic of constraint satisfaction in Optimality Theory, such derivations will be well-formed (*ceteris paribus*) if Phase Balance outranks Last Resort.

It follows from this reasoning that intermediate steps in long wh-movement can apply freely (without featural motivation and in violation of Last Resort) but still be part of successful derivations. As a consequence, no "spurious" wh-features need be postulated which drive intermediate applications of wh-movement. It also follows that an important analytical wedge is driven between the final step of long wh-movement (featurally driven) and intermediate steps (not featurally driven).

The attractiveness of these proposals lies in their ability to rid the theory of the apparent embarrassment of spurious wh-features, while maintaining the essence of the principle of Last Resort (its effects buried in the constraint rankings but detectable in the absence of higher-ranked constraints).

However, the core strength of this proposal is also, it seems to me, its core weakness. If one looks at all the known cases in which the intermediate steps of wh-movement are morphologically marked, a striking, and as far as I know exceptionless, generalization emerges. It is always the case that the mark deposited on the intermediate C-positions is the same mark which is deposited on the topmost C-position. For Irish, this can be seen by reexamining (4) and (5). The complementizer *aL* must head each clause in which there has been an application of wh-movement – the lower parts of the dependency (in which according to Heck and Müller (2000) movement is not featurally driven), as well as the topmost part (*cp* (6)) in which the movement is, on all assumptions, featurally driven.

In this respect, the Irish case is completely typical. It is a feature of every such case that I have seen described that the morphosyntax of the intermediate positions is the same as the morphosyntax of the highest C-projection in the dependency (Chung 1998: 234ff.). This pattern is sufficiently general and clear that it would be wrong, in my view, to treat it as accidental or epiphenomenal. The conclusion it suggests is that the mechanisms which are in play in the intermediate positions of A'-dependencies are the same as the mechanisms which are in play in the highest positions. In other words, if we interpret the morphosyntax as reflecting the presence of a movement-inducing feature on the topmost C of the dependency (for detailed discussion of this in the Irish case, see McCloskey 2001), then it is question-begging not to assume the same for the same morphosyntax in intermediate positions. This implies in turn that the intermediate movements must indeed also be feature-driven.

This conclusion is my starting point here. That is, I work from the assumption that since the morphosyntactic consequences of movement look the same in all positions – intermediate positions and topmost positions – we should assume that the same featural mechanisms are at play.

For Irish, in addition, all of this interacts in an important way with the syntax of resumption, in ways that are clearly relevant for the larger issues. For that reason, the second assumption that I work from here is that we should aim to construct an analysis of the morphosyntax of complementizers which, to the extent possible, integrates what happens under movement with what happens under resumption. The basic facts have been well described before. They are summarized in the following section.

3   The form of complementizers

Speaking informally, we can say that the form of the complementizer in a finite clause in Irish depends in the first place on whether or not a relation of

A'-binding reaches into the clause. In the second place, the form of the complementizer depends on what kind of A'-binding reaches into the clause. In the absence of any A'-binding, we have (as we saw at (3) above) a form of the particle *go*:

(8) Creidim gu-r   inis sé bréag.
     I-believe go–[PAST] tell he lie
     "I believe that he told a lie."

If the clause hosts A'-binding of a trace ((9a)), it is headed by the particle *aL*; if the clause hosts A'-binding of a resumptive pronoun, it is headed by the particle conventionally represented as *aN* ((9b)).[3]

(9) a. an ghirseach a ghoid na síogaí
         the girl   aL stole the fairies
         "the girl that the fairies stole away"

     b. an ghirseach a-r   ghoid na síogaí í
         the girl   aN-[PAST] stole the fairies her
         "the girl that the fairies stole away"

This fundamental pattern holds for the full range of A'-dependencies – relative clauses ((9)), constituent questions ((10)), clefts ((11)), and so on (see McCloskey 1985; Mac Cana 1985; McCloskey 1990; McCloskey 2001 for more detailed discussion and exemplification).[4]

(10) a. Céacu ceann a dhíol tú?
         which one   aL sold you
         "Which one did you sell?"

     b. Céacu ceann a bhfuil dúil agat   ann?
         which one   aN is   liking at-you in-it
         "Which one do you like?"

(11) a. Teach beag a cheannaigh muid.
         house little aL bought   we
         "It was a little house that we bought."

     b. Teach beag seascair a-r   mhair muid ann.
         house little snug   aN-[PAST] lived we   in-it
         "It was a snug little house that we lived in."

In summary, we need to make a three-way distinction among finite clause-introductory particles – one form is associated with the binding of a trace (*aL*), one with the binding of a pronoun (*aN*), and one with the absence of A'-binding (*go*). I will continue to assume here that the relevant clause-initial particles are instances of the category C. This claim has been uncontroversial in the case of *go* and *aN*, but somewhat controversial in the case of *aL*. McCloskey (2001) is a detailed defense of the position that all three elements are complementizers and I will take that conclusion as a given here. Given that starting point, the task becomes that of understanding how the form of C is shaped by the particular derivational functions served by the specifier position of CP.

Examples (8)–(11)   illustrate the facts for simple one-clause cases. It will be important to establish the facts for multi-clause structures also. For the case in which the variable-position is occupied by a gap, we have already established the basic facts (see (4), (5), repeated here as (12) and (13)):

(12)   XP$_j$ [$_{CP}$ *aL* . . . [$_{CP}$ *aL* . . . [$_{CP}$ *aL* . . . t_j . . .]]]]

(13)   a.   an t-ainm <u>a</u> hinnseadh dúinn <u>a</u> bhí _ ar an áit
          the name *aL* was-told to-us *aL* was   on the place
          "the name that we were told was on the place"

    b.   cuid den   fhilíocht <u>a</u> chualaís ag do   sheanmháthair
          some of-the poetry   *aL* heard [s2] by your grandmother
          á rá   <u>a</u> cheap   an sagart úd   _
          being-said *aL* composed the priest DEMON
          "some of the poetry that you heard your grandmother saying that that priest composed "

That is, the particle *aL* must introduce *each* clause which contains the gap.

For the case in which the variable position is occupied by a resumptive pronoun, the pattern schematized in (14) is by far the commonest and the least marked:

(14)   DP [$_{CP}$ *aN* . . . [$_{CP}$ *go* . . . *pro* . . .]]

That is, *aN* (the form of C normally associated with the binding of a resumptive pronoun) appears in the topmost specifier of CP-position, while all the lower C-positions are occupied by *go*:

(15)   cúpla muirear   a bhféadfá a rá   go rabhadar bocht
        couple household *aN* you-could say [–FIN] go were [P3] poor
        "a few households that you could say were poor"

(16)   fir   ar shíl   Aturnae an Stáit go rabh siad díleas do'n Rí
        men *aN* thought Attorney the State go were they loyal to-the King
        "men that the Attorney General thought were loyal to the King"

(17)   An t-ór seo   ar chreid   corr-dhuine go raibh sé ann
        the gold DEMON *aN* thought some-people go was it there
        "this gold that some people thought was there"

(18) postaí ar maoidheamh go rabh siad sócamhlach agus buan
      jobs *aN* was-claimed go were they comfortable and permanent
      "jobs that were claimed to be comfortable and permanent"

(19) an rud a dtug sé orm mionnughadh go gcoinneóchainn
      the thing *aN* brought he on-me swear [–FIN] go keep [COND] [S1]
      ceilte   é
      concealed it
      "the thing that he made me swear that I would keep hidden"

Note that the pattern is the same whether the resumptive element is realized
as a free-standing element ((16)–(19)), or as *pro* identified by agreement morphology (as in (15)) These issues are considered in detail in McCloskey and
Hale (1984) and McCloskey (1986).

4 An earlier analysis

This all makes a comforting kind of sense. There are two classes of cases. In
one ((4)/(5)), we have the following clustering of properties:

(i)   a gap (trace) in the variable position;
(ii)   all the standard properties of movement to an A′-position –
       island effects, weak crossover, and so on (McCloskey 1979, 1985,
       1990; Chung and McCloskey 1987);
(iii) morphosyntactic evidence for successive-cyclic movement.

In the other set of cases we have a complementary set of properties:

(i)   a pronoun in the variable position;
(ii)   evidence that movement plays no role in the derivation – immunity
       from islands, absence of weak crossover effects (McCloskey 1990);
(iii) morphosyntactic evidence (in the form of the default complement-
       izer *go*) that intermediate C-positions play no role in establishing
       the binding relation.

   It is the aim of the analysis developed in McCloskey (1990) to capture these
clusterings of properties. It is assumed there that appearance of *aL* is associated
with an application of (successive-cyclic) wh-movement within a CP – movement
through the specifier of CP signaled by the form *aL* (see also McCloskey 2001).
   For the second set of cases ((14)), the assumption is that there is an operator
(null) in the highest Spec-CP-position of the A′-dependency – an operator which
binds the resumptive pronoun. Featural properties of that operator determine
(by way of the specifier–head relation) the form of C, which is realized as
aN. Since the relation between the operator and the resumptive pronoun is
mediated by binding and not by way of movement, the intermediate specifier

of CP-positions are irrelevant and unoccupied. Since they are unoccupied, the associated C-head is realized as the default form *go*. Hence the clusterings of properties.

Reassurance, however, is short-lived. When we look more closely at the mechanisms that must be assumed to make this analysis work, certain very troublesome things emerge.

For this analysis of the determination of C-form to work, the operator which binds resumptive pronouns must be distinct in its properties from whatever element it is that determines the form of the *aL* complementizer. Those differences, furthermore, must be of a type that features of the C-head could be sensitive to. What could these distinguishing features be? There seem to be two candidates:

(i)   there could be some intrinsic difference (lexically specified) between the element which determines the form *aL*, and the element which determines the form *aN*;

(ii)   the operator which binds resumptive pronouns could inherit some features from the bound pronoun along the A'-chain that links them – features which are distinct in some detectable way from those of the wh-operator which, by hypothesis, determines the form *aL*. This is the suggestion made briefly in McCloskey (1990).

Two kinds of issues arise if the second approach is adopted. The first is that it is very unclear what the relevant features might be; the second is the nonlocality of the relation between the pronoun and the element in Spec-CP whose featural make-up it must determine or agree with.

Consider the former issue first. What feature might be inherited from a resumptive pronoun that would allow its binder to force C to take on the form *aN*?

The relevant feature is unlikely to be a distinctive mark associated with pronouns in their resumptive use. A remarkable but little commented on property of resumptive pronouns is that they simply *are* pronouns. I know of no report of a language that uses a morphologically or lexically distinct series of pronouns in the resumptive function. If we take this observation to be revealing, there can be no syntactic feature which distinguishes resumptive pronouns from "ordinary" pronouns, and any appeal to such a feature must be construed as, at best, an indication of the limits of understanding.

The formal features which define resumptive pronouns will then just be the formal features which define pronouns in general. Could some or all of these features be passed up to the binding operator, and ultimately affect the featural make-up of C? Two considerations make this unlikely. The first is that there is straightforward evidence that person-number features at least are not in fact inherited from a resumptive pronoun. Consider the examples in (20). These are cases in which there is a mismatch between the featural constitution of the pronoun and that of its ultimate binder.

(20) a.   A Alec, tusa a   bhfuil an Béarla   aige
                    you *aN* is   the English at-him
           "Hey, Alec – you that know(s) English"

b. Is   sinne an bheirt ghasúr a–r   dhíol tú ár lóistín.
    COP[PRES] we   the two boy   aN-[PAST] paid you our lodging
    "We are the two boys that you paid our lodging."

Here, we have resumptive pronouns (third person singular in (20a), first person plural in (20b)) which fail to match the person-number features of their (ultimate) binders. If person-number features are inherited from bound pronouns by the elements which bind them, such mismatches are unexpected.

Consider now the issues of locality. Whatever element it is that occupies the specifier-position associated with *aN* must be able to detect, in some direct or indirect sense, the presence of a resumptive pronoun within its c-command domain.

But the relation between the null element in Spec-CP and the pronoun which it supposedly binds is very nonlocal, potentially reaching across many clause-boundaries, across DP-boundaries, PP-boundaries, into possessor positions, across island boundaries and all combinations of these (McCloskey 1979, 1985, 1990 and many examples to be cited below). It would be an unusual and disturbing thing, in current contexts, if morphosyntactic information of the kind we are dealing with here could be shared across such syntactic distances.

If there is no distinctive feature for "resumptive" pronouns (as argued above), the problem is more severe – because the search for the right pronoun to bind may bypass many pronouns which are more prominent than, and thus more accessible than, the pronoun which is in fact bound:

(21) an fear a–r   shíl   sé go dtabharfadh sé an duais dó
      the man aN–[PAST] thought he go would-give he the prize to-him
      "the man to whom he thought he would give the prize"

It seems unlikely, then, that the distinctive properties of the element which triggers appearance of *aN* could be inherited from the resumptive pronoun.

If appearance of *aN* is a reflection of specifier–head agreement, then the differences between the element which forces appearance of *aL*, and the element which forces appearance of *aN* must be intrinsic to those elements.

But it turns out that this approach too is untenable, for there is strong evidence that there can be no relevant featural difference between the element which determines the form *aN* for C, and the element which determines the form *aL*. To see this, we must look at some more unusual and less well studied instances of "long binding." That is the business of the next section.

5 Mixed chains – movement and binding

There are two assumptions from previous work that I mean to carry forward into the discussion which immediately follows. The first is that when we see the pattern:

(22) $[_{CP}\ aL\ [_{TP}\ldots t\ldots]]$

the gap in TP is produced by movement to an A'-position. This is not, as far as I know, a controversial assumption. For concreteness, I will follow most work in the area and assume that what is moved from the position of the gap is a null operator. Following much earlier work (see especially Browning 1987) I will assume that that operator is a subtype of the null pronominal *pro*. We will shortly consider some data relevant to the issue.

The second assumption is more controversial. It is that when we see the pattern:

(23) $[_{CP}\ aN\ [_{TP}\ldots pro\ldots]]$

we are not dealing with movement from the position of *pro*. This assumption has been widely accepted but also occasionally questioned (Kayne 1994; Noonan 1997; Bianchi 1999: 241–2, 2000; Boecks 2001). I will, however, maintain it here for two principal reasons:

(i)   The relation between *pro* and its binder shows no sensitivity to the locality constraints characteristic of movement (subjacency and ECP phenomena). The relevant evidence is presented in McCloskey (1979, 1985, and 1990). The general pattern will also be apparent from the examples we consider here.

(ii)   Weak crossover effects are not observed in structures like (23).

In a later section, I will consider the property of Irish resumptive pronoun structures which has principally suggested that there might be some sense in which they are movement-derived. It will be argued there that the relevant property has been misinterpreted (and see note 9 for additional relevant material). That argument will be more easily developed when certain other elements are in place. For the moment I want only to point out that the insensitivity to islands stands as a severe difficulty for analyses according to which resumptive pronouns are spelled-out traces, or represent, say, a stranded D, whose complement has been moved (see Koopman 1999 for relevant discussion). The rethinking of the theory of island-hood that this view makes necessary is not yet in prospect.[5]

With this much in hand, we can go on to consider the patterns of interaction among C-form, movement and resumptive binding.

5.1   *Pattern 1*

The patterns we have already examined for long-distance A'-dependencies ((4) and (14), repeated here as (24a) and (24b) respectively) are by far the most productive.

(24)   a. $XP_j\ [_{CP}\ aL\ldots[_{CP}\ aL\ldots[_{CP}\ aL\ldots t_j\ldots]]]$
         b. $DP\ [_{CP}\ aN\ldots[_{CP}\ go\ldots pro\ldots]]$

Examples of both patterns turn up with great frequency in published texts and in speech, formal and informal. But many other example-types turn up as well in written and oral usage. Many of these examples seem to represent only "noise" – errors of production, the consequence of ill-informed copy-editing, or nonce productions which aren't replicable. Others, however, represent patterns which recur and which can be investigated in a systematic way with native speaker consultants.[6] These are the patterns to be investigated in what follows. Empirically, the investigation is tricky. Although these constructions turn up in speech and writing, they are rarer than the two in (24). The patterns are real, but are liminal parts of the language, lying at the edge of people's competence and at the edge of their experience. Some of them have been described in the literature before, but some have not.

What the patterns have in common is that they all involve a resumptive pronoun but they also have a "successive-cyclic" character in the sense that they involve distinctive morphosyntactic marking of intermediate C-positions.

We can begin with structures like (25). These are structures which should invoke the Complex Noun Phrase Constraint of Ross (1967):

(25)

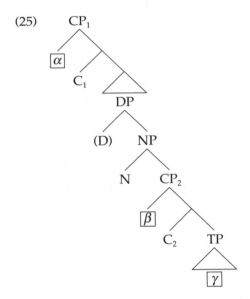

CP_2, being a complement to N, should make extraction difficult, and such structures are indeed islands[7] – see especially McCloskey (1985), and for the case in which N of (25) is a psych-noun, see McCloskey and Sells (1988).

We are interested in three positions in such structures (boxed in (25)) – γ is the variable position of an A'-dependency, α is the highest Spec-CP position of the dependency and is linked ultimately with the head of a relative clause construction, or the focus of a cleft, or the interrogative phrase of a question and so on. β is the intermediate Spec-CP position. What are the grammatical realizations of this schematic structure? Unsurprisingly, the commonest way to realize this structure is by way of (24b), as we can see in (26):

(26)   a.   achan rud   a   rabh dóchas aca   go dtiocfadh   sé
             every thing *aN* was hope   at-them go come [COND] it
             "everything that they hoped (that it) would come"

       b.   Mícheál sin   a   raibh dóchas acu   uilig go bpósfadh
                   DEMON *aN* was hope   at-them all go marry [COND]
             sé Róise
             he
             "that Mícheál that they all hoped (that he) would marry Róise"

In this case, position γ is occupied by a resumptive pronoun, C_1, related to position α, is occupied by *aN*, and C_2, linked with the intermediate position β is occupied by the default complementizer *go*. The grammaticality of (26) corresponds to expectation – use of the resumptive pronoun makes the island-hood of CP_2 irrelevant; use of the pronoun triggers the appearance of *aN* in the highest C-position (C_1 here), and the intermediate Spec-CP position is unoccupied (resulting in the appearance of default *go* in C_2). (27), however, is also a possibility, as shown by the (attested) examples in (28)–(31):[8]

(27) $[_{CP}$ *aN* $[_{TP}$ ... $[_{DP}$ (D) $[_{NP}$ N $[_{CP}$ *aL* $[_{TP}$ ... *t* ... $]]]]]$

(28)   rud   a   raibh coinne   aige   a   choimhlíonfadh _ an aimsir
       thing *aN* was   expectation at-him aL fulfill [COND]   the time
       "something that he expected time would confirm"

(29)   biseach   ... a   raibh súil   agam a   bhéarfá   _
       recovery   *aN* was   hope at-me aL get [COND] [s2]
       "a recovery that I hoped you would stage"

(30)   rud   a   raibh tuairim láidir agam a   bheadh   _ aige
       thing *aN* was   opinion strong at-me aL be [COND]   at-him
       "something that I strongly suspected he would have"

(31)   rud   a   raibh dóchas láidir agam a   bhí _ fíor
       thing *aN* was   hope   strong at-me aL was   true
       "something that I strongly hoped was true"

In (28)–(31), C_1 is occupied by *aN*, suggesting the presence of a resumptive pronoun somewhere in its domain, but C_2 is occupied by *aL*, suggesting that wh-movement has applied into its specifier position.

   Now there is a certain sense in which this is an expected outcome. CNPC structures are different from other islands, in the sense that movement within the complement CP itself should not be in any way prohibited. That is, local movement from position γ to position β of (25) will not violate any principle. Therefore the application of wh-movement which is signaled by the presence of *aL* in C_2 should be well-formed. At this point, however, one might have expected the derivation to stall, faced with the barrier of the island boundary represented by CP_2 of (25); movement from position β to any higher position will be impossible. But the derivation does not stall – it proceeds, with aN occupying the highest C-position. If the presence of aN in C_1 can be taken – in this case, as in other cases – to signal the presence of a resumptive pronoun in the domain of C, then what we have in the "second half" of the derivation of (28)–(31) is routine. This is just another instance of the use of resumptive pronoun binding to cross an island boundary (to speak informally). Where is this resumptive pronoun? The simplest assumption would seem to be that it occupies position β of (25) – the intermediate Spec-CP position. If this interpretation is right, then what we have in (28)–(31) is a derivation of the schematic form in (32):

(32) $[_{CP}$ XP_j aN $[_{TP} \ldots [_{DP}$ (D) $[_{NP}$ N $[_{CP}$ *pro$_j$* aL $[_{TP} \ldots t_j \ldots$ $]]]]]$

in which a "composite" A'-dependency is formed, the two lower positions linked by movement, and the two higher positions linked by binding of a resumptive element. The existence of such composite chains has in fact already been established, on entirely different grounds, for Selayarese (Finer 1997).

The existence of this possibility is interesting in its own right (and we will return to its implications), but for our narrower present purposes, the relevant conclusion is this: the element which undergoes A'-movement in constructions characterized by appearance of the aL-complementizer can itself be bound as a resumptive pronoun.

Notice that this possibility is in some sense expected, if (as we have assumed) what undergoes movement in aL-constructions is in fact a null pronominal.

The implications for our understanding of the mechanisms governing the form of C are these. We have been considering the possibility that the choice of aL over aN, and vice versa, is triggered by featural characteristics of the element which occupies the specifier of CP. One mechanism for ensuring that the two elements would be featurally distinct would be to assume that they inherit certain features from the elements they bind (trace or resumptive pronoun). But in the light of (32) ((28)–(31)) this seems very dubious. In such cases, we would have to assume that the element in the intermediate Spec-CP-position (corresponding to position β of (25)) would have to pass up to the higher Spec-CP-position features which it itself did not bear (since it locally determines an occurrence of the C aL, not aN). This seems paradoxical.

5.2   Pattern 2

We can probe these issues further by examining a second mixed chain type. Unlike (32), this pattern has been known about since the beginning of work on the topic (McCloskey 1976; McCloskey 1979: 167–8; Sells 1984; Harlow 1981; McCloskey 1985; McCloskey 1990) but has always resisted understanding. This pattern is, in a sense, the mirror image of the previous, in that it inverts the order of the two complementizers. In this pattern, we find a pronoun in the lower clause which is in a position inaccessible to movement; we find the

form of C appropriate to binding of a resumptive pronoun (*aN*) in the intermediate position, and we find the form of C associated with an application of
wh-movement in the higher of the two clauses. Schematically:

(33) $[_{CP} \ aL \ [_{TP} \ldots [_{CP} \ aN \ [_{TP} \ldots pro \ldots]]]]$

The examples in (34)–(38) are typical:

(34)   aon duine a cheap sé a raibh ruainne tobac aige
       any person *aL* thought he *aN* was scrap tobacco at-him
       "anyone that he thought had a scrap of tobacco"

(35)   Cé is   dóigh leat   a bhfuil an t-airgead aige?
       who *aL*–cop[PRES] likely with-you *aN* is   the money   at-him
       "Who do you think has the money?"

(36)   an galar   a chuala mé ar cailleadh bunadh an oileáin   leis
       the disease *aL* heard I   *aN* died   people the island [GEN] by-it
       "the disease that I heard that the people of the island died of (it)"

(37)   faoi pháistí a cheapadar   a raibh breoiteacht orthu
       about children *aL* they-thought *aN* was   illness   on-them
       "about children that they thought were ill"

(38)   rud   ar bith a cheapann siad a bhfuil baint   aige le   saol
       thing any   *aL* think [PRES] they *aN* is   connection at-it with life
       na   Gaeltachta
       the [GEN] Gaeltacht [GEN]
       "any thing that they think has to do with the life of the Gaeltacht"

In the "lower half" of this pattern we have the characteristic association between resumptive pronoun (in a position inaccessible to movement) and the
appearance of the complementizer *aN*. At the top of the dependency, however,
we have the complementizer routinely associated with an application of wh-
movement. The natural way to understand this pattern is to suppose that we
have binding of a resumptive pronoun in the lower clause by an element in
the intermediate Spec-CP, followed by movement of that binder into the higher
Spec-CP position, forcing an appearance of the complementizer *aL*. This is
exactly the interpretation suggested for some similar structures in Selayarese
by Finer (1997).

   Under such an interpretation, this structure is the reverse of the one we
looked at earlier.

(39)   a. $[_{CP} \ aN \ [_{TP} \ldots [_{CP} \ aL \ldots t \ldots]]]$

       b. $[_{CP} \ aL \ [_{TP} \ldots [_{CP} \ aN \ldots pro \ldots]]]$

Whereas in (39a) we have movement in the lower clause, followed by binding of a resumptive pronoun in the higher clause, in (39b) we have binding of a resumptive pronoun in the lower clause, followed by movement in the higher clause.

Again we will consider later the broader implications of the existence of such a pattern. For present purposes, however, it suggests certain conclusions about the mechanisms governing the form of C. Specifically: the element which binds a resumptive pronoun can itself undergo A'-movement – determining an *aN*-complementizer in its lower position, an *aL*-complementizer in its higher position. That is, the *same* element determines one form of C in its lower position, a different form of C in its higher position. Unless the raised element loses or acquires featural content as a consequence of raising, this is incompatible with the view that intrinsic properties of the element in Spec-CP determine the form of C. But we have already seen that it is implausible that the relevant features could be inherited from the bound element.

5.3   Pattern 3

To complete the picture, and to see the same point in a slightly different way, we should note finally that there is a third possibility here: one in which *aN* appears in both C-positions of a two-clause A'-dependency. There is, in these cases, a resumptive pronoun in the lower of the two clauses – in a position inaccessible to movement (see especially (44)). The appearance of that pronoun is, as usual, associated with the appearance of *aN* – in this case, in the finite clause which most immediately contains it:

(40)   [$_{CP}$ *aN* [$_{TP}$ ... [$_{CP}$ *aN* [$_{TP}$ ... *pro* ...]]]]

(41)   an bhean   a   raibh mé ag súil   a   bhfaighinn   uaithi   é
       the woman *aN* was   I   hope [PROG] *aN* get [COND][S1] from-her it
       "the woman that I was hoping that I would get it from (her)"

(42)   an méid den   dán   ar mheas   sé a   raibh feidhm leis
       the much of-the poem *aN* thought he *aN* was   need   with-it
       "as much of the poem as he thought was needed"

(43)   san   áit   ar dúradh   leis   a   bhfaigheadh sé Jim ann
       in-the place *aN* was-told with-him *aN* find [COND] he   in-it
       "in the place where he was told that he would find Jim"

(44)   na cuasáin thiorma ar shíl   sé a   mbeadh   contúirt ar bith uirthi
       the holes   dry   *aN* thought he *aN* would-be danger any   on-her
       tuitim   síos   ionnta
       fall [–FIN] down into-them
       "the dry holes that he thought there might be any danger of her falling
          down into them"

The existence of this pattern was first noted by Tomás de Bhaldraithe (de Bhaldraithe 1956); see also McCloskey (1985), McCloskey (1990). Its existence is expected, given the observations already made. We know already (from pattern (33)) that a resumptive pronoun in an embedded clause may trigger the appearance of *aN* in the lower C-position. But we also know (from (32)) that the higher link in these two-clause binding structures may be signaled by the appearance of *aN* in the highest Spec-CP position. (40), then, represents the expected combinatorial possibility.

Finally, note how the existence of these more complex patterns compromises the treatment of even the simplest cases in which we want to establish a correlation between type of A'-binding and the form of C – a simple case of object extraction, for example:

(45) a.   an bhean   a   chonaic Seán –
           the woman *aL* saw
           "the woman that John saw"

      b.   *an bhean   a   bhfaca Seán –
           the woman *aN* saw
           "the woman that John saw"

      c.   *$[_{CP} \, aN \, [_{TP} \ldots t \ldots]]$

The trick here (on the approach being criticized) is to have the choice of *aN* in C-position reflect an illegitimate interaction between the featural content of C and the featural content of the element in its specifier position. But what could go wrong here? We know (from the existence of Pattern 1 – (32) above) that the element which undergoes movement to Spec-CP is "pronominal enough" that it can itself be bound as a resumptive element (because it is itself a null pronominal *pro*, we have hypothesized). It must then (be able to) have the distinctive featural properties of a resumptive pronoun, whatever they are. Either those properties are the same as the properties of the binder of resumptive pronouns, or they are not. If the featural constitution of binder and bound pronoun are the same, then (45b) should be legitimate (counter to fact). If the relevant properties of binder and bound pronoun are different, then (33) (repeated here as (46)):

(46) $[_{CP} \, aL \, [_{TP} \ldots [_{CP} \, aN \, [_{TP} \ldots pro \ldots]]]]$

becomes mysterious. For in this instance, the element which binds a resumptive in the lower CP must undergo movement into the specifier of the higher CP. But in this higher specifier-position, it forces an appearance of *aL*. Unless it can acquire or lose features in the course of that movement, there will be no way for it to determine *aN* in the lower position, but *aL* in the higher position.

I conclude that there is no internally consistent way to have the form of C determined by featural properties of the element which occupies its specifier position.

5.4 Implications

What are the implications of all this?

The first conclusion is that UG must allow for the existence of composite chains of the type first mooted by Finer (1997) – complex chains in which some pair-wise links are negotiated by way of movement, and some are negotiated by way of binding of a resumptive element.[9] The system seems to allow for completely blind and opportunistic choices at each phase of the derivation.[10]

The second (and more parochial) conclusion is that it seems at best unlikely that the difference between clauses headed by *aN* and clauses headed by *aL* in Irish can be determined on the basis of featural properties (inherent or inherited) of the element which occupies Spec-CP. We need to distinguish between them on some other basis. A natural hypothesis suggests itself if we continue to assume that *aL* signals an application of wh-movement, and that the appearance of *aN* is associated with the absence of movement properties. What is needed is something with the effect of (47), which is in turn very close indeed to the proposals of Shlonsky (1992):

(47)   C whose specifier is filled by Move is realized as *aL*.
       C whose specifier is filled by Merge is realized as *aN*.
       C whose specifier is not filled is realized as *go*.

I continue to assume that in resumptive pronoun structures, Spec-CP is occupied. I will also continue, for concreteness and for simplicity, to assume that the element which occupies Spec-CP in this circumstance is *pro*, which can in turn then act both as binder for a lower occurrence of *pro* and as bound element for a higher occurrence; recall the mixed bindings of Pattern 1 ((32), (28)–(31)) and Pattern 3 ((40), (41)–(44)). Even for those cases in which *aN* occupies an intermediate C-position, there is evidence that its associated specifier is occupied. As pointed out in McCloskey (1979 and 1990), these cases resemble simpler structures in giving rise to the effect known as the Highest Subject Restriction. In Irish, and in many other languages which have a fully grammaticized resumptive strategy, the only position from which resumptive pronouns are excluded is the highest subject position within the relative clause (McCloskey 1979; Harlow 1981; Borer 1984; Shlonsky 1992; Aoun and Choueiri 1997 and many others):

(48)   a.   *an fear a   raibh sé breoite
             the man *aN* was   he ill
             "the man that (he) was ill"

       b.   an fear a-r   shíl   muid go raibh sé breoite
             the man *aN*-[PAST] thought we   go was   he ill
             "the man that we thought was ill"

This effect has usually been understood as reflecting an antilocality effect (of the kind characteristic of pronouns) governing the relation between a resumptive pronoun and an operator which binds it.[11] When *aN* appears in intermediate positions, the Highest Subject Restriction holds (McCloskey 1990: 219, 1979: 168). Compare (48b) with (49):

(49)   a.   *an fear a-r   shíl   mé a   raibh sé breoite
            the man *aN*-[PAST] thought I   *aN* was   he ill
            "that man that I thought (that he) was ill"

       b.   *an bhean   a mheas   mé a   raibh sí   tinn
            the woman *aL* thought I   *aN* was   she sick
            "the woman that I thought (that she) was sick"

If the Highest Subject Restriction derives from an antilocality requirement governing the relation between a binding operator and the pronoun which it binds, then we have in these old observations confirming evidence for the presence of a binding operator in the intermediate positions in which we find *aN* in C-position.

The proposal in (47), then, has a certain appeal, but it is (as far as I know) unprecedented in theoretical terms, since its core claim is that the morphosyntactic make-up of a head is influenced not by the syntactic material with which it is in a local relation, but rather by the mode of introduction of that material. While it may be unprecedented, the proposal has a number of striking merits: it is very simple at its core, and, whatever other strange properties that it has, it involves an interaction no more distant than that between C and the specifier of C. Worries about locality disappear. It is also empirically successful in that it resolves certain analytical problems that have remained unresolved since the mid-1970s. Furthermore, it provides the basis for an understanding of certain properties of adjunct-extraction in Irish, which have not been described before, let alone analyzed.

6   Analysis

The proposal seems worth developing, then. Perhaps it would be right to take (47) at face value, and to allow the morphosyntactic constitution of C to be determined directly by the mode of introduction of material into Spec-CP (see Chomsky 2001a for discussion along these lines).[12]

I want, however, to develop the basic idea in a slightly different way, here, making use of some ideas developed in Chomsky (2000, 2001b). One of the core concerns of those two papers is the issue we have been grappling with here – how to make sense of "intermediate" movements. The strategy pursued is to take seriously the need for "spurious" wh-features and to explore the consequences (for larger questions of language-design) of their existence.

6.1   Two features

A central concept in these two papers is that of a "phase" of a derivation. When the system finishes the construction of a phase (CP in the case of present interest), everything within the phase, except the edge components, is inaccessible to further operations. The edge components are the head C and material in the specifier of C. At exactly this point (when all the lexical material which defined the phase has been used up), the head (C for present purposes) may freely be assigned two additional features – a wh-feature and an "EPP-feature" (these are the "spurious wh-features" of our earlier discussion). The wh-feature enters into an agreement relation with a wh-phrase in TP. The second feature (the "EPP-feature") forces overt movement of that phrase into Spec-CP. Postulating this feature represents a rethinking of the older and problematical notion of feature "strength;" rather than say that movement is forced by the presence of a feature on C with the "strength" property (a feature of a feature), we say that overt movement is forced by the joint presence of a feature which needs to be eliminated and an EPP-feature (which demands that the associated specifier-position be occupied). Jointly, these two features force an application of wh-movement.

The postulation of these two properties provides us with a simple and plausible way of differentiating the three forms of finite C in Irish. We can understand (47) as in (50):

(50)   C which bears both the *Op*-feature and the EPP-feature is realized as *aL*.
       C which bears only the EPP-feature is realized as *aN*.
       C which bears neither the *Op*-feature nor the EPP-feature is realized as *go*.

Consider how such a system will work.[13] Let us begin with the notion "Op-feature." I will assume that this feature identifies operators – scope-taking elements which must command their scope. I assume that this feature appears on wh-operators and on null pronominal operators at least, and that it is interpretable (see (52) below).

There must be some matching feature on C. This is what the distinctive distribution and behavior of *aL* in Irish indicates. I will take it here that this matching feature on C is also simply "*Op*." Other assumptions are possible; all that is crucial is that the two features (that on operator *pro* and that on C) be paired. In Irish, C bearing the *Op*-feature, when it is combined with the finiteness property, is realized as *aL* (for more discussion, see McCloskey 2001). C bearing *Op* will enter into an agreement relation with *pro* bearing *Op*, in a way that is exactly analogous to the identification of interpretable person and number features on nonoperator *pro* by a c-commanding head bearing uninterpretable person and number features (McCloskey and Hale 1984).

In the case of *go* (C lacking both relevant features), nothing of interest happens.

In the case of *aL* (C endowed with both the *Op*-feature and the EPP-feature), the feature *Op* on C will enter into an agreement relation with *pro* bearing *Op* within its c-command domain. Since *aL* also bears the EPP-feature, raising of the operator *pro* to Spec-CP will be forced, as in the system of Chomsky (2001b). As a consequence, appearance of *aL* will always be associated with A'-movement properties.

In the case of *aN* (C bearing only the EPP-feature),[14] the presence of the EPP-feature will mean that the specifier position of C must be filled. But economy considerations (the relative complexity of Move as compared to Merge) will demand that this requirement be satisfied by Merge rather than by movement from within TP. The appearance of *aN* will as a consequence be associated with the absence of movement properties.

Consider other possibilities. Could C bearing both the *Op*-feature and the EPP-feature *(aL)* have its requirements met by way of Merge? If this were a possibility, we would have (incorrectly) an occurrence of *aL* associated with the absence of movement properties. This, however, will not be possible if we maintain that the agreement relation can only hold between a head and an element within its c-command domain (see Chomsky 2001b and especially Chomsky 2001a). Merging operator *pro* into Spec-CP would leave the *Op*-feature on C (which is surely uninterpretable) unchecked. If the language possessed Spec-CP expletives, then other possibilities might exist, given the right initial choice of lexical items. I assume that Irish possesses no such items, but the invariant elements (such as *was* in German), which appear above the "real" wh-phrase in partial wh-movement constructions, could well be understood in such terms (McDaniel 1989; Rizzi 1991).[15]

6.2   Successive cyclic effects

The "long" derivations work as expected. To see this, consider a simple clause in which the mechanisms of the previous section have done their work. There are three possible outcomes:

(51)   a.   [$_{CP}$ *pro aL* [$_{TP}$ . . . *t* . . .]]

     b.   [$_{CP}$ *pro aN* [$_{TP}$ . . .]]

     c.   [$_{CP}$ *go* [$_{TP}$ . . .]]

At this point, *pro* in (51a) and (51b) retains its Operator feature (since that is interpretable), but the features of C have been checked.

If these structures are then further embedded within a larger CP, the same options arise again. If the higher C is given both relevant features (*Op* and the EPP-feature), C will agree with *pro* in the intermediate specifier of CP position and attract it. This will give rise either to the classic "long movement" pattern of Irish ((4), (5)), or to Pattern 1 of the "mixed" patterns discussed above ((46), (34)), depending on whether we have (51a) or (51b) in the lower clause. If we have (51c) in the lower clause, then the derivation can proceed only at the cost of incurring a violation of the locality constraints on movement.

If, on the other hand, the higher C is given only the EPP-feature (and consequently realized as *aN*), then that requirement can only be met by way of Merge. If an element is merged which will allow for semantic interpretation (see (52) below), we will have either Pattern 1 of the mixed bindings ((27), (28)–(31)), Pattern 3 ((40), (41)–(44)), or the more common pattern of long binding of a resumptive element ((14)), depending on whether the lower clause is of type (51a), (51b), or (51c).

Finally, if no feature is added to the higher C, no element will appear in its specifier and the structure will be uninterpretable (see (52)).

6.3   Implications

This general approach to the problem of complementizer choice in Irish has a number of implications which are worth highlighting.

The first is that (50) provides the system with a number of free choices. When a phase has been constructed, one can choose not to add any features to its head, one can add one feature, or one can add two. This freedom corresponds to (and derives) two freedoms which are a fundamental feature of the Irish system. The first is that the choice between using a resumptive pronoun and using a trace is free (McCloskey 1990). This choice reflects the choice between adding an *Op*-feature to C or not. The second freedom is the freedom to construct A'-chains successive cyclically or not (to the extent permitted by locality constraints on movement). This freedom reflects the fact that it is a locally optional matter whether any features at all are added to the heads of phases.

The second is that we might assume that the presence of a lexical form corresponding to the Irish complementizer *aN* is the property which distinguishes languages which have a productive and grammaticized resumptive pronoun strategy from those which do not. Irish, Hebrew, Arabic and so on would possess such a lexical item; English would not. This is surely too crude a proposal as it stands (more distinctions are required than are provided by this simple binary choice), but it might be a place to start. It has the advantage of letting us understand what is otherwise a truly mysterious difference among languages (whether or not they deploy resumptive pronouns as a grammatical device) in terms of the availability or unavailability of a particular morphosyntactic form. The proposal thus assimilates this parametric difference to others which have yielded to similar kinds of understanding.[16]

A third feature of the proposal is that it does not in any direct way force the appearance of a resumptive pronoun within a clause headed by *aN*. This, as we will soon see, is one of the principal strengths of the proposal, in that it provides a way of understanding an otherwise very mysterious aspect of adjunct-extraction. For the case in which pronouns do appear, I will assume that among the elements that can be merged to satisfy the EPP-feature of C is a null operator (which we can continue to identify with the element *pro*), and that other choices, though syntactically unobjectionable, will yield uninterpretable results in the general case (though see p. 210 below). For concreteness, we might assume the following principle of interpretation (for a fuller and more detailed treatment, see for instance Heim and Kratzer 1998: 86–130):

(52)   CP $[[CP]] = \lambda v_i^e \ [[TP]]$

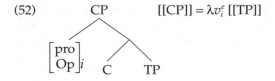

in which the notation v_i^e indicates the *i*-th variable of type *e*. That is, the presence of an operator (*pro* bearing the *Op*-feature) in Spec-CP triggers an application of predicate abstraction over some variable contained within TP – a variable supplied, in the general case, by a pronoun or by the trace of *pro*. This general account assumes no syntactic or morphosyntactic relation between the resumptive pronoun and an element in Spec-CP. It thus avoids the worries about locality that we considered in connection with the earlier analysis but still lets us account for the distribution of *aL* and *aN*. We return to some empirical concerns in section 8.

7   Adjunct extraction

Adjunct extractions also often trigger an appearance of *aN*:

(53) a.   An t-am a-r   tháinig sé, bhíodar   díolta ar fad.
            the time *aN*-[PAST] came   he they-were sold   all
            "(By) the time he came, they were all sold."

      b.   Sin an áit   a   bhfuil sé ina   chónaí
            that the place *aN* is   he living
            "That's where he's living."

      c.   Sin an dóigh a   bhfuil sé
            that the way   *aN* is   it
            "That's the way it is."

      d.   Sin an fáth   a-r   fhág sé an   baile.
            that the reason *aN*-[PAST] left he home
            "That's why he left home."

No account of these facts currently exists, even though no theory of the distribution of the complementizers can be considered complete unless they are integrated. It also turns out that closer examination of these matters sheds further light on the theory of complementizer form developed here.

It seems fairly clear that not every use of *aN* can be traced to a single grammatical principle or device (McCloskey 2001). However, the use of *aN* in adjunct extraction and its use under resumption seem to be unified. The evidence suggests this has to do with certain patterns of dialect variation. Munster varieties and some southern Connacht varieties use the "default" complementizer *go*, instead of *aN*, in resumption structures.[17] This is illustrated briefly in (54):

(54) a. Tigh beag caol   gu-r   mhaireamar ann.
          house little narrow go-[PAST] we-lived   in-it
          "It was a little narrow house that we lived in."

      b. fear gu-r   buaileadh le   camán   é
          man go-[PAST] was-struck with hurley-stick him
          "a man that was struck with a hurley-stick"

But these varieties have *aN* in the other contexts in which it occurs – in headless relatives, for instance, and in certain cases of arbitrary selection by a governing head (a preposition or conjunction; see McCloskey 2001):

(55) a. Bhí a   raibh san   Oileán ag féachaint ar na naomhóga
          was *aN* was in-the Island look [PROG] on the currachs
          "Everyone who was in the Island was watching the currachs."

      b. sar   a   raibh an dinnéar leath-chríochnuighthe
          before *aN* was   the dinner half-finished
          "before the dinner was half finished"

It is not the case, then, that these varieties have simply eliminated *aN* from their inventories. But in these dialects we also find *go* rather than *aN* under adjunct extraction. This is illustrated for various adjunct-types in (56)–(59):

(56) an oíche gur baitheadh   é
      the night go was-drowned him
      "the night that he was drowned"

(57) ar an slí   go raibh ag éirí   leo
      on the way go was   rise [PROG] with-them
      "in the way that they were succeeding"

(58) áit   go mbeadh   an tUachtarán ag bualadh leis an bpobal
      place go be [COND] the President meet [PROG] with the community
      "a place where the President would be meeting the community"

(59) an fáth   gu-r   dhúirt sí sin
      the reason go-[PAST] said   she that
      "the reason she said that"

This pattern of co-variation suggests strongly that a unified account is called for. A crucial clue about how to construct this unified account emerges from a closer look at adjunct extraction. For the second pattern that emerges is that *aL* and *aN* alternate freely in a number of types of adjunct extraction. This is illustrated for locatives in (60), in (61) for manner adverbials, and in (62) and (63) for temporals:[18]

(60)   a.   Siúd an chéad áit   a   chuala mise mé
            that the first   place *aL* heard I   it
            "that's the first place I heard it"

       b.   Sin an áit   a   bhfuair mé é
            that the place *aN* got   I   it
            "that's the place that I got it"

(61)   a.   an dóigh chéanna a   mhair a   réim
            the way   same   *aL* lasted their rule
            "(in) the same way that their rule lasted"

       b.   Sin an dóigh a   bhfuil   sé
            that the way *aN* be [PRES] it
            "That's the way it is."

(62)   a.   am   ar bith ar   raiceáladh   árthach
            time any   *aN*-[PAST] was-wrecked vessel
            "any time that a vessel was wrecked"

       b.   lá   amháin a bhí sé féin ...
            day one   *aL* was he himself
            "one day that he himself was ..."

(63)   a.   san   am a   deachaigh mise inti
            in-the time *aN* went   I   in-it
            "at the time when I joined it"

       b.   an t-am a chuaigh an dá   bhuíon ceoil ar bun
            the time *aL* went   the two band   established
            "the time when the two bands were established"

Even coordinated relative clauses permit *aL* in one conjunct and *aN* in the other:

(64)   an lá a fuair a   fear   bás   agus a-r   fágadh ina
       the day *aL* got   her husband death and *aN*-[PAST] was-left in-her
       baintreach í
       widow   her
       "the day that her husband died and she was left as a widow"

The optionality documented here is, however, limited to certain classes of adverbials. It is found only, as far as I can tell, with temporals, locatives, and manners. Duratives and frequency adverbials take only *aL*:

(65) a. Cá fhad   a bhí   tú ann?
        how-long *aL* be [PAST] you there
        "How long were you there?"

     b. *Cá fhad   a   raibh   tú ann?
        how-long *aN* be [PAST] you there
        "How long were you there?"

(66) a. Cá mhinice   a dúirt mé leat   é?
        WH frequency *aL* said I   with-you it
        "How often did I say it to you?"

     b. *Cá mhinice   a-r   dhúirt mé leat   é?
        WH frequency *aN*-[PAST] said   I   with-you it
        "How often did I say it to you?"

Reason adverbials, by contrast, take only *aN*:

(67) a. Cén fáth   a-r   dhúirt tú   sin?
        what reason *aN*-[PAST] said   you that
        "Why did you say that?"

     b. *Cén fáth   a dúirt tú   sin?
        what reason *aL* said you that
        "Why did you say that?"

(68) a. Cad chuige a-r   dhúirt sí   sin?
        why   *aN*-[PAST] said   she that
        "Why did she say that?"

     b. *Cad chuige a dúirt sí   sin?
        why   *aL* said she that
        "Why did she say that?"

This initially bewildering array of facts falls into place given the analysis so far developed, along with a couple of other assumptions that I believe are fairly plausible on independent grounds. The reasoning is as follows.

We have seen that a unified analysis of the form of complementizers under resumption and under adjunct extraction is required.

There is reason to believe that there are pronominal elements corresponding at least to temporal and locative adverbials. This is suggested by the relative ease with which such adverbials can be extracted from weak islands (Huang 1982) and by the strong connection known to exist between such extractability and the availability of corresponding (often null) pronouns (Cinque 1990; Postal 1998).

Irish, we know, has a rich array of null pronouns alongside its overt pronouns (McCloskey and Hale 1984; McCloskey 1986). It is plausible then to think that there will be null pronouns corresponding to temporal and locative adverbials.

That being so, the fact that both *aN* and *aL* are possible under adjunct extraction is just a reflection of the choice between movement and resumption (with consequences for the form of C) that we are now familiar with. (62b) and (63b) will involve movement of an adverbial element into Spec-CP and consequent realization of C as *aL*; (62a) and (63a) will involve the presence of a temporal pronoun (a null version of *then*) within TP, and the merge of a binding operator into Spec-CP, with consequent realization of C as *aN*. On this general conception, there is nothing in this data that we have not already dealt with.

There are no pronouns corresponding to other adverbial types (frequency and duration especially), and so the resumption option is unavailable. Movement is, as a consequence, the only possible outcome in such cases, and we see only the complementizer *aL* in (65) and (66).

Where do reason adverbials fit into the picture? Luigi Rizzi has argued (Rizzi 1990, 1996) on the basis of a number of phenomena, that the interrogative forms of reason adverbials are always base-generated in Spec-CP. If this is correct, there will be no resumptive element within TP in "why"-clauses. But there will be an element in Spec-CP, and that element will have been placed there by Merge, rather than by Move. If that is so, our principles of C-realization ((47)/ (50)) will necessarily lead us to expect *aN* in such cases, even in the absence of a resumptive element. Recall that what (47)/(50) require is that C be realized as *aN* when an element is merged in (rather than moved into) Spec-CP.

Long extraction of reason adverbials, as has often been noted, takes the form in (69):

(69) Cén fáth   a   dúirt Pól a   raibh Seán ann
      what reason *aL* said   *aN*   there
      "Why did Paul say that John was there?"

We can now understand this pattern as involving merge of the reason adverbial in the lower Spec-CP (resulting in the C-form *aN* in the lower position), followed by raising to the higher Spec-CP (resulting in realization of the higher C as *aL*).

This general line of analysis will also allow us to understand certain other apparent mysteries – in particular, a puzzle concerning long adjunct extraction pointed out to me some years ago by Sandy Chung. We have seen, and it is well known, that for argument extraction, each C between the variable-position and its ultimate binder must be realized as *aL*:

(70) XP$_j$ [$_{CP}$ *aL* . . . [$_{CP}$ *aL* . . . [$_{CP}$ *aL* . . . t$_j$ . . .]]]

(71) Aon bhliain déag is   dóigh liom a deireadh   m'
      one year   ten *aL*-cop[PRES] I-think   *aL* say [PAST-HABIT] my
      athair a bhí sé nuair . . .
      father *aL* was he when
      "It's eleven years old that I think that my father used to say that he was when . . ."

Exceptions to this pattern do occur (Chung and McCloskey 1987: 223–4) but they are very rare. One might have expected, given the general history of work on island-hood and ECP phenomena in the 1980s, that for adjunct extraction, exceptions would be even rarer. The opposite, however, is in fact the case. That is, examples of the general type in (72) are extremely common in both informal and formal usage, but only for temporal and locative adjuncts:[19]

(72)   DP [$_{CP}$ *aN* . . . [$_{CP}$ *go* . . . *adj-gap* . . .]]

A few attested examples are cited in (73):

(73)   a.   insan áit   ar   cheap   an fear eile   go raibh an
             in-the place   *aN*-[PAST]   thought   the man other   go was   the
             t-airgead curtha
             money   buried
             "in the place where the other man thought the money was buried"

       b.   ar an áit   a-r   shamhail mé go rabh   na
             on the place   *aN*-[PAST]   imagined I   go be [PAST] the
             créatúir   ag troid
             creatures   fight [PROG]
             "to the place where I thought that the creatures were fighting"

We can now understand this pattern as simply another instance of the (very common) pattern in (74) discussed earlier:

(74)   DP [$_{CP}$ *aN* . . . [$_{CP}$ *go* . . . *pro* . . .]]

(75)   fir   ar shíl   Aturnae an Stáit go rabh siad díleas
        men   *aN* thought   Attorney the State go were they loyal
        "men that the Attorney General thought were loyal"

In addition, all the more unusual patterns documented in section 5 also turn up in adjunct extraction of locatives and temporals (as observed in part already in Ó Nolan 1920: 133–4), although much less commonly (as we would expect) than (72)/(73):

(76)   XP$_j$ [$_{CP}$ *aL* . . . [$_{CP}$ *aL* . . . [$_{CP}$ *aL* . . . t_j . . .]]]

(77)   Cathain a   deirir   a   dhíolfir   mé
        when   *aL* you-say *aL* you-will-pay me
        "When do you say that you will pay me?"

(78)   [$_{CP}$ *aL* [$_{TP}$ . . . [$_{CP}$ *aN* [$_{TP}$ . . . *pro* . . .]]]]

(79)   Cá háit   seo a dúirt tú   a   raibh an gluaisteán?
        WH place this *aL* said you *aN* was   the car
        "Where's this you said the car was?"

(80)   [_{CP} *aN* [_{TP} . . . [_{CP} *aN* [_{TP} . . . *pro* . . .]]]]

(81)   an áit   a-r   inis an seanduine dó   a   rabh an t-ór
       the place *aN*-[PAST] told the old-man   to-him *aN* was the gold
       "the place where the old man told him the gold was"

Finally, and as expected, extraction of a locative or temporal from an island is grammatical:[20]

(82)   a.   mar   a   raibh tuairim mhaith aige   go raibh sí
            where *aN* was   idea   good   at-him go was   she
            "where he had a good idea that she was"

       b.   an treo baill a   mbeadh   aon dealramh go dtiocfaimis   suas
            the direction *aN* would-be any chance   go we-would-come up
            leis
            with-him
            "the direction where there is any chance that we could catch up with him"

All of these observations, and the relative frequency of the attested patterns, fall into place on the assumption that extraction of a temporal or locative adjunct (at least in Irish) can involve the binding of a null pronominal.

These proposals are sketchy and unsatisfactory in several respects. It is a mystery (to me at any rate) why manner adverbials pattern with temporals and locatives in permitting the syntactic patterns associated with resumption.[21] It is also unclear what licensing requirements the postulated null pronominals are subject to.[22] Finally, the island data needs to be explored much more thoroughly than in (82).

Nevertheless, in outline at least, the proposals seem plausible enough to be worth developing further. If they turn out to be broadly correct, then the goal of integrating adjunct extraction with resumption in Irish will be realized, and the core proposals developed here will be further supported. Note especially that the proposal developed here ((47)/(50)) in which what is crucial is whether Spec-CP is filled by Merge or by Move, allows us to unify the initially surprising similarity between resumption and wh-movement of a reason adverbial.

A final empirical observation may be worth making. If one looks at the form of the interrogative complementizer in Irish (the element which marks a Yes-No question), it turns out that it is indistinguishable in its phonological and morphophonological properties from *aN* (McCloskey 2001):[23]

(83)   a.   A'   mbíonn   tú ag caint   leis?
            INTERR be [PRES-HABIT] you talk [PROG] with-him
            "Do you talk to him?"

       b.   A-r   labhair tú leis?
            INTERR-[PAST] speak   you with-him?
            "Did you speak to him?"

(84) a.   fear   a   mbíonn   tú   ag caint   leis
          man *aN* be [PRES-HABIT] you talk [PROG] with-him
          "a man that you talk to"

    b.   fear   a-r   labhair tú   leis
          man *aN*-[PAST] spoke   you with-him
          "a man that you spoke to"

If Yes-No questions, as frequently assumed, involve the "base generation" of an interrogative operator in the specifier of CP, then this case, too, falls into place.[24]

8   A final challenge

A central assumption of the analysis developed here has been that when a resumptive pronoun appears in an A'-binding structure, that pronoun is not created by movement. We have reviewed the evidence for this position, claiming that such structures show none of the usual properties of A'-movement. There is one phenomenon, though, which has been taken to challenge this generalization (Noonan 1997; Bianchi 1999: 241–2, 2000). In questions, under certain conditions, beside (85a), which is expected given all that we have said so far, (85b) is also possible.

(85) a.   Cé   a   raibh tú   ag caint   leis?
          who *aN* were you talk [PROG] with-him
          "Who were you talking to?"

    b.   Cé   leis   a   raibh tú   ag caint?
          who with-him *aN* were you talk [PROG]?
          "Who were you talking to?"

The crucial property of (85b) is that an inflected preposition whose agreement properties reflect the presence of a resumptive pronoun may appear to the right of the interrogative pronoun and to the left of the complementizer (McCloskey 1979: 94–7; McCloskey 1990: 226–35; Shlonsky 1992: 463).

    (85b) bears a striking initial resemblance to pied-piping structures such as (86):

(86)   With who(m) were you talking?

and this resemblance has been taken to reveal enough of a kinship that one should assume pied-piping for the Irish cases also. If pied-piping is a property of movement constructions, then from this one can conclude in turn that cases like (85b) (and by extension perhaps resumption structures in the language more generally) are best regarded as being derived by movement. I am not aware of any developed treatments which go beyond this initial conclusion and deal with the island phenomena, or with the form of complementizers, but the argument clearly has a certain force nonetheless.

On closer examination, however, the argument turns out to be flawed, because its starting point – the identification of (85b) with pied-piping – is mistaken, I believe.

The core properties of (85b) are discussed and documented in McCloskey (1990). As shown there, the possibility in (85b) is limited by a number of prosodic factors. The sequence of interrogative pronoun and inflected preposition forms a single prosodic unit, with the syllable corresponding to the preposition being by far the more prominent of the two. The interrogative pronoun, furthermore, must be stress-less and monosyllabic:

(87)   a.   Cá   leis   a   ndearna tú   é?
            what with-it *aN* did   you it
            "What did you do it with?"

       b.   Goidé a   ndearna tú   leis   é?
            what *aN* did   you with-it it
            "What did you do it with?"

       c.   *Goidé leis   a   ndearna tú   é?
            what with-it *aN* did   you it
            "What did you do it with?"

The normal word for "what" is *goidé* in Northern varieties (as seen in (87b)), but, because it is disyllabic and has a stress on its second syllable, it may not combine with a fronted pronoun. The form *cá* (phonetically [ka] or [kə]) appears instead. Because of its prosodic weakness, however, this form may not itself appear unsupported by the inflected preposition:

(88)   *Cá   a   ndearna tú   leis   é?
        what *aN* did   you with-it it
        "What did you do it with?"

That is, *cá* is a kind of allomorph of the inanimate interrogative pronoun, which has the very particular property that it must have an inflected preposition on which to depend prosodically.

In this clustering of properties, (85b) does not resemble pied-piping, but it bears a close and detailed resemblance to the phenomenon recently dubbed "Swiping" in Merchant (2000). "Swiping" is a name for the word order pattern found under sluicing in many Germanic languages, in which one has a reversal of the "normal" order of preposition and interrogative pronoun:

(89)   a.   She spoke to somebody, but I don't know <u>who to</u>.

       b.   Peter went to the movies but I don't know <u>who with</u>.

Merchant (2000) is the most comprehensive and successful treatment of this phenomenon to date (see also Ross 1969 and Rosen 1976). Merchant shows clearly that what is involved here is prosodic incorporation of D (the interrogative pronoun) into P, a process which he takes to involve head movement in the derivation between Spell Out and PF.[25] Given the prosodic restrictions on "PP Preposing" in Irish, and given its detailed similarities with Swiping, as described by Merchant, I propose that the Irish case also involves prosodic incorporation – head movement of the inflected preposition to right-adjoin to the D-head of the interrogative pronoun, an incorporation triggered by phonotactic properties of the host D, and producing an output like (90):

(90)

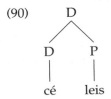

Incorporation of this kind is straightforwardly compatible with the observation (McCloskey 1990: 229) that the inflected preposition must appear between the interrogative pronoun and the modifier *eile* ("other"):

(91) a. Cá   leis   eile   a   mbeifeá   ag dúil?
          what with-it other *aN* you-would-be expect [PROG]
          "What else would you expect?"

      b. Caidé eile a   mbeifeá   ag dúil   leis?
          what else *aN* you-would-be expect [PROG] with-it
          "What else would you expect?"

      c. *Cá h- eile leis   a   mbeifeá   ag dúil?
           what other with-it *aN* you-would-be expect [PROG]
          "What else would you expect?"

This much gets us a certain distance in understanding the phenomenon, and it also suggests that a connection with pied-piping is not crucial in that understanding, but many puzzles and difficulties remain. Two related puzzles in particular now come to the fore.

The first again concerns questions of locality. From what position does the inflected preposition incorporate into the interrogative pronoun? Prosodically-motivated head movement is, one would think, a very local process; if this is so, then the inflected preposition must have adjoined to D not from its base-position (complement to the progressive verb *ag dúil* in (91a)) but from some other position much closer to the interrogative pronoun.

There is in fact evidence for an independent process fronting PPs containing resumptive pronouns. The pattern we have been examining here ((85b), (93)) in the surviving Irish dialects is restricted to interrogative clauses. This restriction, however, does not reflect any deep connection between the PP-fronting operation(s) and the appearance of an interrogative pronoun; it is rather a contingent historical fact about which dialects have survived and which have not. For there are now extinct, but nonetheless relatively well documented, varieties in which the same (or a clearly related) phenomenon appears in relative clauses. Ó Cadhlaigh (1940: section 476, 398–401) (see also McCloskey 1979: 96) discusses the phenomenon and cites examples such as (92):

(92)   a.   go dtógfá   an té air   go dtuitfeadh an crann
            go you-would-take the one on-him go would-fall the lot
            "that you would take the one to whose lot it fell"

       b.   an dream acu   a mbíonn   meas mór orra   féin
            the group at-them *aN* be [PRES-HABIT] respect great on-them [REFL]
            "the ones who have great respect for themselves"

       c.   an spiorad céanna leis   a ndearnadh é
            the spirit   same   with-it *aN* was-made it
            "in the same spirit in which it was made"

This phenomenon is surely to be related to (85)/(93) and also to the phenomenon of topicalization of resumptive pronouns in Modern Hebrew (Borer 1984: 220; Doron 1982; Shlonsky 1992), in Polish (Bondaruk 1995) and in Swiss German (van Riemsdijk 1989), in which a resumptive pronoun moves to an IP-external position immediately to the right of C. Doron (1982) and Shlonsky (1992) analyze this phenomenon as involving movement of the resumptive to a Topic position to the right of C, but external to IP. To make the appropriate typological link, it seems right to analyze the Irish phenomenon in the same way.[26] Putting these observations together, we can maintain that the option of topicalizing a (PP containing a) resumptive pronoun is available within the Irish dialect continuum, surfacing as such in some extinct varieties ((92)) and serving as an intermediate step in the derivation of (85) in surviving varieties (where it applies only in the domain of an interrogative C).

On this view, the existence of (85) and its like does not reflect the operation of pied-piping, but rather the interaction of two independent operations – topicalization of a PP, and subsequent head-movement, which incorporates the P-head of the fronted PP into the interrogative D (as in "Swiping"), this last driven by fundamentally phonotactic considerations.

But at this point the second of the two puzzles alluded to above arises urgently, and it is one which is at the heart of the concerns of this paper. How does the operation which topicalizes PP in cases like (85) and (92) detect and target exactly that PP which corresponds to the resumptive pronoun? Because of course it is not the case that *any* prepositional phrase can be targeted. Rather that prepositional phrase must be targeted which contains the pronoun which will be bound by the interrogative phrase. The example in (93) has only the interpretation indicated:

(93)   Cé   roimhe   aN bhfuil eagla air?
       who before-him *aN* is   fear on him
       "Who is he afraid of?"

(93) is based on the psych-noun *eagla* ("fear") whose argument structure can be seen more clearly in the simple example (94):

(94)   Tá eagla orm   roimhe.
       is fear on-me before-him
       "I am afraid of him."

where (the surface order notwithstanding) *roimhe* ("before him") realizes an internal argument and *orm* ("on me") realizes an external argument (McCloskey and Sells 1988).

   The PP that fronts in (93), then, corresponds to a less prominent, internal argument of the head noun *eagla*. But what is impossible is to interpret (93) in such a way that the unfronted prepositional phrase *air* is the one that contains the resumptive pronoun (i.e. so that the interpretation would be: "Who is afraid of him?"). But it has been argued earlier that resumptive pronouns have no formal features distinct from those which attach to pronouns generally. One can maintain that what the fronting rule targets is an indexed pronoun (this is the proposal tentatively made in McCloskey 1990: 235), but ceding to movement operations the power to detect and respond to such indices seems like a very dubious move (and one that is in violation of the principle of "inclusiveness" advocated in Chomsky 1995). Identical worries arise in the case of resumptive pronoun topicalization in Hebrew and in Swiss German (where pied-piping is not at issue).

   Given the conclusions of this section, though, an alternative view suggests itself. In that context (and in the context of McCloskey 1996), (85) appears as in (95) at the relevant level of representation:

(95)

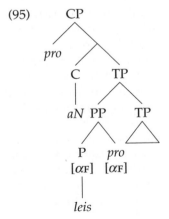

(96) represents the structure of (85) before the operation of prosodically induced movements obfuscates matters (lowering of C to T, as in McCloskey

1996, and incorporation of P into the higher interrogative pronoun discussed above).[27] Assuming a structure like (95) makes the relation of the Irish phenomenon to that of resumptive pronoun topicalization in Hebrew and in Swiss German particularly clear. The two are in effect assimilated – a welcome result, given the commonalities that unite the constructions in the various languages.

With this much in place, the task is to ensure that the only interpretation assigned to (95) is one in which the pronoun which is bound by the operator in Spec-CP is the pronoun contained within the topicalized PP, not some random other pronoun within TP. But the connection just made with fronting of resumptive elements in Hebrew and Swiss German now provides us with a way of understanding this restriction. There is a long-established connection between topicalization and relativization (see, among many others, Schachter 1973; Kuno 1976; Bresnan and Mchombo 1987), the fronted wh-phrase in relative clauses sharing many properties with clause-internal topics. But the literature on Hebrew especially is unanimous in identifying the fronting of resumptive elements in relative clauses with topicalization. If the fronted element in all of these cases is a topic, and if the bound element within a relative clause must be a topic, then it is natural that the binding capacity of the null operator of (95) in Irish should be restricted in the way just illustrated.[28] If this approach to the problem turns out to be tenable, we can maintain the position (*contra* McCloskey 1990) that resumptive pronouns (*qua* resumptive pronouns) cannot be targeted by syntactic operations.

9   Summary and conclusion

We are now fairly distant from our starting point and have been enmired in some of the gorier details of Irish morphosyntax. It is probably time to raise our sights a little and take stock.

The chapter has been concerned with successive cyclic effects in Irish and with what we can learn from them about how "long" A'-movement and "long" A'-binding work in general. The analysis developed goes a good deal farther than previous efforts in the area in its empirical coverage – in integrating the "Mixed Binding" patterns of section 5, and in at least partially integrating observations about adjunct extraction that have not previously been dealt with. Yet its conceptual basis (principally (47) and (50)) is fairly simple, and it avoids some fairly serious conceptual worries that attach to earlier analyses of some of the same material (worries having to do especially with the locality of syntactic operations and with the status of indexing as a syntactically visible property). At the heart of the analysis is the understanding of intermediate movements developed in Chomsky (2000) and in Chomsky (2001b). To the extent that the proposals offered here succeed, the more basic proposals on which they depend are supported.

A striking feature of the system as a whole is its locally blind character. At the completion of each phase (or at least at the completion of each CP), features are distributed on its defining head which cause Spec-CP, by one means or another, to be occupied. The ultimate effect is semantic. The presence of an appropriate element in that position (the null pronominal *pro* we have assumed) will trigger an application of Functional Abstraction (see (52) above), an operation which is necessary if the content of the wh-clause is to be integrated into the larger semantic structure of which it is a part. This must in some sense be why syntactic devices exist whose effect is to fill Spec-CP – ultimately to cause clauses to be turned into predicates.

This operation will apply appropriately at the "top" of A'-dependencies. But if it applies in intermediate positions, the result will be uninterpretable (the embedded CP will denote a predicate, rather than the proposition which the embedding verb expects to encounter in its complement position). Some extra piece of technology needs to be introduced to ensure that interpretation can proceed at these intermediate points. One might imagine that the Functional Abstraction operation could be regarded as optional in some sense, but the concept of "optional" rules of semantic composition is not obviously a coherent one.

It might be that the offending element is deleted by some mechanism from the structures that semantic composition operates on.[29] Or it might be that the mechanisms of semantic composition should themselves be enriched in such a way that interpretation of certain elements can be postponed until a point is reached in the larger compositional process at which they can be folded in. We know how to do this. It can be accomplished, for instance, by way of the mechanisms of "Cooper storage" developed by Robin Cooper in work of the late 1970s and early 1980s (Cooper 1975, 1983). And a good part of the semantics of Gazdar et al. (1985) (see especially Chap. 6, pp. 229–36) is, in essence, devoted to the same problem.

But whatever move is made, real complications seem to be required. The semantic system of natural language is clearly one that is rich enough and powerful enough to allow for the construction of arbitrarily complex properties – "the property of being an x such that they said that they wanted to hire x," for instance (cf. (1) above). But the locality requirements that are an integral part of the syntactic system mesh poorly with this power, and there is, as a consequence, a certain awkwardness in the fit between syntactic and semantic representations. The ungainly morphosyntax of the complementizer system (which Irish gives us an uncommonly clear glimpse of) can, perhaps, be viewed as a response to this mismatch.

Acknowledgments

My thanks to Jason Merchant, to Joseph Aoun, and most especially to Sandy Chung, all of whom have helped me a lot over the years with the issues dealt with here. Thanks also to Eddie Ruys, Cedric Boeckx, Kleanthes Grohmann, Anders Holmberg, Valentina Bianchi, Kyle Johnson, Norbert Hornstein, Chris Potts, Daniel Seely and Sam Epstein for discussion, questions, and commentary which helped shape the final version. I am particularly grateful to Noam

Chomsky for a very detailed and penetrating commentary on an earlier version of the chapter. Not all of the issues which arose in that correspondence can be dealt with in the space of this revision.

Notes

1 See, among many others: McCloskey (1976), McCloskey (1979), Harlow (1981), Sells (1984), McCloskey (1985), Chung and McCloskey (1987), McCloskey (1990), Duffield (1995), Noonan (1997), Noonan (1999), McCloskey (2001), Adger and Ramchand (2001).

2 As has become conventional, I use the symbol *aL* as a quick abbreviation for what is in fact a very complex clustering of phonological and morphophonological properties. For detailed discussion of those properties, see Sells (1984), Duffield (1995), McCloskey (2001).

   All of the nonroutine examples in the paper are cited from published sources. I have not encumbered the text with relevant references, but these and other details can be obtained on request by e-mail.

3 Like *aL*, *aN* is a convenient cover-symbol for a complex clustering of phonological and morphophonological properties.

   As frequently noted, in the speech of many younger speakers, the distinction between *aL* and *aN* is not observed. I will concentrate here on the more conservative varieties in which the distinction is preserved. See, however, note 16 below.

4 However, all of the particles are intrinsically finite and have no overt nonfinite counterparts. Investigation of properties of C for nonfinite wh-constructions is therefore more difficult.

5 I do not intend a general claim here (i.e. that resumptive pronouns are never derived by movement). There are languages in which pronouns pretheoretically called "resumptive" are found in structures which show many of the hallmarks of movement (Koopman 1982; Engdahl 1985). These cases stand in rather stark contrast to the Irish cases.

6 I am grateful in particular to Lillis Ó Laoire of the University of Limerick for his very patient and very knowledgable help with the investigation of these constructions.

7 Or they are at least when the clause is finite. Nonfinite complements to N, as expected, are more porous.

8 (31) has been simplified slightly to make it easier to parse.

9 Jason Merchant points out that the existence of such structures makes much more complex than previously thought the task of establishing whether or not one gets reconstruction effects with resumptive elements. Consider the kind of data used by Joseph Aoun and Lina Choueiri in an important series of recent papers (Aoun and Choueiri 1997, 2000; Aoun et al. 2001). The examples whose properties they probe typically have the structure in (i):

(i) $[_{XP} \ldots pro \ldots] \, [_{TP} \ldots QP \ldots [_{CP} \ldots resum \ldots]]$

in which XP binds a resumptive element *resum*. They then ask if *pro* within XP can be bound by the quantifier QP. If the answer is yes, then the conclusion is that there is reconstruction of XP into the position of *resum*. But given the existence of the kinds of composite chains that we have, with Finer, just argued for, the conclusion does not so easily follow. If there were a resumptive link between an element in the lower Spec-CP and *resum*, followed by a movement link between that position and the higher Spec-CP, then reconstruction to the intermediate position alone would be enough to place *pro* of (i) within the c-command domain of QP. Under this interpretation, the only mechanism needed to account for the properties of such examples is (uncontroversial) reconstruction under A'-movement.

Even for simpler cases in which there is supposedly reconstruction into a position occupied by a resumptive pronoun in VP, and binding of a pronoun within the reconstructed phrase from a quantifier in subject position, questions now arise. If (as in Chomsky 2000, 2001b) *v*P is a phase, then exactly the same issues and questions arise – with CP in (i) now replaced by *v*P.

10   We must ask why the patterns we have been concerned with are so much rarer and so much more marked than the core patterns (24). My assumption here will be that the three patterns we have seen are fully well-formed but that they involve extra processing complexity and are therefore less likely to be pressed into use. This is hardly satisfactory.

11   Though see Shlonsky (1992) for a different kind of account based on the idea that Spec-CP is sometimes an A-position and so will give rise to locality effects typical of A-movement (specified subject condition effects especially). This idea is in turn grounded in the claim that a fully-fledged agreement relation, similar enough to that which holds between a subject and a finite verb, say, holds between Spec-CP and its head.

12   On such an account, the basic idea would be that C can have the EPP-feature freely, but that the element in its specifier must have the *Op*-feature. If the specifier material is added by Internal Merge (in the sense of Chomsky 2001a), C is *aL*; if the specifier material is added by External Merge (again in the sense of Chomsky 2001a), C is *aN*.

13   Discussions with Norbert Hornstein and with Noam Chomsky were very helpful in forcing some needed clarification in this section of the paper.

14   Cedric Boeckx and Kleanthes Grohmann point out that it might well be illegitimate to think of the EPP "property" as being a formal feature in the same sense as Case, Agreement, or *wh*. All that is required for our core proposal, though, is that this "property" or "feature" be capable of having morphosyntactic consequences for the head which bears it.

15   The EPP property of C must be satisfied after CP (the phase) has been constructed. This proposal therefore implies either that phases are not defined by lexical subarrays (as in Chomsky 2000) or else that the system has access to the subarray which will define the next phase, as soon as the lower phase has been constructed. That is, the order of events must be: (i) combine C with TP, forming CP; (ii) add the additional features to C; (iii) gain access to the next set of lexical choices – that defining *v*P. This second view is largely consistent with the discussion in Chomsky (2001b), as far as I can tell. Note that there is no threat here of reintroducing "Marantz' problem:"

(i)   There was assumed to be a reason why a man was in the garden.

where the presence of expletive *there* in the higher clause might incorrectly preempt raising of the DP *a man* into the lower specifier of TP. At the point where that raising applies, the expletive is not in the lexical subarray and so has no influence on whether or not Move may apply within the limits of TP. The earliest point at which the system could gain access to the expletive will be at the completion of the next highest phase above TP – namely CP.

16   For the more innovative Irish varieties which make no distinction between *aL* and *aN* (see note 3), we can say that *aL* is the form taken by C when it bears the EPP-feature (alone or in combination with a wh-feature).

17   As a consequence, the "mixed" A'-bindings of section 5 take on a slightly different look in these dialects. Pattern 1 (section 5.1, (27)), which involves a Complex NP Island and has *aN* in the top clause and *aL* in the lower, appears as in (i):

(i)   an chaint go raibh súil   agam a gheobhaimis _
      the talk   go was hope at-me *aL* we-would-get
      "the talk that I hoped we would hear"

Pattern 2 (section 5.2, (46)), which has *aL* in the higher clause and *aN* in the lower clause, appears as in (ii)–(iii):

(ii)   an rud   a   cheapfadh san   gur-bh   fhiú   cuimhneamh
       the thing *aL* would-think that-guy go–COP[COND] worthwhile think [–FIN]
       air
       on-it
       "the thing that he would think would be worth thinking of"

(iii) Éireannaigh eile   a dúirt Holland go raibh aithne   acu   air
       Irish-people others *aL* said   go was   acquaintance at-them on-him
       "other Irish people that Holland said knew him"

And Pattern 3 (section 5.3, (40)), which has *aN* in both clauses and a resumptive pronoun in the lower, emerges as in (iv) (indistinguishable from (14)):

(iv)   an simné   gu-r   dhóigh leat   go leagfadh   gálaí an
       the chimney go-[PAST] you-would-think go would-knock-over gales the
       gheimhridh é
       winter [GEN] it
       "the chimney that you'd think the winter gales would topple"

18   The two examples in (60a,b) were produced within seconds of one another by the same speaker in a taped interview (Ó Laoire 1999: 62).
      Informal commentary often links the use of *aL* in adjunct extraction with the tendency already mentioned (see notes 3 and 16) for younger speakers to abandon the distinction between *aL* and *aN*. This linkage is mistaken, however. The same very conservative speakers (such as the people whose speech is represented in (62b), (63) or in (60)), who are scrupulous in distinguishing *aL* from *aN* under resumption, freely permit the alternation for adjunct extraction.

19   I have noted some 20 examples of this type in published texts (all involving temporal or locative adverbials), as opposed to three for the case of argument extraction.

20   On the island-hood of the structures of (82), see the references cited on p. 195 above.

21   It is easy enough to propose a null pronominal corresponding to English *thus*, but it is harder to reconcile this with the extreme island-sensitivity documented in the literature for extraction of manner adverbials.

22   Compare the strict requirement of identification under agreement that personal pronouns are subject to. See McCloskey and Hale (1984) and McCloskey (1986).

23   The two, however, are distinguished orthographically and have distinct historical origins. For this reason, and probably also because of their apparent difference of function, they are never identified in traditional or current descriptions.

24   A potential difficulty is that in the Munster and South Connacht varieties discussed above, this complementizer does not appear as *go*.

25   The restriction of the phenomenon to sluicing contexts in Germanic remains mysterious on all accounts. There is no such requirement in Irish. Under sluicing, however, the preposition "survives" along with the interrogative pronoun, further suggesting incorporation of some kind:

(i)   Bhí sé ag caint   le   duine inteacht ach níl fhios agam cé   leis
      was he talk [PROG] with person some   but I-dont-know who with-him
      "He was talking to somebody but I don't know who to."

26   The position of the complementizer in (85b) (to the right of the fronted P(P)) will reflect either or both of the head movements discussed earlier or the complementizer lowering to T argued for in detail in McCloskey (1996).

27   Other assumptions about the structure of (85) are, of course, possible, assumptions which would, for instance, deny the legitimacy of one or other of the prosodically-induced movements alluded to here. All of the plausible alternatives I can imagine, however, make the statement of the claim I am about to make simpler and more natural rather than more complicated.

28   Interrogative clauses in Irish seem to involve a relative clause as a subpart. See McCloskey (1979: Chapter 3).

29   Recall (49) though. If the ungrammaticality of those examples reflect LF configurations (which seems at least plausible), then the operator which induces the violation in its relation with the subject resumptive must still be present at that level.

References

Adger, David and Gillian Ramchand. 2001. "Phases and interpretability." In *WCCFL 20 Proceedings*, ed. K. Megerdoomian and L. A. Bar-el, 101–14. Somerville, MA: Cascadilla Press.

Aoun, Joseph and Lina Choueiri. 1997. "Resumption and last resort." MS, University of Southern California.

Aoun, Joseph and Lina Choueiri. 2000. "Epithets." *Natural Language & Linguistic Theory* 18: 1–39.

Aoun, Joseph, Lina Choueiri, and Norbert Hornstein. 2001. "Resumption, movement, and derivational economy." *Linguistic Inquiry* 32: 371–404.

Bianchi, Valentina. 1999. *Consequences of Antisymmetry: Headed Relative Clauses*. Berlin: Mouton de Gruyter.

Bianchi, Valentina. 2000. "Resumptive relatives and LF chains." MS, Scuola Normale Superiore, Pisa.

Boecks, Cedric. 2001. "Resumption and derivation." MS, University of Connecticut.

Bondaruk, Anna. 1995. "Resumptive pronouns in English and Polish." In *Licensing in Syntax and Phonology*, ed. Edmund Gussmann, 27–55. Lublin: Folium.

Borer, Hagit. 1984. "Restrictive relatives in Modern Hebrew." *Natural Language & Linguistic Theory* 2: 219–60.

Bresnan, Joan and Sam Mchombo. 1987. "Topic, pronoun, and agreement in Chicheŵa." *Language* 63: 741–82.

Browning, Marguerite. 1987. "Null operator constructions." Doctoral dissertation, MIT, Cambridge, MA.

Chomsky, Noam. 1973. "Conditions on transformations." In *A Festschrift for Morris Halle*, ed. Stephen R. Anderson and Paul Kiparsky, 232–86. New York: Holt, Rinehart and Winston.

Chomsky, Noam. 1995. *The Minimalist Program*. Cambridge, MA: MIT Press.

Chomsky, Noam. 2000. "Minimalist inquiries, the framework." In *Step by Step: Essays on Minimalist Syntax in Honor of Howard Lasnik*, ed. Roger Martin, David Michaels, and Juan Uriagereka, 89–156. Cambridge, MA: MIT Press.

Chomsky, Noam. 2001a. "Beyond explanatory adequacy." MS, MIT, Cambridge, MA.

Chomsky, Noam. 2001b. "Derivation by phase." In *Ken Hale: A Life in Language*, ed. Michael Kenstowicz, 1–52. Cambridge, MA: MIT Press.

Chung, Sandra. 1998. *The Design of Agreement: Evidence from Chamorro*. Chicago: University of Chicago Press.

Chung, Sandra and James McCloskey. 1987. "Government, barriers and small clauses in modern Irish." *Linguistic Inquiry* 18: 173–237.

Cinque, Guglielmo. 1990. *Types of A'-dependencies*. Cambridge, MA: MIT Press.

Cooper, Robin. 1975. "Montague's semantic theory and transformational syntax." Doctoral dissertation, University of Massachusetts, Amherst.

Cooper, Robin. 1983. *Quantification and Syntactic Theory*. Dordrecht: Kluwer.

de Bhaldraithe, Tomás. 1956. "Nótaí comhréire." *Éigse* 8: 242–6.

Doron, Edit. 1982. "On the syntax and semantics of resumptive pronouns." *Texas Linguistic Forum* 19: 1–48.

Duffield, Nigel. 1995. *Particles and Projections in Irish Syntax*. Dordrecht: Kluwer.

Engdahl, Elisabet. 1985. "Parasitic gaps, resumptive pronouns, and subject extractions." *Linguistics* 23: 3–44.

Finer, Daniel. 1997. "Contrasting A'-dependencies in Selayarese." *Natural Language & Linguistic Theory* 15: 677–728.

Gazdar, Gerald, Ewan Klein, Geoffrey Pullum, and Ivan Sag. 1985. *Generalized Phrase Structure Grammar*. Cambridge: Harvard University Press and London: Basil Blackwell.

Harlow, Stephen. 1981. "Government and relativization in Celtic." In *Binding and Filtering*, ed. Frank Heny. Cambridge, MA: MIT Press.

Heck, Fabian and Gereon Müller. 2000. "Successive cyclicity, long-distance superiority and local optimization." MS, University of Stuttgart and University of Tübingen.

Heim, Irene and Angelika Kratzer. 1998. *Semantics in Generative Grammar*. Oxford: Basil Blackwell.

Huang, James. 1982. "Logical relations in Chinese and the theory of grammar." Doctoral dissertation, MIT, Cambridge, MA.

Kayne, Richard S. 1994. *The Antisymmetry of Syntax*. Cambridge, MA: MIT Press.

Koopman, Hilda. 1982. "Control from comp and comparative syntax." *The Linguistic Review* 2: 365–91.

Koopman, Hilda. 1999. "The internal and external distribution of pronominal DPs." In *Beyond Principles and Parameters: Essays in honor of Osvaldo Jaeggli*, ed. Kyle Johnson and Ian Roberts, 91–132. Dordrecht: Kluwer.

Kuno, Susumu. 1976. "Subject, theme, and the speaker's empathy." In *Subject and Topic*, ed. Charles N. Li. New York and San Diego: Academic Press.

Mac Cana, Proinsias. 1985. "Varia xii: a note on the prepositional relative." *Ériu* 36: 210–12.

McCloskey, James. 1976. "Conditions on transformations in Modern Irish." In NELS VII, *Proceedings of the Seventh Annual Meeting of the North Eastern Linguistics Society*, ed. J. Kegl, D. Nash, and A. Zaenen. Cambridge, MA: Department of Linguistics, MIT.

McCloskey, James. 1979. *Transformational Syntax and Model Theoretic Semantics: A Case-study in Modern Irish.* Dordrecht: Reidel.

McCloskey, James. 1985. "The Modern Irish double relative and syntactic binding." *Ériu* 36: 45–84.

McCloskey, James. 1986. "Inflection and conjunction in Modern Irish." *Natural Language & Linguistic Theory* 4: 245–81.

McCloskey, James. 1990. "Resumptive pronouns, A'-binding and levels of representation in Irish." In *Syntax of the Modern Celtic Languages,* ed. Randall Hendrick, volume 23 of *Syntax and Semantics,* 199–248. New York and San Diego: Academic Press.

McCloskey, James. 1996. "On the scope of verb raising in Irish." *Natural Language & Linguistic Theory* 14: 47–104.

McCloskey, James. 2001. "The morphosyntax of Wh-extraction in Irish." *Journal of Linguistics* 37: 67–100.

McCloskey, James and Kenneth Hale. 1984. "On the syntax of person number marking in Modern Irish." *Natural Language & Linguistic Theory* 1: 487–533.

McCloskey, James and Peter Sells. 1988. "Control and A-chains in Modern Irish." *Natural Language & Linguistic Theory* 6: 143–89.

McDaniel, Dana. 1989. "Partial and multiple wh-movement." *Natural Language & Linguistic Theory* 7: 565–604.

Merchant, Jason. 2000. "Swiping in germanic." To appear in Jan-Wouter Zwart and Werner Abraham, eds., *Studies in Comparative Germanic Syntax.* Amsterdam: John Benjamins.

Noonan, Máire. 1997. "Functional architecture and wh-movement: Irish as a case in point." *Canadian Journal of Linguistics* 42: 111–39.

Noonan, Máire. 1999. "What is the true nature of successive cyclic wh-movement?" MS, York University, Toronto. Paper Presented to the Eighteenth Annual Meeting of the West Coast Conference on Formal Linguistics, University of Arizona, Tucson.

Ó Cadhlaigh, Cormac. 1940. *Gnás na Gaeilge.* Dublin: Oifig an tSoláthair.

Ó Laoire, Lillis. 1999. "'Ar chreag i lár na farraige': Próiseas an chultúir i leith sheachadadh agus láithriú na namhrán i dToraigh." Doctoral dissertation, University College Cork.

Ó Nolan, Gerald. 1920. *Studies in Modern Irish, part 1.* Dublin: The Educational Company of Ireland, Limited.

Postal, Paul. 1998. *Three Investigations of Extraction.* Cambridge, MA: MIT.

Rizzi, Luigi. 1990. *Relativized Minimality.* Cambridge, MA: MIT Press.

Rizzi, Luigi. 1991. "Argument/adjunct (a)symmetries." MS, Université de Genève and SISSA, Trieste.

Rizzi, Luigi. 1996. "Residual verb second and the *wh*-criterion." In *Parameters and Functional Heads: Essays in Comparative Syntax,* ed. Adriana Belletti and Luigi Rizzi, 63–90. Oxford and New York: Oxford University Press.

Rosen, Carol. 1976. "Guess what about?" In *NELS 6: Papers from the Sixth Annual Meeting of the Northeastern Linguistics Society,* ed. A. Ford, J. Reighard, and R. Singh, 205–11. Montreal: Montreal Working Papers in Linguistics.

Ross, John R. 1967. "Constraints on variables in syntax." Doctoral dissertation, MIT, Cambridge, MA. Published as *Infinite Syntax!* Norwood, NJ: Ablex (1986).

Ross, John R. 1969. "Guess who?" In *CLS 5: Papers from the Fifth Regional Meeting of the Chicago Linguistic Society,* ed. R. Binnick, A. Davison, G. Green, and J. Morgan, 252–86. Chicago: Chicago Linguistic Society.

Schachter, Paul. 1973. "Focus and relativization." *Language* 49: 19–46.

Sells, Peter. 1984. "Syntax and semantics of resumptive pronouns." Doctoral dissertation, University of Massachusetts, Amherst.

Shlonsky, Ur. 1992. "Resumptive pronouns as a last resort." *Linguistic Inquiry* 23: 443–68.

van Riemsdijk, Henk. 1989. "Swiss relatives." In *Sentential Complementation and the Lexicon*, ed. D. Jaspers, W. Klooster, Y. Putseys, and P. Seuren, 343–54. Dordrecht: Foris.

Chapter nine

Very Local A' Movement in a Root-first Derivation

Norvin Richards

In Richards (1999), following an approach developed by Phillips (1996, to appear), I pursued the idea that the syntactic derivation involves creation of the material at the top of the tree first, and adds new material to the bottom of the existing structure. I offered an account in those terms of some of the conditions on the relation between an expletive and its associate, which are exemplified in (1):

(1) a. There seems to be a man in the room
     b. *There seems a man to be in the room
     c. There was heard a rumor [that a man is in the room]
     d. A rumor [that there is a man in the room] was heard

The account I developed of the facts in (1) made a surprising prediction about A' movement: that under certain circumstances, such movement should be very local, essentially unable to skip an intervening A-position. In this paper I will try to show that this prediction is in fact correct, and accounts for a number of recalcitrant facts. In the next two sections I will review some salient properties of the theory in Richards (1999), which make the prediction that A' movement should be very local: section 1 reviews Richards' (1999) proposal about expletive–associate relations, and section 2 outlines the way successive-cyclic movement was handled, via a mechanism known there as Sinking. In section 3, I will try to show that A' movement is indeed very local in a certain range of cases.

Before I continue, I should briefly outline some of my assumptions about how the root-first derivation works. I will be assuming a version of movement which is essentially identical in all relevant respects to that assumed in bottom-up derivations; the Move operation creates a copy of some subpart of an existing tree and attaches it to the tree somewhere else. In a root-first derivation, this copy, like all other material, will be added at the bottom rather than at the top of the tree, and thus will be c-commanded by the material of which it is a copy. In the case of what is standardly called "overt movement," the new copy will not be pronounced. It may be helpful to think of this operation as involving insertion of a trace, and I will often refer to it that way. In other words, movement chains in a root-first derivation will involve insertion of the head of the chain first, and subsequently of the tail of the chain, rather than the other way around as in a bottom-up derivation.

In Richards (1999) I discuss several imaginable variants on the general theme of a root-first derivation, and interested readers should look there for a fuller discussion of this topic. For most of this paper I will simply be assuming a derivation which is essentially the reverse of that standardly assumed in work on Minimalism, with new objects introduced into the tree in the opposite of the order in which they appear in a bottom-up derivation. While this assumption has the virtue of simplicity, it does involve a certain amount of lookahead. Consider, for example, the derivation for the embedded clause of an example like (2), which would begin as in (3):

(2)   I think [that he ate the mackerel]

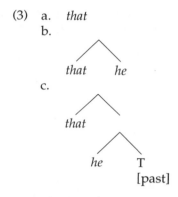

(3)   a.   *that*
      b.
      c.

The derivation in (3) is essentially a Minimalist derivation run backwards; it begins with C, the last thing that a Minimalist derivation would add to the embedded clause, and will end with the most deeply embedded constituent. New syntactic objects are added to the tree essentially in the order in which they would be heard, which seems attractive if we are concerned with parsing.

On the other hand, steps like (3b) above seem to crucially implicate some kind of knowledge of the future. There is no selectional relation between *that* and *he*, and no obvious reason to have chosen *he* as the particular lexical item to be inserted here. These considerations might prompt us to adopt a root-first derivation more like that proposed by Schneider (1999), in which new material is always inserted as a response to selectional or feature-checking properties of material already present in the tree. Such a derivation for the embedded clause of (2) might begin, as does (3) above, with the complementizer *that*. The next step, in response to selectional properties of this C, would be to Merge T:

(4)

Next, the features to be checked on T would license insertion of a specifier for T:

(5)

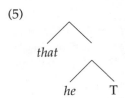

Thus, the derivation would proceed in a way that avoids "lookahead" (and note that the essential "top-down" nature of the derivation is unaffected; every node is being inserted in a position as low as possible in the tree, c-commanded by all existing material in the tree). The distinction between these two kinds of derivations will not be important in what follows; I include it here only in order to address concerns about the degree of lookahead that is necessary for derivations of this kind.

1 Expletive–associate relations

Consider again the facts in (1), repeated as (6):

(6) a. There seems to be a man in the room
    b. *There seems a man to be in the room
    c. There was heard a rumor [that a man is in the room]
    d. A rumor [that there is a man in the room] was heard

In Chomsky (1995, 1998), the facts in (6) are accounted for in terms of a bottom-up derivation and a preference for Merge over Move. Consider the derivation of an example like (6a). The derivation begins at the bottom of the tree, and proceeds until it reaches the first EPP-position, namely the specifier of the embedded infinitival TP:

(7) __ to be a man in the room

At this point, we could in principle either take *there* from the Numeration and insert it or move *a man*; either option would satisfy EPP. A preference for Merge over Move requires that we take the first option, inserting *there*:

(8) there to be a man in the room

The derivation then continues until the higher EPP-position is reached, at which point *there* must move to check EPP (assuming that *man* is prevented from moving at this point, by familiar locality constraints on movement):

(9)   there seems __ to be a man in the room

This derivation correctly yields (6a), and not (6b). It encounters difficulties, however, with examples like (6c) and (6d). In (6c), the derivation begins by constructing the embedded clause, and eventually reaches the EPP-position:

(10)   __ is a man in the room

At this point, we might expect to be forced to insert *there*. Insertion of *there* is certainly possible, as the well-formedness of (6d) shows, but is not forced. Chomsky's (1998) solution to this problem is to divide the Numeration for the sentence into smaller Numerations. In particular, the embedded clause of (6c) has its own Numeration, which does not contain *there*. As a result, we have no choice but to move *a man* to satisfy EPP at the point in the derivation shown in (10), and the derivation gives the correct result.

In Richards (1999) I proposed an alternative to this approach which does not require the use of sub-Numerations, or even of a Numeration.[1] Consider the derivation of (6a), beginning at the top. At some point, we reach a structure in which an EPP-feature will need to be satisfied:

(11)   There seems __ to

Here I suggest that there is a preference for Move over Merge; we might think of this as a preference for manipulating objects already on the "workspace," as opposed to accessing the lexicon to get new material. Thus, we prefer to create a trace of *there* in the EPP-position. The derivation then continues until the theta-position is reached:

(12)   There seems to be __

Here, again, we would prefer to create a trace of *there*, but this option is blocked by whatever well-formedness conditions on theta-assignment prevent the assignment of theta-roles to expletives. We have no option, then, but to access the lexicon for the material necessary to construct *a man* and insert it.

This account has no problem with the well-formedness of (6c). The derivation proceeds from the top down until the EPP-position of the embedded clause is reached:

(13)   There was heard [a rumor that __]

At this point, as always, we would prefer copying *there* to inserting new material from the lexicon. However, copying *there* is not an option here; locality conditions on A-movement prevent the creation of a trace of *there* in this context. Again, we are forced to insert *a man*:

(14)   There was heard [a rumor that a man . . .]

The derivation can then proceed as desired.

This account seems to encounter empirical difficulties, though, when we begin to consider A' movement. Consider the examples in (15):

(15)   a.   Who did John kiss __?
      b.   Who __ kissed John?

When the derivation of an example like (15a) reaches the subject position, we have a choice of a familiar kind; we could create a copy of *who*, or access the lexicon so that we can construct and Merge the DP *John*. As the theory has been developed thus far, we expect that the first of these options should always be preferred; Move is preferred over Merge in this system (perhaps, as I suggested, because accessing the lexicon is avoided). If there is a preference for creation of copies over all other possibilities, then why can A' movement skip A-positions in which it could land? In this particular case, why is (15a) not blocked by (15b)?

Of course, the sentences in (15) are not synonymous, and we might appeal to this as an overriding factor. This move would not harm the above account of the facts in (6), where the relevant sentences would presumably have the same meaning if they were both grammatical.

In fact, however, I want to explore the possibility that this odd prediction is correct. The fact is that there are a number of cases of A' movement which cannot skip an A-position in which it could land. This theory makes such a condition on A' movement look very natural; what we have to try to develop now is an understanding of when A' movement should be subject to this condition.

2 Sinking and non-Sinking

To begin with, I will try to develop a way for this account to permit examples like (15a). This will be the kind of movement referred to as "Sinking" in Richards (1999). I will then try to show that in a number of cases in which Sinking is not available, A' movement is in fact very local.

Consider the beginning of a derivation for an example like (15a):

(16)

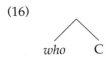

who   C

The grammar prefers, on this theory, to make copies of objects already in working memory whenever possible. In (16), there is a copying operation we can perform which will contribute to feature-checking. It is determinable by inspection of *who* that it has features which will need to be checked later; Case features, for instance, if nothing else. Since the position of *who* in (16) is not one in which its Case feature can be checked, checking the Case feature of *who* will require two steps: the insertion of a head which can check *who*'s Case feature, and the creation of a copy of *who*. There is no a priori reason for these operations to be required to occur in a particular order. In fact, we are entertaining the possibility that creation of copies, when licit, is preferred over all other options. We are therefore entitled (in fact, compelled) to create this copy immediately:

(17)

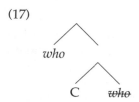

Obviously the preference for copying over other operations must be limited in some way; if it were not, derivations would simply consist of long strings of copies of the first lexical item accessed, and would never converge. Suppose we assume that the preference for creating copies is overridden by a requirement that operations serve some syntactic purpose: perhaps a requirement that they contribute to feature-checking or to satisfaction of selectional restrictions.[2] In (17), we could avoid forcing the system to copy *who* over and over again by making the Case feature ineligible to trigger the creation of copies once it had been copied once. This could be formalized in a number of ways, but in the interests of concreteness, suppose we borrow Chomsky's (1995) terminology of *checking* and *deletion*, where checking makes a feature unable to trigger further syntactic operations and deletion actually removes it from the representation. We can say, then, that a feature is checked when it triggers creation of a copy (and is thenceforth unable to trigger creation of more copies), and deleted when it enters into a local relation with another feature of the same kind.[3] The terminology is unfortunately somewhat confusing, since "checking", in the technical sense intended here, takes place before a "checking relation" with another feature is established. But this is purely a terminological problem; the goal is to disqualify the Case feature of *who* in (17) from causing (and, in fact, forcing) the creation of infinite numbers of copies.

In (17), then, we have exhausted our options for creating copies for the time being, since the Case feature of *who* has been "checked" by copying. We can now introduce new material from the lexicon. The new material must be as low as possible in the tree (this is the condition which forces the derivation to proceed from the top down). We might, for instance, insert a new object X, as in (18):

(18)

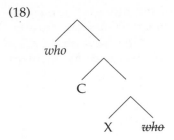

X is as low as possible in the tree, as required; it is c-commanded by all the other objects in the tree, for instance, and c-commands as few of them as possible.[4] Further insertion of the same kind will separate the two copies of *who* further:

(19)

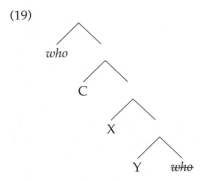

The effect of this kind of derivation is to allow *who* to "move" successive-cyclically down the tree until its Case-checking position is reached and its Case feature is deleted. I put "move" in scare quotes because there is in fact only one copying operation, which occurs near the beginning of the derivation; each step in the successive-cyclic movement happens as a result of the way in which new material is inserted, with no need to posit ad hoc features to drive the movement. I discuss this kind of movement, which I refer to as "Sinking," in Richards (1999).

One property of Sinking is worth emphasizing here: it should be impossible for intersecting movement paths to both involve Sinking. Consider a derivation in which we try to have two intersecting paths both undergo Sinking. At some point in such a derivation, we might have a tree with two copies of wh-phrases at the bottom:

(20)

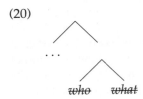

At this point in the derivation a new object must be introduced. If it must be introduced as low as possible in the tree, and if binary branching must be respected, then one of the wh-paths will stop Sinking; the new object must c-command as few things in the existing tree as possible, and this involves c-commanding only one thing:

(21)

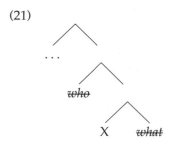

Thus, one of the wh-copies (in this case, the copy of *who*) will no longer be at the bottom of the tree, and will be unable to Sink further. In cases of intersecting wh-paths, then, one path will be able to Sink, but the other will have to undergo movement of a more traditional kind, waiting to create a copy until a checking position is created.[5]

Another case in which Sinking might be unavailable concerns properties of the head of the dependency. At the beginning of this section I noted that it is detectable by inspection, for certain wh-phrases, that they bear a feature that needs to be checked. If the grammar avoids lookahead, we might expect to discover cases in which it is not detectable by inspection that an operator has features that will be checked later. Such cases would then be ineligible for Sinking. Suppose we make the conservative assumption that movement is driven by the kinds of features that standardly drive it in Minimalism; the ones which will be important for this chapter will be Case features and wh-features. A wh-phrase introduced in Spec-CP, then, has Case and wh-features, and has its wh-feature deleted immediately by C, leaving its Case feature, which can drive Sinking, as we have seen. An NP introduced in a Case-checking position, on the other hand, would start the derivation with a Case feature, which would be deleted immediately once it was inserted in the tree. As long as there are no such things as "theta-features" on the argument receiving a theta-role,[6] then, the head of an A-movement chain would be a case in which it is not detectable by inspection that movement will take place; the head of an A-movement chain should never have unchecked features, assuming that improper movement is somehow ruled out.

It is in cases in which Sinking is unavailable that the surprising prediction with which this chapter began should be realized. If a position created in the course of the derivation could be filled by a copy of a syntactic object which is already present in the tree, then copying should be forced; we have seen that copying is always preferred when it is an option. More simply, non-Sinking movement should be unable to skip possible landing sites. Consider, for example, the head of an A-chain, which should be unable to Sink, as we have just seen:

(22)

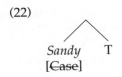

Sandy   T
[~~Case~~]

In (22), an NP has been inserted in a Case-checking position, thus deleting the only feature that could license immediate copying. The derivation must then access the lexicon in order to proceed to the next stage, which might involve inserting the *v* head for which T selects:

(23)

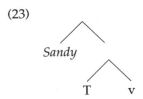

Sandy

T   v

If *v* is transitive and hence a theta-assigner, then we have a familiar choice of ways in which to satisfy the theta-assignment properties of *v*; we could create a copy of *Sandy*, or we could access the lexicon in order to create a new NP to receive *v*'s theta-role. As before, our desire to avoid lexical access should force copying of *Sandy*; insertion of another NP should not be an option. In other words, we predict that A-movement, because it can never involve Sinking, should be unable to skip A-positions, and this prediction seems to be correct.

Note that this line of reasoning does not apply to Sinking, which ought to be able to skip positions in which it could land. Consider a stage in a derivation involving Sinking like the one in (24), where T is a head that could in principle have the landing site of the Sinking path in its specifier:

(24)

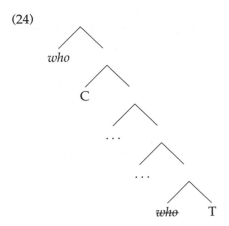

who

C

. . .

. . .

~~who~~   T

At this point in the derivation there are two options. We could take *who* as the specifier of X; we would then need to access the lexicon in order to Merge the next head in the tree, presumably one selected by X. Alternatively, we could access the lexicon in order to Merge something else as the specifier of X, allowing *who* to keep Sinking. Whichever of these options we choose, we must access the lexicon. As far as the goal of avoiding lexical access is concerned, then, the two options are tied; Sinking paths ought to be able to either stop at A-positions or not, which seems to be the result we want.

We have seen, then, that A-movement cannot skip A-positions, because it cannot involve Sinking. A' movement, by contrast, which typically can involve Sinking, ought to be able to skip A-positions. But we also saw above that we might expect to see cases in which A' movement is unable to involve Sinking; for instance, I claimed that Sinking should be banned in cases of intersecting A' movement paths. I will now try to show that A' movement which is not Sinking, like A-movement, cannot skip A-positions.

3   Very local A' movement

In this section I will discuss a number of cases of very local A' movement, and will try to show how their distribution and properties follow from the theory developed above.

3.1   *Inner* tough-*movement*

Jacobson (2000) points out a surprising property of *tough*-movement. *Tough*-movement generally seems to exhibit locality properties typically associated with A' movement (Jacobson 2000):

(25)   That sonata is hard to imagine John playing __ on that violin

However, when *tough*-movement intersects with another A' movement, it becomes more local:[7]

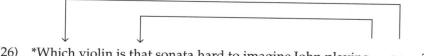

(26)   *Which violin is that sonata hard to imagine John playing __ on __?

As Jacobson points out, (26) contrasts sharply with a similar example with no *tough*-movement:

(27)   Which violin is it hard to imagine John playing that sonata on __?

There also appears to be a contrast between (26) and the minimally different (28), where PRO appears instead of *John*:[8]

(28)   ?Which violin is that sonata hard to imagine playing __ on __?

The contrast between (26) and (28) suggests a relevant generalization; if a *tough*-movement path intersects with another A′ movement path, it cannot cross an A-position in which it could land. Assuming for the moment that it is possible to identify the subject position of a control infinitive as an impossible landing site for an A′ moving operator, the contrasts in (26–28) follow. As we saw in the previous section, this is one of the contexts in which we should expect Sinking to be impossible; intersecting paths cannot both involve Sinking, and non-Sinking paths should be very local. In (26), on this approach, at the point in the derivation at which the subject of *playing* is to be inserted, we should prefer creating a copy of the head of the *tough*-movement chain to accessing the lexicon in order to construct and insert *John*. By allowing *tough*-movement to skip a position which it could in principle fill, this derivation has failed to avoid lexical access, and is therefore ruled out. In (28), by contrast, the subject position of *playing* is not a possible landing site for *tough*-movement, since it is a control infinitive; the *tough*-movement path is therefore not skipping any positions in which it could land.

3.2   Vacuous movement

Chung and McCloskey (1983) and Chomsky (1986) pursue the hypothesis that string-vacuous wh-movement does not occur. Their arguments are based on contrasts like the one in (29):

(29)   a.   This is a paper [that we need to find someone [who __ understands __]]
       b.   *This is a paper [that we need to find someone [who we can intimidate __ with __]]

The idea is that in (29a), string-vacuous movement of *who* does not occur and therefore does not create a wh-island.

The contrast in (29) could also be understood in terms of the theory under development here, however, as another instance in which an A′ path is forced to be very local just when it intersects with another A′ path. In (29b), on this account, the offending A′ dependency is the one headed by *who*, which skips the A-position occupied by *we*.

These two approaches make different predictions in cases in which the shortest possible movement path is not string-vacuous. The contrast in (30), for instance, seems to argue in favor of the alternative under development here:

(30)   a.   This is a paper [that we need to find someone [to persuade __ [to ask John to read __]]
       b.   *This is a paper [that we need to find someone [to persuade John [to ask __ to read __]]

The contrast in (30) is subtle, but seems to go in the expected direction. Here the inner path in (30b) crosses the A-position occupied by *John*. In (30a), by contrast, movement is not string-vacuous, but crucially does not skip any A-positions in which it could land.

3.3 *Contained relative clauses in Japanese*

Kuno (1973), Hasegawa (1984), and Ochi (1997) investigate a condition on relativization in Japanese. They note that when relativization paths intersect, one of the paths is required to be very local. Hasegawa (1984) offers the following generalization about the facts:

(31) The relativization or topicalization of a phrase in a relative clause is allowed only if
    a. the phrase is the subject of the relative clause, and
    b. the head of that relative clause is the subject of the higher clause.

I will refer to relative clauses that are contained in larger relative clauses as "contained relative clauses." (31a) is meant to account for the contrast in (32); in (32a) the movement path from the outermost head noun involves the subject of the contained relative clause, while in (32b) it is the object that is so relativized:[9]

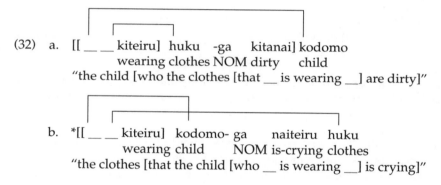

(32) a. [[__ __ kiteiru] huku -ga   kitanai] kodomo
               wearing clothes NOM dirty   child
          "the child [who the clothes [that __ is wearing __] are dirty]"

    b. *[[__ __ kiteiru] kodomo- ga   naiteiru huku
              wearing child   NOM is-crying clothes
          "the clothes [that the child [who __ is wearing __] is crying]"

(31b) accounts for the contrast in (33); in (33a), the contained relative clause modifies the subject of the relative clause in which it is contained, while in (33b) the contained relative clause modifies the object:

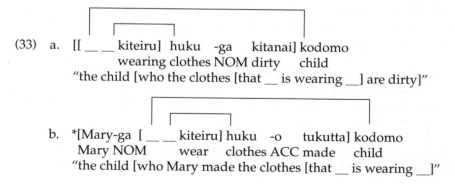

(33) a. [[__ __ kiteiru] huku -ga   kitanai] kodomo
               wearing clothes NOM dirty   child
          "the child [who the clothes [that __ is wearing __] are dirty]"

    b. *[Mary-ga [__ __ kiteiru] huku -o   tukutta] kodomo
        Mary NOM   wear   clothes ACC made   child
        "the child [who Mary made the clothes [that __ is wearing __]"

The condition in (31) imposes a requirement which is familiar to us by now; when A' paths intersect, one of them is forced to be very local, and is rendered unable to skip A-positions in which it could in principle land. In (33b), for instance, the offending path is that connected to *kodomo* "child;" this path is unable to skip the position occupied by the NP *Mary.*[10]

Ochi (1997) makes the point that these locality conditions on relativization are specifically conditions on relativization paths which intersect with other relativization paths. Simply crossing an island does not impose this kind of locality on relativization in Japanese, as we can see in examples like (34a), where the CED is violated, and (34b), where a wh-island is crossed (Ochi 1997: 215)

(34) a. [[John-ga __ katte   kita node]   minna   -ga   yorokonda]
          John NOM bought came because everyone NOM was-glad
          hon
          book
          "the book [that everyone was glad [because John bought __]]"

      b. [FBI-ga   [sono otoko-ga __ tsukatta ka dooka]   sirabeteiru]
          FBI NOM that man   NOM used   whether investigate
          naihu
          knife
          "the knife [that the FBI is investigating [whether that man used]]"

There is an intriguing difference between this case and the other cases reviewed in the previous sections. In the examples discussed above, when A'-paths intersect, the path which is required to be very local is the one whose eventual landing site is lower (that is, the inner path, in nested paths). Consider, for example, the contrast in (30), repeated as (35):

(35) a. This is a paper [that we need to find someone [to persuade __ [to
          ask John to read __]]
      b. *This is a paper [that we need to find someone [to persuade John [to
          ask __ to read __]]

In (35), the relativization path associated with *someone* is required to be very local, because it intersects with the relativization path associated with *paper*. (35b) is therefore ruled out, because the relativization path for *someone* crosses the A-position occupied by *John*. In (35a), however, we can see that the relativization path for *paper* is *not* required to be very local; it can skip *John* with impunity. Thus, the very local path is the "inner path," the one headed by the operator whose landing site is structurally lower.

In Japanese, on the other hand, the very local path is the one whose operator is structurally higher. We saw in (33) above, for instance, that the path associated with *kodomo* "child," the outermost head noun, is required to be very local when it intersects with another relativization path. This contrast between English and Japanese will presumably be relevant for investigating the derivation of dependencies in Japanese in this kind of model. One descriptive generalization that would cover both English and Japanese is that the chain of the intersecting chains which must be very local is the one whose head is linearly rightmost. If this chain is the one created last in the derivation, and if Sinking is preferred over non-Sinking movement when both are available (as seems reasonable, assuming the approach sketched in section 2 above), then we may be in a position to explain these facts. I will leave this issue for further work.

3.4   Tense islands

It is sometimes suggested (e.g., by Chomsky 1986; Frampton 1990b; Manzini 1991; Boyd 1992) that tense plays a role in strengthening island effects. This suggestion is based on contrasts like the one in (36):

(36)   a.   What do you know how [to repair __]
       b.   *What do you know how [you repaired __]

The literature on this contrast has suggested a connection between island-hood and tense: the island in (36b) is more impermeable to extraction than the one in (36a), because the island in (36b) is tensed while the island in (36a) is infinitival.
    There is, of course, another difference between the examples in (36), which is that the island in (36b) has a subject position of the kind which could in principle be occupied by a wh-trace, while the island in (36a) has a subject position which is occupied by PRO and could not be an origin for wh-movement. If islands have the effect of preventing Sinking paths from entering them, then the contrast in (36) might follow from the theory under development in this paper; the path of *what* in (36a) is very local (once it enters the island), but the corresponding path in (36b) is not. In order for the account to work, we will have to assume that the path of *what* in (36) is allowed to Sink down to a position just above the island, and is required to stop sinking at that point.[11,12] Neither of the examples in (36) involves a path which is very local all along its length; both of these paths skip the matrix subject position.
    Evidence that it is the presence of *John*, rather than of tense, which makes (36b) ill-formed comes from triples like the following:

(37)   a.   What are you wondering [how to try to repair __]
       b.   *What are you wondering [how John tried to repair __]
       c.   *What are you wondering [how to persuade John to repair __]

(37c) is an example of the type for which the theories about the examples in (36) make different predictions; the island is infinitival, but the potentially offending path does cross an A-position which it could in principle fill (that of *John*). English-speakers generally agree that (37c) seems worse than (37a), which is encouraging for the theory under development here. Some of my informants find (37b) worse than (37c); we may be forced to concede that Tense does play a role in worsening island effects, and that (37b) violates both this Tense-imposed condition and the requirement that A' paths into islands be very local, while (37c) only violates this strict requirement of locality. Careful examination of a wider range of data seems to be in order.

3.5 Persian scrambling

The sections above have described instances in which an intersection beween A' movement paths forces A' movement to be very local. This section, and the following one, will consider types of A' movement which must apparently always be very local, whether they intersect with other A' movement paths or not.

The first has to do with long-distance scrambling. Karimi (1999) notes an intriguing constraint on long-distance scrambling in Persian; it is blocked by any intervening NP with the same case as the NP being long-distance scrambled. This is demonstrated for subjects in (38a), for indirect objects in (38b), and for direct objects in (38c) (Karimi 1999: 174–6):

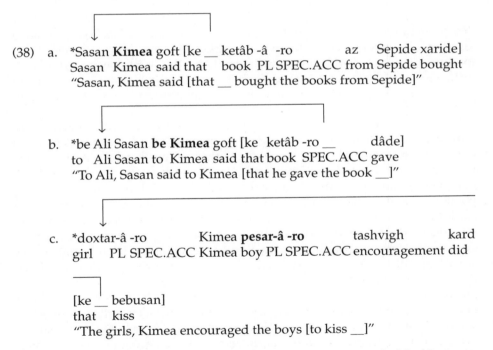

(38) a. *Sasan **Kimea** goft [ke __ ketâb -â -ro   az   Sepide xaride]
          Sasan Kimea said that   book PL SPEC.ACC from Sepide bought
          "Sasan, Kimea said [that __ bought the books from Sepide]"

      b. *be Ali Sasan **be Kimea** goft [ke ketâb -ro __   dâde]
          to Ali Sasan to Kimea said that book SPEC.ACC gave
          "To Ali, Sasan said to Kimea [that he gave the book __]"

      c. *doxtar-â -ro   Kimea **pesar-â -ro**   tashvigh   kard
          girl   PL SPEC.ACC Kimea boy PL SPEC.ACC encouragement did

          [ke __ bebusan]
          that   kiss
          "The girls, Kimea encouraged the boys [to kiss __]"

Preliminary investigations suggest that these properties may hold of Japanese as well. Saito (1985: 185) notes that long-distance scrambling of a subject past another subject is impossible in Japanese:

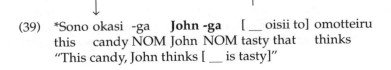

(39) *Sono okasi -ga   **John -ga**   [__ oisii to] omotteiru
      this   candy NOM John NOM tasty that   thinks
      "This candy, John thinks [__ is tasty]"

Several informants agree that datives are subject to a similar restriction, finding scrambling of a dative past a c-commanding dative (40a) quite awkward, and clearly worse than long-distance scrambling of a dative when the matrix dative follows (hence, presumably fails to c-command) the embedded clause (Shogo Suzuki, Shigeru Miyagawa, Shinichiro Ishihara, Ken Hiraiwa, personal communication):

(40)   a.   *Taroo-ni   John-ga   **Mary-ni**   [Hanako -ga __ hana   -o
           Taroo DAT John NOM Mary DAT Hanako NOM flower ACC
           ageta to]   itta
           gave that said
           "To Taroo, John said to Mary [that Hanako gave a flower __]"

       b.   Taroo-ni John-ga [Hanako-ga__ hana-o ageta to] **Mary-ni** itta

These phenomena certainly seem to have something in common with those described in the previous sections, in that A' movement is blocked by (certain kinds of) A-positions. There are two obvious differences, however. One is that locality is restricted only by nouns that have the same case as the long-distance scrambled noun. Another is that there is only a single A' movement path in this example, whereas the previous examples involved intersecting A' movement paths.

Recall that the reason for the "very local" nature of certain kinds of A' movement, in this theory, has to do with a preference for copying material already in the tree (that is, for Move) over other options (such as Merge of new material from the lexicon). Unless an A' movement path involves Sinking, then, we should be required to copy the head of the A' dependency as soon as possible. These Persian and Japanese examples suggest that in some cases, at least, the set of possible positions in which an A' trace can be created is constrained by the case of the head of the A' dependency. This difference between Persian and Japanese on the one hand and English on the other might simply stem from the difference with respect to case morphology; all of the long-distance scrambled NPs in the Persian and Japanese examples above bear morphological evidence of the Case they bear. English case, by contrast, is famously impoverished.[13] The Persian and Japanese facts call into question standard assumptions about the role of Case in syntax, namely that "narrow syntax" is unconcerned with the particular value of Case, only with its presence or absence (see Chomsky 1999 for some discussion). We see here that either this standard assumption is not correct or the effects under consideration here, contrary to the theory being developed, should not be analyzed as part of "narrow syntax".

Why long-distance scrambling should be very local in the relevant sense is far from clear; why does long-distance scrambling differ from wh-movement, for instance, in this regard? Considering the two types of movement from the point of view of a parser, we might expect that a parser is able to postulate the existence of an A' movement chain as soon as a wh-phrase at the beginning of a clause is reached, and begin movement (that is, Sinking) immediately. In the case of long-distance scrambling, on the other hand, it might not be clear that long-distance scrambling has taken place until later in the derivation; a clause beginning with a dative NP, for instance, might be the result of local scrambling, or pro-drop of any c-commanding arguments. Since it is non-Sinking paths that are very local, it is possible that this distinction between the two types of movement is the relevant one.

3.6 Tagalog extraction

Another apparent instance of very local A' movement comes from Tagalog, in which all A' movement of arguments appears to have very local properties. Tagalog sentences typically require that one argument be made the "topic;" topicalization has (arguably) no effect on word order but is associated with morphology on the verb and on the topicalized noun. The topic is underlined in the following examples:

(41) a. Nagbigay <u>ang magsasaka</u> ng   bulaklak sa kalabaw
          AT-gave T farmer   Unm flower   L water-buffalo
          "The farmer gave a flower to a/the water buffalo"

      b. Ibinigay ng   magsasaka <u>ang bulaklak</u> sa kalabaw
          TT-gave Unm farmer   T   flower   L water-buffalo
          "A/the farmer gave the flower to a/the water buffalo"

      c. Binigyan ng   magsasaka ng   bulaklak <u>ang kalabaw</u>
          LT-gave Unm farmer   Unm flower   T   water-buffalo
          "A/the famer gave a/the flower to the water buffalo"

The syntactic nature of topicalization is disputed (cf. Schachter 1976, 1996; Guilfoyle, Hung, and Travis 1992; Richards 2000, and references cited there) but it is generally agreed that it involves the topic undergoing movement of some kind to a position above the base positions of the arguments of the sentence, and this is all the understanding of the phenomenon we will need.
    Relativization requires that the relativized noun be topicalized:

(42) a. bulaklak [na ibinigay ng   magsasaka sa kalabaw]
          flower   that TT-gave Unm farmer   L water-buffalo
          "the flower that the farmer gave to the water buffalo"

      b. *bulaklak [na nagbigay ang magsasaka sa kalabaw]
          flower   that AT-gave T   farmer   L water-buffalo

      c. *bulaklak [na binigyan ng   magsasaka ang kalabaw]
          flower   that LT-gave Unm farmer   T   water-buffalo

When an extraction site is more deeply embedded, the clause in which it is embedded must be the topic of the higher clause, and the extraction site must still be the topic of its clause. Thus, (43b) is ruled out because the topic of the higher clause is *Maria* rather than the clausal complement, and (43c) is ruled out because the topic of the lower clause is *magsasaka* "farmer" rather than the relativized NP:

(43) a. bulaklak [na sinabi   ni   Maria [na ibinigay ng   magsasaka
          flower   that TT-said Unm Maria that TT-gave Unm farmer
          sa kalabaw]]
          L water-buffalo
          "the flower that Mary said the farmer gave to the water buffalo"

      b. *bulaklak [na nagsabi si Maria [na ibinigay ng   magsasaka sa
          flower   that AT-said T Maria that TT-gave Unm farmer   L
          kalabaw]]
          water-buffalo

      c. *bulaklak [na sinabi ni   Maria [na nagbigay ang magsasaka
          flower   that TT-said Unm Maria that AT-gave T   farmer
          sa kalabaw]]
          L water-buffalo

These conditions on Tagalog relativization strongly resemble the conditions on Japanese contained relative clauses discussed earlier; essentially, the relativization site must be the highest position in the relative clause, with no c-commanding nominals. In other words, the movement is very local, in the sense defined here. These facts could be made to follow, then, if we could guarantee that Tagalog A′ extraction could not involve Sinking.

Unfortunately, it is not clear how to do this. At the end of the previous section, I briefly discussed the idea that Sinking might be ruled out in cases in which the parser has no way of diagnosing the presence of an A′ dependency until after structure has already been inserted under the head of the dependency. The idea would be that at this point it is too late to begin Sinking. This was supposed to account for the distinction between wh-movement in a language like English, which is not very local except under the circumstances explored above, and long-distance scrambling, which does appear to be very local (once the effects of differences in Case are taken into account). We would need to say, then, that wh-movement can be diagnosed from the outset, as soon as a clause beginning with a wh-phrase is encountered, while long-distance scrambling is more difficult to detect.

This line of reasoning could in principle be expanded to deal with the Tagalog facts, but I think that it may ultimately lead to unfortunate consequences. It is generally the case that Tagalog relative clauses are not identifiable as relative clauses until after the verb has been introduced; the morpheme *na* which introduces the relative clauses in the examples above would also be used to introduce a postnominal adjective:

(44)   bulaklak na   maganda
       flower   NA beautiful
       "beautiful flower"

On the other hand, there are certainly circumstances, even in English, in which relative clauses are not identifiable as such until late in their construction, but this does not seem to lead to very local movement. For instance, the material following *the man* in (45a) could be a complement clause or a relative clause, as the continuations in (45b–c) make clear:

(45)   a.   I told the man [I saw
       b.   in the park yesterday] a story
       c.   a burglar]

Similarly, Japanese relativization is not normally very local, but relative clauses are quite generally unrecognizable as such until the head noun is reached. The clause in (46a), for instance, could be a complete (informal) sentence with pro-drop, or it could be a relative clause, as it is in (46b):

(46)   a.   hon-o   katta
            book ACC bought
            "He bought a book"

       b.   [hon-o   katta]   gakusei
            book ACC bought student
            "the student who bought a book"

Thus, it is not clear to what extent we can trace properties of the grammar back to properties of the parser. Still, we now seem to have a theoretical means at our disposal for relating the Tagalog facts to facts from other languages; all we need now is some way of preventing Tagalog relative operators[14] from Sinking.

4   Conclusion

In this chapter I have suggested that under certain circumstances, A' movement exhibits a kind of strict locality which is more typically associated with A-movement. I have also tried to show that the account sketched in Richards (1999) of how dependencies are created in a top-down derivation makes this phenomenon appear fairly natural. It is always the case, I have suggested, that copying of existing material is preferred to retrieving new material from the lexicon (that is, Move is preferred over Merge). This principle was used in Richards (1999) to explain facts about the relation between expletives and their associates, as we saw in section 1 above. I have suggested that this principle holds for A' movement as well, and is realized in one of two different ways.

When possible, the head of the A' dependency is created immediately, and new lexical material is inserted above the copy until the copy reaches its destination; this is the kind of very successive-cyclic "movement" I referred to as Sinking. When Sinking is impossible for some reason (and we have seen that the reasons are not always clear, though I have offered theories of some of the relevant cases), then A' movement is very local, just like A-movement.

Acknowledgments

Many thanks to audiences at MIT, the University of Maryland, the University of California at Irvine, and WECOL 2000, and especially to David Pesetsky, Norbert Hornstein, and Sam Epstein, for helpful comments on this material. Responsibility for any errors is entirely mine.

Notes

1   For other attempts to eliminate Numerations, see Collins (1997), and Frampton and Gutmann (1999).
2   It seems clear that obedience to this requirement could be enforced by local inspection of the syntactic structure at the point in the derivation at which copying takes place; if the object copied has an unchecked feature, or checks a feature on something else by virtue of being copied, then copying is legitimate.
3   There will also be cases in which features are checked under Merge; we may regard these as involving deletion without checking, or alter the definition of checking slightly to accommodate these cases. Nothing crucial hinges on the choice, as far as I can see.
4   In derivations where the moving wh-phrase is phrasal, we would have the additional option of Merging new material within the wh-phrase. The question of how to rule this out is essentially equivalent to that of determining how much material should pied-pipe under movement; I have nothing new to say about the problem, but it seems clear that it is a familiar one.
5   This contrast between distinct types of wh-movement is highly reminiscent of Manzini's (1992) distinction between address-based and categorial index dependencies (and see also Marantz (1994) for a discussion of intriguing locality distinctions made by that theory).
6   This approach is consistent with there being theta-features on theta-assigning heads; thanks to Norbert Hornstein for pointing this out to me.
7   It is unimportant for our purposes here whether *tough*-movement involves movement of the NP *that sonata* or of an operator associated with it.
8   Jacobson (2000) actually denies this; she would accord (26) and (28) the same status.
9   Here I draw relativization paths connecting the relativization site with the head noun; this is simply for ease of representation, and is not meant to be a stance on the question of whether a null operator is involved.
10   This reasoning might lead to an account of the contrast in (32) as well, depending on whether the other relativization path is understood as involving Sinking. If neither path is Sinking, then the conditions on the derivation should be satisfied in (32b); at each of the trace positions, a copy is made of an operator, and the lexicon

is not accessed. On the other hand, the contrast in (32) might be susceptible to explanation by other means; in general, it seems to be the case that intersecting movement paths prefer to cross (speaking hierarchically) in Japanese; the hierarchically higher operator moves to the hierarchically higher landing site. For some discussion, see Nishigauchi (1990), Saito (1994), Grewendorf and Sabel (1996), Richards (1997, 2001), Tanaka (1998).

11   This is not the assumption defended in Richards (1999), where I assumed that the wh-phrase from the higher clause is able to Sink into the island. The account given there of Path Containment Condition effects crucially hinged on this assumption; if the account sketched in this section is to be pursued, some other way of dealing with those effects will have to be found.

12   This requirement is reminiscent of the conditions on scope reconstruction imposed by islands; as noted by Longobardi (1987), Frampton (1990b), and Cresti (1995), a wh-phrase extracted from the island cannot undergo reconstruction into the island, though it can reconstruct to positions outside the island and below its eventual landing site. In terms of the theory sketched here, we might conclude that scope reconstruction is limited to positions along Sinking paths.

13   This line of reasoning leads to the intriguing prediction that in a language with rich Case marking on nouns, the phenomena discussed in the previous sections should become somewhat less local than they are in English; the A' movement paths should be blocked only by intervening A-positions with the same Case features.

14   Tagalog argument wh-questions exhibit similar locality conditions, but such questions are invariably clefts involving a (sometimes headless) relative clause (see Schachter and Otanes 1972; Kroeger 1993; Richards 1998 for arguments to this effect), so it seems reasonable to collapse this problem with the one discussed in the text.

References

Boyd, John. 1992. "Exceptions to island constraints and syntactic theory." Doctoral dissertation, University of Massachusetts, Amherst.

Chomsky, Noam. 1986. *Barriers*. Cambridge, MA: MIT Press.

Chomsky, Noam. 1995. *The Minimalist Program*. Cambridge, MA: MIT Press.

Chomsky, Noam. 1998. "Minimalist inquiries: the framework." MIT Occasional Papers in Linguistics 15, MIT Working Papers in Linguistics, Cambridge.

Chomsky, Noam. 1999. "Derivation by phase." MIT Occasional Papers in Linguistics 18, MIT Working Papers in Linguistics, Cambridge.

Chung, Sandra and James McCloskey. 1983. "On the interpretation of certain island facts in GPSG." *Linguistic Inquiry* 14: 704–13.

Collins, Chris. 1997. *Local Economy*. Cambridge, MA: MIT Press.

Cresti, Diana. 1995. "Extraction and reconstruction." *Natural Language Semantics* 3: 79–122.

Frampton, John. 1990a. "The fine structure of wh-movement and the proper formulation of the ECP." MS, Northeastern University, Boston, MA.

Frampton, John. 1990b. "Parasitic gaps and the theory of *wh*-chains." *Linguistic Inquiry* 21: 49–78.

Frampton, John and Sam Gutmann. 1999. "Cyclic computation, a computationally efficient minimalist syntax." *Syntax* 2: 1–27.

Grewendorf, Günther and Joachim Sabel. 1996. "Multiple specifiers and the theory of adjunction: on scrambling in German and Japanese." *Sprachwissenschaft in Frankfurt Arbeitspapier* 16.

Guilfoyle, Eithne, Henrietta Hung, and Lisa Travis. 1992. "Spec of IP and Spec of VP: two subjects in Austronesian languages." *Natural Language and Linguistic Theory* 10: 375–414.

Hasegawa, Nobuko. 1984. "On the so-called 'zero pronouns' in Japanese." *The Linguistic Review* 4: 289–341.

Jacobson, Pauline. 2000. "Extraction out of *tough.*" *Snippets* 1: 9–10.

Karimi, Simin. 1999. "Is scrambling as strange as we think it is?" *MITWPL 33: Papers on Morphology and Syntax, Cycle One*, ed. Karlos Arregi, Benjamin Bruening, Cornelia Krause, and Vivian Lin. Cambridge, MA: MIT Working Papers in Linguistics.

Kroeger, Paul. 1993. *Phrase Structure and Grammatical Relations in Tagalog.* Center for the Study of Language and Information, Stanford.

Kuno, Susumu. 1973. *The Structure of the Japanese Language.* Cambridge, MA: MIT Press.

Longobardi, Giuseppe. 1987. "Extraction from NP and the proper notion of head government." In Alessandra Giorgi and Giuseppe Longobardi, eds., *The Syntax of Noun Phrases*, 57–112. Cambridge: Cambridge University Press,

Manzini, Maria Rita. 1991. *Locality.* Cambridge, MA: MIT Press.

Marantz, Alec. 1994. "The two modes of A' binding are not tied to the argument/adjunct distinction." MS, MIT, Cambridge, MA.

Nishigauchi, Taisuke. 1990. *Quantification in the Theory of Grammar.* Dordrecht: Kluwer.

Ochi, Masao. 1997. "On the nature of relativization in Japanese." *Proceedings of CONSOLE V*, ed. Tina Cambier-Langeveld, João Costa, Rob Goedemans and Ruben van de Vijver. Sole, Leiden, pp. 213–28.

Phillips, Colin. 1996. Order and structure. Doctoral dissertation, MIT.

Phillips, Colin. To appear. "Linear order and constituency." *Linguistic Inquiry.*

Richards, Norvin. 1997. "What moves where when in which language?" Doctoral dissertation, MIT, Cambridge, MA.

Richards, Norvin. 1998. "Syntax versus semantics in Tagalog wh-extraction." *UCLA Occasional Papers 21: Recent Papers in Austronesian Linguistics*, ed. Matthew Pearson. UCLA Department of Linguistics, Los Angeles.

Richards, Norvin. 1999. "Dependency formation and directionality of tree construction." *MITWPL 34: Papers on Morphology and Syntax, Cycle Two*, ed. Vivian Lin, Cornelia Krause, Benjamin Bruening, and Karlos Arregi. Cambridge, MA: MIT Working Papers in Linguistics.

Richards, Norvin. 2000. "Another look at Tagalog subjects." *Formal Issues in Austronesian Linguistics*, ed. Ileana Paul, Vivianne Phillips, and Lisa Travis. Dordrecht: Kluwer.

Richards, Norvin. 2001. *Movement in Language: Interactions and Architectures.* Oxford: Oxford University Press.

Saito, Mamoru. 1985. "Some asymmetries in Japanese and their theoretical implications." Doctoral dissertation, MIT, Cambridge, MA.

Saito, Mamoru. 1994. "Additional-wh effects and the adjunction site theory." *Journal of East Asian Linguistics* 3: 195–240.

Schachter, Paul. 1976. "The subject in Philippine languages: actor, topic, actor-topic, or none of the above." In Charles Li, ed., *Subject and Topic*, 491–518. New York: Academic Press.

Schachter, Paul. 1996. "The subject in Tagalog: still none of the above." *UCLA Occasional Papers in Linguistics* 15.

Schachter, Paul and Fe Otanes. 1972. *Tagalog Reference Grammar.* Berkeley: University of California Press.

Schneider, Dave. 1999. "Parsing and incrementality." Doctoral dissertation, University of Delaware.

Tanaka, Hidekazu. 1998. "Conditions on logical form derivations and representations." Doctoral dissertation, McGill University.

Chapter ten

Arguments for a Derivational Approach to Syntactic Relations Based on Clitics

Esther Torrego

1   Introduction

The purpose of this article is to conduct a case study of three syntactic problems associated with subject-to-subject raising over the Experiencer argument. The proposed solutions involve a strict derivational approach to the M(inimal) L(ink) C(ondition), thereby providing evidence for a strong derivational system of the sort argued by Epstein and Seely (1999). The MLC is a principle of grammar that ensures that a certain grammatical operation occurs in an optimal manner. Determining the application of the MLC to a given structure often requires solving a problem not directly connected to the MLC. Subject-to-subject raising over an Experiencer represents a case in point.

Research on this topic for the last 15 years provides evidence that variation in the morphosyntactic expression of the Experiencer plays a significant role in the possibilities of subject-to-subject raising over an Experiencer. Two types of related facts support this finding. One involves differences in the realization of the Experiencer, e.g., a moved wh-Experiencer, a clitic, a nontopicalized lexically realized DP. The other involves cross-linguistic differences in whether or not subject-to-subject raising over the Experiencer is possible at all. When subject-raising is sensitive to the movement of the Experiencer we suspect that the structure has changed during the course of the derivation, making it possible to evade a MLC violation. Something similar happens with the cross-linguistic variation found in the morphosyntactic expression of the Experiencer *vis-à-vis* the possibilities of raising over the Experiencer altogether. In frameworks that restrict syntactic objects to lexical items and to objects recursively built from them (see Chomsky 1995), what operations can take place and when they apply depends largely on the form and featural content of the items already assembled. By now, several studies have explored connections between the featural content of the Experiencer and those of relevant functional categories in the structure, especially T.

Boeckx (2000) has suggested that the Experiencer bears a [person] feature along with T, reflecting its semantic association with point of view (see also Chomsky 2000).[1] Arguably the bearer of the [person] feature linked to Experiencers that encodes point of view is the functional head that checks the Experiencer's Case feature. In this study I explore the idea that the functional category housing the [person] feature associated with the Experiencer is a null P. Variation in the feature content of the null P, and in its location within the structure, are extremely important with respect to the role played by the Experiencer in regard to T and V. Significantly, verbs such as *seem* do not display a uniform cross-linguistic syntactic behavior; *seem* is found as a copula in a variety of languages, including English, French, and Spanish (see Moro 1993); in French and Spanish, *seem* can (arguably) be a control verb with certain realizations of the Experiencer (Rouveret and Vergnaud 1980; Kayne 1984), and in Spanish the syntactic possibilities of subject-to-subject raising vary depending on the nature of the complement clause, in ways to be explained. We are led to suspect that *seem*-structures are highly variable, and that the form and function of the Experiencer yield these different choices.

1.1   Background

There is a discrepancy between the c-commanding facts exhibited by the English sentences in (1) and subject-to-subject raising. As Chomsky (1995: 304) notes, English sentences with a raising verb and an Experiencer such as (1a) pose a problem for the Minimal Link Condition. The subject of these sentences raises from the infinitival to the matrix clause, but the Experiencer appears to be "closer" (Chomsky 1986: 181):

(1) a. they seem to each other [to admire the artist]
     b. it seems to him [that John is a failure]
     c. it seems to his friends [that John is a failure]

In (1b) *John* is interpreted as disjoint from *him*. By condition C, *him* c-commands *John*. Since *him* c-commands into the embedded TP, the PP [to *him*] does not prevent *him* from c-commanding *John*; rather the Experiencer behaves as a NP/DP Case-marked by *to*. Thus, in (1a) *each other* c-commands the trace of *they*. Since *they* binds *each other* and *each other* in turn binds the trace of *they*, *each other* is the closest attractable category to the matrix Infl. We then expect the Experiencer to block subject-raising, contrary to fact.

The MLC forces movement of the closest DP:

(2) *Minimal Link Condition*
     K attracts α only if there is no β, β closer to K than
     α, such that K attracts β.

Nonetheless, for the reasons presented at the outset, we suspect that the MLC holds for these structures as it holds for many other movement phenomena (Kitahara 1997).

Ferguson (1994), Kitahara (1997), and Epstein et al. (1998: 2.5) present a solution for English (1) in derivational terms. They argue that the c-command properties of the intervening Experiencer are not the same throughout the derivation. At the derivational point in which the infinitival subject raises, the Experiencer is within a PP, and, as such, it does not c-command the embedded subject. The Experiencer NP/DP, however, is "promoted" at LF where Binding Condition C applies. The two main syntactic problems I will discuss here can also be seen in this light, as providing arguments for a derivational system in the domain of the MLC.

1.2   Background assumptions

Right from the beginning we need to address the following question: Where does the Experiencer merge in the structure? This question has generated much recent debate because the position where the Experiencer merges is likely to impact the possibilities of subject raising.[2] I argue that the initial position of the Experiencer in the derivation is only partially relevant for the satisfaction of the MLC in the structure. It seems that it is the functional head P that checks the Case of the Experiencer that is central, both with respect to the position where P merges and with respect to its feature content.

The literature discusses two main positions for the merger of the Experiencer: outside VP, as a subject, or inside VP, as a complement. I will assume that the Experiencer merges as a subject, an idea that goes back to Perlmutter (Perlmutter 1984). The plausibility of this assumption is enhanced by several cross-linguistic facts, including that the Experiencer of *seem* is not required (in contrast, for instance, to psych predicates), and that *seem* enters into multiple structures (copula, raising and, arguably, control). In a number of respects, the Experiencer of raising verbs is closer to what in the nominal system is the possessor than to a complement. For instance, possessors are the highest arguments within the DP, tend to be animate, and hold a weak thematic connection with N. The Experiencer of raising verbs shares with the possessor the [person] feature of participants, and also its weak thematic connection with V.[3]

Once we assume that the Experiencer of *seem* merges as a subject, the next important question is where the category that houses the feature [person] associated with point of view merges. Boeckx and Chomsky have [person] in T. However, I use a different category to house this feature, one that I label P. For a number of reasons, I take it that the site of P in raising predicate constructions is higher than T. With these assumptions as background, I will briefly discuss English in the face of this general approach. English may present a problem for the hypothesis that the functional head P that checks the Experiencer's Case feature checks dative, especially if *to*-datives bear inherent Case and inherent Case is not checked.

1.3   English

Previous accounts of subject-to-subject raising over the Experiencer in English (Ferguson 1994; Kitahara 1997; Epstein et al. 1998: 2.5) have succeeded in accounting for the absence of syntactic effects of the English Experiencer in subject-raising. They hypothesized that the Experiencer is a PP at the point in which the infinitival subject raises to T.[4] Here I want to speculate why at the particular derivational point in which T attracts the infinitival subject the Experiencer is a PP. Previous accounts simply assert that it is a PP.

Assuming that the Experiencer in English is within a PP, let us ask whether the Case of the Experiencer needs to be checked or not. If the Experiencer in English has inherent Case, the head P that encodes the [person] feature in association with the Experiencer cannot possibly have uninterpretable features. Taken in isolation, this is not necessarily problematic. However, it raises the question of how P establishes an agreement relation with the Experiencer. I would like to suggest that in English it is the dative preposition *to* of the *to*-Experiencer that plays a fundamental role in licensing point of view. What is crucial is that *to* be a P that has a [person] feature along with the Experiencer. Null P above T will be to able to enter into an agreement relation with *to* so long as *to* has (some) inflectional features. My conjecture is that P has an empty slot to be filled, in the spirit of Koopman (1995), and that attracts *to* to move covertly, deriving: [5]

(3)   [to^1-P [T [[to^2 [him]]   [v [seems [the child is happy]]]]]]
      PP   TP vP PP   vP VP

Assuming bottom-up cyclic rule application (Chomsky 1993, 1995, 2000, 2001), at the derivational point in which T attracts the subject over the [[P-DP] P], null P has not merged yet. This being so, subject-to-subject raising over the Experiencer incurs no violation of the MLC. If this is on the right track, this could provide an argument for the strict derivational character of the MLC. I turn to Romance, for which I argue P has inflectional features that need to enter into checking.

2   Strict derivationality: the first two arguments from Romance

The next three arguments for strict derivationality concern Romance sentences containing Experiencer-Subject verbs and clitics. Informally, clitics display a richer array of movement possibilities than nonclitics. This makes the exploration of a radical derivational system of the sort argued by Epstein and Seely (1999) particularly fruitful, as new structures can be formed as the derivation unfolds.

2.1   The first argument: French and Italian

One well-known contrast from Italian and French is illustrated in (4) and (5), respectively:[6]

(4)   *Italian*
    a.   Gianni gli sembra essere stanco.
         Gianni to him-seems to be tired
         "Gianni seems to him to be tired."

    b.   *Gianni sembra a Maria essere stanco.
         Gianni seems to Maria to be tired
         "Gianni seems to Maria to be tired."

(5)   *French*
    a.   Ce conducteur me semble être fatigué.
         This driver to me-seems (to) be tired
         "This driver seems to me to be tired."

    b.   ??Marie semble à Jean être fatiguée.
         Marie seems to Jean (to) be tired
         "Marie seems to Jean to be tired."

As first noted and analyzed by Torrego (1989 – partially published in 1996a), lexical Experiencers in Romance interfere with subject-to-subject raising. Under present assumptions, this fact suggests that in Romance, datives are DPs at the relevant level, with the dative preposition *a* being the Spell Out of a Case feature.[7]

Let us consider the contrasts in (4) and (5). It appears that clitic movement makes it possible for T to attract the infinitival subject, as in the analysis of McGinnis (1998). In order to arrive at the structures of the sentences in (4a) and (5a), we need to invoke the assumption that clitics are both X^{max} and X^{min}. Their X^{max} and X^{min} status will play a significant role in the analysis of sentences like (4a) and (5a).

Within a Bare Phrase Structure theory, clitics are assumed to be both maximal and minimal (Chomsky 1995). The clitic is maximal because it does not project, and is minimal because it does not dominate anything. Assuming the X^{max} and the X^{min} status of clitics to be correct for Italian and French, the acceptability of examples (4a)/(5a) provides one more argument for strict derivationality. Let us discuss why.

In the structure of sentences like (5a), the clitic merges, receiving the Experiencer thematic role. At this particular derivational point, the clitic c-commands into the lower TP:

(6)   [me [v [semble [ce conducteur être fatigué]]]]
       vP   vP VP   TP

In the next step, T merges. At this point, the clitic moves to T as an X^0 and adjoins to T (for whatever reasons clitics move, which are not clear[8]). Next, T attracts the infinitival subject to its Specifier without interference from the clitic, which, due to its incorporation into T, no longer c-commands the infinitival subject:[9]

(7)   [[me^1 -T] [me^2 v [semble [ce conducteur être fatigué]]]]
      TP T   vP   VP

If this analysis is correct, the facts that clitics do not bar subject-to-subject raising in French and Italian provides another argument for strict derivationality; in particular, for the derivational application of the MLC.[10]

2.2   The second argument: Spanish versus French/Italian

Intrinsic to the proposed account for Italian (4a) and French (5a) is that clitics are both X^{max} and X^{min}. Movement of a clitic during the derivation can change the structure in ways that movement of nonclitics cannot.

Torrego (1989, 1996a) discusses data from Spanish (and the other clitic doubling Romance languages of Western Romance), leading to the conclusion that clitics in Spanish (and these other languages) do not help in the derivation of subject-to-subject raising. Consider the contrast in (8):

(8)   a.   *Ese taxista les parece estar cansado.
           That taxi-driver to-them-seems (to) be tired
           "That taxi-driver seems to them to be tired."

      b.   Les parece que ese taxista está cansado.
           to-them seems that that taxi-driver is tired
           "It seems that that taxi-driver is tired."

The ill-formedness of Spanish (8a) is surprising. Everything else being equal, movement of the clitic in (8a) should raise the Experiencer to T, just as movement of the clitic raises the Experiencer to T in Italian and French, making attraction of the infinitival subject by T possible.

In Torrego (1989, 1996a), I attributed the failure of the clitic to license subject-raising in Spanish (8a) to its status as a "doubling" clitic, arguing that the Experiencer argument is not the clitic; instead a null *pro* is. Here I continue to assume that *pro* rather than the clitic is the argument, but I will suggest a new perspective on the Spanish facts that provides a better understanding of the apparent exception to the clitic effect in derivations involving subject-to-subject raising across an Experiencer.

My treatment of doubling clitics will make them functional heads or, more exactly, part of heads (see section 2.2.1). I assume that doubling clitics fail to receive a thematic role in languages of the Spanish type, hence movement of a doubling clitic does not raise the Experiencer to T in these languages. Given this difference in the syntactic status of clitics in the two groups of languages (French/Italian–Spanish) the analysis proposed for Italian (4a) and French (5a) is not threatened by the Spanish data.

2.2.1   The light v of subject-Experiencer verbs

Chomsky (2000, 2001) proposes that v and T can have inflectional features. Case-checking requires that v and T have a complete set of inflectional features. The inflectional features of v and T are uninterpretable and must be deleted for legibility. The inflectional features of v and T delete by establishing an agreement relation with an element with a full set of inflectional features and Case. Importantly, the v of the vP-structure of English *seem* does not have a full set of φ-features: it is defective. It is crucial to the derivation of subject-to-subject raising not to encounter an intervening functional head such as v able to check Case on the infinitival subject. A key question to investigate here is whether the v of Spanish *parecer*+Experiencer is also defective.

The possibility that the light verb of Spanish *parecer*+Experiencer may be nondefective arises from an empirical fact that holds of subject-Experiencer verbs. Namely, that a dative clitic doubling the Experiencer is required with these verbs. This is shown in (9a) for the raising predicate *parecer* ("seem"), and in (9b) for the psych predicate *gustar* ("like"):

(9)   a.   (*Le) parece (a esta gente) que ese taxista está cansado.
                (to them)-seem (to these people) that this taxi-driver is tired
            "It seems to these people that the taxi-driver is tired."

        b.   (*Le) gustaron los juguetes (al niño)
                (to-him)-pleased the toys (to the child)
            "The child liked the toys."

I want to pursue the intuition that the doubling clitic is housed in v, and provides v, the subject-Experiencer light verb, with inflectional features. On this approach (put forward in Torrego 1998), the requirement that subject-Experiencer verbs have a doubling clitic can be seen as a parametric property of light verbs licensing an Experiencer subject.

Assuming the φ-features of the v analysis of clitics, as in Torrego (1998), the structure that corresponds to sentences (9a) and (9b) will be (10a) and (10b), respectively:

(10)   a.   [EXP [[Cl-v] [V(*parecer*) [T [EA [v [V . . .]]]]]]]]
                vP   vP   VP   TP vP vP VP

          b.   [EXP [[Cl-v] [V(*gustar*) THEME]]]
                  vP   vP   VP

Structures of the form [[v] [V-TP]], with nondefective v, correspond to ECM structures. In ECM structures, an infinitival subject moves to the edge of vP and checks accusative in this position. If the combination "[Cl-v]" amounts to having nondefective v, structure (10a) could be a raising-to-object structure, although not one of raising-to-subject.

The state of affairs obtained, though, suggests that this picture is only partially right. When we consider structures with psych predicates such as (10b) more closely (which are, in relevant respects, like (10a) but less complex) we find evidence for displacement of the object to the edge of vP, but not for Case-checking. Taking specificity effects on an object to signal Object shift, we must assume that the Theme of psych predicate *gustar* ("like") undergoes movement:[11]

(11)   a.   Le gustaron al niño *juguetes/los juguetes.
             To him-pleased to the child toys/the toys
             "The child liked toys."

       b.   Les gustó a los niños un juguete.
             To them-pleased to the children a toy
             "The children liked a toy."

In (11a), the Theme of *gustar* cannot be realized as a bare plural, and in (11b), the Theme is an indefinite and must be interpreted as specific: there is a specific toy that the children liked. The natural assumption is that the complex [Cl-v] of the structure represented in (10b) has an EPP-feature that attracts the Theme to raise to the outer Specifier of vP, yielding (12):[12]

(12)   [un juguete^1 [a los niños   [[les-v]   [gustó un juguete^2]]]]
        vP   vP   vP v   VP
        a toy   to the children [them-v] pleased a toy

Interestingly, Object Shift is an instance of movement associated with light verbs that have a full set of inflectional features (Chomsky 2001). Yet, the raised Theme is nominative rather than dative (finite V shows person and number agreement with the Theme). Thus, though the intuition is clear that the doubling clitic provides inflectional features to v, it is also clear that the raised object satisfies an EPP-feature without Case-checking.[13]

Conceptually, the fact that the raised Theme is nominative rather than dative fits well with our earlier proposal that dative is checked by a P. Nonetheless, I want to consider another factor pertaining to the structures in (10), one that may be relevant to the absence of dative Case in the structure: a hidden *pro*.

The class of heads that license *pro* in Romance involves pronominal inflection. Suppose, then, that the complex head [*les*-v] licenses *pro*, and that the Experiencer of subject-Experiencer predicates in Spanish is therefore *pro*. An assumption I make that will drive my analysis of the intricate facts of subject-to-subject raising in Spanish (and similar languages) is that *pro* is a head, and, as such, *pro* is able to probe the clitic, deleting its Case feature and the clitic's inflectional features.[14] On this approach, the structure that corresponds to sentence (11b) will not be (12), but the following:[15]

(13)   [un juguete¹ [(a los niños) pro [[les-v]   [gustó un juguete²]]]]
       vP   vP   vP v   VP
       a toy   to the children   [them-v] pleased a toy

Before discussing various important consequences that may follow from this analysis, let us consider some evidence in support of the claim that the clitic of subject-Experiencer verbs is housed in v.

Torrego (1989) discusses a number of contrasts in the Tense-inflectional possibilities of *parecer* depending on whether the Experiencer is present or absent. All of these differences reflect an impoverished verbal structure of *parecer* with no Experiencer, as predicted by the proposal. The following is a summary of such contrasts.

When no Experiencer is present, *parecer* cannot be in the progressive (**Está pareciendo que Juan cocina muy bien* versus *Nos está pareciendo que Juan cocina muy bien* "It is seeming (to us) that Juan cooks very well"); cannot appear in compound tenses with *have* (**Ha parecido que Juan cocina muy bien* versus *Nos ha parecido que Juan cocina muy bien* "It has seemed (to us) that Juan cooks very well");[16] and cannot be in the preterit (**Pareció que Juan cocina muy bien* versus *Nos pareció que Juan cocina muy bien* "It seemed (to us) that Juan cooks very well").

Such tense restrictions make sense if the absence of the Experiencer argument implies absence of a light verb v altogether. Under the approach taken here, absence of the dative clitic in the structure reflects absence of v altogether since the dative clitic is part of v. On this view, *parecer* must be considered a species of T (i.e., a Modal).[17]

By comparison, absence of a clitic with psych predicates such as *gustar* ("like") cannot possibly reflect absence of v in the structure (cf. *Gustan mucho los juguetes a los niños* "Children like toys a lot").[18] This difference between *parecer* ("seem") and *gustar* ("like") may be relevant in other areas as well (see section 3.1).

2.2.2   Subject-to-subject raising

Next, let us compare (8a) (**Ese taxista les parece estar cansado* "That taxi-driver seems to them to be tired") with (9b) (*Le gustaron los juguetes (al niño)* "The child liked the toys"). The question we must now ask is why raising-to-subject over the Experiencer is ill-formed, whereas in the structure of the psych-predicate *gustar* ("like") the Experiencer does not cause any problems. Within present assumptions, there is, of course, an important difference between these two structures: the first has a syntactic head P that needs to check its inflectional features. However, this head is missing from the the structure of psych predicates.[19]

In what follows I argue that the ill-formedness of instances of subject-to-subject raising with Spanish *parecer*+Experiencer derives from the impossibility of P checking its uninterpretable feature(s). Consider the ill-formed sentence given in (8a), repeated below:

(8)   a.   *Ese taxista les parece estar cansado.
           That taxi-driver to-them-seems (to) be tired
           "That taxi-driver seems to them to be tired."

My analysis assumes that raising structures with an Experiencer argument have a functional head P above T, which is active. Thus, at some point of the derivation, computation constructs the following:[20]

(14)   P [ese taxista¹ T [pro [[le-v] [V(*parecer*) [ese taxista² estar cansado]]]]]
        TP   vP vP   VP   TP

The question that arises is whether P can check its inflectional features against the Experiencer in this structure. For Spanish the answer is clearly negative. The Case of *pro*, the Experiencer, is checked against the dative clitic at the point in which *pro* merges in the structure. On the other hand, we must assume that the infinitival subject checks its Case against matrix T. As discussed earlier, the Experiencer *pro* in the structure of the psych predicate *gustar* "like," does not interfere in the attraction of the Theme by T. Assuming that matrix T establishes a checking relation with the infinitival subject in (14) (we return to a possible reason why immediately below), at the point in which P merges in the structure, no element remains "active." Hence P cannot check its uninterpretable features, and the resulting derivation does not converge at LF.[21]

There are several reasons for favoring some version of this approach. Consider the contrast in (15), from Torrego (1989):

(15)   a.   María me pareció inteligente.
           Maria to me-seemed intelligent
           "Maria seemed to me intelligent."

       b.   *María me pareció descalza.
            Maria to me-seemed barefoot
            "Maria seemed barefoot to me."

On the basis of binding facts, Ausin (2000) argues convincingly (against Torrego 1989) that (15a) is an instance of subject raising.[22]

The various syntactic factors already discussed in this section are responsible for the grammaticality difference between (15a) and (15b). Let us consider them one by one. First, in both structures the Experiencer is *pro*. Second, the method of feature-checking for *pro* is "privileged:" *pro* probes the clitic, checking its Case feature against the clitic. Third, T checks the Case feature of the subject. It must therefore be that the structure of (15a) lacks the peripheral functional head P, since if P were present, P could not check its features and the derivation would not to converge, contrary to facts since, clearly, (15a) is well-formed. To illustrate, consider the hypothetical derivation given in (16):

(16)   [Maria¹ T [Maria² [pro [me v] [pareció [María³ inteligente]]]]]
        TP   vP   vP   VP   sc

Given the absence of P in structure (16), the syntactic elements "pro [me-v] pareció]" derive a meaning for *parecer*+clitic that is compatible with an individual level small clause complement (the meaning that corresponds to (15a)), and is incompatible with a stage level small clause complement (the meaning that corresponds to (15b)).[23] Let us consider one more aspect of (15a) *vis-à-vis* derivation (16).[24]

Intuitively, in structures such as (15a) *pro* has incorporated into the verb. Whatever the mechanics of this instance of incorporation may be, *pro*-incorporation seems to be key in the possibility of T attracting the infinitival subject. Thus, although there is subject-to-subject raising over an Experiencer in some Spanish sentences, in the structure of such sentences the Experiencer "is buried," and this may well be crucial to its invisibility. I leave this suggestion as an informal account.

In sum, what is critical to the well-formedness of instances of subject-to-subject raising over an Experiencer in Spanish is, one, that the higher head that encodes point of view be absent, and two, that the Experiencer be realized as *pro*.

The proposed analysis raises a question with respect to well-formedness of sentences involving *parecer*+Experiencer in matrix clauses, as in (8b), repeated below:

(8)   b.   Le parece (a esta gente) que ese taxista está cansado.
           to-them seems (to people) that that taxi-driver is tired
           "It seems to these people that that taxi-driver is tired."

How are the inflectional features of P checked in (8b)? The only answer consistent with the analysis is that P is absent altogether from the structure of these sentences. Given this, the interpretation of *parecer* +Experiencer in matrix clauses should correspond to that of internal perception/opinion. A positive sign in this direction is that there exist grammaticalized forms such as *me parece* (the clitic must be first person) with the meaning "I think;" thus, in *Yo me parece que no voy a ir* (I to me-seem that I am not going to go "I think I am not going to go"), the verbal form is *me parece*, as suggested by the fact that the subject pronoun *Yo* is nominative. Similarly, the question: *Qué te parece?* means "What do you think?;" and an appropriate comment to a statement such as *María se va a enfadar* ("Mary is going to get mad") is *No, no me parece* – not to me-seems "I don't think so."

The analysis of subject-to-subject raising of this section provides another argument for strict derivationality. In particular, the establishment of the checking relation between *pro* and the clitic must take place at the derivational point in which the clitic has not moved. Movement of the clitic to T (and perhaps to P) will destroy the configuration in which *pro* probes the dative clitic.

In the next section we will discuss some other structures involving clitics and "seem" for French and Spanish. In all of them, the combination "seem"+ clitic has the meaning of a verb of internal perception rather than the meaning of external perception or point of view that corresponds to the English raising predicate "seem"+Experiencer.

3   The third argument

Strikingly, as the French contrast in (17) shows, clitics make the following construction possible (Rouveret and Vergnaud 1980, from Ruwet 1975):

(17)   a.   Il lui semble avoir résolu toutes les difficultés.
            it seems to him to have solved all the difficulties

       b.   *Il semble à Pierre avoir résolu toutes les difficultés.
            it seems to Pierre to have solved all the difficulties

As shown in (18) Spanish also has the French type of construction in (17a):[25]

(18)   Le parece haber resuelto todas las dificultades.
       to him/her seem to have resolved all the difficulties
       "S/he believes to have solved all the difficulties."

Our previous dicussion of clitics will provide the background assumptions needed for the analysis of French (17a) and Spanish (18).

3.1   Raising-to-object or control?

The analysis of clitics as both X^{max} and X^{min} allows us to treat the clitic in French (17a) on a par with Spanish doubling clitics. If we analyze the French dative clitic *lui* in (17a) as an X^0, we arrive at a structure in which the clitic is a functional head rather than an argument. The clitic (maybe in conjunction with v) will need to enter into a checking relation with a DP since it has uninterpretable inflectional features, and if it has an EPP feature, the clitic will attract the infinitival subject to move to its Spec.
   The derivation of French (17a) will then be as follows:

(19)   a.   [lui [v [semble [DP avoir compris]]]]
            vP   VP   TP

       b.   [T [DP^1 [lui [v [semble [DP^2 . . .]]]]]]]
            TP vP   VP   TP

       c.   [[lui^1-T] [DP^1 [lui^2 [v [semble [DP^2 . . .]]]]]]]
            TP   vP   VP   TP

       d.   [Il [lui^1-T] [DP^1 [lui^2 [v [semble [DP^2 . . .]]]]]]]
            TP   vP   VP   TP

Here, the embedded infinitival subject is attracted to the position of the Experiencer, which is the Specifier position of *lui* (or of the complex "[*lui*-v]"), if French were to receive the analysis proposed in the previous section for Spanish.

Crucially, movement of the infinitival subject must take place at the derivational point where the clitic *lui* merges: that is, before T merges in the structure, since finite T has the expletive *Il* as subject (*Il lui semble avoir résolu toutes les difficultés*). If this analysis is correct, sentence (17a) provides another argument for a derivational system of the sort argued by Epstein and Seely (1999). The analysis is not obviously replicable in representational terms. We could not motivate movement to the Specifier of *lui* in representation (19d), with the clitic already moved to T, unless some extra assumption is made concerning the trace of the clitic.

However, there are three possible objections to this analysis. Let us start with the one that I consider the less serious: Is the v-VP configuration necessarily a theta-marking configuration? If it is, the moved infinitival subject would receive two thematic roles: the Experiencer role, plus the role received from the infinitival predicate. We could, however, adopt the movement analysis of control phenomena put forward by Hornstein (1999) and assume that an argument picks up more than one theta-role as it moves.

The second possible objection to the analysis of (17a) concerns the type of null element that raises. Since no overt DP appears in the example, it is difficult to see whether the infinitival subject has moved at all, and where. It is doubtful that the infinitival subject be *pro*, since I have assumed that *pro* is a head. The third possible objection to the analysis is closely related to this one, and concerns Case. What Case does the raised null subject check?

The assumptions adopted earlier strongly favor a control analysis of both French (17a) and Spanish (18). On the basis of Spanish, I have argued that dative clitics license *pro* (perhaps in conjunction with v), and that *pro* is a head that probes the clitic. Structures of the form "[cl-v]-VP" could therefore be phases, in Chomsky's (2001) sense. Being a phase, the V of structure "[cl-v]-VP" could have a complete set of inflectional features and select a CP rather than (a defective) TP (see Chomsky 2001 for discussion). Of course, whether or not control can be reduced to raising is a different matter.

French, however, has closely related infinitival structures that do appear to instantiate the raising-to-object analysis rejected for (17a) and Spanish (18). Consider the following example from Kayne (1984: chapter 5, fn. 7), who credits Gross (1968: 91) for it:

(20)   Il semble à Jean y être allé déjà.
       It seems to Jean there be gone already
       "It seems to John (that he) has gone there already."

Example (20) is particularly interesting in the context of the present discussion. Prima facie, (20) does not fall together with (17a) (*Il lui semble avoir résolu toutes les difficultés*), which has a clitic raised to T.

Importantly, example (20) contains *y*, a pronominal form that replaces locatives and, according to Kayne (1975: 2.7, fn. 49), replaces dative clitics extensively in nonstandard French. Since the expletive pronoun *Il* fills the subject position, and the dative *à Jean* intervenes between T and the infinitival clause, plausibly, (20) can be analyzed as an instance of raising to the Specifier of *y*.[26]

My hypothesis is that *y* has the ambiguous X^{max} status proposed by Chomsky (1995) for clitics. This assumption allows me to treat *y* as a pronominal form merging with v-VP as a head, and attracting the infinitival subject to its Specifier:

(21) a.   [à Jean¹ [y [v [semble [à Jean² . . .]]]]]
           vP   VP   TP

      b.   [T [à Jean¹ [y [v [semble [à Jean² . . .]]]]]]
           TP vP   VP   TP

      c.   [Il [T [à Jean¹ [y² [v [semble [à Jean² . . .]]]]]]]
           TP TP vP   VP   TP

If *à Jean* is attracted to move by *y* (perhaps in conjunction with v), and its dative Case is checked in this position, we expect the raised DP *à Jean* to become inert. The fact that the subject position of (20) must be filled with an expletive is consistent with the derivation proposed for this example.[27]

Still, certain aspects of the French example in (17a) (*Il lui semble avoir résolu toutes les difficultés*) and the analysis of Spanish (18) (*Le parece haber resuelto todas las dificultades*) remain to be discussed.

Sentence (17a) has the expletive *Il* in subject position. However, the pronoun *Il* in (17a) can also be interpreted as a masculine singular pronoun meaning *he*, as observed in the literature (Rouveret and Vergnaud 1980):

(22) Il lui semble avoir résolu toutes les difficultés.
      "He seems to him to have understood all the difficulties."

Since *Il* is argumental (as reflected in the gloss) *Il* must have raised all the way from the embedded infinitival clause to the Specifier of the matrix Tense. On present assumptions, this means that (22) cannot have the same analysis as (17a).

Example (22) seems to be an instance of subject-to-subject raising over an Experiencer clitic, like the phenomena analyzed in section 2.1. The relevant steps of the derivation are illustrated below:

(23) a.   [lui [v [semble [il avoir résolu . . .]]]]
           vP   VP   TP

      b.   [T [lui [v [semble [il avoir résolu . . .]]]]]
           TP vP   VP   TP

      c.   [[lui¹-T] [lui² [v [semble [il avoir . . .]]]]]
           TP T   vP   VP   TP

    d.   [il^1 [lui^1-T] [lui^2 [v [semble [il^2 . . .]]]]]
        TP T   vP   VP   TP

At derivational stages (23a) and (23b), the Experiencer clitic *lui* c-commands *il*, the subject of the embedded infinitival. Once T merges in the structure, T c-commands both *lui* and *il*, as illustrated in representation (23b). At step (23c), *lui* moves to T. Once *lui* moves to T, *lui* no longer c-commands outside T, whereas T continues to c-command *il*. Hence, after derivational step (23c), T can attract the infinitival subject *il* without interference from the clitic *lui*.

    Given that a clitic moved to T no longer c-commands outside T, the empirical data analyzed in this article are evidence against May's (1985) segmental analysis, which was designed to allow c-command in configurations of this form. Simply put, the derivational approach to c-command disallows the segmental theory of c-command proposed by May (1985).[28]

    Let us now return to Spanish (18) (*Le parece haber resuelto todas las dificultades* "It seems to him/her to have solved all the difficulties") and compare it to French (20) (*Il semble à Jean y être allé déjà* "It seems to John (that he) has gone there already)."

    Importantly, the word order allowed for the dative argument in the French example (20) is not permitted in Spanish, as illustrated below,

(24) a. ??   Le parece (a Juan) haber resuelto todas las dificultades.
                To him-seems (to Juan) to have resolved all the difficulties

      b. (A Juan) le parece haber resuelto todas las dificultades.
           (To Juan) to him-seems to have resolved all the difficulties

Example (24a) is far less natural than (24b), which may be a sign that the derivation proposed for French (20) should not be adopted for Spanish (18).

    In fact, if *pro* rather than the lexical dative is the argumental Experiencer in Spanish, the location of the lexical dative in (24) may simply reflect the site of *pro*:

(25)   pro [[le-v] [V(*parecer*) [C [PRO haber resuelto todas las dificultades]]]]
        vP   VP   CP TP

Being adjunctal to *pro*, the lexical dative *a Juan* will have to be adjacent to *pro*. Since *pro* is incorporated to the verb, and the verb in Spanish finite clauses raises to T, the lexical dative *a Juan* cannot appear lower than T.

    Finally, we may note that the clausal complement in examples such as Spanish (18) can cliticize as accusative: *Se lo* (accusative) *pareció* (to them- it -seemed), where *lo* stands for the clause *Les pareció haber resuelto todas las dificultades* "They believe to have resolved all the difficulties." This may be evidence that, as suggested, Spanish (18) (and French (17a)) are instances of control.

4   Conclusion

In this study I have selected several syntactic contexts relevant to the MLC in the empirical domain of subject-raising, concentrating on Romance. We have seen that certain derivations involving dative clitics are incorrectly excluded by the MLC if applied representationally. Invoking the X^{max} and X^{min} status of clitics proposed by Chomsky (1995), I have argued for a derivational approach to syntactic relations, deriving numerous syntactic asymmetries in this manner, especially for Spanish. I have shown that, in each and every case, the interaction between the clitic and the moving infinitival subject gives us interesting arguments for the bottom-up, step-by-step nature of derivations. Replicating the results in representational terms might be possible, but not without losing naturalness in the approach. Since clitics move, keeping track in the representation of the syntactic operations established by a given clitic, if at all possible, will be at the cost of obscuring syntactic explanation.

Acknowledgments

I thank S. Epstein and D. Seely for their detailed and helpful comments and specific suggestions. I am grateful to C. Boeckx for generously sharing his work with me, and N. Moreno for discussion. Thanks also to C. Piera, and to my students at the Ortega y Gasset Institute for their comments and questions.

Notes

1   Boeckx (2000) relies here on work by Uriagereka (1995), who, in the context of clitic-placement, proposes a syntactic head F peripheral to the sentence that encodes a speaker's or an embedded subject's point of view. See his article for details and the references cited within.

2   Divergent views of this issue can be found throughout the literature, including my (1998) approach, which differs significantly from the proposals of the present article.

3   The possessor and the Experiencer also share their Case-array. Possessors tend to appear in the genitive (Spanish *el libro de Juan*[GEN] – "the book of John's"), or in the dative (French *le livre à moi*[DAT] – the book to me "My book"). Across languages, the Experiencer of *seem* verbs appears in the genitive (Greek *O Jannis tis*[GEN] *fenete arostos* "John seems to her to be sick"), or in the dative, as in English and in the Romance languages.

4   McGinnis (1998) and Anagnostopoulou (1999) also make crucial use of the DP/PP distinction, but they do not capitalize on the strict derivational approach advocated by Epstein et al. (1998: 2.5).

5   The hypothesized head P above T recalls proposals about the prepositional nature of C (Emonds 1985). It might be possible to collapse P with C, specially if preposition-like elements turn out to be complementizers.

6   There seems to be disagreement among French speakers concerning acceptability judgments in sentences with subject-to-subject raising over a lexical Experiencer

(see Chomsky (2000) for discussion). Rouveret and Vergnaud (1980) give the following example as acceptable: *Paul semble à Marie avoir résolu toutes les difficultés* "Paul seems to Marie to have solved all the difficulties." For the purposes of this presentation I will treat French and Italian alike, but this may be the wrong move (see Boeckx 1999, 2000). Naturally, the analysis proposed for Italian (4) should be disregarded for French if acceptability judgments differ for French and Italian. See note 7.

7   It is not clear whether in French, Experiencers should be considered to be DPs at the time in which T attracts the infinitival subject to Spec-TP. The evidence that they are comes from the unacceptability of instances of subject-to-subject raising over a dative Experiencer, but, as noted in note 6, speakers' judgments vary considerably. For speakers who accept these examples, datives may be PPs. I leave this issue open.

8   McGinnis (1998) assumes that clitics move attracted by T, checking their features against T. Her approach is incompatible with the present analysis, where the clitic checks its features prior to moving to T in many instances. For an approach to clitic-placement compatible with present assumptions, see Uriagereka (1995).

9   Potentially problematic for this approach is that in derivations such as (7), *me²*, the trace of the clitic, intervenes between T and the infinitival subject. However, traces have been called into question in recent developments of the theory. Epstein et al. (1998) speculate that there are no traces, and Lasnik (1999) proposes that A-traces can be dispensed with. If (at least) A-traces do not exist, the representation obtained at derivational point (6) is destroyed once the derivation reaches stage (7). For the remainder of this paper, I will assume that traces can be dispensed with.

10 Under this approach, the fact that anaphoric clitics are excluded from raising-to-subject sentences (see Rizzi 1982; Epstein 1986) must be derived from a different set of assumptions. I assume that the exclusion of anaphoric clitics is to be explained on some other syntactic grounds.

11 The same conclusion was reached by N. Moreno in unpublished work.

12 I assume that the surface word order of the sentence *Les gustó a los niños un juguete* obtains as a result of V moving to v and the resulting complex moving to T.

13 See Chomsky (2001) for the proposal that EPP and Case assignment are two independent phenomena.

14 My proposal is not entirely original. Chomsky (in his class lectures of Spring 2001) advanced this hypothesis for French expletive *il*.

15 For the purposes of this article, I assume that instances of obligatory doubling with dative clitics involve a phonologically null pro regardless of whether or not a lexical dative appears in the sentence. Though there are certainly other well-known approaches to doubling in the literature, for the phenomena discussed here (as well as those discussed in Torrego 1996b) the present approach yields the desired results.

16 Apparently, English *seem* is not entirely exempt from Tense restrictions, judging from contrasts such as (i) and (ii):

(i)   ??It has seemed that Juan was sick.
(ii) It has seemed for a while that Juan was sick.

17 An epistemic modal, according to Bosque and Torrego (1995). (See also Ausín and Depiante 2000). The fact that *parecer* allows clitic-climbing with certain verbs is consistent with this approach (cf. *Parece haberlo resuelto/Lo parece haber resuelto* "S/he seems to have-it resolved/it-seemed to have resolved "S/he seems to have resolved it").

18 The absence of a dative clitic with *gustar* is limited to sentences with a generic interpretation. Plausibly, there is a phonologically null clitic in the structure.

19 This is all that is needed for Spanish (and the other clitic-doubling Romance languages of Western Romance). For languages of a different type, it may be important to determine the site of the head that checks dative in structures containing psych predicates, provided that dative is a structural Case in these languages. I leave them aside. In agreement with Boeckx, my treatment of dative Experiencers distinguishes between what he calls "T-oriented" Experiencers and "V-oriented" Experiencers. In this article I concentrate on the first type of Experiencers.

20 I omit from structure (14) the intermediate step of the infinitival subject moving to the edge of the matrix vP. See section 2.2.1 for discussion of this type of movement with psych predicates.

21 Presumably, P has the inflectional features of the dative doubling clitic, namely person and number. Dative clitics agree with their doubles in these two features (*les* (pl.3rd) *a los niños* (pl.3rd) them-to the children).

22 Ausin's binding facts include Condition C violations with pronominal clitics as well as Condition C violations with anaphoric clitics. Compare: *le$_i$ pareció [el amigo de Juan$_i$ inteligente]* – to him-seemed [the friend of John intelligent] with **El amigo de Juan$_i$ le$_i$ pareció inteligente* – the friend of John to him-seemed intelligent; and this, in turn, with *El amigo de Juan$_i$ le$_i$ dio un libro* – the friend of John to-him gave a book. Also, *Juan se considera inteligente* "Juan considers himself intelligent" versus **Juan se pareció inteligente* "Juan seems to himself intelligent." Leaving aside several theoretical issues of importance engendered by these results, these are a good diagnosis for Ausin's raising analysis of (15a).

23 Roughly, the meaning that corresponds to internal perception/opinion; in fact, the Spanish expression *A mi parecer* means "In my opinion," as observed in Torrego (1989).

24 Ausin and Depiante (2000) stipulate this result. In discussing Torrego's (1996a, 1998) analysis of raising constructions, these authors argue that there are two verbs *parecer*: one modal, that is raising, and another verb that is a "regular" main verb that can take an Experiencer with no raising (i.e., it does not take a TP complement). But these (and several other syntactic contrasts such as (15)) ought to be the object of inquiry. The facts still need to be explained.

25 It is significant that the meaning of *parecer+Cl* here corresponds to that of internal perception discussed in the previous section for other sentences. Compare the highly deviant example in (i) with (ii), which is perfect:

   (i)   ???Le parece ver la televisión.
            to him-seems to watch television
   (ii) Le parece ver visiones.
         to him-seem to see visions
         "He seems to see visions."

26 For discussion concerning the properties of the French clitic *y* see Kayne (1975).

27 The details concerning the Case-checking of the dative by the clitic *y* remain to be worked out. One possibility is that the clitic *y* is attached to a null P. I leave this open.

28 I thank S. Epstein for pointing out to me this theoretical consequence of my analysis of clitic movement. As he observes, the issue is more general, since all head movement violates the Proper Binding Condition. For relevant discussion of issues pertaining to this analysis, see Epstein (1986).

References

Anagnostopoulou, E. 1999. "Datives." MS, University of Crete.

Ausin, A. 2000. "A-chains, anaphoric clitics and the derivational-representational debate." Paper presented at Harvard–MIT Student Conference on Linguistics, Cambridge, MA, August 31, 2000.

Ausin, A. and M. Depiante. 2000. "On the syntax of *parecer* ("to seem") with and without an Experiencer." In *Hispanic Linguistics at the Turn of the Millennium: Papers from the 3rd Hispanic Linguistic Symposium*, ed. H. Campos, E. Herburger, A. Morales-Front, and T. J. Walsh. Somerville, MA: Cascadilla Press, pp. 155–70.

Boeckx, C. 1999. "Quirky agreement." MS, University of Connecticut.

Boeckx, C. 2000. "Raising and Experiencers, cross-linguistically." MS, University of Connecticut.

Bosque, I. and E. Torrego. 1995. "On Spanish *haber* and tense." In *Proceedings of the Conferences Language and Grammaire 1*, Université de Paris VIII.

Chomsky, N. 1986. *Barriers*. Cambridge, MA: MIT Press.

Chomsky, N. 1993. "A minimalist program for linguistic theory." In *The View from Building 20: Essays in Linguistics in Honor of Sylvain Bromberger* ed., Kenneth Hale and Samuel J. Keyser. Cambridge, MA: MIT Press.

Chomsky, N. 1995. *The Minimalist Program*. Cambridge, MA: MIT Press.

Chomsky, N. 2000. "Minimalist inquiries: the framework." In *Step by Step*, ed. Roger Martin, David Michaels, and Juan Uriagereka. Cambridge, MA: MIT Press.

Chomsky, N. 2001. "Derivation by Phase." In *Ken Hale: A Life in Language*, ed. Michael Kenstowicz, Cambridge, MA: MIT Press.

Emonds, J. 1985. *A Unified Theory of Syntactic Categories*. Dordrecht: Foris.

Epstein, S. D. 1986. "The Local Binding Condition and LF chains." *Linguistic Inquiry* 17: 187–205.

Epstein, S. D., E. Groat, R. Kawashima, and H. Kitahara. 1998. *A Derivational Approach to Syntactic Relations*. Oxford: Oxford University Press.

Epstein, S. D. and D. Seely. 1999. "SPEC-ifying the GF 'subject'; eliminating A-chains and the EPP within a derivational Model." MS presented at the LSA Summer Institute Workshop on Grammatical Relations, July 1999.

Ferguson, S. 1994. "Deriving the invisibility of PP nodes for command from AGR^0+P^0 Case checking." In *Harvard Working Papers in Linguistics* 4, ed. S. Epstein, H. Thráinsson, and S. Kuno. Department of Linguistics, Harvard University, Cambridge, MA, 30–6.

Gross, M. 1968. *Grammaire transformationnelle du français: Syntaxe du verbe*. Paris: Larousse.

Hornstein, N. 1998. "Movement and chains." *Syntax* 1, 99–127.

Hornstein, N. 1999. "Movement and control." *Linguistic Inquiry* 30, 69–96.

Kayne, R.-S. 1975. *French Syntax*. Cambridge, MA: MIT Press.

Kayne, R.-S. 1984. *Connectedness and Binary Branching*. Dordrecht: Foris.

Kitahara, H. 1997. *Elementary Operations and Optimal Derivations*. Cambridge, MA: MIT Press.

Koopman, H. 1995. "On verbs that fail to undergo V-second." *Linguistic Inquiry* 26: 137–63.

Lasnik, H. 1999. *Minimalist Analysis*. Oxford: Blackwell Publishers.

McGinnis, M. 1998. "Locality in A-movement." PhD dissertation, MIT, Cambridge, MA.

May, R. 1985. *Logical Form: Its Structure and Derivation*. Cambridge, MA: MIT Press.

Moro, A. 1993. *I predicati nominali e la struttura della frase*. Padova: Unipress.

Perlmutter, D. 1984. "Working 1s and Inversion in Italian, Japanese and Quechua." In D. Perlmutter and C. Rosen, *Studies in Relational Grammar 2*. Chicago: University of Chicago Press.

Rizzi, L. 1982. "On chain formation." in H. Borer, ed., *The Syntax of Pronominal Clitics*. Orlando, FL: Academic Press.

Rouveret, A. and J.-R. Vergnaud. 1980. "Specifying reference to the subject: French causatives and Conditions on Representations." *Linguistic Inquiry* 11, 97–202.

Ruwet, N. 1975. "Montée du sujet et extraposition." *Le français moderne* 43, 97–134.

Torrego, E. 1989. "Experiencer and Raising Verbs." Presented at "Second Princeton Workshop on Comparative Grammar," April 1989, Princeton University.

Torrego, E. 1996a. "Experiencer and raising verbs." In R. Freidin, ed., *Current Issues in Comparative Grammar*, Dordrecht: Kluwer Academic Publishers.

Torrego, E. 1996b. "On quantifier float in control clauses." *Linguistic Inquiry* 27, 111–26.

Torrego, E. 1998. *The Dependencies of Objects*. Cambridge, MA: MIT Press.

Uriagereka, J. 1995. "Aspects of the syntax of clitic placement in Western Romance." *Linguistic Inquiry* 26, 79–123.

Chapter eleven

Issues Relating to a Derivational Theory of Binding

Jan-Wouter Zwart

1   Introduction

The derivational approach to syntactic relations (DASR, see Epstein 1995; Epstein et al. 1998; Epstein and Seely 1999) entails that an interpretive relation between two elements α and β is a function of an operation M merging α and (a constituent containing) β. In many cases, it appears to be impossible to maintain the stronger version, where M merges α directly with β, illustrated in (1a), forcing one to also acknowledge the weaker version, where M merges α not with β directly, but with a constituent γ containing β, illustrated in (1b).

(1)   a. $[\alpha\ \beta]$

    b. $[\alpha\ [\gamma\ [\dots \beta \dots]]]$

The situation in (1a) applies to phrase structure relations, to the extent that they are reducible to the sisterhood relation, as well as to relations of argument structure and predication defined in terms of phrase structure, *casu quo* sisterhood. For example, in (2), the interpretive relation between a verb *love* and its internal argument *Mary* exists precisely because *Mary* has been merged with *love*:[1]

(2)   [I [love Mary]]

The situation in (1b) applies to all cases where there is no sisterhood, but c-command is relevant; for example, movement cases like (3), where the moved category *who* must c-command the position where *who* was first merged (indicated by a copy of *who* in angled brackets):[2]

(3)   (You wonder) [who [I [love <who>]]]

In (3), the interpretive relation between *who* and *<who>* (namely that one is a "trace" of the other) is not a function of merger of *who* to *<who>*, but of merger of *who* to a constituent containing *<who>*.

On its strongest implementation, DASR restricts interpretive relations to the configuration in (1a), excluding the c-command case (1b). This requires a re-thinking of many of the most elementary syntactic relations in grammatical theory, not least movement and binding. But the very idea that information may be accrued in the course of a stepwise derivation, crucial to DASR, already provides a solution to some of the most immediate problems.

For example, the movement illustrated in (3) need not involve a relation between *who* and *<who>*, if we consider *who* to be a single element which is merged more than once, and which acquires additional information with each merger (see Epstein and Seely 1999). From this perspective, there is no need to compute the properties of *who* by a process of reconstruction of *who* in its base position at an interpretive "level" Logical Form (LF). All that is needed at the point of interpretation is an inspection of the various features acquired by *who* in the course of the derivation of the sentence (features relating to argument status and grammatical function (Case), as well as additional ("A'") features relating to its status as an interrogative element).[3] As noted by Epstein and Seely (1999), this approach potentially eliminates typically representational notions like "chain" and "trace," as well as conditions governing the well-formedness of the relevant entities.[4]

In the present contribution, I want to consider the question whether binding relations can be redefined in a similar derivational vein. Binding of an anaphor (4), local obviation of a pronoun (5), and obviation of a referential expression (R-expression) (6) typically involve a c-commanding antecedent (in the a-examples, the antecedent c-commands the dependent element in the binding relation, in the b-examples, it does not):

(4)   a.   John loves himself   (anaphor binding)
      b.   *John's mother loves himself   (no anaphor binding)

(5)   a.   John loves him   (obviation)
      b.   John's mother loves him   (no obviation)

(6)   a.   He loves John   (obviation)
      b.   His mother loves John   (no obviation)

But unlike the relation between an antecedent and its trace, the binding/obviation relation cannot obviously be reformulated without reference to c-command (i.e. to a configuration like (1b)).

Yet this is what I am attempting here. My point of departure is the proposal by Kayne (2000, this volume), according to which (nonaccidental) coreference of α and β, where β is a pronominal element, ensues if and only if α and β are merged together yielding a constituent like (1a). This appears to be the strongest implementation of the derivational approach to binding, meriting priority consideration. I consider the consequences of this proposal for local anaphor binding first (unlike Kayne 2000, this volume, where it is applied mostly to nonlocal pronominal coreference). As the antecedent moves away from the anaphor in the course of the derivation, a movement necessitated by standard licensing requirements, conditions on local anaphor binding reduce to conditions on local noun phrase movement ("A-movement"). This in turn makes reference to c-command superfluous, as with all movement, as discussed in connection with (3).

I have found that this approach, counterintuitive though it may seem, allows one to address fundamental questions connected with theories of binding, which seemed out of reach before. These questions are:

(7)   *Some fundamental questions of binding theory*
   a.   Why is binding limited to A-positions?
   b.   Why is there a morphological distinction between anaphors and pronouns (and not, generally, between bound pronouns, coreferential pronouns, and pronouns interpreted deictically)?
   c.   Why is binding subject to locality, and why are the locality conditions the way they are?

Like Kayne (2000, this volume), I propose that these questions become tractable once binding phenomena have been reduced to movement phenomena (in this case, A-movement phenomena).

Contra Kayne (2000, this volume), I am led to believe that all other forms of coreference, including pronoun binding, as in (5b), are accidental. This is because the conditions on pronoun binding are not identical to the conditions on noun phrase movement.

The derivational approach to binding attempted here, like DASR in general, makes it unnecessary to resort to "reconstruction" at LF of earlier stages in the derivation. For example, (8) is interpretable, not because we can reconstruct the displaced anaphor *himself* in its original position indicated by *<himself>*, but because *John* and *himself* were merged together at some (early) point in the derivation (represented by (9)):

(8)   Himself, John loves <himself>

(9)   [John himself]

Example (8) is derived from (9) through a succession of steps, merging *loves* to *John himself*, extracting *John* from *John himself* and merging it again to *loves <John> himself*, and, finally, raising *<John> himself* and merging it again to *John loves <<John> himself>*. The reasoning is the same as with (3): with each new operation Merge the element merging to the structure acquires additional features which are interpreted at LF, but no "trace" or "chain" is created, and no information can be gathered from these entities.

The article has the following structure. Section 2 presents anaphoricity as a feature acquired by pronouns in the course of the derivation, leading to Spell Out and interpretation of the pronoun as an anaphor. Section 3 lists nine advantages of viewing anaphoricity in this way, addressing the fundamental questions of the binding theory in (7). Section 4 explores to what extent other types of anaphoricity, such as bound variable anaphora, can be viewed as "accidental." Section 5 discusses various effects of reconstruction (and anti-reconstruction), to see if they can be accounted for in the derivational approach. Finally, a number of remaining problems are briefly mentioned in section 6.[5]

2   Anaphoricity as acquired information

In most approaches to binding phenomena, it is taken for granted that in the lexicon there are (at least) three types of noun phrases, listed in (10), which are subject to various requirements, the binding conditions (listed in (11)).

(10)   a.   anaphors (English *himself*)[6]
       b.   pronouns (English *him*)[7]
       c.   R-expressions (English *the man, Bill*)

(11)   Given a local domain D,
       a.   anaphors are bound in D,[8]
       b.   pronouns are free in D, and
       c.   R-expressions are free.

(11a) and (11b) represent the local binding and local obviation requirements illustrated in (4) and (5), respectively, and (11c) represents the general obviation requirement illustrated in (6). Following the introduction of the classical binding theory (Chomsky 1981), much discussion addressed the question at what level of representation the conditions in (11) apply. In the Minimalist approach (Chomsky 1993), conditions can apply only at the interface levels (PF and LF), and hence it was concluded that the conditions in (11) must apply at LF, yielding a slight reformulation of (11) as interpretive procedures (Chomsky and Lasnik 1993: 100):

(12)   Given a local domain D,
       a.   if α is an anaphor, interpret it as coreferential with some c-commanding phrase in D,
       b.   if α is a pronoun, interpret it as disjoint from every c-commanding phrase in D, and
       c.   if α is an R-expression, interpret it as disjoint from every c-commanding phrase.

Both the classical formation in (11) and the reformulation in (12) raise the question in (13):

(13)   What makes an element an anaphor/pronoun/R-expression?

This question is relatively easy to answer for the category of R-expressions. R-expressions are referential expressions, they represent a concept, a projection in the sense of Jackendoff (1983), expressable in terms of lexico-semantic features.[9] But for anaphors and pronouns the situation is much less clear.

The classical binding theory stipulates an ontology of noun phrase types based on the features [anaphoric] and [pronominal] (Chomsky 1982: 78):

(14)

Overt	Anaphoric	Pronominal	Covert
	+	+	PRO
anaphor	+	−	A-trace
pronoun	−	+	pro
R-expression	−	−	A'-trace

This classical inventory is curious in that it defines anaphors and pronouns as being maximally distinct in feature value specifications, each having more in common with R-expressions than with the other. However, the morphology of anaphors and pronouns suggests that they have much in common, as anaphors can be analyzed as pronouns with added focus markers, as in (15a), or as grammaticalized inalienable possessive noun phrases containing a pronominal possessor, and often a body-part noun, as in (15b):[10]

(15) a. pronominal *him*, anaphor *him-self*   (*English*)
      b. z'n eigen   (*colloquial Dutch*)
          his own   "himself"
          koye *men*   (*Fulani*)
          heads our "ourselves"

These considerations suggest that the inventory of noun phrase types is more like (16) than like (14):[11]

(16) ±REFERENTIAL

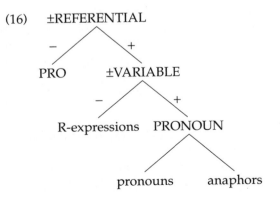

Ignoring PRO, the subject of control infinitives, the major cut-off point in (16) appears to be between [−variable referential] elements (i.e., R-expressions), and [+variable referential] elements (pronouns and anaphors). These vary only in that in local contexts, one is chosen over the other (where pronouns are the underspecified "elsewhere" category).[12]

This leads me to believe that syntax recognizes just a single category of [variable referential] elements, PRONOUN, which acquires features in the course of the derivation, which in turn yield a particular Spell Out (at the interface component PF (Phonetic Form)) and a particular interpretation (at LF). Since pronouns are the underspecified category, the binding theory only needs to specify the conditions under which the generic category PRONOUN acquires the features that would yield the Spell Out and interpretation of an anaphor.[13]

In this context, body-part anaphors are instructive, since they can be used both as anaphors (17a) and as referential expressions (17b) (examples from Fulani (Peul), Sylla 1993: 149):

(17)   a.   en tooñ-ii   koye men   *(Fulani)*
            we harm-ASP heads our
            "We have harmed ourselves."

       b.   koye men kell-ii
            heads our hurt-ASP
            "Our heads hurt."

The expression *koye men* "our heads" may be used referentially or as an anaphor, a grammaticalized element with bleached semantics. This suggests that anaphoricity is not a lexical property of certain expressions, but a feature that arises in a certain syntactic context. If so, anaphoricity is a property *acquired in the course of a derivation*, rather than a lexical feature which is present from the outset.[14]

On the strictest implementation of the derivational approach to syntactic relations, the features relevant to anaphoricity can only be acquired in a sister-hood configuration like (1a). This leads to the following coreference "rule" (cf. Kayne 2000, this volume):

(18)   A PRONOUN α is coreferential with β iff α is merged with β

Thus, a construction like *John hurt his head* may have the two derivations in (18):

(19)   a.   John hurt [<John> [his head]]
       b.   John hurt [his head]

In a language using body-part anaphors, (18) forces an interpretation of *his head* as "himself" in (19a), but not in (19b).

My proposal differs from Kayne's in assuming that a coreferential PRONOUN (i.e. a [+coreferential] variable referential element) is invariably spelled out at

PF and interpreted at LF as an anaphor. We may think of this in terms of the antecedent bestowing a feature [+coreferential] upon the PRONOUN, which is then interpreted accordingly at PF and LF.[15] In Kayne's proposal, both anaphors like *himself* and bound pronouns like *he* in the relevant reading of (20), are merged with their intended antecedent (cf. (20b)):

(20) a.   John thinks that I like him   (*no obviation*)
      b.   [John him]

In my proposal, *him* is present in the syntax only as the generic variable referential element PRONOUN. Assuming (18), a derivation including (20b) would have to add [+coreferential] to the PRONOUN's set of features. While this would have the correct effect at LF, where the PRONOUN is interpreted as coreferential with *John*, it would have the wrong effect at PF, where Morphology (by (18)) would interpret the PRONOUN as an anaphor and generate an anaphor (*himself*) instead of a pronoun (*him*)(see note 13). We return to the difference between anaphors and pronouns below.

In conclusion of this section, I have proposed that what makes a variable referential element an anaphor is that it is merged with its antecedent. Other variable referential elements are spelled out as pronouns by default.

3   Consequences

A number of standard properties of anaphor binding fall out immediately from the idea that anaphors are merged with their antecedent (more exactly, are the morphological Spell Out of a generic variable referential element PRONOUN which is merged with its antecedent), illustrated in (21)

(21)   [$_{XP}$ [antecedent] [PRONOUN]]

These properties are discussed in the subsections below.

3.1   *Asymmetry*

As pointed out by Kayne (2000, this volume), asymmetries of the type observed in (22), showing that anaphors must be c-commanded by their antecedents and not vice versa, are explained on the assumption that the PRONOUN is the head of XP in (21).

(22) a.   I expect John to like himself
      b.   *I expect himself to like John

Following the line of argumentation in Kayne (2000, this volume), (22a) is derived by extracting *John* from the XP headed by (the PRONOUN ultimately spelled out as) *himself* and (re)merging it in the Exceptional Case Marking position. In order to derive (22b), either we would have to merge *John himself* in the Exceptional Case Marking position and lower *John* to the position of the internal argument of *like* (which is not allowed in most current approaches, including DASR), or we would have to raise the head *himself*, stranding its specifier *John*. But this would involve movement of a head into a specifier position, which is also not allowed. Thus, the asymmetry between anaphors and their antecedents follows from standard conditions on movement.

3.2   Obviation (Principle C)

Also following Kayne (2000, this volume), we derive the effects of Principle C of the Binding Theory (cf. (11c) and (12c)) immediately, since nonaccidental coreference is obtained only when two coreferential elements are merged together yielding a constituent like (21). Two noun phrases that are merged to the structure independently can be interpreted as coreferential only by accident, not as a fact of grammar.

This derives the standard Principle C effects illustrated in (23)–(24):

(23) a. John likes John
      b. John thinks that I like John

(24) a. He likes John
      b. He thinks that I like John

The two instances of *John* in the sentences in (23) are interpreted as disjoint by default. In order to be able to interpret the two instances of *John* in the sentences in (23) as coreferring, we would have to assume that they are merged together as a constituent, as in (25):

(25) [[John] [John]]

But since neither instance of *John* is a variable referential element, coreference is impossible to obtain.[16]

In (24), the disjoint interpretation of *he* and *John* is forced along the same lines, if *he* and *John* are merged as in (26a), or, if *he* and *John* are merged as in (26b), by the condition on movement prohibiting raising of a head (*he*) to a specifier position (Kayne 2000, this volume; cf. section 3.1):[17]

(26) a. [[he] [John]]
      b. [[John] [he]]

Note that locality is not a factor here, as the pair of examples in (23) shows, since the disjoint interpretation is obtained by default.

As is well known since Evans (1980), the general obviation requirement expressed in standard formulations of Principle C of the binding theory may be lifted in circumscribed contexts, yielding "accidental coreference." Some examples are given in (27):[18]

(27) a. (Not many people like John, but I believe) John likes John
      b. (Surely if everybody likes John, then) John likes John

The relevance of these examples is that they show that the binding conditions cannot be applied mechanically to a representation of a completed derivation (say, at LF). Principle C, if applied mechanically at LF, must rule out the examples in (27) under the intended interpretation. In the theory of Kayne (2000, this volume), there simply is no Principle C, since disjoint interpretation is given by default.

Typically, accidental coreference appears to be facilitated in contexts giving rise to ellipsis. Thus, next to (27) we have (28):

(28) a. Not many people like John, but I believe John does.
      b. Surely if everybody likes John, then so must John.

Ellipsis constructions involve a (accented) focus segment combined with a (deaccented) "topic" segment which is either repeated from previous contributions to the discourse or otherwise understood. In (27a), for example, the first instance of *John* is in focus, and the verb phrase *likes John* is understood. The part that is understood can also be left out, yielding (28a), suggesting that ellipsis is just an extreme form of deaccenting (cf. Tancredi 1992). In short, what happens is that a single element is introduced both as "old" and as "new." Precisely in this situation we seem to get "accidental coreference" (see Demirdache 1997: 76 and references cited there).[19] It is not immediately clear how Principle C could be made sensitive to these discourse considerations, suggesting that phenomena of accidental coreference are better handled in a theory that makes no recourse to a requirement of obligatory disjointness like Principle C.[20]

Other cases of accidental coreference, though perhaps not standardly viewed that way, involve non-c-commanding antecedents:[21]

(29) a. John's mother thinks John is an idiot
      b. His mother thinks John is an idiot

We return to cases like (29) in section 4.

To conclude, standard effects of Principle C follow automatically from the theory of Kayne (2000, this volume), so that Principle C itself can be dispensed with.

3.3 Obligatoriness

An anaphor *must* be bound. This follows on the theory proposed here, since anaphoricity is a nonlexical, syntactically enduced property, acquired by a variable referential element (a PRONOUN) only when merged with an anteced-ent (as in (21)).

3.4   Uniqueness

An anaphor must be bound by a unique antecedent. Thus, a sentence like (30) cannot be interpreted as involving a split antecedent *John, Bill* to the anaphor *himself*:[22]

(30)   John heard Bill curse himself.

This follows since *Bill* and *John* cannot both be the antecedent in the structure (21), which I take to obey a binary branching requirement (i.e., merger is an operation that relates two categories).[23]

3.5   C-command

An anaphor must be bound by a c-commanding antecedent, as illustrated in (4), repeated here as (31):

(31)   a.   John loves himself   (*anaphor binding*)
        b.   *John's mother loves himself   (*no anaphor binding*)

In order to derive (31b), with intended coreference of *John* and *himself*, from (21), fleshed out here as (32a), *John* would have to be extracted from (32a) and merged internal to the noun phrase (DP) *(John)'s mother* (32b):

(32)   a.   [[John] [PRONOUN]]
        b.   [$_{DP}$ _ 's [mother]]

If the DP in (32b) is already merged to the structure containing *John* at the moment of its extraction out of (32a), the derivation violates the Extension Condition of Chomsky (1993: 190), which states that Merge must extend exist-ing structure:

(33)   *Extension Condition*
        No operation Merge applying to a phrase marker α targets a node dom-inated by α.

If the DP in (32b) has not yet been merged to the structure containing *John* at the moment of its extraction out of (32a), the displacement operation targets two independent phrase markers (yielding an "interarboreal operation"). I take the impossibility of coreference in (31b) to provide clear evidence that such a derivation is disallowed.[24]

3.6 Locality

It has been clear since Chomsky (1981) that the locality conditions on anaphor binding are strikingly similar to the locality conditions on noun phrase movement (A-movement).[25] In the present framework, the similarity is not surprising, assuming that the noun phrase antecedent in (21) is forced to move away from the anaphor into an A-position.

I assume here that noun phrases, in order to be interpretable at LF, need to acquire in the course of the derivation features relating to argument structure status (thematic roles) and grammatical function (subject/object, Case).[26] The antecedent noun phrase in (21) has neither. It must therefore be extracted from the constituent in (21) and be merged to the structure in positions where the relevant features may be acquired. Since these positions are (by definition) A-positions, the relevant noun phrase movement must be A-movement.[27]

A-movement is in principle clause bound, with the exception of Exceptional Case Marking (ECM) configurations, where two (or more) verbs share a single functional domain (composed of the set of functional projections where grammatical functions are licensed ("where Case is assigned")). This is more easily illustrated in Dutch than in English (where the syntax of Exceptional Case Marking is still somewhat obscure):

(34) *Exceptional Case Marking*
     . . . dat Jan   Piet Marie niet <Jan> zag <Piet> kussen <Marie>
     that   John Pete Mary not   saw   kiss-INF
     ". . . that John did not see Pete kiss Mary."

In (34), the negation *niet*, interpreted as a matrix clause element, serves to indicate the lower boundary of the matrix clause functional domain. The matrix clause functional domain contains projections licensing *Piet* and *Marie* as grammatical objects (they receive accusative Case when pronominal) and *Jan* as a grammatical subject.[28] As these positions are apparently sufficiently local for A-movement of the arguments of the embedded verb, the local domain for A-movement of α may be defined in terms of the maximal functional domain associated with the verb projecting the functional projection in which α is licensed. If the association of a verb and its functional domain is expressed as "L-relatedness" (following Chomsky and Lasnik 1993: 64), the definition of the local domain for A-movement becomes:

(35) *Local domain for A-movement (the L-domain)*
     The local domain for A-movement of α is the maximal projection of the highest functional head f L-related to a verb V L-related to a functional head f' licensing α

According to (35), if the argument of an embedded verb is licensed in a functional projection associated with a matrix verb, then the maximal functional projection L-related to the matrix verb is the local domain for A-movement.

As is well known, the extension of the local domain in ECM configurations is also needed to account for anaphor binding by an argument of a higher verb, as in (36):

(36) a. John saw himself kiss Mary
      b. . . . dat Jan   zichzelf Marie zag kussen   (*Dutch*)
          that   John himself Mary saw kiss-INF

Both A-movement and binding beyond the L-domain as defined in (35) is impossible:

(37) a. *John believes that we expect himself to kiss Mary
      b. *John seems (that) will kiss Mary

The locality effects of A-movement and binding raise two questions:

(38) 1. Why are anaphor binding and A-movement subject to the same locality conditions?
      2. What explains the definition of the local domain?

Within the theory advanced here, the answers are clear.

First, anaphor binding and A-movement are subject to the same locality conditions because anaphoricity is established by merging a PRONOUN with its antecedent as in (21), after which the antecedent must move out and merge again in positions where it can acquire features indicating its thematic role and grammatical function. These positions are A-positions by definition (note 27).

Second, the local domain for A-movement is defined by the maximal functional projection in which a noun phrase acquires the features it needs (i.e. thematic features and Case features). I would like to propose that movement out of that functional projection can only serve the purpose of acquiring additional features. This excludes merger in additional A-positions. Thus, A-movement is limited by an economy condition reminiscent of the principle of "Greed" of Chomsky (1993: 201). On our theory, the locality of anaphor binding is likewise a result of Greed.[29]

This view on locality implies that functional projections L-related to V must be realized in close proximity to V, perhaps before any A'-projections are merged to the structure, but certainly before a complementizer is. If this is correct, Principle A of the classical binding theory (cf. (11a)) is deduced from the derivational approach to binding, involving merger of binder and bindee in a construction like (21), in conjunction with the economy condition Greed.

3.7   Binding restricted to A-positions

In the Government and Binding theory, binding is restricted to A-positions (Chomsky 1981: 184). This accounts for the fact that (39) does not induce a

Principle C violation (where *himself* has been fronted into an A'-position c-commanding *John*):

(39)   Himself, John likes

However, simply excluding A'-positions from consideration in computing binding and disjointness does not suffice, witness the contrast in (40):

(40)   a.   John, I like him
       b.   *Him, I like John

Moreover, the restriction of binding to A-positions is unexplained in classical approaches, and somewhat unexpected from the DASR point of view. Other processes resembling binding (in requiring c-command, for instance), such as negative polarity item (NPI) licensing, are not restricted to A-positions (i.e., are not computed over A-positions only):

(41)   a.   Niemand heeft ook maar iets gedaan
            nobody   has   anything-NPI done
            "No one did a single thing."

       b.   *Ook maar iets heeft niemand gedaan
            anything-NPI has noone   done

This raises the question why binding is special in that it is restricted to A-positions.

In our theory, since there is no Principle C, (39) is unproblematic. The coreference of *John* and *himself* is already established at an early stage in the derivation, represented by (42a), after which *John* is extracted and merged in the subject position, and XP may be moved across *John* to the topicalization position (42b):

(42)   a.   [$_{XP}$ John PRONOUN]
       b.   [[$_{XP}$ <John> PRONOUN] [John [likes <[$_{XP}$ <John> PRONOUN]>]]]

Afterwards, the PRONOUN gets spelled out at PF as *himself* and interpreted at LF as anaphoric to *John*.

Nowhere in the description of (39) is it necessary to acknowledge the distinction between A- and A'-positions.[30] Binding *appears* to be restricted to A-positions because, in our theory, the binding relations established when the antecedent and the anaphor are merged together (yielding (21)) cannot be undone by A'-movement (or by any other operation).

Without Principle C, the contrast in (40) is in need of an alternative explanation. A comparison with Dutch suggests that left-dislocation constructions of the type in (40) require a particular division of roles between the left-dislocated element and a variable referential resumptive element (fronted in Dutch, but not in English):[31]

(43) a.   Jan, die   mag ik wel   (*Dutch*)
           John DEM-NNTR may I AFF
           "John, I like him."

      b.   *Die,   Jan mag ik wel
           DEM-NNTR John may I AFF

The example in (43b), the Dutch version of (40b), is characterized by a reversal
of roles, the resumptive element taking up the left-dislocation position, and
the referential expression trying to perform as a resumptive element. I suggest
that nothing else is wrong with (40)/(43).

   The contrast in (41) suggests that the A-movement analysis of anaphoric
binding explored here cannot be extended to NPI licensing. This is supported
by the observation that NPI licensing is not restricted to the L-domain (35):

(44)   Niemand verwachtte dat ook maar iemand iets   zou doen
       noone   expected   that anyone-NPI   something would do
       "No one expected a single person to do anything."

Note that our analysis of (39) needs no recourse to an LF operation reconstructing the stage before topicalization of *himself* ("reconstruction"), a topic to
which we return in section 5 below.

3.8   *Local obviation (Principle B)*

The local obviation effects of pronouns, illustrated in (5), repeated here as (45),
need not be accounted for by a separate Principle B (cf. (11b), (12b)):

(45)   a.   John loves him   (*obviation*)
       b.   John's mother loves him   (*no obviation*)

In our theory, if *John* and *him* in (45a) are to be interpreted as coreferring, they
must be merged together in a constituent like (46) (cf. (21)):

(46)   [$_{XP}$ [John] [PRONOUN]]

Note that on our assumptions, (46) involves no pronouns or anaphors, but
just the generic variable referential element PRONOUN. In the context (46),
the PRONOUN acquires the feature [+coreferential], which is interpreted
by Morphology as an instruction to return the Spell Out *himself* (rather than
the default form *him*; see note 13). Thus, under the intended, coreferential
interpretation, (45a) will always be realized as (47).

(47)   John loves himself.

The absence of obviation in (45b) need not surprise us. Like (29), this is a case of accidental coreference, not reducible to movement by the same reasons that exclude (31b).

Note that our explanation of local obviation effects raises the question how nonlocal coreference, as in (48), is derived.

(48) John thinks that he is a genius.

Kayne (2000, this volume) proposes to describe coreference of *John* and *he* as a function of *John* and *he* being merged together, the original idea that gave rise to the present contribution:[32]

(49) John thinks [CP that [<John> he] is a genius]

However, in order for *John* to raise to the subject position in the matrix clause, it would have to move to the specifier position of CP first, which is an A'-position. The next movement step would take *John* back to an A-position, yielding (disallowed) improper movement. This leads me to believe that the coreference of *John* and *he* in (48) is in fact accidental. We return to cases like (48) in section 4 below.

3.9 Absence of nominative anaphors

The general absence of nominative anaphors (in nominative-accusative languages) is also explained in the theory advanced here.[33]

Note first that, if an external argument is present, an internal argument can only be realized as an object (Burzio's Generalization, Burzio 1986: 178). Thus, if a constituent like (21) is merged in the internal argument position (50i), and the antecedent is extracted and merged in the external argument position (50ii), the remnant noun phrase headed by *himself* will have to be licensed as an object, not as a subject (50iii). As a result, the anaphor will not acquire the nominative Case features connected with the subject position.

(50) *subject position object position* *ext.arg. pos. verb int.arg. pos.*

(i)			V	[John himself]
(ii)		John	V	[<John> himself]
(iii)	[<John> himself] John		V	<[<John> himself]>

Alternatively, (21) could be merged in the external argument position (51i). This will allow the noun phrase headed by *himself* to become a subject (51ii):

(51) *subject position . . . ext.arg. position* *verb . . .*

(i)		[John himself]	V
(ii)	[John himself]	<[John himself]>	V

However, the derivation will succeed only if the antecedent, still locked within the noun phrase headed by *himself*, can move to a position in which it may acquire a thematic role. Such a position must be found within the same L-domain (cf. (35)), which defines the locality conditions on A-movement. The only configuration in which the various conditions are met is the ECM configuration. Assuming, as before, that the arguments of the verb in an ECM complement clause are licensed as objects in the functional domain of the matrix verb, the derivation of an ECM construction with an anaphoric embedded external argument will look like (52):

(52) *object position*   *ext.arg. pos. ECM verb ext.arg. pos.*   *verb* . . .
   (i)   V   [John himself]   V
   (ii)   John   V   [<John> himself]   V
   (iii) [<John> himself] John   V   <[<John> himself]> V

In both (50) and (52) the only element ending up in the subject position (to the left of the object position in (52)) is *John*, not (the noun phrase headed by) *himself*. As a result, syntax never yields a PRONOUN marked by a combination of the features [coreferential] and [nominative], and Morphology will never be forced to return a nominative anaphor for a PRONOUN.[34]

Note that previous discussions of the absence of nominative anaphors have mentioned the possibility that an (accidental) gap in the pronoun paradigm might be (partially) responsible for the lack of nominative anaphors (cf. Everaert 1990 and references cited there). The approach advocated here explains this gap in the pronoun paradigm.[35]

3.10   Conclusion

Following Kayne (2000, this volume), and consonant with the derivational approach to syntactic relations, I have proposed that coreference is a function of merger. More precisely, I have proposed that (nonaccidental) coreference of α and β results if and only if α has been merged with β in a structure like (21), where α is the antecedent of the PRONOUN β, and β is the head of the noun phrase XP containing α:

(21) $[_{XP}$ [antecedent] [PRONOUN]]

The antecedent, a noun phrase, needs to move out of XP into a position in which it may acquire features indicating its argument structure status ("thematic role") and grammatical function ("Case"). Since the target for the noun phrase movement is an A-position (by definition), anaphor binding is essentially reduced to A-movement.

This theory of anaphor binding explains a number of fundamental properties of binding which had to be stipulated in earlier approaches (see (7)). The fact that binding is restricted to A-positions is explained because the antecedent in (21) needs to move to an A-position. The fact that the local domains for binding and A-movement coincide is also explained by the reduction of binding to A-movement. And finally, the fact that there is a morphological distinction between anaphors and pronouns (such that anaphors are marked variants of pronouns), but not among the various types of pronouns, follows from the assumption that anaphors are in fact pronouns that acquire an additional feature [+coreferential] in the configuration (21), in conjunction with the idea that morphological realization is a postsyntactic process (note 13).

The circumstance that these fundamental questions receive a relatively straightforward answer suggests to me that the current approach is on the right track.

4   Other types of anaphora

Various other types of anaphoric reference have not been discussed so far, and cannot be discussed in great detail within the confines of this contribution. What follows is a brief discussion of their properties, from the point of view of the theory of anaphoric binding explored here.

With the exception of reflexive pronouns of the type of *zich* in Dutch (SE-reflexives in the terminology of Reinhart and Reuland 1993) and reciprocals (English *each other*, Dutch *elkaar*), other types of anaphoric binding, such as binding of logophors/long-distance anaphors, pronouns, and bound variable anaphora, are not necessarily local (i.e. contained within the L-domain (35)). This suggests that the relation between these other types of anaphors and their antecedents is not in fact established by merging the anaphor with its antecedent in a constituent like (21) and displacing the antecedent via A-movement (*pace* Kayne 2000, this volume). This raises the question of how the anaphoric interpretation can be derived in these cases.

To start with SE-reflexives, the crucial observation is that SE-reflexives (Dutch *zich*) do not alternate freely with true anaphors (Dutch *zichzelf*):

(53) a.   Jan   haat   zichzelf/*zich   (Dutch)
           John hates SE-SELF/SE
           "John hates himself."

      b.   Jan   schaamt zich/*zichzelf
           John shames SE/SE-SELF
           "John is ashamed."

      c.   Jan   wast   zichzelf/zich
           John washes SE-SELF/SE
           "John washes himself."

In (53a), only the anaphor *zichzelf* can be used, and in (53b) only the reflexive. In (53c) both the anaphor and the reflexive can be used, but the interpretation is not the same in the two cases (Rooryck and VandenWyngaerd 1998; Ter

Meulen 2000). For example, the anaphor, but not the reflexive, can be used in a situation where John is washing a statue of himself. Thus, *zichzelf* represents a separate participant ("the self as other," in the expression of Rooryck and VandenWyngaerd 1998), and *zich* does not.

The observation that the anaphor represents a separate participant is not incompatible with the view of anaphoric binding explored here. The anaphor in (21) heads a noun phrase independently of the antecedent, which sits in the specifier position of the noun phrase but must collect its thematic role and grammatical function elsewhere.

Reflexives, like anaphors, cannot be bound outside the L-domain (35):

(54)   Jan   liet toe [dat ik hem/*zichzelf/*zich waste]   (*Dutch*)
       John let to that I him/se-self/se   washed
       "John allowed that I washed him."

Both reflexives and anaphors can be bound in the "subject" position in ECM-constructions:[36]

(55)   Jan   zag zichzelf/zich/*hem mij (al)   wassen   (*Dutch*)
       John saw se-self/se/him   me already wash
       "John saw himself wash me"/"John could already see himself wash me."

As the object of the perception verb *zien* "see" in this construction is an argument of the embedded verb *wassen* "wash," this example shows that *zich* need not be a co-argument of its antecedent. The observations suggest that *zich* is generated as the head of a separate noun phrase, just like *zichzelf*.

I would like to propose that *zich* is one of the two possible Spell Outs of a [+coreferential] PRONOUN, and that its special properties (i.e. the special interpretation at LF and the Spell Out by Morphology as a se-reflexive) derive from what happens to *zich* after the antecedent has been extracted. As is well known, *zich* shows the properties of a clitic, suggesting that it is adjoined to a lexical or functional head in the course of the derivation (cf. Zwart 1991).[37] If this adjunction involves the further acquisition of features, the possibility is expected that in the Spell Out procedure Morphology will not return *zichzelf*, but a special clitic form.

Reciprocals (English *each other*, Dutch *elkaar*) show the same locality effects as true anaphors (although English *each other* can also be logophoric, see below):

(56)   a.   De jongens haten elkaar   (*Dutch*)
            the boys   hate   each other

       b.   *De jongens denken dat ik elkaar   haat
            the boys   think   that I each other hate
            "The boys think that I hate each other."

       c.   De jongens zagen elkaar   lopen
            the boys   saw   each other walk

This suggests that reciprocal binding be described in the same way as anaphor binding, i.e. as resulting from the merger of the reciprocal with its antecedent in a configuration like (21). However, we must ensure that the PRONOUN in case of reciprocity is spelled out as *elkaar* and in cases of nonreciprocity as *zichzelf*:

(57)   a.   De jongens zagen [<de jongens> zichzelf]   *(Dutch)*
           the boys   saw   themselves

       b.   De jongens zagen [<de jongens> elkaar]
           the boys   saw   each other

I would like to propose that a reciprocal is not the Spell Out of a generic PRONOUN, but of a different element, derived through grammaticalization of a more complex category involving a floating quantifier (*elk* "each," *each*) and a noun phrase (*aar<ander* "other," *other*). Thus, although syntax does not distinguish anaphors and pronouns before Spell Out, it does recognize the separate category RECIPROCAL. As before, interpretation of the RECIPROCAL in connection with a particular antecedent (i.e., interpretation of the antecedent–reciprocal relation) can only take place if the antecedent and the reciprocal have been merged together in a constituent like (21).[38]

It seems that the default (nonanaphoric) Spell Out of the RECIPROCAL in Dutch is *de ander* "the other:"

(58)   a.   *De jongens haten de ander   *(Dutch)*
           the boys   hate   the other

       b.   De jongens denken dat ik de ander haat
           the boys   think   that I the other hate

In our theory, *de ander* would be the form returned by Morphology when encountering a RECIPROCAL that was never merged with an antecedent, i.e., the reciprocal variant of the (nonanaphoric) pronoun. *De ander* is also used in subject position (59a) and inside a subject noun phrase (59b):

(59)   a.   De jongens denken dat de ander   een genie is   *(Dutch)*
           the boys   think   that the other   a   genius is
           "The boys each think that the other is a genius."

       b.   De jongens denken dat de ander z'n vriendin   het leukst is
           the boys   think   that the other his girlfriend the cutest is
           "The boys think that each other's girlfriend is the cutest."

As expected, *de ander* is not obligatorily bound, any more than an ordinary pronoun would be:

(60)   De jongens denken dat ze   genieën zijn   *(Dutch)*
       the boys   think   that they geniuses are

Ze "they" in (60) can be interpreted as "the boys" or as some other persons familiar in the discourse. Likewise, *de ander* "the other" in (59) can be interpreted as some discourse familiar person who is not the same as some other person previously mentioned.

It seems that in English, *each other* can also be used logophorically, in examples like (61):[39]

(61)   They knew that pictures of each other would be on sale.

Because of the fact that logophors are bound nonlocally, they cannot be analyzed along the same lines as true, locally bound anaphors in our approach. Logophors behave differently from true anaphors, in that their antecedents may be picked up in the course of a derivation, as in (62a), contrasted with the case of a true anaphor in (62b), from Dutch:

(62)   a.   John wonders which pictures of himself Bill saw

(himself = Bill or John)

     b.   Jan   vroeg zich af welke foto's   van zichzelf Piet gezien had
         John asked SE   off which pictures of   SE-SELF Pete seen had
         "John wondered which pictures of himself Pete saw."

(zichzelf = Piet)

This supports the idea that the relation between a logophor and its antecedent is established in a way quite different from true anaphor binding (see Sells 1987).

This raises the question, not resolved here, why English has no morphological distinction between logophors and true anaphors.[40] In the morphology-after-syntax approach adopted here (cf. note 13), it is not immediately expected that Morphology returns the special [+coreferential] form (i.e., the true anaphor) in other contexts as well. Perhaps this is an accidental fact of English pronoun paradigms, where the anaphor appears to be a grammaticalized emphatic pronoun.

Pronouns can be nonlocally bound, as in (63):

(63)   John thinks that he is a genius.

We have seen that local binding of a pronoun (the Principle B effect) is an effect of Spell Out. A PRONOUN that is marked [+coreferential] will always be spelled out as an anaphor. Local coreference of a pronoun with an antecedent can only come about accidentally, in cases like (64):

(64)   (As for John, if everyone likes him, then surely) John must like him.

It is a consequence of our theory that the coreferential interpretation in (63) is accidental as well, even if much easier to obtain than in local contexts like (64).

Note first of all that coreference in (63) is optional, raising the question what factors assist in biasing a coreferential or noncoreferential interpretation. One factor that might be important is that *he* in (63) may be regarded as a "self-oriented" pronoun, where the "self" is not the speaker uttering (63) but the creator of the proposition selected by the verb *think* (Tancredi 1997). The phenomenon of "self-orientation" is more familiar from reference to the speaker (by first person pronouns), but occurs equally in contexts like (65):

(65)   Chris frowned. Now he would be all alone.

In both (63) and (65), *he* refers not directly to an antecedent, but to the person responsible for the utterance in which it occurs, in much the same way as first person pronouns do. This carries over to cases like (66), where the antecedent is a quantified noun phrase:

(66)   Every student thinks he is a genius.

As is well known, (66) lacks the reading that would be expected under a naive conception of coreference, namely that every student thinks that every student is a genius. If *he* is viewed as a self-oriented pronoun, it refers to the individual owner of each instance of the thought "I am a genius," yielding the correct interpretation. This obviously cannot be the whole story, but it serves to indicate the kind of factors that may be involved.

Pronouns like *he* in (66), which are interpreted in connection with a quantified noun phrase ("bound variable anaphora"), need not be bound by a c-commanding antecedent:

(67)   [Everyone's mother] thinks he is a genius

This suggests that the binding relation between *he* and its antecedent (*everyone* in (66)–(67)) is not established by merging *he* and *everyone* in a constituent like (21). As discussed in section 3.5, the option of merging an antecedent in the specifier of a DP must not be allowed, in order to exclude binding of a true anaphor by a non-c-commanding antecedent:

(68)   *[Everyone's mother] likes himself

This supports the idea, advanced here, that the proposal of Kayne (2000, this volume) to describe coreference as a function of sisterhood of the antecedent and the dependent element applies to anaphor binding only, and that pronoun binding comes about in a different way.

Bound pronouns (bound variable anaphora) are a separate phenomenon in that the relation between the pronoun and its antecedent is mediated by an expression which is referentially dependent on the antecedent (Rullmann 1988). Thus, in (67), the expression *everyone's mother* evokes a set containing all and only the persons who are the mothers of the persons referred to by *everyone*. In terms of Jackendoff (1983), we may think of *everyone's mother* as projecting a TYPE consisting of a number of TOKENS, where the TOKENS are (projections of) individuals (mothers) identified by the reference of *everyone* (i.e., the projection of a collection of understood individuals). I would like to suggest that this situation makes the reference of *everyone* sufficiently salient for the relevant individuals to be interpreted as referred to by *he*. But the coreference is still optional and hence accidental. In contrast, the coreferential interpretation of an anaphor and its antecedent is not optional and is not sensitive to referential dependency (witness the ungrammaticality of (68)).

Various other properties of "bound" vs. "(accidentally) coreferential" pronouns are discussed in the literature (e.g. Lasnik 1976; Reinhart 1976, 1983; Evans 1980; Higginbotham 1980), but although the differences are clear, they do not automatically lead to the conclusion that pronoun binding is not accidental. Thus, backward linking is allowed with ordinary pronouns, but not with bound pronouns:

(69)   a.   [People who know him] say John/*every linguist is a genius
      b.   [His mother] loves John/*everyone

Likewise, although strict c-command by its antecedent is not required for bound variable anaphora (see (67)), it seems that bound variable anaphora must be c-commanded by an element referentially dependent on the antecedent (Rullmann 1988). This is not the case with pronouns that are interpreted as coreferential with nonquantified expressions:

(70)   a.   People who know every linguist believe he is a genius (no bound
         interpretation)
      b.   People who know John believe he is a genius (coreferential interpretation allowed)

Furthermore, contexts disallowing bound pronouns do not admit of a sloppy interpretation of pronouns in ellipsis (Lasnik 1976: 20):

(71)   People who know John believe he is intelligent and people who know
      Bill do, too (sc. believe John/*Bill is intelligent)

Discussion of each of these differences would take us too far afield at this point. To us, the more telling observation is that the PRONOUNS are spelled out the same in all of these cases, whether interpreted as bound variable anaphora or not. In each case, the PRONOUN gets the default Spell Out of an ordinary pronoun. Moreover, the morphological identity of bound variable anaphora and ordinary pronouns does not appear to be an isolated fact of English.[41] This suggests that a PRONOUN does not acquire any additional features in the course of the derivation when a bound variable interpretation is intended, hence that the interpretation of a pronoun is not determined by its derivational history.[42]

5   Reconstruction

The theory of Kayne (2000, this volume), according to which α is (nonaccidentally) interpreted as coreferential with β if and only if α and β are merged together in a constituent like (21) – which I have argued applies to true anaphoric binding only – entails that coreference is established once and for all at the moment of merger of the antecedent and the dependent element (see also Epstein et al. 1998: 63f.). This eliminates the need for a reconstruction operation at LF, accounting for anaphoric binding of displaced dependent elements, as in (72a):

(72) a. Himself, John knows well
       b. [knows [$_{XP}$ John PRONOUN]]

As discussed above, the derivation of (72a) involves the earlier stage (72b), where coreference of *John* and PRONOUN is established through sisterhood (after which *John* moves to the subject position and the remnant XP is topicalized to yield (72a)). As a function of the sisterhood configuration, the PRONOUN acquires the feature [+coreferential], which leads to Spell Out as an anaphor at PF and interpretation as an anaphor at LF.

Since the theory of binding explored here involves no disjointness conditions like Principle B and C of the classical binding theory (see (11)–(12)), it is not entirely unexpected that disjointness effects (whatever their cause) may be lifted in the course of a derivation. This is indeed what we find ("anti-reconstruction," see Van Riemsdijk and Williams 1981):

(73) a. He likes every book that John wrote   *(obviation)*
       b. [Which book that John wrote] does he like best   *(no obviation)*

Example (73b) is problematic for a theory which involves reconstruction of displaced elements at LF, feeding the interpretation of variable referential elements (like *he* in (73)). Reconstruction of *which book that John wrote* would restore *John* to a position c-commanded by *he*, yielding a violation of Principle C of the binding theory (11c).[43] In our theory, disjointness is not marked at any stage in the derivation (unlike coreference), and it is not excluded that in the course of the derivation, circumstances arise which favor an (accidental) coreference interpretation.

It seems to me that one crucial factor facilitating (accidental) coreference in cases like (73b) is identified in Heycock (1995: 558f.). Heycock notes contrasts like (74):[44]

(74) a. Which stories about Diana did she most object to?   *(no obviation)*
       b. How many stories about Diana does she want us to invent?
                                                               (obviation)

As Heycock points out, the fronted noun phrases in (74a) and (74b) differ in that *which* in (74a) signifies the presupposed existence of a set of stories about Diana, whereas the fronted noun phrase in (74b) is "nonreferential" (in the sense that such a presupposition is not signified). This makes it much easier to interpret *Diana* as a discourse familiar entity in (74a) than in (74b), allowing a reading of (74a) in which both *Diana* and *her* "hark back" to the same discourse familiar entity.[45]

More exactly, the intonational properties of the fronted noun phrase in (74a), where *Diana* is deaccented, present (the projection of) Diana as a discourse familiar entity. The deaccenting signals familiarity, whether Diana was mentioned prior to the utterance (74a) or not. This appears to be typically the case with coreferential R-expressions contained in sentence-level adjuncts, which generally precede the main clause containing the pronoun, but not always (Klein 1980: 217):

(75) a. Voordat Eline er erg in had, was ze   haar verloofde al   kwijt
                                                                    (*Dutch*)
          before   Eline it noticed   was she her fiancé   already rid
          "Before Eline noticed it, she had already lost her fiancé."
                                                              (*no obviation*)

      b. Ze was haar verloofde al   kwijt, voordat Eline er erg in had
          she was her fiancé   already rid   before   Eline it noticed
          "She had already lost her fiancé, before Eline noticed it."
                                                              (*no obviation*)

I would like to suggest that the fronted noun phrases in (73b) and (74a), by their displacement into a sentence-level A'-position, acquire the status of an adjunct facilitating a coreferential interpretation under the relevant intonation.[46]

The issue of reconstruction is closely related to the question of where the binding conditions apply. It is within the spirit of the DASR program that the binding conditions apply at each point in the derivation, whereas it is within the spirit of the Minimalist Program more generally that the binding conditions apply at LF only. Lebeaux (1998) argues that the "positive" binding condition Principle A applies at LF, whereas the "negative" conditions Principles B and C apply throughout the derivation (cf. (11)–(12)).[47] Part of the evidence for this division is derived from examples like (76), where *himself* in (76b) can ignore the "lower" antecedent *Bill* and pick *John* as its antecedent at a late stage in the derivation, while *Bill* must be interpreted as disjoint from *he* in (76a):

(76) a. John wondered which pictures of Bill he saw   (obviation *Bill – he*)

      b. John wondered which pictures of himself Bill saw
                                      (binding *John – himself* or *Bill – himself*)

In fact, the situation is much more complicated, since, as we have just seen, the obviation in configurations like (76a) is not always enforced, and *himself* in (76b) is a logophor rather than an anaphor (see (62); see note 25).

On the theory advanced here, the question of where the binding principles apply evaporates. There is just a single binding condition, namely that coreference is established only by merging the antecedent and the anaphor (in fact, the generic PRONOUN) yielding a constituent as represented in (1a)/(21) at an early point in the derivation. Coreference relations thus established are fixed once and for all time (i.e., until the interface levels PF/LF). Disjointness is not governed by principles, but is the default interpretation, which can be overruled under the influence of various factors and at various points in the derivation.

This theory also excludes the possibility, argued for in Branigan (2000), that anaphor binding is established in covert syntax (i.e., after the Spell Out point in the derivation). In the theory advanced here, if an anaphoric relation would be established at LF it would have the effect that an element *not* spelled out as an anaphor at *PF* (i.e., an element spelled out as an ordinary pronoun) be interpreted as an anaphor at *LF* (see note 13 on the architecture of the grammar assumed here). Indeed, evidence showing that anaphoricity can be established at LF appears to be hard to come by, a circumstance which our theory explains immediately.[48]

6   A few words on remaining problems

The theory of local anaphor binding advanced here meets with a serious problem involving interaction of binding and raising. The relevant cases are illustrated in (77), where the anaphor is contained within an adjunct PP in the matrix clause, and the antecedent is taken to originate inside the embedded clause:

(77)   a.   John seems to himself [to be a genius]
       b.   John was expected by himself [to become class president]

It is standardly assumed that in these constructions the antecedent *John* originates within the embedded clause indicated with brackets in (77), as *John* is interpreted as the external argument of the predicate *a genius/class president*.[49] Therefore, the source of the coreference with *himself* cannot be that *John* and *himself* are merged together as in (21), unless the adjunct PPs are generated in a lower position than currently assumed.

It seems to me that the phenomena in (77) can only be reconciled with the theory of local anaphor binding explored here if the standard assumption that these examples involve raising out of the embedded clause is abandoned. Such a serious digression from the standard analysis of the relevant phenomena cannot be defended within the confines of this article. I can, however, indicate why I think such a digression would be worth pursuing (leaving the actual pursuing to another occasion).

As for the raising example (77a), it is interesting to note that verbs like *seem* appear to lose their raising characteristics in the presence of an experiencer PP.[50] This is suggested by the facts in (78), discussed by Lebeaux (1998), where the presence of the Experiencer PP blocks a "downstairs" interpretation of the matrix clause subject:

(78)   a.   Two computer experts seem [to be expected to crash every system]
       b.   Two computer experts seem to each other [to be expected to crash
            every system]

Whereas (78a) has a reading in which *every system* takes scope over *two computer experts*, yielding the interpretation "two arbitrary computer experts for each system," (78b) does not, yielding only the interpretation "two given computer experts for the entire set of systems." This would be accounted for if *seem* loses its raising characteristics when an Experiencer PP is present.[51]

As for the passive case (77b), the analytic passive of the later stages of most Indo-European languages seems to lend itself to an analysis where the past participle is regarded as an adjectival predicate taking the subject as its external argument (79a), as with ordinary adjectival predication (79b):

(79)   a.   was [John [arrested]]
        b.   was [John [sick]]

The possibility of coreference in (77b) would then be accounted for if the *by*-phrase were contained within the adjectival predicate, as in (80).

(80)   was [John [arrested by himself]]

In a structure like (80), our analysis of coreference as resulting from the merger of the antecedent with the anaphor (as in (21)) can be implemented without problems:

(81)   was [John [arrested by [<John> himself]]]

This analysis makes the clear prediction that languages featuring true morphological passivization should not allow anaphors to appear in the *by*-phrase. This prediction finds initial support in Anagnostopoulou and Everaert (1996: 14), according to whom Greek (which has a morphological passive) observes a "thematic prominence" requirement disallowing binding of an agent (in a *by*-phrase) by a theme (the subject of the passive):

(82)   *O monos kureas pu   ksiristike   pote apo ton eafto tu itan o Figaro
                                                                              (*Greek*)
        the only   barber who shave-PASS ever by   himself   was Figaro
        "The only barber who was ever shaved by himself was Figaro."

A more thorough discussion of the phenomena illustrated in (77) and their relevance to the theory of local anaphor binding explored here would require further study.

7   Conclusion

In this paper I have argued that a locally bound anaphor is the marked Spell Out of a generic variable referential element ("PRONOUN") which has acquired, in the course of the derivation of the sentence in which it occurs, a special feature indicating its coreferentiality with an antecedent. I have explored the possibility, consonant with the strictest implementation of the derivational approach to syntactic relations (Epstein et al. 1998; Epstein and Seely 1999), that the PRONOUN acquires the feature [+coreferential] as an automatic consequence of a derivational procedure which merges the PRONOUN with its antecedent, as proposed by Kayne (2000, this volume). I have argued that if we take this procedure to apply to locally bound anaphors only, a number of properties of local anaphor binding are explained, most importantly the fact that it is subject to the locality conditions on A-movement. These results require that we take the coreferential interpretation of an unmarked pronoun (i.e. a pronoun not marked for anaphoricity) to be essentially accidental, i.e. not an automatic consequence of the derivational procedure as proposed by Kayne (2000, this volume).

The proposal discussed here shares with Kayne's the important consequence that almost all of the traditional binding theory (see Chomsky 1981, 1982) disappears. Coreferentiality is a function of the operation Merge, not of some interpretive procedure to be captured by various principles. There is no issue of the level of representation at which the binding theory applies, as coreferentiality is fixed once and for all at the stage in the derivation where the PRONOUN is merged with its antecedent. Finally, it is explained that the local domain for anaphor binding coincides with the local domain for A-movement, on the assumption that the antecedent, after being merged with the PRONOUN, needs to be extracted and remerged in an A-position (the thematic and Case positions needed for the antecedent's proper interpretation).

These considerations suggest to me that the computational system of human language establishes grammatical relations only by merging the relevant entities in a sisterhood configuration like (1a), repeated here for convenience:

(1a) $[\alpha\ \beta]$

Acknowledgments

My thanks to Sam Epstein, Daniel Seely, Howard Lasnik, David Lebeaux, Richard Kayne, Jan Koster, Hanneke Ramselaar, Eric Reuland, and Mark de Vries. The research leading to this article was sponsored by the Netherlands Organization for Scientific Research, grant no. 300-75-027, which is gratefully acknowledged.

Notes

1 The example is chosen for illustrative purposes. I follow Hale and Keyser (1998) in assuming a more detailed structure of the verb phrase than the one employed here.

2 α c-commands β iff α is merged with (a constituent containing) β (see Epstein 1995).

3   Note that this raises the question why elements can only be merged in positions c-commanding their previous position (i.e. the c-command requirement). To a large extent this can be derived from the Extension Condition of Chomsky (1993), limiting merger to the top node of existing structure. See Epstein et al. (1998: 139ff.) for discussion.

4   This holds as well of notational variants of "traces," such as the "slashes" of Gazdar (1981).

5   The written version of Kayne (2000), which appears in this volume, only came to my attention when the present article was in its final copy-editing stage. Unfortunately, the publication schedule made it impossible for me to address Kayne (this volume) more squarely and to eliminate unnecessary restatements of Kayne's proposals and arguments.

6   Anaphors are standardly taken to include reciprocals (English *each other*) and reflexives (Dutch *zich*), but these elements each have their own distribution and interpretation, not necessarily coinciding with that of anaphors in the strict sense. Bound pronouns are not generally taken to be in this class, although the term "anaphora" may be used to refer to bound pronouns as well ("bound variable anaphora").

7   I use the term "pronoun" in the restricted sense of a variable referential element that is not locally bound (the term "pronominal" is used elsewhere). Reinhart and Reuland (1993) take reflexives (Dutch *zich*) to be nonreferential pronouns rather than anaphors. This view of reflexives is not adopted here.

8   An element is "bound" if there is a binder for it, i.e. an element that c-commands it and corefers with it. An element is "free" if it is not bound.

9   A projection is created by the mind on the impulse of sensory data or thought processes. The linguistic entities that have referential properties are taken not to refer to real-world entities directly, but to projections (which may or may not be based on real-world entities).

10 See Jayaseelan (1997) for extensive discussion of the idea that anaphors are modified pronouns.

11 The classical inventory derives its charm mainly from the circumstance that it covers both overt and covert categories. However, traces are currently no longer viewed as separate entities from their antecedents, but as copies of their antecedents. Hence, they can be of any noun phrase type, regardless of the type of movement. Also, the idea that *pro* is a pronominal anaphor has been contentious from the start (see Koster 1984). See Zwart (1999b) for the idea that *pro* stands out as a nonreferential element.

12 Reinhart and Reuland (1993: 659) describe pronouns as being less referentially defective than anaphors. For our purpose, the crucial distinction is between fully referential elements (R-expressions) and variable referential elements (pronouns and anaphors), regardless of the ability of pronouns to stand on their own in a given discourse setting or by virtue of some process of accommodation. That anaphors are variable referential rather than nonreferential is shown by various tests, discussed in Zwart (1999b), showing different behavior of anaphors compared to reflexives or *pro*. For example, in (i), the anaphor, but not the reflexive, allows an interpretation where Sally is listening to a recording of her own speech (Rooryck and VandenWyngaerd 1998), and in (ii) the anaphor allows a "de re" interpretation, unlike PRO (cf. Chierchia 1989):

(i)   Sally hoorde zich/zichzelf praten   (*Dutch*)
      Sally heard   SE/SE-SELF   talk

(ii) The unfortunate expects himself/*pro* to get a medal

13 The view on Spell Out and the role of the lexicon here is inspired by the frame-
    work of Distributed Morphology of Halle and Marantz (1993), and more generally
    by recent theories which assume a morphology-after-syntax approach. In such an
    approach, the Spell Out procedure takes a syntactic terminal and converts it into a
    string of phonemes. The module performing the conversion, called Morphology,
    yields a form from the (paradigms stored in the) lexicon that best matches
    the morphosyntactic features present on the terminal. The approach to binding
    explored here assumes that the lexicon contains paradigms of pronouns, that
    anaphoricity is a pronominal feature which may be acquired in the course of a
    derivation and prompts Morphology to yield an anaphor when encountered on
    a terminal node in the Spell Out procedure. Note that coreferentiality on this
    approach is not introduced at LF by an interpretive procedure, but is already present
    as a syntactic feature, acquired by the PRONOUN in a sisterhood configuration with
    its antecedent. As pointed out by the editors, this is compatible with the notion,
    entertained in DASR and in Chomsky (2001b), of continuous communication be-
    tween the computational system (syntax) and the interface components LF and PF.
14 Cf. Postma's (1997: 303) discussion of similar cases, where he argues that the
    semantic bleaching needed to turn a referential expression into an anaphor is not
    an inherent lexical property but a function of syntactic structure.
15 To be more exact, the proposal made here does not necessarily imply that
    anaphoricity should be marked on the PRONOUN rather than on the antecedent. A
    cursory glance at anaphoricity across languages suggests that the entire range of
    possibilities is attested: anaphoricity marking on the PRONOUN (English), on the
    antecedent (i), on both the PRONOUN and the antecedent (ii), and on neither (iii):

    (i)   Irail pein duhp-irail   (*Ponapean*, Rehg 1981: 301)
           they self bath-them
           "They bathed themselves."

    (ii)   Ada   wiči   wič   alzurar-zawa   (*Lezgian*, Haspelmath 1993: 186)
           he-ERG self-ERG self-ABS deceive-IMPF
           "He is deceiving himself."

    (iii) Nrâ   dreghe nrî   fadre rroto   (*Tiri*, Osumi 1995: 207)
           he-SUBJ injure he-OBJ with car
           "He injured himself in a car."

16 More precisely, *John* is neither a variable referential element, nor does it contain a
    variable referential element, as is the case with inalienable possessive (body-part)
    noun phrases used as anaphoric expressions.
17 Note that in the version of Kayne's theory advanced here, *he* would have to be
    spelled out as an anaphor if its coreferentiality with *John* were to derive from the
    circumstance that *he* and *John* form a constituent as in (26). This alone would
    suffice to exclude the sentences in (24) on the relevant reading.
18 See also Heim (1998) for a recent discussion of these facts. Heim introduces the
    useful notion of a "guise," an individual concept, i.e. a function from worlds to
    individuals, and proposes that reference is always to a guise. Binding principles B
    and C can then be reformulated as prohibiting (local) coreference to the same
    guise. Heim does not, however, propose to describe all cases of accidental
    coreference as reference of identical noun phrases to different guises. A solution
    along these lines might be feasible for the examples in (27), for instance, if dis-
    course new elements (elements in focus) are taken to refer to a different guise/

projection than (identical) discourse old elements (elements lending themselves to ellipsis). In (27), the first instance of *John* is in focus, whereas the second is deaccented, showing discourse old status. See Demirdache (1997) for relevant discussion.

19   It seems to me that the curious exception to Principle C in (i), discussed in Fiengo and May (1994: 265), Fox (1995), and Zwart (1998b), must also be described with reference to focusing and defocusing effects.

(i)   I gave him everything John wanted me to (give him)

Here, *him* and *John* may be understood as coreferring, in violation of Principle C. In Zwart (1998b), I suggested that the overt *him* is (for its interpretation) parasitic on the elliptical *him* in the part in parentheses, which itself, being deaccented, is introduced as discourse old. In terms of Tancredi (1992), there is a "focus related topic" *give someone something* which allows *give him* to be deaccented and even deleted. At the same time, the overt *him* is of necessity interpreted as identical to the elliptical *him*, yielding accidental coreference of the overt *him* and *John*. In my present view, the phenomena are slightly more complicated, because the interpretation of the elliptical *him* can now no longer be viewed as an instance of coreference (which is restricted to anaphors), for which see below.

20   Demirdache (1997: 75) argues that Principle C should not be understood as prohibiting accidental coreference, but as excluding an anaphoric interpretation of accidental coreference. Thus in (27a), although *John* may like *John*, the information that John is a "self-liker" is not conveyed. In our theory, the anaphoric interpretation is automatically excluded because *John* is not a variable referential element.

21   In earlier work (Zwart 1999a), I proposed to derive Principle C effects, and absence thereof in non-c-commanding configurations, from a reference assignment procedure working in tandem with the operation Merge, to the effect that every noun phrase newly merged to the structure is contraindexed to (referential) noun phrases already in the structure. This essentially incorporates Lasnik's (1976) obviation principle, a precursor to Principle C. I now believe that the strongest implementation of the derivational approach to binding should eliminate Principle C altogether, and should not involve any mechanism of reference assignment other than the mechanism yielding coreference discussed here.

22   Number is not an issue here, witness the equally ungrammatical (i):

(i)   The boys heard the girls curse themselves.

23   Note that the uniqueness requirement does not exclude recursive anaphoricity, as in:

(i)   John heard himself curse himself.

As pointed out by Kayne (2000), the derivation of examples like (i) may involve a constituent like (ii), where *John himself* is first extracted from XP, and *John* is then extracted out of YP:

(ii)   [XP [YP John himself] himself]

24   Interarboreal operations have been proposed as a solution to the problem that head movement typically violates the extension condition (Bobaljik and Brown

1997). In Zwart (2001) I suggest a different approach to this problem, namely to abandon the idea that head movement (feature movement) involves adjunction.

25 I take English *himself* inside representational noun phrases like *pictures of himself* to be logophors rather than anaphors (see also Reinhart and Reuland 1993: 681f.). If so, the impossibility of A-movement out of representational noun phrases illustrated in (i) does not affect the noted parallelism of anaphor binding and A-movement.

(i) *John seems that [pictures of <John>] are on sale

26 Although this assumption looks familiar from the perspective of the Government and Binding theory (Chomsky 1981), it is actually a novel assumption which requires further support. The Case Filter of the Government and Binding theory applies to all noun phrases, but does not exclude escape mechanisms, such as default or inherent Case assignment, which might be applied to the antecedent in (21) as well. In addition, the Government and Binding theory does not require every *noun phrase*, but every *argument* to acquire a thematic role.

27 A-positions are defined here as positions where thematic roles and (structural) Cases may be assigned.

28 In English, Exceptional Case Marking (ECM) constructions (*John saw Bill kiss Mary*) do not obviously involve NP-raising into the functional domain associated with the matrix verb (*pace* Johnson 1991), unless the raising takes place at LF (Branigan 1992) or involves the entire VP (Koster 2000). In the classical Government and Binding theory analysis, the extension of the local domain for A-movement and binding in ECM constructions was described as a function of government of the embedded subject by the higher verb (cf. Chomsky 1981: 188). In the Minimalist framework, the local domain can no longer be defined with recourse to the notion "government."

29 This may be derived from the idea expressed in Chomsky (2001a) that interpretation takes place in phases, where CP constitutes a phase.

30 Cases like (i) are excluded because *John*, extracted from the noun phrase headed by *himself*, lacks a thematic role and a Case.

(i) *John, himself likes Mary

31 The abbreviations used in the glosses are: DEM = demonstrative, NNTR = nonneuter, AFF = affirmative. See Zwart (1998a) for a comparison of Dutch and English left-dislocation constructions.

32 Kayne (2000, this volume) does not appear to start from the assumption that the derivation starts out with a generic variable referential element PRONOUN, which is spelled out either as an anaphor or as a pronoun.

33 Absolutive anaphors are widely attested, both in the pronominal variant (e.g. Lezgian, Haspelmath 1993: 184f.) and in the inalienable possessive noun phrase variant (e.g. Basque, Saltarelli 1988: 104).

34 Nominative-accusative languages with nominative objects, such as Icelandic, deserve additional comment. In Icelandic, nominative anaphors are excluded in object position as well (Everaert 1990: 281), including the object position occupied by embedded external arguments in ECM constructions (Schütze 1997: 119). I leave this subject for further study. One possibility is that the dative subject typically required in these constructions is contained within a preposition phrase (PP) headed by an empty preposition. Being inside a PP, the dative subject could not originate as a sister to the PRONOUN, eliminating the only possible source of coreference in our approach.

35 Note that nominative "long-distance anaphors" (not bound inside the L-domain) are widely attested (see Jayaseelan 1997 for a survey). This leads me to believe that long-distance anaphors are not anaphors in the sense defined here, i.e. PRONOUNS merged with their antecedent. That long-distance anaphors are not true anaphors is supported by the distribution of the long-distance anaphor *taan* in Malayalam, which cannot be bound locally, as shown in (i)–(ii) (data from Jayaseelan 1997: 190f).

(i)   taan waliya aaḷ   aaṇə ennə raaman-ə   toonni   (*Malayalam*)
      self great person is   COMP Raaman-DAT seemed
      "It seemed to Raman that he (sc. Raman) was a great man."

(ii) *raaman tan-ne aṭiccu
      Raman   self-ACC hit-PAST
      "Raman hit himself."

36 The modal particle *al* facilitates the interpretation of the verb *zien* "see" as "imagine," which is the necessary interpretation if the ECM-subject is *zich* rather than *zichzelf*.
37 Hence the development of the SE-reflexive into a grammaticalized reflexivity marker in many languages, e.g. Norwegian.
38 It is tempting to consider the construction in (i) as resulting from movement of the antecedent and the floating quantifier out of the noun phrase headed by *the other*. However, as (ii) shows, the locality conditions on A-movement are not met, suggesting that a different analysis applies to these cases.

(i)   The boys each hated the other
(ii) The boys each knew that I hated the other

39 Crucially, the creator of the pictures in (61) may be different from the persons indicated by *they*, so that we know that *each other* is not bound by an empty *pro* subject.
40 Other languages do, like Dutch (anaphor *zichzelf*, logophor *'mzelf*) and Malayalam (anaphor *tanne-tanne*, logophor *tanne* (ACC)).
41 Languages featuring weak and strong pronoun paradigms must use the weak paradigm (including the empty pronoun *pro*) when a bound reading is intended (Montalbetti 1984). But, crucially, weak pronouns are not used *exclusively* in bound readings.
42 The relevance of (a weak version of) c-command to bound variable anaphora (i.e., the pronoun must be bound by its antecedent or by a noun phrase referentially dependent on its antecedent) suggests that the antecedent (or a noun phrase referentially dependent on the antecedent) must be merged to a constituent containing the pronoun for a bound variable anaphora interpretation to obtain. This can be understood if the pair-list reading characteristic of bound variable anaphora (i.e. *every x thinks x is a genius* is interpreted as x_1 *thinks* x_1 *is a genius,* x_2 *thinks* x_2 *is a genius,* etc.) requires merger of two elements involving some kind of multiplicity. The quantified noun phrase is inherently multiplicitous, and its sister can be interpreted as such if it contains a multiplicitous element, such as a variably (i.e. nondeictically) interpreted pronoun. (As shown by Higginbotham 1980, the pair-list reading disappears when the pronoun is interpreted deictically in examples like *Every musician will play some piece that you ask him to play*.) If so, bound variable

anaphora requires a configuration like (1a), but in a different way from true anaphor binding.

43 Following Lasnik (1998), I assume that the complement/adjunct asymmetry often noted in connection with this type of anti-reconstruction effects (see Lebeaux 1988) is spurious.

44 Note that the presence of a *pro* subject in the fronted (representational) noun phrases is irrelevant in the crucial case of (74a), as *Diana* is not the author of the stories (Heycock 1995, note 15).

45 In introducing discourse familiarity, I deviate from Heycock's (1995) explanation of the pattern in (74). Heycock (1995: 561) proposes to represent nonreferential noun phrases at LF as involving a split between a fronted part (*how many*) and a reconstructed part (*stories about Diana*), explaining the Principle C effect through c-command at LF. She shows that *how many*-phrases also permit a referential interpretation where the entire *how many*-phrase is interpreted in the fronted position at LF. On this interpretation, *how many stories about Diana* asks for the cardinality of a given set of stories about Diana. Again, the notion "given" appears to be crucial here, and, in our view, sufficient to facilitate an (accidental) coreferential reading. The observation in Fox (1999: 166) that effected objects (of a verb like *build*) trigger a nonreferential interpretation and hence reconstruction effects, whereas noneffected objects (of a verb like *rebuild*) do not, again supports the significance of the notion "given" in this domain:

(i)   How many houses in John's city does he want the government to (re)build?
(obviation only with *build*)

46 The relevance of deaccenting to coreference was noted as early as Lakoff (1968), Akmajian and Jackendoff (1970).

47 Lebeaux's conclusions are adopted in Epstein et al. (1998: 62), albeit that in their approach communication between syntax and LF is continuous. Hence, Principle A must be satisfied at any point in the derivation, whereas Principle B/C must be satisfied throughout the derivation.

48 Branigan (2000) argues in support of binding effects created by covert movement on the basis of examples like (i):

(i)   Perry proved [Jill and Tony to have lied] during each other's trials

The argument assumes covert movement of the ECM "subject" *Jill and Tony* to an object licensing position c-commanding *each other*, a movement established overtly in languages like Dutch (see (34)). But the argument begs the question whether such covert movement exists (on which see Koster 2000), and whether *each other* in (i) is a "true" rather than a logophoric or even pronominal reciprocal.

49 This eliminates the possibility that a constituent [John himself] is merged in the embedded clause and raises to the adjunct position, after which *John* is extracted and merged in the matrix clause subject position. In such a derivation, *John* would not be interpreted as the external argument of the predicate, but *John himself* would.

50 *Pace* Martin (1996: 112).

51 As discussed by Torrego (1996), McGinnis (1998), and Ura (2000), languages seem to differ as to whether the experiencer blocks raising. In Dutch, no blocking effect occurs, but, interestingly, reflexive experiencers appear to be excluded with raising verbs (i), unlike with nonraising verbs of appearance (ii):

(i)   Jan   lijkt   mij/$^{??}$zich(zelf) een genie te zijn   (*Dutch*)
       John seems me/SE(self)   a genius to be
       "John seems to me/himself to be a genius."

(ii)   Jan   komt mij/zichzelf voor een genie te zijn
       John comes me/himself fore a genius to be
       "John appears to me/himself to be a genius."

References

Akmajian, Adrian and Ray S. Jackendoff. 1970. "Coreferentiality and stress." *Linguistic Inquiry* 1: 124–6.

Anagnostopoulou, Elena and Martin Everaert. 1996. "Asymmetries in binding: configurational and thematic effects on anaphora." *GLOW Newsletter* 36: 14–15.

Bobaljik, Jonathan D. and S. Brown. 1997. "Interarboreal operations: head movement and the Extension Requirement." *Linguistic Inquiry* 28: 345–56.

Branigan, Phil. 1992. "Subjects and complementizers." Dissertation, MIT, Cambridge, MA.

Branigan, Phil. 2000. "Binding effects with covert movement." *Linguistic Inquiry* 31: 553–7.

Burzio, Luigi. 1986. *Italian Syntax: A Government-binding Approach*. Dordrecht: Kluwer.

Chierchia, Gennaro. 1989. "Anaphora and attitudes 'de se'." In R. Bartsch, J. van Benthem, and P. van Emde Boas, eds., *Semantics and Contextual Expression*. Dordrecht: Foris, pp. 1–31.

Chomsky, Noam. 1981. *Lectures on Government and Binding*. Dordrecht: Foris.

Chomsky, Noam. 1982. *Some Concepts and Consequences of the Theory of Government and Binding*. Cambridge, MA: MIT Press.

Chomsky, Noam. 1993. "A minimalist program for linguistic theory." In N. Chomsky, 1995, *The Minimalist Program*, Cambridge: MIT Press, pp. 167–217.

Chomsky, Noam. 2001a. "Derivation by phase." In M. Kenstowicz, ed., *Ken Hale: A Life in Language*. Cambridge, MA: MIT Press.

Chomsky, Noam. 2001b. "Beyond explanatory adequacy." MS, MIT, Cambridge, MA.

Chomsky, Noam and Howard Lasnik. 1993. "The theory of principles and parameters." In N. Chomsky, 1995, *The Minimalist Program*, Cambridge, MA: MIT Press, pp. 13–127.

Demirdache, Hamida. 1997. "Condition C." In H. Bennis, P. Pica, and J. Rooryck, eds., *Atomism and Binding*. Dordrecht: Foris Publications, pp. 51–87.

Epstein, Samuel D. 1995. "Un-principled syntax and the derivation of syntactic relations." MS, University of Harvard. In S. D. Epstein and N. Hornstein, eds., 1999, *Working Minimalism*, Cambridge, MA: MIT Press, pp. 317–45.

Epstein, S. D., Erich M. Groat, Ruriko Kawashima, and Hisatsugu Kitahara. 1998. *A Derivational Approach to Syntactic Relations*. New York: Oxford University Press.

Epstein, Samuel D. and Daniel Seely. 1999. "SPEC-ifying the GF 'subject': eliminating A-chains and the EPP within a derivational model." MS, University of Michigan.

Evans, Gareth. 1980. "Pronouns." *Linguistic Inquiry* 11: 337–62.

Everaert, Martin. 1990. "Nominative anaphors in Icelandic: morphology or syntax?" In W. Abraham, W. Kosmeijer, and E. Reuland, eds., *Issues in Germanic Syntax*. Berlin: Mouton de Gruyter, pp. 277–305.

Fiengo, Robert and Robert May. 1994. *Indices and Identity*. Cambridge, MA: MIT Press.

Fox, Danny. 1995. "Condition C effects in ACD." *MIT Working Papers in Linguistics* 27: 105–19.

Fox, Danny. 1999. "Reconstruction, binding theory, and the interpretation of chains." *Linguistic Inquiry* 30, 157–96.

Gazdar, Gerald. 1981. "Unbounded dependencies and coordinate structure." *Linguistic Inquiry* 12: 155–84.

Hale, Kenneth and Samuel J. Keyser. 1998. "The basic elements of argument structure." *MIT Working Papers in Linguistics* 32: 73–118.

Halle, Morris and Alec Marantz. 1993. "Distributed morphology and the pieces of inflection." In K. Hale and S. J. Keyser, eds., *The View from Building 20: Essays in Linguistics in Honor of Sylvain Bromberger*. Cambridge, MA: MIT Press, pp. 111–76.

Haspelmath, Martin. 1993. *A Grammar of Lezgian*. Berlin: Mouton de Gruyter.

Heim, Irene. 1998. "Anaphora and semantic interpretation: a reinterpretation of Reinhart's approach." *MIT Working Papers in Linguistics* 25: 205–46.

Heycock, Caroline. 1995. "Asymmetries in reconstruction." *Linguistic Inquiry* 26: 547–70.

Higginbotham, James. 1980. "Pronouns and bound variables." *Linguistic Inquiry* 11: 679–708.

Jackendoff, Ray. 1983. *Semantics and Cognition*. Cambridge, MA: MIT Press.

Jayaseelan, K. A. 1997. "Anaphors as pronouns." *Studia Linguistica* 51: 186–234.

Johnson, Kyle. 1991. "Object positions." *Natural Language and Linguistic Theory* 9: 577–636.

Kayne, Richard S. 2000. "How movement, binding, and agreement are related." Paper presented at the 19th West Coast Conference on Formal Linguistics, Los Angeles, February 4. Also presented as "Toward an understanding of Condition C effects" at the 15th Workshop on Comparative Germanic Syntax, Groningen, May 27.

Kayne, Richard S. This volume. "Pronouns and their antecedents."

Klein, Maarten. 1980. "Anaforische relaties in het Nederlands." In M. Klein, ed., *Taal kundig beschouwd*. The Hague: Martinus Nijhoff, pp. 206–21.

Koster, Jan. 1984. "On binding and control." *Linguistic Inquiry* 15: 417–59.

Koster, Jan. 2000. "Pied piping and the word orders of English and Dutch." *Proceedings of NELS* 30: 415–26.

Lakoff, George. 1968. "Pronouns and reference." In J. McCawley, ed., 1976, *Notes from the Linguistic Underground*. New York: Academic Press, pp. 273–335.

Lasnik, Howard. 1976. "Remarks on coreference." *Linguistic Analysis* 2: 1–22.

Lasnik, Howard. 1998. "Some reconstruction riddles." *University of Pennsylvania Working Papers in Linguistics* 5: 83–98.

Lebeaux, David. 1988. "Language acquisition and the form of grammar." Dissertation, University of Maryland.

Lebeaux, David. 1998. "Where does the binding theory apply?" MS, NEC Research Institute, Princeton, NJ.

Martin, Roger. 1996. "A minimalist theory of PRO and control." Dissertation, University of Connecticut.

McGinnis, Martha-Jo. 1998. "Locality in A-movement." Dissertation, MIT, Cambridge, MA.

Montalbetti, Mario. 1984. "After binding: on the interpretation of pronouns." Dissertation, MIT, Cambridge, MA.

Osumi, Midori. 1995. *Tinrin Grammar*. Honolulu: University of Hawaii Press.

Postma, Gertjan. 1997. "Logical entailment and the possessive nature of reflexive pronouns." In H. Bennis, P. Pica, and J. Rooryck, eds., *Atomism and Binding*. Dordrecht: Foris Publications, pp. 295–322.

Rehg, Kenneth L. 1981. *Ponapean Reference Grammar*. Honolulu: University of Hawaii Press.

Reinhart, Tanya. 1976. "The syntactic domain of anaphora." Dissertation, MIT, Cambridge, MA.

304   *Jan-Wouter Zwart*

Reinhart, Tanya. 1983. *Anaphora and Semantic Interpretation*. London: Croom Helm.
Reinhart, Tanya and Eric Reuland. 1993. "Reflexivity." *Linguistic Inquiry* 24: 657–720.
Rooryck, Johan and Guido VandenWyngaerd. 1998. "The self as other." *Proceedings of NELS* 28: 359–73.
Rullmann, Hotze. 1988. "Referential dependency." MA thesis, University of Groningen.
Saltarelli, Mario. 1988. *Basque*. London: Croom Helm.
Schütze, Carson. 1997. "INFL in child and adult language: agreement, Case and licensing." Dissertation, MIT, Cambridge, MA.
Sells, Peter. 1987. "Aspects of logophoricity." *Linguistic Inquiry* 18: 445–79.
Sylla, Yèro. 1993. *Syntaxe peule: contribution à la récherche sur les universaux du langage*. Dakar: Les Nouvelles Éditions Africaines du Sénégal.
Tancredi, Christopher. 1992. "Deletion, deaccenting and presupposition." Dissertation, MIT, Cambridge, MA.
Tancredi, Christopher. 1997. "Pronouns and perspectives." In H. Bennis, P. Pica, and J. Rooryck, eds., *Atomism and Binding*. Dordrecht: Foris Publications, pp. 381–407.
Ter Meulen, Alice G. B. 2000. "On the economy of interpretation: semantic constraints on SE-reflexives in Dutch." In H. Bennis, M. Everaert, and E. Reuland, eds., *Interface Strategies*. Amsterdam: KNAW, pp. 239–55.
Torrego, Esther. 1996. "Experiencers and raising verbs." In R. Freidin, ed., *Current Issues in Comparative Grammar*. Dordrecht: Kluwer, pp. 101–20.
Ura, Hiroyaki. 2000. "On the typology of subject raising and English." *English Linguistics* 17: 417–26.
van Riemsdijk, Henk and Edwin S. Williams. 1981. "NP-structure." *The Linguistic Review* 1: 171–217.
Zwart, Jan-Wouter. 1991. "Clitics in Dutch: evidence for the position of INFL." *Groninger Arbeiten zur germanistischen Linguistik* 33: 71–92.
Zwart, Jan-Wouter. 1998a. "Where is syntax? Syntactic aspects of left-dislocation in Dutch and English." In P. Culicover and L. McNally, eds., *The Limits of Syntax (Syntax and Semantics 29)*. San Diego: Academic Press, pp. 365–93.
Zwart, Jan-Wouter. 1998b. "A note on 'Principle C' in ellipsis constructions." MIT Press Chomsky Celebration web site (http://mitpress2.mit.edu/celebration)
Zwart, Jan-Wouter. 1999a. "A dynamic theory of binding." In E. van Gelderen and V. Samiian, eds., *Proceedings of the Western Conference on Linguistics 10*, Fresno: California State University, pp. 533–52.
Zwart, Jan-Wouter. 1999b. "'Referentie' en de typologie van NPs: de status van PRO." *Tabu* 29: 49–66.
Zwart, Jan-Wouter. 2001. "Syntactic and phonological verb movement." *Syntax* 4: 34–62.

Index